Law and Social Policy in the Global South

The book is an in-depth study of the origins and the trajectories of the law governing social policies in Brazil, China, India, and South Africa, four middle-income countries in the global South with a history in social policy making that starts in the 1920s.

The policies of these countries affect almost half of the world's population. The book takes the legal framework of the policies as a starting point, but the main interest lies behind the letter of the law: What were the objectives and goals of social policy over the course of the last 100 years? What were the ideas, ideologies, and values pursued by relevant actors? The book comprises four country studies and a comparative study. The country studies concentrate on the political and social context of social policy making in Brazil, China, India, and South Africa as well as on the ideas, ideologies, and values underpinning the constitution, statutory laws, and case law that frame and shape social policy at the national level. The country studies are complemented by a comparative study exploring and describing the commonalities and differences in the ideational approaches to social policies across the four countries, nationally and – in the formative decades – internationally. The comparative study also identifies the characteristics that make Brazilian, Chinese, Indian, and South African social policies distinct from European social policies. With its emphasis on law and drawing on legal scholarship, the book adds a new dimension to the existing accounts on welfare state building, which, so far, are dominated by European narratives and by scholars with a background in sociology, political science, and development studies.

This book is relevant to specialists and peers and will be invaluable to those individuals interested in the fields of comparative and international social security law, human rights law, comparative constitutional law, constitutional history, law and development studies, comparative social policies, global social policies, social work, and welfare state theory.

Ulrike Davy is Professor of Constitutional and Administrative Law, German and International Social Security Law, and Comparative Law at the Faculty of Law, Bielefeld University, Germany, and Visiting Professor of Law at the University of Johannesburg, South Africa.

Albert H.Y. Chen is the Cheng Chan Lan Yue Professor and Chair of Constitutional Law at the University of Hong Kong.

Law and Social Policy in the Global South

Brazil, China, India, South Africa

Edited by Ulrike Davy
and Albert H.Y. Chen

Routledge
Taylor & Francis Group
a GlassHouse Book

First published 2023
by Routledge
4 Park Square, Milton Park, Abingdon, Oxon OX14 4RN

and by Routledge
605 Third Avenue, New York, NY 10158

Routledge is an imprint of the Taylor & Francis Group, an informa business

A GlassHouse book

British Library Cataloguing-in-Publication Data
A catalogue record for this book is available from the British Library

ISBN: 978-1-032-15167-0 (hbk)
ISBN: 978-1-032-15172-4 (pbk)
ISBN: 978-1-003-24282-6 (ebk)

DOI: 10.4324/9781003242826

Typeset in Bembo
by Apex CoVantage, LLC

To all unsung heroes and heroines

Contents

Contributors

Albert H.Y. Chen is the Cheng Chan Lan Yue Professor and Chair of Constitutional Law at the University of Hong Kong (HKU). He studied law at HKU and Harvard University and began teaching at HKU in 1984. He served as Dean of HKU's Faculty of Law in 1996–2002. His recent publications include *An Introduction to the Chinese Legal System* (5th ed 2019) and *The Changing Legal Orders in Hong Kong and Mainland China* (2021). He is also the editor or co-editor of *Constitutionalism in Asia in the Early Twenty-First Century* (2014) and *Constitutional Courts in Asia (2018).*

Ulrike Davy is Professor of Constitutional and Administrative Law, German and International Social Security Law, and Comparative Law at the Faculty of Law, Bielefeld University, and Visiting Professor of Law at the University of Johannesburg, South Africa. She is also a Principal Investigator participating in the Collaborative Research Center (SFB) 1288, funded by the German Research Foundation (DFG). Ulrike Davy is a leading scholar in European welfare state theory, German and European law relating to social policies, and international human rights law. Her most recent publications include the co-edited book *Imaging Unequals, Imaging Equals* (2022) and a book chapter on EU social policy (2020).

Octávio Luiz Motta Ferraz is Professor of Law at the Dickson Poon School of Law, King's College London, United Kingdom, where he is also the Co-director of the Transnational Law Institute, and Senior Global Fellow at the Fundação Getúlio Vargas in São Paulo, Brazil. He has extensive expertise in the field of social and economic rights, in particular on the right to health and the role of courts in their implementation. His main research focuses on exploring the relationship between law, in particular public law and human rights, and sustainable human development, from an interdisciplinary and transnational perspective. He is the author of *Health as a Human Right. The Politics and Judicialisation of Health in Brazil* (Cambridge University Press 2021) and the Co-editor of the Oxford Compendium of National Legal Responses to COVID-19.

Letlhokwa George Mpedi is Professor and Vice-Chancellor and Principal (Designate), University of Johannesburg, South Africa, and Visiting Professor of Law, University of Cape Coast, Ghana. Before becoming Vice-Chancellor and Principal (Designate), Professor Mpedi served as Deputy Vice-Chancellor: Academic and Executive Dean (Faculty of Law) of the University Johannesburg. He has published widely in the fields of social security and labour law in South Africa, Southern Africa, and Anglophone Africa. His most recent publications include a co-authored book *Labour Law in Ghana* (2022) published by LexisNexis, South Africa.

Sarbani Sen is Professor and Executive Director of the Center for Constitutional Law Studies at Jindal Global Law School, Jindal Global University, New Delhi, India. Her teaching and research interests broadly lie in the areas of Indian constitutional law, comparative public law, legal theory, and constitutional history. Specific interests include issues of constitutional foundings/transformations; constitutional and judicial formulations of 'social welfare'; judicial interpretive strategies of constitutional provisions; standards of judicial review of legislative action; and secularist approaches to problems of diversity and plurality.

Preface and Acknowledgements

This edited volume is the fruit of years of research collaboration on social policy in the global South, organised under the auspices of the *Zentrum für interdisziplinäre Forschung* (ZiF, or Centre for Interdisciplinary Research), Bielefeld University. Most of the chapters in this volume are revised versions of papers presented at a conference on 'Understanding Southern Welfare: Social Policies in Brazil, India, China and South Africa', taking place at the ZiF from 11 through 12 July 2019.

The July 2019 conference was the culmination and concluding event of the activities of the ZiF Research Group on 'Understanding Sothern Welfare: Ideational and Historical Foundations of Social Policies in Brazil, India, China and South Africa'. The Research Group – an international research team – was approved by the ZiF in July 2016 and convened by Ulrike Davy, Faculty of Law, Bielefeld University, and Lutz Leisering, Faculty of Sociology, Bielefeld University, as the heads of the group. Two subgroups were formed under the Research Group – the 'sociology subgroup' headed by Lutz Leisering, and the 'law subgroup' headed by Ulrike Davy. The contributors to the present volume were members of the 'law subgroup'.

The members of the Research Group were all invited to stay at the ZiF as Fellows for five months during the period from March through July 2018. Before the Research Group gathered for the longer period of stay at the ZiF, three research workshops on issues that subsequently constituted the main themes of the Research Group had already been held at the ZiF in November 2014, November 2015, and December 2016. The 'law subgroup' met additionally in December 2017 to prepare for the activities of the group in the following year.

The 'residence-phase' of the Research Group at the ZiF in 2018 was devoted to sessions of intense joint readings and exchange of views among jurists, sociologists, political scientists, historians, and economists who are eminent scholars in the study of social policies in the West and the global South. The participants included the Fellows of the Research Group itself and other scholars invited to visit the ZiF and to participate in the seminars and workshops organised by the Research Group. The 'law subgroup' organised two ZiF workshops, one in April 2018 and the other in July 2018, during which valuable inputs were provided by guest speakers and commentators who were external to the Research Group. The comparative study written in 2020 and 2021 additionally drew on discussions and many insights gained in the context of the Collaborative Research Center (SFB) 1288 on Practices of Comparing, funded by the German Research Foundation (DFG).

We are much indebted to all those who contributed to, participated in, facilitated, funded, provided administrative support for, or otherwise made possible the numerous workshops, seminars, and conferences of the research project of which this volume forms a part. In particular, we take this opportunity to express our gratitude to the following institutions: The ZiF itself, its directors (Michael Röckner, Véronique Zanetti, Philippe Blanchard, Martin Egelhaaf, and Joanna Pfaff-Czarnecka), and Britta Padberg for funding the group and for giving us much encouragement and support; the Faculty of Law, Bielefeld University, for funding a workshop and for sponsoring the publication of this edited volume as an open access publication; the Stellenbosch Institute for Advanced Study, South Africa, and its director Hendrik Geyer for generously providing two fellowships that were crucial for the preparation of our ZiF application.

Our warmest gratitude extends to the ZiF staff – Marina Hoffmann, Trixi Valentin, Mo Tschache, and Daniela Brinkmann – who were always there when needed and did miracles to make things run smoothly, and to Stefan Adamick whose posters for our workshops and conferences were pieces of art, each time.

Maria Virginia Lorena Ossio Bustillos was for more than a year the coordinator of the Research Group, steering us, like a guardian angel, through all sorts of weathers, with wisdom, joyfulness, humour, and admirable insights in the human soul. Lorena could laugh away easily all oddities and difficulties we have encountered and shared during our joint endeavours. We are and remain grateful for her friendship. Thank you very much, Lorena!

We owe a big 'thank you' to our fellow Fellows from the 'sociology subgroup': Lutz Leisering, Aiqun Hu, Lena Lavinas, Gabriel Ondetti, Sony Pellissery, Jeremy Seekings, Shi-Jiunn Shi, and Marianne Ulriksen. They helped us understand social policies in Europe and the global South from their particular specialisations. They also made us aware of differences in perspectives and approaches. Through the lens of differences and diversity, we could better grasp how we should proceed in describing why and to what extent welfare states emerged and developed in Brazil, China, India, and South Africa, while bearing in mind Europe from a comparative perspective. Although Europe cannot be left out of our narrative, our interest was and is on the ideational foundations of the domestic policies and politics in the four countries as expressed in constitutions, statutory laws, and court adjudication. These developments may at times have been inspired by European models of the welfare state, but not necessarily or always so. Developments at the domestic level also mirror local ideas, values, and preferences. And the domestic level is what we chose to be the starting point for our common project of understanding Southern welfare, as it took shape historically in Brazil, China, India, and South Africa.

We are also grateful to the scholars who came to the ZiF to share their expertise with us over the years: Ravi Ahuja, Daniel Brinks, Sarah Cook, Benjamin Davy, Vivek Nenmini Dileep, Virgilio Afonso da Silva, Andries du Toit, Eberhard Eichenhofer, Sonia Fleury, Peter Ho, Mingtao Huang, Niraja Gopal Jayal, Evance Kalula, Sandra Liebenberg, Frances Lund, Marcelo Medeiros, Marcus André Melo, James Midgley, Kinglun Ngok, Leila Patel, Shitong Qiao, Prerna Singh, Göran Therborn, Arun Thiruvengadam, André van der Walt, Sue-Mari Viljoen, Yitu Yang, Li Zhang, and Augusto Zimmermann. Their inputs proved invaluable.

And, last but not least, we want to thank our fellow contributors to this volume, who, together with the two of us, constituted the 'law subgroup' of the Research Group: Octávio Luiz Motta Ferraz, Letlhokwa George Mpedi, and Sarbani Sen. We have spent many hours together, at ZiF workshops, during our stay at the ZiF as resident Fellows, and via Zoom in preparing for the publication of this edited volume. We cherish all these moments and memories! We also cherish their commitment, dedication, and perseverance. Thank you very much Letlhokwa, Octávio, and Sarbani!

We regard the work of producing this volume to be a labour of love – both as a testimony to the efforts made over the course of many decades of social policy development in the four countries covered by this volume, and as a memorial to the friendship and collegiality that have been built up among the members, friends, and supporting staff of our Research Group during years of sharing and collaboration in research. We hope that this volume can serve as a useful work of reference for scholars and students in the field for years to come.

This book's dedication to 'all unsung heroes and heroines' is inspired by a passage in the judgement of the Constitutional Court of South Africa in *Sylvia Bongi Mahlangu and South African Domestic Service and Allied Workers Union v Minister of Labour and others* ([2020] ZACC 24). The judgement links social policy to ideas of dignity and equality that dominate, time and again, the emergence and the trajectories of social policies in Brazil, China, India, and South Africa.

Ulrike Davy and Albert H.Y. Chen
Co-editors
October 2022

Chapter 1

Law and Social Policy in the Global South

Setting the Stage

Ulrike Davy

Background

Scholarly accounts on the emergence and the trajectories of the European welfare states abound, for more than a hundred years.[1] Scholarly interest focuses particularly on the German and the British welfare states. Generally, Germany and Great Britain are deemed forerunners instituting distinct and differing welfare state models that were subsequently promoted at the international level, mainly by the International Labour Organisation (ILO). The forerunner models often served as points of reference for other countries.[2] Germany and Great Britain have a tradition of poor laws, ie of a legal framework ensuring that people receive help in case they are not able to provide for themselves. The British poor law is often traced back to the beginning of the seventeenth century, when Elizabeth I introduced the first comprehensive system of parish churchwardens and overseers tasked with providing relief for

1 See eg John Graham Brooks, *Compulsory Insurance in Germany* (Rev edn, Government Printing Office 1895); Lee K. Frankel and Miles M. Dawson, *Workingmen's Insurance in Europe* (Russell Sage Foundation 1910); Henry Rogers Seager, *Social Insurance. A Program of Social Reform* (Macmillan Company 1910); I.M. Rubinow, *Studies in Workmen's Insurance: Italy, Russia, Spain* (Dissertation, Columbia University 1911); I.M. Rubinow, *Social Insurance* (Henry Holt and Company 1913); Karl Polanyi, *The Great Transformation* (Beacon Press 1944); T.H. Marshall, 'Citizenship and Social Class' in T.H. Marshall (ed), *Citizenship and Social Class and Other Essays* (Cambridge University Press 1950) 1; Gøsta Esping-Andersen, *The Three Worlds of Welfare Capitalism* (Polity Press 1990); Franz-Xaver Kaufmann, *European Foundations of the Welfare State* (Berghahn 2012); Franz-Xaver Kaufmann, *Variations of the Welfare State. Great Britain, Sweden, France and Germany between Capitalism and Socialism* (Springer 2013).

2 For an account on the role of the International Labour Organisation in dispersing the idea of the 'welfare state' see Sandrine Kott, 'Constructing a European Social Model: The Fight for Social Insurance in the Interwar Period' in Jasmien van Daele and others (eds), *ILO Histories: Essays on the International Labour Organization and Its Impact on the World During the Twentieth Century* (Peter Lang 2010) 173; Kaufmann, *European Foundations* (n 1) 97; Gerry Rodgers, 'India, the ILO and the Quest for Social Justice since 1919' (2011) 46 Economic & Political Weekly 45, 46; Daniel Maul, *Human Rights, Development and Decolonization. The International Labour Organization 1940–70* (Palgrave 2012).

DOI: 10.4324/9781003242826-1

the poor in 1601.[3] The 1601 Act for the Relief of the Poor was an early act of state requiring that towns, parishes, and hamlets support 'their' poor.[4] In the sixteenth and the seventeenth century, Germany still relied mainly on *Bettelverbote* (regulations by the Emperor, territorial rulers, or local authorities prohibiting the begging in the cities and requiring local authorities to expel all non-resident beggars).[5] The first German statute announcing that providing poor relief was within the responsibilities of the state was the Prussian *Allgemeine Landrecht* of 1794 (ALR).[6] The ALR also detailed the responsibilities of the local authorities and the requirements for the provision of relief. Yet, the decisive move toward what was later termed the 'welfare state' occurred in Germany in the 1880s.[7] War-torn Great Britain followed suit in the early 1940s, after some experimenting at the beginning of the twentieth century,[8]

3 See eg George Nicholls, *A History of the English Poor Law in Connexion with the Legislation and other Circumstances Affecting the Condition of the People*, vol 1 (John Murray 1854) 192; Anthony I. Ogus, 'Landesbericht Großbritannien' in Peter A. Köhler and Hans F. Zacher (eds), *Ein Jahrhundert Sozialversicherung in der Bundesrepublik Deutschland, Frankreich, Großbritannien, Österreich und der Schweiz* (Duncker & Humblot 1981) 269, 276, 294; Derek Fraser, *The Evolution of the British Welfare State. A History of Social Policy since the Industrial Revolution* (2nd edn, Macmillan 1984) 31; Ulrike Davy, Chapter 6 in this volume, p. 190. Earlier poor relief acts were more piecemeal, less systematic. The Elizabethan poor law was superseded by a major poor law reform in 1834. For details on the Poor Law Amendment Act of 1834 see Sidney Webb and Beatrice Webb, *English Local Government: English Poor Law History: Part II. The Last Hundert Years*, vol 1 (Longmans, Green and Co. 1929) 90.

4 Nicolls (n 3) 197.

5 The rules prohibiting the begging in the cities and communes were part and parcel of the various (imperial, territorial, or local) *Policeyordnungen* (decrees making provision for a good public order) of the sixteenth and seventeenth century. The decrees regularly emphasised that non-resident beggars as well as able-bodied resident beggars ought not to be tolerated in the cities. Rather in passing, the decrees referred to the cities and communes as the pertinent local authorities carrying some responsibilities for 'their' poor. When implementing these responsibilities, the cities and communes relied on the willingness of their (wealthy) burghers to provide the means (alms) necessary to implement these responsibilities; providing a framework for giving alms was the traditional realm of the Church. The responsibilities of the Church and the responsibilities of the secular authorities were still quite closely entwined. On the legal framework of *Fürsorge* (welfare relief) in early modern Germany see Karl Otto Scherner, 'Das Recht der Armen und Bettler im Ancien régime' (1979) 96 Savigny-Zeitschrift, Germanistische Abteilung 55.

6 *Allgemeines Landrecht für die Preußischen Staaten* (General Laws Applicable in the Prussian States), 1 June 1794 <https://opinioiuris.de/quelle/1621> accessed 28 February 2022. ALR, II 19 § 1 read: 'It is incumbent on the state to provide food and care for those citizens who cannot provide for themselves, and who do not receive aid from other private persons who are obliged by law to do so' (translation by the author).

7 See eg Detlev Zöllner, 'Landesbericht Deutschland' in Peter A. Köhler and Hans F. Zacher (eds), *Ein Jahrhundert Sozialversicherung in der Bundesrepublik Deutschland, Frankreich, Großbritannien, Österreich und der Schweiz* (Duncker & Humblot 1981) 83.

8 David Gladstone, 'The Welfare State and the State of Welfare' in David Gladstone (ed), *British Social Welfare. Past, Presence, Future* (UCL Press 1995) 1, 2; John Stewart, 'The Twentieth Century: An Overview' in Robert M. Page and Richard Silburn (eds), *British Social Welfare in the Twentieth Century* (Macmillan 1995) 15, 17.

subsequently to the release of the Beveridge report.[9] The German model, created by a series of (social) insurance laws relating to health, industrial accidents, and old age, is often classified as 'conservative',[10] as the German system of (income replacing) benefits mirrors the economic hierarchies established through the market forces, some redistributive features of the system notwithstanding: The ones who fare better in the labour market pay higher contributions and receive higher benefits; women and children are conceived of as recipients of benefits based on dependency. By contrast, following the Beveridge report, Great Britain institutionalised a 'liberal' welfare state,[11] ie a welfare state showing only restrained ambition to balance fate, risks, or the market forces. One of the main principles underpinning the social policies introduced in Great Britain in the 1940s was that social security ought to be achieved by the 'co-operation between the State and the individual'.[12] State responsibility was conceptualised as being limited to some sort of defined minimum and, consequently, social policies were supposed to leave 'room and encouragement for voluntary action by each individual to provide more than that minimum'.[13] In short, German policy makers were concerned with finding peace with the labour movement.[14] British policy makers were concerned with fighting want.[15] Even though the original intentions faded into the background later or were supplanted by other intentions, the original intentions still dominate scholarly classifications.

More recently, scholarly attention has turned to the social policies in the global South, in particular in political science, sociology, development studies, and economy.[16] Attention grew in the 1990s and the 2000s, when some countries in the global South started to introduce social policy measures that

9 William Beveridge, *Social Insurance and Allied Services. Report* (Cmd 6404, 1942).

10 Esping-Andersen (n 1) 27, 53.

11 Esping-Andersen (n 1) 26, 48; Stewart (n 8) 19.

12 Beveridge (n 9) para 9.

13 ibid.

14 Lutz Leisering, 'The Welfare State in Postwar Germany' in B. Vivekanandan and Nimmi Kurian (eds), *Welfare States and the Future* (Palgrave Macmillan 2005) 113.

15 Beveridge (n 9) para 11.

16 For an overview see Lutz Leisering, Benjamin Davy, and Ulrike Davy, 'The Politics of Recognition: Changing Understandings of Human Rights, Social Development and Land Rights as Normative Foundation of Global Social Policy' (2014) 18 Max Planck YB of UN Law 565; see also Carina Schmitt, 'External Actors and Social Protection in the Global South: An Overview' in Carina Schmitt (ed), *From Colonialism to International Aid External Actors and Social Protection in the Global South* (Palgrave Macillan & Springer Nature Switzerland 2020) 3; Christian Aspalter, 'Introduction' in Christian Aspalter (ed), *The Routledge International Handbook to Welfare State Systems* (Routledge 2017) 1. The term 'global South' is contested and not clearly defined, and it has more than geographical implications. For a critical stance see eg Nour Dados and Raewyn Connell, 'The Global South' (2012) 11 Contexts 12. Here, the term is used to refer to so-called low- and middle-income countries (according to United Nations parlance) and the term implies a history of colonisation.

were seen as novel and innovative, at times as politically overdue.[17] The introduction of cash transfers, tied to certain duties relating to school attendance, health, or work (so-called conditional cash transfers, according to the terminology used by the World Bank) or not so tied and generally means-tested, absorbed most of the attention. The first comparative studies appeared in the 2000s, but studies comparing countries in the global South or Southern and Northern welfare are still rare, even in political science, sociology, or development studies.[18] Most existing comparative efforts strive to adjust concepts, models, or classifications capturing European welfare regimes so that they also capture Southern social policies, or tend to suggest new taxonomies or welfare models.[19]

Aims

This book takes a different approach. For one, all contributors are legal scholars. The legal approach pursued in this book adds a distinct and new perspective to the existing literature: We aim to enhance the understanding of the social policies in four, and thus a limited number of, countries in the

17 See eg Anis A. Dani and Arjan de Haan (eds), *Inclusive States. Social Policy and Structural Inequalities* (The World Bank 2008); James Midgley and Kwong-leung Tang (eds), *Social Policy and Poverty in East Asia* (Routledge 2010); James Midgley and Mitsuhiko Hosaka (eds), *Grassroots Social Security in Asia* (Routledge 2011); Ingrid Wehr, Bernhard Leubolt, and Wolfram Schaffar (eds), *Welfare Regimes in the Global South* (mandelbaum 2012); Katja Bender, Markus Kaltenborn, and Christian Pfleiderer (eds), *Social Protection in Developing Countries. Reforming Systems* (Routledge 2013); Rebecca Surender and Robert Walker (eds), *Social Policy in a Developing World* (Edward Elgar 2013); Khayaat Fakier and Ellen Ehmke (eds), *Socio-Economic Insecurity in Emerging Economies* (Routledge 2014).

18 See eg Ian Gough and Geof Wood, *Insecurity and Welfare Regimes in Asia, Africa and Latin America* (Cambridge University Press 2004); Jeremy Seekings, 'Welfare Regimes and Redistribution in the South' in Ian Shapiro, Peter A Swenson, and Daniela Donna (eds), *Divide and Deal. The Politics of Distribution in Democracies* (New York University Press 2008); OECD, *Tackling Inequalities in Brazil, China, India and South Africa. The Role of the Labour Market and Social Policies* (OECD Publishing 2010); Miguel Niño-Zarazúa, Armando Barrientos, Samuel Hickey, and David Hulme, 'Social Protection in Sub-Saharan Africa: Getting the Politics Right' (2012) 40 World Development 163; Jeremy Seekings, 'Pathways to Redistribution. The Emerging Politics of Social Assistance across the Global "South"' in Ingrid Wehr, Bernhard Leubolt, and Wolfram Schaffar (eds), *Welfare Regimes in the Global South* (Mandelbaum 2012) 14; James Midgley and David Piachaud (eds), *Social Protection, Economic Growth and Social Change. Goals, Issues and Trajectories in China, India, Brazil and South Africa* (Edward Elgar 2013). More recently and comprehensively Lutz Leisering, *The Global Rise of Social Cash Transfers: How States and International Organizations Constructed a New Instrument for Combating Poverty* (Oxford University Press 2018).

19 For an overview see Rianne Mahon, 'Rethinking Welfare Regimes: Challenges from the South' (2018) Centre for Social Science Research Working Paper No. 148 <www.cssr.uct.ac.za/sites/default/files/image_tool/images/256/Publications/Mahon-wp418.pdf> accessed 28 February 2022. Focusing on the role of global actors Moritz von Gliszczynski and Lutz Leisering, 'Constructing New Global Models of Social Security: How International Organizations Defined the Field of Social Cash Transfers in the 2000s' (2016) 45 Journal of Social Policy 325.

global South – Brazil, China, India, and South Africa – from the particular angle of law.[20]

Secondly, and because the emphasis is on 'understanding', the book is not conceptualised as a doctrinal effort elaborating on the content of the various statutory laws that combine to what could be termed 'social security law'. Our main interest lies beyond the letter of the law. The book seeks to understand the law in its political and social context: We investigate the ideational foundations of the law relating to the social policies in the countries involved. With putting our emphasis on ideational processes and their outcomes, we follow a recent branch in social policy research that stresses the particular relevance of 'ideas' for explaining the emergence of social policies and, hence, welfare states, European and non-European alike.[21] The notion of 'ideas' is deliberately kept broad, capturing ideologies, concepts, values, beliefs, or perceptions by actors as they make their arguments or claims with regard to certain policy issues.[22] Obviously, ideas may impact policy making at various levels of abstraction: Ideas may influence the very construction of what the problem is and, therefore, influence the setting of an agenda (low wages may be conceived of as a symbol of class struggle or the result of market forces). Ideas may influence the choice of policy instruments (eg benefits in kind or cash benefits). And ideas may determine need for reform (eg perceived changing family patterns).[23] While social policy literature is much concerned with how to prove the specific impact of ideas (causality) – for example, vis-à-vis power structures or institutions – our ambition and task is different.

20 Starting from a similar point of departure, but from a sociological and political science perspective, see the contributions of the Fellows of our twin ZiF-project in Lutz Leisering (ed), *One Hundred Years of Social Protection. The Changing Social Question in Brazil, India, China, and South Africa* (Palgrave Macmillan 2021).

21 See eg Daniel Béland and Randall Hansen, 'Reforming the French Welfare State: Solidarity, Social Exclusion and the Three Crises of Citizenship' (2000) 23 West European Politics 47; Craig Parsons, 'Showing Ideas as Causes: The Origins of the European Union' (2002) 56 International Organization 47; Birgit Pfau-Effinger, 'Culture and Welfare State Policies: Reflections on a Complex Interrelation' (2005) 34 Journal of Social Policy 3; Daniel Béland, 'Ideas and Social Policy: An Institutionalist Perspective' (2005) 39 Social Policy & Administration 1; Wim van Oorschot, 'Culture and Social Policy: A Developing Field of Study' (2007) 16 International Journal of Social Welfare 129; Daniel Béland, 'Ideas, Institutions, and Policy Change' (2009) 16 Journal of European Public Policy 701; Daniel Béland, 'Ideas and Institutions in Social Policy Research' (2016) 56 Social Policy & Administration 734; Privilege Haang'andu and Daniel Béland, 'Transnational Actors and the Diffusion of Social Policies: An Ideational Approach' in Carina Schmitt (ed), *From Colonialism to International Aid External Actors and Social Protection in the Global South* (Palgrave Macmillan & Springer Nature 2020).

22 Béland, 'Ideas and Institutions' (n 21) 736–738.

23 On conceptualising social policy ideas see also Lutz Leisering, 'Social Protection in the Global South. An Ideational and Historical Approach' in Lutz Leisering (ed), *One Hundred Years of Social Protection. The Changing Social Question in Brazil, India, China, and South Africa* (Palgrave Macmillan 2021) 3, 22.

We want to develop narratives, ie accounts of events relating to the social policies occurring in Brazil, China, India, and South Africa, that equal the well-known narratives linked to Western welfare states, in particular Western European welfare states.[24] The 'ideas' we will be dealing with derive from constitutional rights and values, the legal framework for social benefits and, when and where existent, relevant case-law.

Thirdly, we combine the ideational approach with a historical approach. Goals, objectives, and values of actors, and the perception of problems evolve over time, change over time, and may create (sometimes unforeseen or unexpected) path-dependencies. Elements of former social policies may become so entrenched that policy makers are barely able to effectively opt for a change.[25] Of course, history has to start somewhere. The timeline underlying our book generally starts in the 1920s, a decade that marks the emergence of social policies in all countries involved. The timeline ends at the present. Thus, the book gives an in-depth account, from a legal, ideational, and historical point of view, of the emergence and the development of social policies in Brazil, China, India, and South Africa.

Finally, based on comparisons across the four countries and in relation to social policies in Europe (Germany, Great Britain), the book contributes to welfare state theory which has so far mainly drawn on European history. The book is not about adapting the concepts or models relating to European welfare regimes in order to somehow integrate the developments originating in the global South. The book is about giving an account on how social policies emerged in four countries in the global South and how these countries subsequently developed their own pathways, even though links to European social policies were always close and the colonial pasts always present. But European social policies are seen as the periphery, while the social policies in Brazil, China, India, and South Africa are in the forefront.

Countries

Brazil, China, India, and South Africa have, for a number of reasons, been chosen to be the probing grounds for exploring the social policies in countries in the global South. The four countries are significant in terms of the size of the population. The social policies of the four countries affect almost half of the world's population. The four countries are significant from the perspective of economic development. China, India, and Brazil are among

24 For a European perspective see Jens Alber, *Vom Armenhaus zum Wohlfahrtsstaat. Analysen zur Entwicklung der Sozialversicherung in Westeuropa* (Campus Verlag 1982); Kaufmann, *European Foundations* (n 1); Michael Stolleis, 'The European Welfare State. A Model under Threat' (2017) 46 Quaderni Fiorentini 17.

25 See eg Paul Pierson, 'The New Politics of the Welfare State' (1996) 48 World Politics 143, 175.

the twelve largest economies in the world; South Africa is among the economically most advanced countries in Africa.[26] Economic growth indicates the availability of resources and institutions that might stimulate social policies. The four countries are significant from the perspective of social policy trajectories. The countries have – tentative and *ad hoc* as this may have been at first – a history of social policies that reaches back to the 1920s and 1930s.[27] Among the countries in the global South, they were among the first to introduce social policies, broadly understood as state action (reflected in the constitution, statutes, regulations, judgements, doctrine, or policy papers) meant to meet the needs of people relating to economic security, social security, work, housing, food, clothing, health, or education.[28] And in the 2000s, some of the social policy instruments introduced in Brazil, China, India, or South Africa have become role models for other countries in the global South. Most famously, conditional cash transfers spreading in the global South often emulate the Brazilian *Programa Bolsa Família*.[29] The Indian 2005 National Rural Employment Guarantee Act was remodelled in South Africa under the terms of the Community Work Programme.[30] Also, constitutional frameworks align. In all four countries, today's constitutions enshrine socio-economic individual rights, the differences in their constitutional histories and in the interpretation of those rights notwithstanding. In Brazil, India, and South Africa – China has no comparable institutional system – courts are willing to adjudicate in matters governed by constitutionally embedded

26 World Bank national accounts data, GDP (current US$) 2020.

27 On early social policies in Brazil see A. Tixier, 'The Development of Social Insurance in Argentina, Brazil, Chile, and Uruguay' (1935) 32 International Labour Review 610 (part 1) and 751 (part 2); Paula Lopes, 'Social Problems and Legislation in Brazil' (1941) 44 International Labour Review 493. On India see Rajani Kanta Das, 'Labour Legislation in India' (1930) 22 International Labour Review 599; Atul C. Chatterjee, 'Federalism and Labour Legislation' (1944) 49 International Labour Review 415. On China see the early account by John Dixon, *The Chinese Welfare System 1949–1979* (Praeger Publishers 1981). And on the policies of the Union of South Africa enacted by a National Party-Labour Party coalition government see Jeremy Seekings, '"Not a Single White Person Should be Allowed to Go under". *Swartgevaar* and the Origins of South Africa's Welfare State, 1924–1929' (2007) 48 Journal of African History 375.

28 Stephan Haggard and Robert R. Kaufman, *Development, Democracy, and Welfare States. Latin America, East Asia, and Eastern Europe* (Princeton University Press 2008) 3 stress the economic dimension of social policy, holding that 'social policy' is primarily about 'how governments choose to redistribute income, either through insurance schemes that mitigate risk or through spending on basic social services that are of particular significance to the poor'. Bent Greve, 'What is Welfare and Public Welfare?' in Bent Greve (ed), *Routledge Handbook of the Welfare State*, 2nd edn (Routledge 2019) 4 also stresses 'well-being' and the understanding of what 'a good society' means.

29 On the rise of social cash transfers see eg Armando Barrientos, 'Social Protection and Poverty' (2011) 20 International Journal of Social Welfare 240; Rachel Slater, 'Cash Transfers, Social Protection and Poverty Reduction' (2011) 20 International Journal of Social Welfare 250; Leisering (n 18) 139.

30 Khayaat Fakier, 'The Community Work Programme and Care in South Africa' in Fakier and Ehmke (n 17).

socio-economic rights and values.[31] And the four countries have become global players, a status that is epitomised by their being part of a loose network linking Brazil, Russia, India, China, and South Africa (BRICS) and by their role in advancing South-South cooperation.[32]

Against the backdrop of our aim – understanding the social policies and law developed in Brazil, India, China, and South Africa from their very start – we have to be selective with regard to the social policies we cover, and, given space limitations, we have to refrain from going into the specifics and intricacies of the various legal frameworks. We will focus on certain core fields of social policies.

For one, we focus on social insurance, ie contribution-based systems providing benefits in the case of certain risks or contingencies, such as industrial accidents, spells of ill-health, unemployment, or old age. These benefits aim primarily to replace (individual) income loss when one or more contingencies materialise.[33] For another, we focus on tax-financed (often) means-tested benefits addressing basic needs, in particular the need for food, clothing, housing, water, and health care. At the national level, tax-financed and means-tested benefits addressing basic needs come under a plethora of terms. Some benefits take the form of cash transfers: In Germany, the cash transfers are called *Sozialhilfe* (social assistance) or *Grundsicherung für Arbeitsuchende* (basic security for jobseekers), in France they are called *aide sociale* (social assistance), and in the United Kingdom they come under the general term 'income-related benefits', a term that covers income support, housing benefit, or family credit, to name but a few. In Brazil, the cash transfers are called '*bolsa família*', and the recipients must comply with certain requirements regarding school attendance or health checks (conditional cash transfers). China introduced a 'Minimum Livelihood Guarantee' in major cities in the 1990s. The 'Guarantee' was later expanded to other areas. In India, the National Social Assistance Programme encompasses an 'old age pension scheme', a 'family benefit scheme', and a 'disability pension scheme'. In South Africa, lawmakers used the term 'pension' when they introduced a means-tested old age cash transfer for the first time in 1928[34] and in 1936, when they introduced a means-tested cash transfer payable to blind persons.[35] Later, South African lawmakers preferred to use the term 'grants'. In 1946, a disability grant was introduced.[36] Nowadays, the 2004 Social Assistance

31 Generally, Varun Gauri and Daniel M. Brinks (eds), *Courting Social Justice. Judicial Enforcement of Social and Economic Rights in the Developing World* (Cambridge University Press 2008).

32 Lucia Scaffardi, 'BRICS – A Multi-Centre Legal Network' (2014) 5 Beijing Law Review 140; Rumu Sarkar, 'Trends in Global Finance. The New Development (BRICS) Bank' 2016 13 Loyola University Chicago International Law Review 89.

33 For an early conceptualisation of 'social insurance' see Rubinow, *Social Insurance* (n 1) 8.

34 Act 22 of 1928.

35 Act 11 of 1936.

36 Act 36 of 1946.

Act[37] provides for several 'social grants', including child support grants, disability grants, and older persons' grants. Benefits covering basic needs may also take the form of in-kind benefits, such as school meals, nutritional supplements, the free provision of water or electricity, shelters, or health care. Some of the in-kind schemes operate in times of emergency only (famine relief), some operate longer term (school meals). Finally, some benefits are meant to cover all basic needs, either in cash or in kind, some benefits aim at covering specified needs only (mobility allowances, food allowances, housing benefits). Whatever their name at the national level, all these non-contributory benefits are generally included in our study. Thus, the book's quest – understanding the social policies in Brazil, China, India, and South Africa – relies on the main pillars of what is, at the international level, often termed 'social security'.[38]

Comparing

The centre pieces of any comparative research in law are country studies. Our book presents four such country studies. Clearly, we shall not be able to fully understand 'Southern welfare', once we have come to understand the social policies in Brazil, China, India, and South Africa. Four country studies are too scarce a basis for valid generalisations. Still, our comparative endeavour promises to bear fruit.

In order to keep European concepts and models at the periphery, we opted for a country study format that presents national policies and their historical narratives strictly from the perspective of the 'inside', using vocabulary and concepts prevailing at the respective national levels. That does not mean that European concepts and models will be absent from our country studies. On the contrary, European concepts and models were indeed present at the national levels and often quite influential. We just look at those concepts and models from a Southern perspective. Presenting four country studies in such a manner challenges the reader. The various national narratives avoid using concepts or terminologies known in international or Western contexts, such as 'social protection', 'social assistance', or 'social rights'. Such terms are often loosely defined. Equally often, the terms gloss over national peculiarities and, hence, lack substance at the national level because they fail to grasp the relevant local meaning. Also, legal comparisons across countries are, in any case, delicate. To be meaningful, comparative studies across countries require that, to some extent, the countries share relevant characteristics. Otherwise, comparisons

37 Act 13 of 2004.

38 For the language used in human rights law see Ulrike Davy, 'How Human Rights Shape Social Citizenship: On Citizenship and the Understanding of Economic and Social Rights' (2014) 13 Washington University Global Studies Law Review 201. On the notion of 'social security' more generally Ulrike Davy, Chapter 6 in this volume, p. 203.

will fail because workable *tertia comparationis* cannot be identified (lack of comparability). And there must also be room for variation across the countries. Otherwise, differences and similarities cannot be identified and explained.

In our case, similar economic parameters (all countries involved are middle-income countries), a tradition in written constitutions sketching the outlook of social policies, a tradition of statutory law and government practices that concretise social policies, and – with respect to Brazil, India, and South Africa – relevant case-law secure basic comparability. In addition to that, social policies were, in each of the countries involved, informed by ideas originating in Western countries and by the policies of the ILO. That, again, secures basic comparability. Western and international influence was, however, limited. The social policies introduced in Brazil, China, India, and South Africa remained fragmented for decades and different for urban and rural populations. In South Africa, social policies also followed (perceived) racial lines. Expansion and universalisation of social benefits is a recent phenomenon; informality is still widespread. The difference to European social policies is huge. Lastly, and from a more formal angle, the country studies are similar in their structure. The studies proceed according to pertinent historical periods and thus present a narrative that captures the emergence of social policies as well as the trajectories taken over time. Similarities in structure broaden the ground for reliable cross-country comparisons.

On the other hand, the countries differ in important respects. The countries differ in their political histories. China's history involves left-wing authoritarianism that opened up to marketisation in the late 1970s. Brazil has a history of shifting between right-wing authoritarianism and democracy. South Africa has a long history of racial discrimination and apartheid. India has a history of almost uninterrupted democracy. Colonial histories differ too: In China, colonialism was confined to specified spheres of influence, dominated by Great Britain, France, other Western powers, and Japan. Brazil and South Africa were settler colonies, yet Brazil's independence dates to 1822, whereas South Africa was governed by a racist White minority until the beginning of the 1990s. India was subjugated first to indirect rule, then to direct rule. Last but not least, social policies differ: In Brazil and China, social policies now rely on a strong state engagement. However, Brazil has turned to democracy in 1988, whereas China continues to adhere to authoritarianism. In India, state intervention was marginal, until recently. In South Africa, social policies bear the burden and (to some extent) the markers of apartheid. All this provides fertile ground for comparison.

Analytically, our comparative efforts involve two steps. For one, we engage in comparisons across the four countries. We shall seek for commonalities and differences and try to explain the occurrence of similar or divergent pathways of social policies. For another, we engage in South-North comparisons: The four countries drew on European social policy models, in particular the German and the British welfare state model, which were – at some points in time – propagated by the ILO. When it comes to South-North comparisons, we are, nonetheless, not so much interested in commonalities. We rather want to find out whether the social policies in the four countries share some pertinent features – regarding the emergence of the policies or the trajectories taken – that differ from the European models and concepts. Thus, the outcomes of our South-North comparisons contribute to complementing European narratives on the emergence and the trajectories of welfare states and to welfare state theory more generally.

Four Welfare States

According to a widely used definition of the 'welfare state', the welfare state 'is the institutional outcome of the assumption by a society of legal and therefore formal and explicit responsibility for the basic well-being of all of its members'.[39] Such a 'welfare state' emerges when a society becomes convinced that the welfare of the individual is too important to be left to custom or to informal arrangements and private understandings, or the market forces, and is therefore a concern of government.[40] This definition of the welfare state stresses three elements: First, the assumption of 'state responsibility'; second, the formal – eg legal – recognition of such a responsibility; and, third, individual welfare as the object of that responsibility, as opposed to general welfare or community welfare achieved through measures of public health, public infrastructure, public schools, a common defence, or a police force with the mandate to prevent crimes.

Under that broad definition Brazil, China, India, and South Africa undoubtedly qualify as welfare states, and they do so for a few decades. The first Brazilian constitution containing a whole 'title' with respect to 'the economic and social order' was the Constitution of the United States of Brazil of 1946,[41] promising, *inter alia*, 'work that enables a dignified existence' (Article 145) and 'labour and social security legislation', ensuring, for instance, medical and sanitary aid for the worker, assistance to the unemployed, and social security against the consequences of old age, invalidity, illness, or death (Article 157). The 1946 Constitution of the Republic of China[42] contained a chapter on 'fundamental national policies', including a part on 'social security' listing a number of state duties, among them the duty of the state to 'provide opportunity of employment to people who are capable of work' (Article 153) and the duty of the

39 Harry K. Girvetz, 'Welfare State' in David L. Sills (ed), *International Encyclopedia of the Social Sciences*, vol 16 (The Macmillan Company & The Free Press 1968) 512. See also Johanna Kuhlmann, 'What is a Welfare State?' in Bent Greve (ed), *Routledge Handbook of the Welfare State* (Routledge 2019).

40 ibid.

41 Heinonline, World Constitutions Illustrated <www.heinonline.org/HOL/Page?handle=hein.cow/zzbr0379&collection=cow> accessed 28 February 2022.

42 Amos J. Peaslee (ed), *Constitutions of Nations, vol I Afghanistan to Finland* (Rumford Press 1950) 445.

state to 'enforce a Social Insurance System' in order to promote social welfare (Article 155, first sentence).[43] In a similar vein, the 1954 Constitution of the People's Republic of China[44] – envisioning a 'happy socialist society' – declared in Article 93:

> Working people . . . have the right to material assistance in old age, and in case of illness or disability. To guarantee enjoyment of this right, the state provides social insurance, social assistance and public health services and gradually expands these facilities.[45]

The Indian Constitution, adopted in 1949,[46] proclaimed to institute a 'Sovereign Democratic Republic' and promised in its preamble to assure the dignity of the individual (alongside with the unity of the nation). Moreover, the Indian Constitution declared that 'untouchability' be abolished (Article 17), forced labour prohibited (Article 23), and that, in the governance of the country, it be 'the duty of the State' to apply certain principles, such as the principle to 'promote the welfare of the people' (Article 38) or to direct its policy towards 'securing . . . that the citizens, men and women equally, have the right to an adequate means of livelihood' (Article 39[a]), implying the duty, 'within the limits of its economic capacity and development', to 'make effective provision for securing the right . . . to public assistance in cases of unemployment, old age, sickness and disablement, and in other cases of undeserved want' (Article 41). The current South African Constitution adopted in 1996[47] includes a 'Bill of Rights' guaranteeing traditional freedoms (for instance regarding religion, belief, expression, assembly, association, security of person), political rights, a right to property and equality before the law, but also the right to have human dignity respected and protected, the right to have access to adequate housing, health care, food, water, and social security, so-called socio-economic rights.[48] While it

43 The second sentence of Article 155 promised: 'To the aged, the infirm, and the crippled among the people who are unable to earn a living, and to victims of unusual calamities, the State shall extend appropriate assistance and relief'.

44 Albert P. Baustein (ed), *Fundamental Legal Documents of Communist China* (Fred B Rothman & Co 1962) 1.

45 ibid 30.

46 Amos J. Peaslee (ed), *Constitutions of Nations, vol II France to New Zealand*, 2nd edn (Martinus Nijhoff 1956) 223.

47 Act No 108 of 1996.

48 The Constitution of South Africa 1961 was very different. For the text see Amos J. Peaslee and Dorothy Peaslee Xydis, *Constitutions of Nations, vol I Africa*, 3rd edn (Martinus Nijhoff 1965) 808. On the one hand, the preamble of the Constitution 1961 promised that its aim was, *inter alia*, 'to further the contentment and spiritual and material welfare of all in our midst'. On the other hand, the preamble called on the 'Almighty God', 'Who gathered our forebears together from many lands and gave them this their own', an imaginary that left no doubt that the 'we'-group claiming to have forebears ('our forebears') and a country handed over by God ('our country') did not include

is unclear whether the Brazilian, Chinese, or Indian Constitution-makers of the 1940s drew on some concept of 'individual' or 'subjective' rights and, if so, what exactly that concept implied, it is sufficiently clear that all these constitutions and the current South African Constitution imagine a state bearing responsibility with regard to individual welfare, all explicit or implicit limitations to that responsibility notwithstanding. The 'state' is omnipresent as an institution that is meant to intervene in the course of things or societal relations, and old age, illness, invalidity or disability, or unemployment are risks occurring on the individual level.[49]

Summary

The subsequent four chapters will give a more detailed picture of the various shapes of the welfare state established in Brazil, China, India, and South Africa, concentrating on the ideas and goals that informed these shapes. The chapters follow a timeline that harmonises with the history of the country. For all periods deemed relevant, the chapters provide general information on the social, economic, and political context of legal the developments, move to elaborate on the provisions framing social policies more generally, and then turn to the measures we specifically focus on, social insurance and tax-financed means-tested benefits covering basic needs. The chapters trace the influence of international actors, for instance, the ILO, and of foreign models. A final chapter offers comparative perspectives.

Chapter 2 gives an account on the evolution of social policies in Brazil. Octávio Luiz Motta Ferraz starts the account in the 1930s and ends at present times. Ferraz aims to identify the main causes that led to the legal entrenchment of such policies. His focus is on social policies entrenched in the various Brazilian constitutions and some infra-constitutional developments, such as the Family Grant programme (*bolsa família*). The account on legislative acts is followed by an account concentrating on the most often mentioned causes, including ideas, behind the development of social policy legislation in Brazil during the periods covered. Finally, Ferraz comments on the reality of social policies on the ground and shows that and how realities differ, by some margin, from the legal texts. Yet, Ferraz also argues that, the realities notwithstanding, legal developments have made a non-trivial difference to the well-being of the Brazilian people.

people with local forebears. The constitution did not guarantee individual freedoms or individual rights. Equality was mentioned only in the context of languages. Article 108(1) read: 'English and Afrikaans shall be the official languages of the Republic, and shall be treated on a footing of equality, and possess and enjoy equal freedom, rights and privileges'. Against that background, the commitment to the 'welfare of all in our midst' is very thin and exclusive. The reluctance of the constitution was indicative. The governing White minority preferred a marginal welfare state at best.

49 On state responsibility see also Ulrike Davy, Chapter 6 in this volume, p. 198.

Chapter 3 discusses the social policies in China. Albert H.Y. Chen touches upon the Confucian values and practices of the traditional imperial state relating to care for the most unfortunate members of society and then investigates developments in the Republican period (1911–1949), the Maoist era (1949–1977), and the reform era (1978–) of the People's Republic of China (PRC). Chen highlights the changing thinking and institutions relating to social policy, from the enactment shortly after the PRC's establishment of the Labour Insurance Regulations (1951) (the key legal instrument in this domain in the Maoist era), to the constitutional amendment of 2004 (which expressly provides for the state's responsibility for 'social security') and the making of the Social Insurance Law 2010 (which establishes the legal framework for a comprehensive and universally applicable system of social insurance). The opening and reform period, so it seems, triggered an unprecedented expansion in both the field of social insurance and the field of tax-financed means-tested benefits covering basis needs.

Chapter 4 turns to India. Sarbani Sen describes the emergence of social policies in colonial India under British rule, when the first pertinent laws were enacted, the reaction of nationalist leaders to such policies, and the values and goals behind their own articulation of social policy which culminated in the drafting of the Indian Constitution, especially Part IV (the Directive Principles). These Principles were intended to be guidelines to the state about its approach to problems of workers, lower castes, women, and children, among other groups, and the provisions for reservation of seats in state-run educational institutions and in state services of socially and educationally and other backward communities. The chapter goes on to examine certain time periods identified by its distinctive ideas and values of social policy arising from the surrounding social and political context – which became embodied in statutes and regulations or case law of that period – namely, the 1950s and 1960s (the Nehruvian era); the 1970s and 1980s (Indira Gandhi's era); and the 1990s onwards (coalition governments and neo-liberalism). Sen contends that, for decades, policy makers believed in limitations to the state's financial or institutional capacities. Only in the 1980s, the courts, in particular the Supreme Court of India, moved to accept welfare entitlements. In the 2000s, policy makers eventually also strengthened the idea of welfare entitlements, at first under a Congress-led coalition government, then under governments led by Narendra Modi.

Chapter 5 deals with social policies in South Africa. Letlhokwa George Mpedi analyses the social policies in colonial South Africa, apartheid South Africa, and post-apartheid South Africa. Like in India, social policies emerged already in colonial South Africa. However, Mpedi highlights that, in the era of colonial South Africa, social policy was primarily concerned with the land question, the race problem, and the 'poor White problem'. Black South Africans were dispossessed and marginalised. During the apartheid era, cleavages in social policies remained palpable, although (so-called) Black and Coloured

South Africans were eventually integrated into the regimes of social insurance and social grants, yet not on an equal footing. In post-apartheid South Africa, racial distinctions were eliminated, but legacies remained. The beneficiaries of the grants are still categorised (children, disabled persons, elderly), and the Constitutional Court's push for more encompassing social policies is rather soft.

Finally, Chapter 6 engages in comparisons, across the four countries and between the four countries and European social policies, in particular the social policies in Germany and Great Britain, as those two European countries represent the most important foreign models. Ulrike Davy concentrates on critical junctures, the emergence of social policies (conditions, perceptions, ideational frameworks), the trajectories chosen, and the role of the courts in pushing for new social policy concepts and dimensions. She also gives an account of the labour and social politics pursued by Brazil, China, India, and South Africa at International Labour Conferences at a time when social policies started to emerge at the domestic level, ie in the 1920s and 1930s, exploring the linkages between politics pursued at the ILO and home-made social politics. Davy argues that historically all four countries moved from a rather narrowly conceptualised 'social insurance' framework to a more encompassing regime of 'social security'. That move might, at first glance, resemble European pathways. However, so Davy contends, Southern idiosyncrasies prevailed in conceptualising the meaning of 'social security', when the term became prominent. In fact, the term epitomises core elements of Southern welfare and the aspirations of non-European countries in a post-colonial era.

Chapter 2

Brazil's Social Policies Since the 1930s

From Fragmentation to Universalism

Octávio Luiz Motta Ferraz

Introduction

In this chapter my aim is to provide an account of the evolution of social policies in Brazil's legislation since the 1930s and to identify the main causes (in particular the motivational ideas) that led to the legal entrenchment of such policies. Any minimally comprehensive such account would of course require much more space than I have available, so it will be necessarily incomplete and limited in focus. It will hopefully still be useful as an entry point to this complex topic.

The main focus will be on social policies entrenched in the highest level of legislation in Brazil, ie its constitutions. This is, again, a limited focus, yet one that is in my view justified but in need of some explanation. Firstly, it is important to note that not all social policies in Brazil have a constitutional grounding. The most prominent example is the widely known and discussed conditional cash transfer programme called *Bolsa Família* ('The Family Grant').[1] Yet most of Brazil's most significant social policies since the 1930s have been included in the constitutional text, often when new constitutions were adopted (which happened at least five times since then)[2] so the constitution seems the natural place to focus on. Secondly, I of course do not hold the view that the mere adoption of laws, even constitutions, is sufficient to produce social change. But I equally reject a radical sceptical view that laws make no difference whatsoever in what happens in reality. The actual role and impact of laws in social change is an extremely complex and

1 At the end of 2021, the *Bolsa Família* programme was replaced by '*Auxílio Brasil*' ('Brazil Aid'), which is basically the same programme with a different name (mostly for political reasons, ie to try to delink the programme from the party that created it, the Workers' Party) and a few tweaks such as some extra benefits which are however still unclear and will not apply until further legislation and regulation is adopted in future. See Agência Brasil (Online, 2.12.2021), Senate approves provisional measure creating Brazil Aid. <https://agenciabrasil.ebc.com.br/en/politica/noticia/2021-12/senate-approves-provisional-measure-creating-brazil-aid> accessed 28 February 2022.

2 I say at least because experts disagree on whether the 1969 amendment to the 1967 Constitution was just an amendment or in fact a new constitution given the wide-ranging substantive changes it introduced. See José Afonso da Silva, *Curso de Direito Constitucional Positivo* (Editora Malheiros 2005) 132.

DOI: 10.4324/9781003242826-2

important matter which I cannot even begin to address in this chapter.[3] But if laws are indeed capable to contribute to social change to some degree at least (and this will inevitably vary in different contexts), it seems useful to study these laws and how they come about beyond a purely historical interest.

In my view, one of the main justifications for a study of the development of social policies through an analysis of constitutions and legislation and the ideas that inspired them lies precisely in the potential that these legal instruments have to change the reality on the ground, even if this potential is always mitigated by several obstacles. But I will not be able to offer any comprehensive discussion of this topic here. Due to limitations of space and in line with the other chapters and the scope of this book, my focus will be on a more descriptive and analytical account of the evolution of social policies in Brazilian constitutions and legislation. The issue of actual social impact will appear only incidentally in the text and in my concluding remarks.

The chapter is organised as follows. In section 2, I present a historical account of the evolution of social policies in Brazil's constitution and legislation from the 1930s to the 1988 Constitution (still in force), as well as some important infra-constitutional developments such as the Family Grant programme. In section 3, I discuss some of the most often mentioned causes (including the ideas) behind the development of social policy legislation in Brazil during that period. In the concluding section, I comment briefly on the reality of social policies on the ground and how they differ, by some margin, from the legal text, yet have made a non-trivial difference to the well-being of the Brazilian people.

Social Policy in Brazil's Constitutions and Legislation: A History From the 1930s to the Present Day

The Vargas Period (1930–1945)

It is generally agreed that the origins of what we may call today, with several caveats to be made later on, the 'Brazilian welfare state' date back to the first government of Getúlio Vargas, which spanned fifteen years from 1930 to 1945.[4]

3 I deal with this issue in much more depth in previous publications, such as Octávio Luiz Motta Ferraz, 'The Right to Health in the Courts of Brazil: Worsening Health Inequities?' (2009) 11/2 Health and Human Rights Journal <www.hhrjournal.org/2013/08/the-right-to-health-in-the-courts-of-brazil-worsening-health-inequities/> accessed 28 February 2022; Octávio Luiz Motta Ferraz, 'Health Inequalities, Rights and Courts: The Social Impact of the "Judicialization of Health" in Brazil' in Alicia Yamin and Siri Gloppen (eds), *Litigating the Right to Health: Can Courts Bring More Justice to Health Systems?* (Harvard University Press 2011); Octávio Luiz Motta Ferraz, *Health as a Human Right. The Politics and Judicialization of Health in Brazil* (Cambridge University Press 2021).

4 Although some incipient roots were already in place since the 1824 Imperial Constitution, such as free primary education (1–4 grade), social and health assistance to the needy and charitable houses to orphans and the abandoned. See Articles XXXI, XXXII and XXXIII of the Constitution of 1824.

In the 1920s, there had been a very limited and fragmented experience with retirement and pension funds (the CAPs – *Caixa de Aposentadoria e Pensão*) instituted for distinct sectors of the incipient Brazilian industry – the first in 1923 for the workers of the railways. It was only in the 1930s, though, that for the first time in its history Brazil would witness some national and more comprehensive social policies as opposed to limited and localized initiatives.

The Constitution of 1934 is the central legal document in the first years of that period.[5] It was supposed to leave behind forty years of rule by powerful local landowners (known as *coronelismo*), many of them large coffee farmers (then the main economic product of Brazil), and institute democratic principles of power alternation, secret vote (extended for the first time to women) and the impossibility of re-election of the president, then Getúlio Vargas, who had gained power in 1930 through a military coup that deposed the elected president, Julio Prestes. It was partly influenced by the Constitutionalist Revolution of 1932 and was inspired by the Weimar Constitution of 1919 and the Mexican Constitution of 1915.[6] It marked the end of the 'Old Republic' (*Velha República*) and superseded the first constitution of the republican period, the liberal constitution of 1891.

In the social arena, it is the first to include an 'Economic and social order' chapter, moving emphatically away, thus, from the model of liberal constitutions whose main, if not only function was to restrict state power, in part through so-called negative rights, that is freedoms to be secured to citizens from state interference. The 1934 Constitution, on the contrary, influenced by socialist ideas, attributed significant power to the state to interfere with several sacred aspects of the liberal creed, such as the right to private property, and expressly allowed state intervention in the economy.[7] It was therefore a radical change from the hitherto liberal model of the 1891 Constitution, which had been inspired by the American Constitution.

It also contained several specific clauses of a social nature, ie attributing to the state responsibilities to protect and ensure the wellbeing of the population. In Article 10, it set the broad competence of the federal union and the states to 'look after health and public assistance' (10, II); 'oversee the application of social legislation' (10, V); and 'extend public education in all its levels' (10, VI). In later

5 Before the 1934 Constitution some measures protecting workers' rights were introduced by decree, such as the eight hours working day and the minimum wage guarantee. See Decreto 19.398, 11 November 1930. But the Constitution of 1934 gave these policies the highest possible legal status.

6 There was also influence from the Constitution of Spain of 1931 and of some fascist practices such as the participation of forty trade union representatives in the Constituent Assembly. See entry Constituição de 1934 in CPDOC – Centro de Pesquisa e Documentação de História Contemporânea do Brasil. <https://cpdoc.fgv.br/producao/dossies/AEraVargas1/anos30-37/Constituicao1934> accessed 28 February 2022.

7 It authorised the state to intervene in the economy through monopolisation of activities (Article 116); promotion of popular economy and nationalisation of banks (Article 117); control of private use and progressive nationalisation of water falls, mineral and other resources found underground (Articles 118 and 119); and all other services necessary to implement the new socio-economic order.

articles it guaranteed the 'rights of all Brazilians and resident foreigners to liberty, *subsistence*, individual security and property' (Article 113) (my emphasis), and sets as a duty of the state to facilitate a 'dignified existence' to everyone (Article 115).

But perhaps the most significant development in terms of social policies was the constitutionalisation of the duty of the state to protect workers in article 121, and the inclusion of a long and detailed list of protections that labour legislation ought to be enacted to perform. Noteworthy were the establishment of a minimum wage (Article 121, para 1, b); maximum 8 hours of work per day (c); and annual paid holidays (f).

Specific courts were created to enforce these rights (Article 122, 'Labour Courts' *Justiça do Trabalho*). Social assistance to the needy (Article 138, a), protection to maternity and children (Article 138, c) and education (Articles 149 ff) also gained constitutional status. Complementing the power of the state to intervene in the markets, Article 131 restricted the use of private property in light of social and collective interests and authorised the state to expropriate it with just compensation.

But this generously social constitution was to last very shortly, as already in the end of 1935 Getúlio Vargas suspended all rights of political participation on alleged grounds of communist threats to the Brazilian state, and promulgated, in 1937, a new authoritarian constitution (The '*Polaca*', as it was influenced by the Polish constitution), which was to restrict the right to strike and put all trade unions under the supervision and control of the Ministry of Work, lasting till the end of his dictatorship in 1945.[8] Many of the social protections for workers survived in ordinary legislation though, and Vargas is still praised today as the 'Father of the Poor'. His famous Consolidation of Labour Laws, a codification in ordinary legislation of all labour laws, (*Consolidação das Leis do Trabalho* – CLT) was promulgated in 1943 and survives to this day.

The 'Second Republic'[9] (1946–1964) – Not Much Happens

The end of the first Vargas period and his authoritarian regime gave way to a brief democratic interregnum of eighteen years in Brazil which operated under another new constitution, enacted in 1946. It brought back the democratic principles suspended during the Vargas dictatorship and established, emphatically, social justice and the promotion of work as the grounds of the Brazilian constitutional social and economic order. Article 157 had a long list of workers' rights not dissimilar to those of the 1934 Constitution. Article 166 established education as a right, with interesting innovations, such as the imposition on companies

8 See Walter Costa Porto, *A Constituição de 1937* (Subsecretaria de Edições Técnicas do Senado Federal 2012).

9 I am using Sérgio Abranches periodisation here, see Sérgio Abranches, *Presidencialismo de Coalizão. Raízes e evolução do modelo político brasileiro* (Cia das Letras 1988).

with more than 100 employees the duty to provide free primary education for workers and their children (Article 168, III) and a duty on the state to invest a minimum of 10 percent of federal income and 20 percent of states and municipal income on education. Also noteworthy was Article 147, repeating that the right to property has limits in 'social well-being' and adding that the state may, through legislation, promote its 'just distribution with equal opportunity for all'.

The changes between the radical (for the period) innovations of the 1934 Constitution and the 1946 one in terms of social policy were not that significant. As we will see in the next section, both fall within what experts delimit as the first wave of social policies in Brazil, characterised by a strong focus on workers' rights and very limited assistance to the destitute. An important non-constitutional social policy during that period, which also followed this 'corporatist' model, was the creation of contributory pension funds for workers divided by category, the IAPs, Institutes of Retirement and Pensions (see next section).[10] Such a model excludes those without formal links to the labour market or public employment, which were the vast majority of the Brazilian population in that period.[11] Indeed, according to estimates, as late as 1950 the percentage of the population covered by these social policies was a meagre 7 percent (or 20 percent of the economically active population).[12]

The Military Dictatorship (1964–1985)

The second phase of social policies starts in 1964, the year of another military coup, yet again justified by its supporters by the alleged threat of communism. As usual, a new constitution followed in 1967, but this time with a long list of individual rights and guarantees in Chapter 4 (which were all but disrespected to different degrees of intensity during the dictatorship). The innovations in social policy were however not insignificant, and thus the view of many that it represented a new phase. The Constitution of 1967 included a larger number

10 With the exception of some clauses that refer to retirement rights of public servants with full salary after thirty years of service. The coverage of the IAPs varied significantly according to workers' category. The most extensive was that of the workers in the banking sector (IAPB), which included pensions due to age, incapacity, pensions for the surviving partner, medical and pharmaceutical assistance, illness and maternity aid, and even funeral and detention aid. The least comprehensive funds covered only pensions for invalidity and illness aid, eg that of industrial workers (IAPI).

11 One limited exception, as we saw, was the right to free primary education, guaranteed in both constitutions, at least on paper. But note that during the second phase of Varga's government the right to education was significantly watered down in the constitution. According to Article 125 of the Constitution of 1937, the integral education of offspring was the first duty and the natural right of parents. The state was supposed to be no stranger to this duty by collaborating, in a principal or subsidiary manner, to facilitate its execution or to address the deficiencies and shortcomings of private education.

12 Célia Lessa Kerstenetzky, O Estado de Bem-estar Social na Idade da Razão. *A Reinvenção do Estado Social no Mundo Contemporâneo* (Elsevier 2012) 195.

of social clauses than its predecessors, as they repeated, often literally, the clauses of the 1934 and 1946 constitutions discussed earlier, but also extended them.[13] Moreover, in terms of constitutional status, these clauses were formulated unambiguously as individual rights for the first time, which reflects a change in ideas as we shall discuss further in the next section.

In terms of workers' rights, the main innovation was the constitutionalisation, for the first time, of a comprehensive right to 'social protection' (*previdência social*), to cover for loss of income due to unemployment, maternity, illness, old age, incapacity, and death, to be funded by contributions from the state, employers, and employees to a unified system to be centrally managed by the National Institute of Social Providence (INPS) (Article 158, XVI). Also noteworthy was the constitutionalisation of a compulsory insurance to be bought by the employer against work related accidents (Article 158, XVII); of a family grant ('*salário família*')[14], which added a small percentage (around 5 percent of the minimum wage) to the workers' salary per child (Article 158, II); of a fund to compensate workers' when dismissed without fair cause (FGTS) (Article 158, XIII); and the extension to women of full-salary pension after thirty years of work (Article 158, XX).

In terms of the right to education, the most significant innovation was the extension of free schooling from primary education only (constitutions of 1934 and 1946) to those up to 14 years of age.

Important non-constitutional policies were also adopted, such as the extension of pensions to rural workers through the Prorural programme in 1971, and to domestic workers and the self-employed in 1972 and 1973. Also important was the creation of a targeted monthly basic income for life for those above the age of 70 who were also poor and incapacitated for work ('*Renda Mensal Vitalícia*').[15]

As we shall see in the next section, though these extensions seem at first in line with progressive ideas of redistributive universalism, the fact is that benefits remained accessible mostly to those employed and extremely unequal within categories of workers, being much lower to rural and domestic workers for instance. Moreover, the military regime also incentivised strongly the development of the private sector (in line with its liberal anti-communist stance) through

13 The 1967 Constitution was amended through several so-called Institutional Acts (Atos Institucionais) issued by the military rulers and then no less than twenty-seven amendments to the constitution, the first of which, in 1969, incorporated in the constitutional text all five AIs and is therefore regarded by many as another constitution, see Silva (n 2). The most infamous, the AI 5, declared a state of emergency, shut the Congress for almost one year and suspended *habeas corpus*.

14 A type of 'family grant' has existed since 1937 and was included in the constitution of 1967 and 1988. It is also interesting to note that it was also during the military regime that the first condition to the family grant was created, namely the requirement to prove children's vaccination, in 1973. A second condition came in 1999: School attendance. Another important change was the targeting of the family grant, which was originally universal, to only those of low income, through Constitutional Amendment 20 in 1998.

15 Federal Law n° 6.179/74.

tax exemptions, a kind of 'fiscal welfare'. This led to the desertion of the middle classes from public education and health services, which we see to this date, creating what Kerstenetzky dubbed a 'basic universalism' in social policies, or what we may name social policies for the poor, or targeted social policies. As she puts it: 'the embryonic universalist-redistributivist project . . . was abruptly aborted by the movement of March 1964'.[16] It is undeniable, though, that social policies, still limited and deficient as they were (and still are as we will see), nonetheless expanded their coverage significantly during the military regime, reaching 20 percent of the population in 1983, from just above 7 percent in 1960.[17]

The 'New Republic' (1985 to Date)

Genuine universalism, at least on paper, would need to wait another two decades for the end of the military regime, re-democratisation, and adoption of yet another new constitution, Brazil's 7th (or 8th for those who regard the 1969 amendment as a new constitution). The Constitution of 1988 not only reintroduced the democratic regime in Brazil, including an even longer list of civil and political rights than those of its predecessors, but also a much more comprehensive catalogue of social and economic rights. Indicating further the prominence that the idea of rights had then acquired, they were moved from their traditional spot at the end of the constitution to its very beginning, to Articles 5 to 14.

Dubbed the 'Citizen Constitution', reflecting another shift in ideas underlying social policies, that of 'citizenship' (more on this in the next section), it goes much further than any previous constitution in terms of the recognition of social rights, including the rights to health, housing, education, work, leisure, social security, and assistance to the needy (Article 6), well beyond the traditional (though also longer now) list of workers' rights. Moreover, it also establishes in greater detail which policies, and of what nature, are required from the state to implement these rights, through an entire section of the constitution, now exclusively dedicated to the 'The Social Order', and comprising no less than 40 articles.[18]

Its inaugural article, 193, starts by stating that 'the social order has as its ground the primacy of work, and as its goals welfare and social justice'.[19] It follows by stating that 'social security' should guarantee the rights related to

16 Kerstenetzky (n 12) 199.

17 ibid 210.

18 For comparison, the 1967 Constitution had a combined title for the economic and social order with 15 articles, as did the 1946 Constitution, with 30. If we add the economic and social orders, separated in different titles in the 1988 Constitution, it adds up to 62 articles, from Articles 170 to 232. Separating the 'Social Order' chapter from the 'Economic Order' chapter reflects the importance that social policies acquired, at least in rhetoric. Moreover, the idea of 'social rights' as the bedrock of social policies became the core idea of the 'Social Order'.

19 Something that, as we saw, was already present in the 1934, 1946 and 1967 constitutions.

health, pensions, and social assistance (Article 194), whose aims are 'universal coverage and delivery' (Article 194, I); 'uniformity and equivalence of benefits and services between the urban and rural population' (Article 194, II); 'selectivity and distributivity in the provision of benefits and services' (Article 194, III); non-diminution of benefits (Article 194, IV); equity in participation and funding (Article 194, V); diversity in the funding basis (Article 194, VI); and democratic and decentralised administration (Article 194, VII).[20]

An important difference should be noted among the three components of the social security system in the meaning of universality. Whereas health is universal in the broadest sense of the term, ie accessible to all irrespective of payment or any other condition beyond simple registration in the health system, pensions are universal 'on condition of contribution' and fulfilment of specific contribution criteria (period of contribution and age), and social assistance, despite being also independent of contribution, like health, is nonetheless conditional on the fulfilment of certain criteria established in the constitution, namely maternity, infancy, adolescence, old age, and disability (Article 203). Of those, however, only old age and disability, as we saw earlier, have been expressly contemplated in the constitution with a specific benefit of one minimum wage. Protection of children and adolescents and maternity and promotion of integration in the job market were left open, which could perhaps help to explain its lesser priority in social policy.

Education, culture, sports, sciences and technology, social communication, environment, family, children, adolescents and elderly, and indigenous people are the other several areas of the social order, regulated in separate chapters of the 1988 Constitution (Chapters III to VIII). Education, like health, is defined as a right of everyone and a duty of the state (but also the family and in collaboration with society, Article 205), and should be free in public institutions from the age of 4 to 17.[21] Pre-school (from 0 to 5 years) is also a duty of the state (Article 208, IV), not necessarily free, although for workers' children this has been included via constitutional amendment.[22] Another important constitutional provision obliges all government units (federal, state, and municipal) to invest a minimum percentage of their tax income in education (18 percent, 25 percent, and 25 percent respectively).[23] A potential source of constitutional conflict is the provision included in Article 227 that states that children and adolescents have

20 This last section was included later through Constitutional Amendment 20/1998 and was further specified in Federal Law N° 8.212, of 24 July 1991.

21 This was an extension done by Amendment 59, of 2009. The original 1988 Constitution stated that education should be free at the fundamental ('primary') level (Article 208, I) and progressively free at the secondary level.

22 Constitutional Amendment 53/2006. Article 7, XXV – free assistance to the children and dependents since birth till 5 (five) years of age in creches and pre-school.

23 Article 212. The Federal government shall invest, annually, never less than eighteen, and the states, federal district, and municipalities twenty-five per cent, at least, of tax revenue, including that originating in transfers, in the maintenance of education development.

'absolute priority' in the protection of their rights to 'life, health, food, education, leisure, professionalisation, culture, dignity, respect, liberty and social and familial contact'. The elderly are also given the right to free transport after the age of 65 (Article 230, para 2). The indigenous people were guaranteed the right to occupy their ancestral land and have them demarcated (Articles 231 and 232).

This is just a very brief account of the vast array of social clauses included in the 1988 Constitution. As we will see in the concluding section, many of these constitutional commitments remain incompletely fulfilled. What is important to highlight here is the significant change in conception, that is, in ideas, about the role of the state and society in providing social security to the population. The 1988 Constitution has brought Brazil clearly into the territory of comprehensive, universalist-redistributivist social policy thinking; ie from the early narrow and fragmented framework of variable benefits to workers according to economic sector and residual assistance to the needy (the corporatist model), through the unified and expanded, but still variable and mostly contributory benefits system of the military period to the further expanded and by and large non-contributory system of today.[24] How it got there, and what difference it has made, are different questions that will be addressed briefly in the conclusion. The following figure attempts to summarise the evolution of the system through these historical phases in visual form.

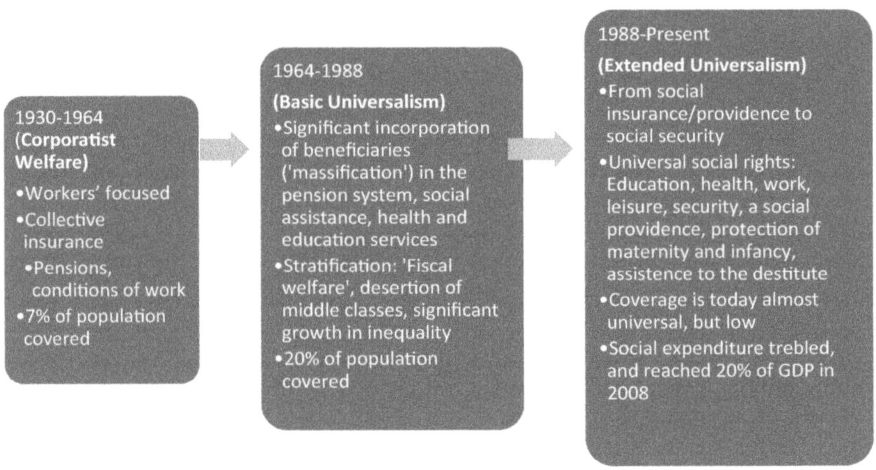

Figure 2.1 Three boxes showing the evolution of welfare in Brazil from corporatist welfare to basic universalism to extended universalism.

Source: By the author.

24 Eduardo Fagnani and Flavio Tonelli Vaz make a similar claim, stating that the 1988 Constitution inaugurated 'a social protection system inspired by the values of the social welfare state'. See Eduardo Fagnani and Flavio Tonelli Vaz, 'Seguridade social, direitos constitucionais e Desenvolvimento, in Ana Fonseca and Eduardo Fagnani (eds), *Politicas Sociais, Desenvolvimento e Cidadania*, vol II (Fundação Perseu Abramo 2014) 92.

The Ideas Behind the 'Brazilian Welfare State'

Preliminary Remarks: Ideas

This chapter aims not only at describing the historical evolution and current state of legally recognized social policies in Brazil but also at investigating the range of 'ideas of the social' that crystallised in the processes of constitution-making and enactment of major statutory law. Why do countries adopt social policies and what influences the shape of the particular policies they adopt, or rather promise to adopt through legislative enactments? As with any human initiative, ideas must necessarily play some role. But what exact ideas and how they influence social policy are of course extremely complex issues. My aim here is to look at some of the debates that took place (and continue to rage) around the adoption of the social policies described in the previous section to see what ideas seem to have been influential in the shaping of what I have been calling, with some exaggeration, the 'Brazilian welfare state'.[25]

The importance of looking at ideas is well explained by Stuart White in the following manner:

> the welfare state is centrally an expression of certain ethical ideals. It is defended in the name of social justice. It is held to violate other ideals, such as individual liberty. Political debate over the future of welfare states taps directly into these claims and counter-claims.[26]

The complexity of the enterprise lies in the fact that 'social justice' is a highly indeterminate and contested concept. Moreover, discussions on social justice necessarily involve a myriad of further equally indeterminate and contested values such as needs, well-being, equality, solidarity, liberty, rights, reciprocity, citizenship etc which, in turn, are influenced by equally contested expectations of the role of the state, different attitudes to risk, and changing knowledge about poverty and deprivation.[27]

Social policies will therefore not be directly and neatly shaped by a single undisputed conception of social justice prevailing universally around the globe at a certain point in time, but rather by the messy politics of each country,

25 As Evelyne Huber and Juan Bogliaccini note, '[t]he concept of the Welfare State (Estado de Bienestar) has come into widespread use relatively recently in Latin American literature. Traditionally, studies of social security dominated the literature. This reflected reality in so far as states – to the extent that they began to take responsibility for the welfare of their citizens – emphasized employment based social insurance, that is, social security, over non-contributory social assistance'. See Evelyne Huber and Juan Bogliaccini, 'Latin America', in Francis Castles and others (eds), *The Oxford Handbook of the Welfare State* (Oxford University Press 2010) 644.

26 Stuart White, 'Ethics', in Castles and others (n 25) 19.

27 See Michael Freeden, 'The Coming of the Welfare State', in Terence Ball and Richard Bellamy (eds), *The Cambridge History of Twentieth-Century Political Thought* (Cambridge University Press 2003) 5.

where different conceptions of these myriad of ideas battle each other and eventually crystalise into legislation. It is not surprising, thus, that the ideal of social justice and the attempt to respond to the so-called social question[28] has led to so many differently shaped 'welfare states' in distinct countries.[29] As Kuhnle and Sander note in their account of the emergence of the Western welfare state, '[s]ocial policies were introduced with different motivations in different places and the various factors have carried different weight in different periods'.[30]

But there is also a great measure of common traits, and this has to do with the transnational exchange of ideas that seem to have started quite early in the history of social policies. As Pierson and Leimgruber note, although the welfare state has usually been understood as

> quintessentially a national phenomenon, as early as 1900 reformers, welfare workers, labour lawyers, insurers and statisticians from many countries met at the social sections of the World Fairs, corresponded through the International Association for Labour Legislation (1901) . . . and attended professional congresses.[31]

It is also important to note that the ideas that underpin social policies change and, with this, the latter's nature and shape, but such shifts are not neat, linear, or irreversible.[32] One important major shift that occurred particularly in Europe after the second world war was that from 'the logic of charity to the logic of citizenship', ie of social policy not as an instrument to help the unfortunate and unlucky but rather to implement their *rights*. Yet that shift, which seemed rather stable for almost thirty years, came under sustained attack after the late 1970s and the spread of 'neoliberal' ideas, prompting many to divide the post-war era into two periods, one of expansion of the welfare state (1945–1973) and one of retrenchment (1973 onwards).[33]

28 For a good intellectual history of the term, see Holly Case, 'The "Social Question," 1820–1920' (2016) 13 Modern Intellectual History 747.

29 Chris Pierson and Matthieu Leimgruber, 'Intellectual roots', in Castles and others (n 25) 32.

30 Stein Kuhnle and Anne Sander, 'The Emergence of the Western Welfare State', in Castles and others (n 25) 67.

31 Pierson and Leimgruber (n 29) 41; see also Kuhnle and Sander (n 30) 75 claiming that 'the idea and practice of social security spread during the interwar period to other regions of the world, most visibly to North, Central, and Latin America. This was often with the help of the International Labour Organization (ILO), established in 1919'.

32 See Pierson and Leimgruber (n 29) 42, noting that many 'of the reforms built upon what had existed in the interwar period and, especially given the financial constraints within which programmes were introduced, the preceding order of conditional payments, user charges, and means-tested assistance lingered on into the brave new world'.

33 For a good critical discussion of this periodisation see Frank Nullmeier and Franz-Xaver Kaufmann, 'Post-War Welfare State Development', in Castles and others (n 25) 81.

Brazil's welfare state has of course been influenced by these international ideational developments and shifts to greater or lesser extent and at varying 'time lags', as we will see in this section.[34] To help organise the discussion I will continue using the periodisation of the previous section, proposed by Kerstenetzky. To recall, she divides the development of social policies in Brazil into *three long waves* of institutional innovation: the years of 'corporatist welfare', which go from 1930 to 1964; the period of 'basic universalism', from the mid-1960s to the mid-1980s, and the current phase of 'extended universalism', which started with the 1988 Constitution.[35] There is a historical tendency, thus, of expansion both in the comprehensiveness of social policies in terms of beneficiaries (from formal workers to anyone in need) and the coverage of risks (from loss of work-related income to any kind of deprivation, not only of income, but also of health, education, housing etc). This periodisation is of course not watertight and neat, and this tendency is of course not linear and inevitable, as I have already cautioned earlier; it faced setbacks in the past and is likely to face them in the future. Many believe that a major setback is currently in course after the impeachment of the Workers' Party president in 2016 and the election of a conservative government in 2018.

Corporatist Welfare (1930s–1964)

As we saw in the previous section, during the first wave, that of 'corporatist welfare' which started in the 1930s with the Vargas regime the focus was very narrow, ie on benefits for workers, at first those employed by the state, civilians and the military, and later also workers of the nascent industries (textile), banking, and commerce. The logic was that of 'collective insurance', ie of cover to the risks associated with formal employment, eg loss of income due to work accidents, illness, and age. Yet even such narrow focus from the standpoint of

34 To cite just a couple of examples, Brazil participated in the Paris conference after the First World War that ended with a number of peace treaties which also contained the constitutions of the League of Nations and the International Labour Organisation. The treaties called on signatory governments (including Brazil) to take initiatives in the area of social and labour policy based on a common minimum ten-point reformist programme aimed as an alternative to the Russian revolutionary approach. As Malloy notes, 'it is impossible to measure the full impact of these international events on Brazil, but most analysists agree that they did have some significant influence in contributing to the political tone of the period'. See James Malloy, *The Politics of Social Security in Brazil* (University of Pittsburgh Press 1979) 38. The internal context was one of growing discontent of workers, but also of the growing urban middle classes with living conditions, inflation of prices etc. Another important potential source of inspiration was Catholic doctrine, recalling that Brazil is the largest Catholic country in the world in terms of population. Two fundamental early texts are the papal Encyclicals Rerum Novarum (1891) and Quadrogesimo Anno (1931).

35 Kerstenetzky (n 12) 181. There are, as usual, disputes about the appropriateness of Kerstenetzky's periodisation. I will not engage with them here. My aim in using it is simply to organise the discussion and make it more manageable.

today's ideas of what a proper welfare state should protect against was a significant improvement on the situation prevailing in Brazil at the time. The question is how these changes came about? A brief look at this important juncture for social policy in Brazil is rather illuminating in terms of how ideas operate.

A central organising idea in those times was that of the 'social question'. As James Malloy notes, the 'manifold problems posed by an emerging working class in the Old Republic were subsumed under the concept of the "social question"'. As he explains:

> By the second decade of this century the social question had become one of the main issues of Brazilian politics. However, the social question increased in salience not simply because of pressure emanating from the working class but from the general internal and external context of the time.[36]

In a speech during his failed presidential campaign in 1919, 'The Social and Political Question in Brazil', Ruy Barbosa, an influential public intellectual and statesmen, strongly denounced the indifference of the economic and political elites to the plight of the 'working plebe', made up significantly of former slaves but also a growing urban working class including immigrants from Italy and elsewhere lured to the country in state sponsored programmes after the abolition of slavery.[37] Other intellectuals and politicians from an also growing urban middle class articulated proposals to deal with the social question, both from the right and from the left of the political spectrum. These proposals were strongly influenced by ideological struggles then current in Europe. On the right, groups called for constitutional reform along 'corporatist' lines, based on the concept of 'class representation' in vogue in Catholic social doctrine and Comtean positivism. On the left, several 'socialist' groups articulated vague Marxist positions. Some in this latter group were elected to the federal legislature and formed a reformist bloc putting forward a series of proposals to reform labour relations along the lines of European labour codes and the provisions of the Versailles Treaty. Many wrote for reformist newspapers and maintained close contact with labour unions, dissident middle-class groups, and disgruntled army officials, forming what James Malloy called an 'incipient multiclass reformist movement'.[38]

Despite this growing reformist mood, it would take almost a decade for the first timid shoots of change to appear and another one for the actual first real wave of social policies to kick off. Here we can clearly see the significance of

36 Malloy (n 34) 37. The external context he refers to was the end of the First World War, the Russian Revolution etc.

37 Rui Barbosa, A Questão Social e Política no Brasil (1919), <www.casaruibarbosa.gov.br/dados/DOC/artigos/rui_barbosa/p_a5.pdf> accessed 28 February 2022.

38 Malloy (n 34) 39. Two prominent figures in these groups were Eloy Chaves, a member of the state parliament in Sao Paulo, and businessman Jorge Street.

what we could perhaps call 'counter-ideas' in the shaping of social policies, as we have already emphasized earlier. The majority of the political and business classes fiercely resisted any kind of reform, as one would perhaps expect.[39] This resistance was often carried out through violent means, ie police repression, as vividly captured by one of the leading painters of the time, Emiliano Di Cavalcanti, in one of his politically engaged drawings where one sees three gigantic and brutal looking policemen holding a minuscule worker and the subtitle 'The social question continues to be a police question'.[40]

But it was also often defended with ideas, again also often borrowed from Europe and America, most notably liberal ones that the state should not intervene in private relationships such as those between employers and employees. On their side was the 1891 liberal Constitution, inspired on the American one, and here is the explanation why constitutional reform was a main aspect in the campaign of the reformist groups. To illustrate, whereas all the constitutions from the 1930s onwards were to state, as we saw earlier, that property ought to play a social function and be necessarily limited by collective and social interests, in the 1891 Constitution, Article 72, para 17 the formulation is much more peremptory: '*the right to property is maintained in all of its plenitude*'.

This battle of ideas echoed of course the one held almost everywhere not only during the emergence of social policies but throughout the history of the welfare state to this date. As Kuhnle and Sander note about the Bismarckian pioneering reforms in imperial Germany in the late nineteenth century, the '*German legislation was a radical break with liberalism*' and were '*still too radical in other national political contexts*'. Yet they were an important precedent for what became gradually accepted as a '*new role for the nation state*', which spread across Europe, across the Atlantic, and reached even the Antipodes, at different paces and intensities.[41]

These ideas eventually reached Brazil, as we saw in the previous section, producing at first more heat than light,[42] but eventually leading to the first wave

39 See Gøsta Esping-Andersen, *The Three Worlds of Welfare Capitalism* (Polity 1990) 22 plausibly stating, 'De-commodification [which is the aim of true welfare states in his view] strengthens the worker and weakens the absolute authority of the employer. It is for exactly this reason that employers have always opposed de-commodification'.

40 Emiliano Di Cavalcanti, 'A questão social continua um caso de polícia – n°7', In 'A Realidade Brasileira'. Nanquim sobre papel, 32.6 cm × 23.1 (Acervo do Instituto de Estudos Brasileiros da Universidade de São Paulo, between 1930 e 1933). For an image of the drawing see <http://200.144.255.59/catalogo_eletronico/fichaDocumentoCAV.asp?Documento_Codigo=2413&Acervo_Nome=m%C3%81rio%20de%20andrade&Acervo_Codigo=1> accessed 28 February 2022.

41 Kuhnle and Sander (n 30) 65–66.

42 Several fragmented initiatives took place before the 1930s, such as autonomous pension funds created at first by the railway companies (Eloy Chaves Law, 1923) and then extended across other industry sectors. Yet, with no direct participation of the state but rather contributions from employers and employees. The language used then was that of 'private social policy'. See Kerstenetzky (n 12) 186–187. Other limited and fragmented initiatives existed since the late nineteenth century,

of 'corporatist welfare', facilitated by the ascendance to power of Getúlio Vargas, in the 1930 revolution that brought an end to the so-called Old Republic (or First Republic, 1889–1930).[43] As well as recognising, and constitutionalising, a large set of workers' rights (see section 2 earlier), it created the national Institutes of Retirements and Pensions (IAPs), organized by professional groups rather than single companies (the maritime workers having been the first) which involved the state directly, as co-founder and administrator, gradually substituting the previous private insurance schemes. The shift in perceptions about the appropriate role of the state is clear. From a 'laissez faire' attitude, through a light touch interference imposing compulsory insurance on employers to a much more extensive role in the administration of the social and economic order and guarantor of workers' protection, in particular pensions and working conditions. This new conception is clearly reflected, as we saw in the previous section, in the language of the constitutions of the period, which included for the first time whole sections on the so-called economic and social order. We are still very far in that period, however, from any strong sense of *democratic citizenship* as the ground for such benefits. In fact, the illiterate, then the majority of the population, could not vote and were virtually excluded from any political participation, and these improvements were conducted in an authoritarian manner, top-down, by the authoritarian government of Vargas, in a spirit of paternalism. Moreover, these benefits were restricted to those in formal employment, either public or private, which, as already mentioned, covered only about 7 percent of the population.[44]

We can talk at most, thus, of what Kerstenetzky aptly calls 'trade-union citizenship' ('*cidadania sindical*'), where workers manage to have some benefits recognized through participation in trade unions heavily controlled by the state and devoid of the right to strike.[45] This model of 'corporatist welfare' was therefore rather fragmented, unequal, and exclusionary. Rather than the universal logic of unconditional citizenship, rights, and equality, it was strongly grounded on ideas of *contribution* and *compensation*, albeit now with the backing of the state. To what extent ideas of social responsibility played a relevant role in those changes is difficult to know. Most analyses choose to highlight political motives linked to the strengthening of the Brazilian state through the

such as the Fund for the Aid of the Workers of the State Railways of 1888 and the Pension Fund of the Personnel of the National Press of 1889.

43 It is important to recall that many of the reformists of the 1910s and 1920s were incorporated in the Vargas government as administrators and advisers. It is also important to remember that, in this battle of ideas eventually won by the reformists against the liberals, there were other potential ideas that 'lost', namely the communist and anarchist approaches. See Malloy (n 34) 39.

44 In 1940, 70 percent of the population was rural.

45 Such control was facilitated by the condition that workers' benefits be accessed only by those in possession of a workers' identity card and the condition of being a member of the trade union to qualify for holidays and to access labour courts.

strategy of industrialisation and import substitution, which could of course not be achieved without healthy workers![46] Authors emphasise the limited redistributive character of such a model, and Kerstenetzky goes further in arguing that such corporatist logic was inimical to the emergence of more universalistic ones. Brazilian sociologist Vera da Silva Telles has a similar view, stating that *'through work the individual acquired a civil existence and was transformed into a citizen to whom the State offered the protection of social rights'*. Yet, as she continues:

> the 'others', those who were outside, who weren't formally workers despite exercising regular productive activities, were not part of the people and did not deserve the protection of the State: unemployed, under-employed, domestic workers, self-employed fell all in the common category of a criminalized and undifferentiated condition that conflated them with outcasts, criminals and subversives.[47]

From 1946 to 1964, the democratic period that followed Vargas' dictatorship, the corporatist welfare model was not altered significantly, as we saw earlier. Yet some initiatives, even if most of them failed, signalled changes that were to come in the future towards a less fragmented and more universal system. They were influenced by foreign important developments such as the Beveridge Report and the Philadelphia Declaration. Noteworthy was the attempt to deal with the social question in the rural areas, with a failed agrarian reform and equally failed extension of non-contributory pensions to rural workers.[48]

'Basic Universalism' (1964–1988)

The second wave, which Kerstenetzky calls 'basic universalism', starts in 1964 with the arrival of the military to power through a coup d'état. As we saw in section 2, significant changes in social policy took place both at the constitutional and non-constitutional levels, such as the creation of the National Institute of Social Providence (INPS) unifying under a single and centralised state bureaucracy all fragmented pension schemes of the Vargas era (the IAPs) and harmonising all hitherto varying benefits, the extension of pensions (though at lower levels) to rural workers, domestic workers, and the self-employed, the small income guarantee to the elderly poor or incapacitated (*Renda Mensal*

46 Kerstenetzky (n 12) 196; Marcelo Medeiros, 'A Trajetória do Welfare State no Brasil: Papel Redistributivo das Políticas Sociais dos Anos 1930 aos Anos 1990' (2001) Texto para Discussão IPEA n. 852. <www.ipea.gov.br/portal/images/stories/PDFs/TDs/td_0852.pdf> accessed 28 February 2022.

47 Vera Da Silva Telles, *Direitos Sociais. Afinal do que se trata?* (Editora UFMG 2006) 124–126.

48 See Tanya de Barcellos (ed), *A Politica Social Brasileira. 1930–64. Evolução Institucional no Brasil e Rio Grande do Sul* (Fundação de Economia e Estatística 1983). <http://cdn.fee.tche.br/digitalizacao/politica-social-brasileira-1930-%2064/politica-social-brasileira-1930-64-texto.pdf> accessed 28 February 2022.

Vitalícia – RMV), the extension of free education to those between 7 and 14 years.

This significant incorporation of beneficiaries ('massification') in the pension system, social assistance, and health and education services was, however, carried out with maintenance of stratification, ie better coverage and services to the better off. The military period was far, therefore, from redistributive universalism, which explains why it was also marked by a significant growth in inequality (the ratio between the income of the top 1 percent and the bottom 40 percent almost doubled in this period), reflecting the non-redistributive character of the welfare system.[49] What was the role played by ideas in the changes to social policies during this second wave?

Under an authoritarian regime that censored and repressed opposition we will not find of course the lively debates about social policies that took place in the 1910s and 1920s.[50] What we see is again a top-down approach, reminiscent of the authoritarian period under Vargas but perhaps intensified. The expansion of social benefits to rural and domestic workers and the self-employed, although they introduced an element of 'universalism' to the hitherto 'corporatist' system (especially as these are non-contributory benefits), were so low so as not to play any significant redistributive role. A leading expert on social policies, Eduardo Fagnani, refers to this period in terms of what he calls a 'conservative strategy'.[51] In his view, this conservative strategy comprises five structural aspects: regressiveness of the financing mechanisms; centralisation of the decision-making process; privatisation of public space; expansion of coverage and offering of goods and services; and restricted redistributive character.[52] The ideas underlying this strategy, according to Fagnani, can be divided into economic ones, mostly what we would today call 'austerity' (reduction of the costs of the state) and political, aiming at the destruction of the support base of the previous nationalist/populist regime through the weakening of its main supporters, eg trade unions, public servants etc and reform of its main instrument of patronage, ie the unification of the pension system.[53]

'Extended Universalism' (1988 to Date)

The Brazilian Constitution of 1988, the 'Citizen Constitution', as we saw earlier, inaugurates the *third wave* of social policies in Brazil, marking a shift towards

49 For a comprehensive study of the history of inequality in Brazil see Pedro H. G. Ferreira de Souza, *Uma História da Desigualdade. A Concentração de Renda entre os Ricos no Brasil 1926–2013* (Hucitec 2018).

50 There were, however, fierce debates intra-government, as noted by Eduardo Fagnani, 'Política Social e Pactos Conservadores no Brasil: 1964/92' (1997) 8 Economia e Sociedade 183.

51 ibid.

52 ibid 185.

53 ibid.

more robust universalism, at least on paper (see concluding section for the reality of welfare policies). Perhaps the most important reflection of such a shift in terms of ideas and concepts is the unification, under the same rubric of 'social security' (note the subtle but important terminological difference between the terms *security* and *insurance*, particular in Portuguese where the terms are very close: respectively *seguridade* and *seguro*), of both contributory schemes such as pensions and non-contributory ones such as social assistance and health, the latter recognized as a fundamental right for the first time. The prevailing logic inaugurated in the 1988 Constitution is therefore clearly one of *social rights*, ie one based on unconditional entitlements of *citizenship* irrespective of contribution or professional affiliation in contrast to the corporatist model. This is well explained by sociologist Vera Telles in the following manner:

> In the horizon of citizenship, the social question was redefined and the 'poor', in fact, stops to exist. Risking some exaggeration, I would say that poverty and citizenship are antinomic categories. Radicalizing the argument, I would say that, within a citizenship perspective, poor and poverty don't exist. What exists indeed are individuals and social groups in specific situations of rights' deprivation. It is another configuration of the social question.[54]

It would be not just naïve, but also inaccurate, however, to conclude that such logic was unopposed, or is now strongly rooted and consolidated simply because the 'Citizen Constitution' was enacted and is now in force. It is one thing (an important one for sure) to include universal social rights in the constitution based on the idea of universal citizenship; it is another to translate them into social policies that implement effectively these ideals. Telles herself admits this, of course, stating that 'the ambiguities and ambivalences in this process . . . show that the path to a more egalitarian and democratic society is tough'.[55]

The myriad of egalitarian clauses peppered across the constitutional document described in section 2, which led to its nickname of the 'Citizen Constitution', should not lead one to the conclusion that ideas of equality, solidarity, and citizenship finally became consolidated and rooted in Brazil (some forty years later than their strengthening in Post-War Western Europe). We need to recall once more, here, the power and resilience of counter-ideas. During the Constituent Assembly itself the majority of the members of Congress represented conservative, right of centre interests, and tried consistently to curtail the initiatives of the most progressive members to pass egalitarian clauses. To the very end of the assembly's operation in 1988 there was a risk that the egalitarian proposals would not pass. It was due to the political ability of a few

54 Telles (n 47) 129.
55 ibid 131.

progressive members of Congress and popular pressure from social movements that the text ended up as egalitarian as it now looks. Yet such egalitarianism is significantly tempered not only by counter-balancing constitutional clauses themselves, such as the continuing recognition of property as a fundamental right, but also by the simple fact, already emphasised a few times in this chapter, of the necessary disconnect between 'law in books' and 'law in action', to which I return in the next, concluding section.[56]

Conclusion: Universalist Constitutional Rhetoric, Selective Policy Practice?

When one focuses exclusively on the text of a constitution, or any legal instrument, one gets a very limited picture of how the ideas that became entrenched in those legal documents actually impact the lives of individuals and groups, which is, in my view, one of the main reasons why we are interested in those ideas and legislation in the first place. To be sure, the mere entrenchment of ideas in law are also important in themselves, ie from a purely symbolic perspective, which partly explains the battles we see in the legislature and constituent assemblies to shape the text of constitutional norms. Especially in democratic regimes, however imperfect, the ideal of the rule of law creates the expectation that the text of the constitution and ordinary laws will directly influence political debates and policies and translate into real consequences, even if always imperfectly. Yet, even in the most developed democracies, a gap is always present between 'law in the books' and 'law in action'. This divergence can be explained by a set of complex and interacting factors such as state capacity, societal values and norms ('culture'), economic and political power etc. If one is interested in knowing whether and to what extent legislative developments have changed things on the ground, one needs to go beyond the text of legal documents and engage extensively with empirical data.

For reasons of scope and space, this broader and necessarily more complex project was not pursued here. The focus was rather on the textual creation and changes in social policies entrenched in laws and the ideas that may have influenced and shaped them. I hope this has been useful as an effort to map out the landscape and encourage further investigation about the actual impact of those ideas and the ensuing legislation in the well-being of the Brazilian population. In these final paragraphs, however, I will make some brief speculations that will hopefully be useful to those interested on this issue.

56 For an insightful account of the battles that took place in the Constituent Assembly of 1987/1988, see José Celso Cardoso Junior (ed), *A Constituição Brasileira de 1988 Revisitada. Recuperação Histórica e Desafios Atuais das Políticas Públicas nas Áreas Econômica e Social* (IPEA 2009), in particular the contribution of Plínio Arruda Sampaio, 'Para Além da Ambiguidade: Uma Reflexão Histórica sobre a CF/1988'.

The first thing to note is that the egalitarian universalistic rhetoric of the current constitutional text is mitigated to an important extent in the reality of the political economy of Brazil. Kerstenetzky's use of the term 'extended universalism' to describe the post-1988 period seems therefore appropriate. Though by no means trivial, the redistributive impact of the social policies entrenched in the 1988 Constitution has been importantly moderated by policies that go in the opposite direction, ie towards more concentration of income and wealth, such as a highly regressive taxation system (focused on indirect consumption taxes rather than direct income and property ones); low investment in universal services such as health and education; tax exemptions to private providers and consumers that undermine further these services; very high salaries and pensions for some public servants, such as judges, public prosecutors, and state lawyers etc.[57] Such policies, which have all but survived reasonably unscathed even during the relatively more progressive governments of the Workers' Party (2002–2016) have significantly blunted the potential transformative impact of the 1988 Constitution.

The ideas and legislative changes that we described to have taken place in the past eighty-five years – the shift from limited, contributory, exclusionary, and fragmented schemes towards comprehensive, non-contributory, inclusive, and unified systems grounded on individual constitutional rights – are therefore much more radical on paper than in the reality on the ground. As Kerstenetzky aptly observes, '[a]fter more than two decades of the Citizen Constitution, Brazil seems finally to move towards the universalisation of its welfare state, though in a non-homogenous and shaky manner'. Expenditure with social policies has gone significantly up, breaching the 20 percent barrier in 2008 and moving towards 30 percent this decade. It covers by and large the whole of the Brazilian population. Yet this expenditure is not as redistributive as it could be, especially in light of what the constitution promises, and is often also inefficient and regressive.[58]

Moreover, although the text of the Brazilian constitution survived reasonably well the strong 'neo-liberal' winds that started blowing in the late 1970s and reached their peak in the 1990s, the same cannot be said of the real world of social policies, which was heavily affected by those ideas. In the past two decades, more attention has been paid to the contributory and targeted parts of the social security system than to universal services. Funding for health has grown

57 Another expert, Marcelo Medeiros, concludes emphatically in an earlier study that the redistributive character of social policies in Brazil has been significantly compromised by economic policies that tend towards income concentration, a lack of unity among workers (especially rural and urban), and by a state bureaucracy with low levels of autonomy from the government. In his view, there was no evidence in the 1990s that the Brazilian Welfare State had become more egalitarian. See Medeiros (n 46), see also Souza (n 49).

58 See Kerstenetzky (n 12) and Carola Pessino, Alejandro Izquierdo and Guillermo Vuletin, *Better Spending for Better Lives How Latin America and the Caribbean Can Do More with Less* (Inter-American Development Bank 2019). <https://publications.iadb.org/publications/english/document/Better-Spending-for-Better-Lives-How-Latin-America-and-the-Caribbean-Can-Do-More-with-Less.pdf> accessed 28 February 2022.

a little but still adds up to a lower percentage of GDP (around 4 percent) and small amounts in terms of GDP per capita when compared to more developed countries and even to some of a similar level of development. Education fairs better in terms of expenditure (6.2 percent) but continues to suffer from low quality. Since 2016 austerity measures have depleted these public services even further of resources. Middle and upper classes have all but deserted them.

This focus on targeted (ie non-universal) policies may well be a tendency in the so-called developing world, what Lena Lavinas has called an 'hegemonic paradigm of the 21st century'. As she argues:

> The social-protection paradigm that emerged at the end of the 19th century and developed, in parallel with the workers' movements, during the 20th, aimed to protect and equalize access and opportunities, irrespective of income level and social status. In this model, the structure of social spending prized not only income security but above all the promotion of equity and convergence. By contrast, the hegemonic paradigm of the 21st century holds that market mechanisms are the key to improving general welfare; cash transfers and expanded household debt, the latter underwritten by the former, are the key elements in this framework, in which decommodified provision is to be pared to the barest bones. What is taking place – spurred on by the 'success story' of CCTs – is a downsizing of social protection in the name of the poor. Over the past six years these programmes have benefited from boom conditions, as surplus capital flooded into 'emerging economies' from the crisis-stricken advanced capitalist zones. Yet how they will weather a reversal of capital flows and tightening of credit, if quantitative easing in the North finally starts to slow, remains to be seen.[59]

Lavinas' piece is about Latin America as a whole, and other developing regions where so-called CCTs (conditional cash transfers), but also UCTs (unconditional cash transfers) have been adopted in recent years, with the backing and praise of the World Bank as effective policies to fight poverty and inequality. I do not disagree with her scepticism about the efficiency of these policies compared to truly universal ones in reducing poverty and inequality. In the case of Brazil, however, one must be careful not to jump to conclusions that universal policies have all but given place to conditional cash transfers. Conditional cash transfers have surely been the most visible and talked about innovation of recent years and the flagship policy of the Workers' Party, in office from 2002 to 2016. It is indeed very limited in terms of expenditure, at less than 0.5 percent of GDP, although not in coverage, reaching directly 13.8 million families, and thus almost 50 million individuals, ie about 1/4 of the Brazilian population.[60]

59 Lena Lavinas, '21st Century Welfare' (2013) 84 New Left Review 5.

60 Tereza Campello and Marcelo Côrtes Neri (eds), *Programa Bolsa Família. Uma Década de Inclusão e Cidadania* (Ipea 2013).

Yet, although universal services have all but stagnated in terms of expenditure, it seems somewhat premature to say that they have been 'pared to the barest bones'. Health and education, as we saw, consume together 10 percent of GDP, not an insignificant amount; the pension system, although less progressive than it ought to be, consumes another 12 percent of GDP, keeping millions of beneficiaries who receive the minimum wage out of poverty; the non-contributory social assistance grant (the 'BPC') is now benefiting more than 4 million elderly and disabled individuals, and the policy of updating the minimum wage in more than 76 percent in the past decade, which is the basic income of some 46.7 million Brazilians, has benefited millions as well. But the period of economic crisis and then austerity that developed since 2014, as well as the pandemic, have made things worse, with extreme poverty growing from a historic record low of 4.7 percent of the population in 2014 to 6.8 percent in 2019 (around 14 million people). With the current public health crisis caused by the new Coronavirus and its economic impact the situation would have deteriorated further and significantly, to 12.9 percent (more than 27 million people), yet was mitigated by an emergency grant which kept the extreme poverty levels at 5.7 percent of the population.[61]

As a whole, thus, the Brazilian welfare system, composed by constitutionalised universal public services (health and education); vague constitutional promises (the right to housing and the social function of property); targeted and specific programmes of a contributory (pensions) and non-contributory nature (BPC); and the non-constitutionalised conditional cash transfers (the Bolsa Família programme), performs a non-trivial but underachieving reduction in the persisting inequalities of the country. According to a recent study by the OECD, 'the redistributive role of the Brazilian tax system is underexploited' and 'actually increases inequality' when both direct and indirect taxes are taken into account.[62]

To go back to a point I made earlier and should perhaps re-emphasise now at the conclusion, although the shape of social policies is in great part a result of the ideas that inspire them, these ideas are contested, changeable, and do not operate, as a consequence, in a neat, linear, and irreversible manner. Even

61 See Leonardo Vieceli, 'Sem Auxílio, Extrema Pobreza Teria Atingido 27 milhôes no Brasil em 2020, diz IBGE', Folha de S. Paulo, 3 December 2021, <https://www1.folha.uol.com.br/mercado/2021/12/sem-auxilio-extrema-pobreza-teria-atingido-27-milhoes-no-brasil-em-2020-diz-ibge.shtml> accessed 28 February 2022.

62 This is due to due to: 'a high reliance on indirect taxes – which are regressive, as in most countries; low progressivity of the personal income tax, partly as a result of significant loopholes that favour those with above-average incomes; and a cap on social security contributions. In Brazil, direct taxes reduce income inequality (measured by the Gini coefficient) by 5%, compared to 12% on average in the OECD area'. See OECD Brazil Policy Brief. Inequality. Improving Policies to Reduce Inequality and Poverty, <www.oecd.org/policy-briefs/brazil-improving-policies-to-reduce-inequality-and-poverty.pdf> accessed 28 February 2022. For a more positive view, see Nora Lustig, Carola Pessino and John Scott, 'The Impact of Taxes and Social Spending on Inequality and Poverty in Argentina, Bolivia, Brazil, Mexico, Peru and Uruguay: An Overview' (2013) *CEQ Working Paper No. 13*. <http://repec.tulane.edu/RePEc/ceq/ceq13.pdf> accessed 28 February 2022.

the mitigated universalism achieved so far in Brazil may suffer setbacks. Many argue, plausibly in my view, that the current conservative wave started since the impeachment of the Workers' Party president in 2016 and strengthened in the elections of 2018 is inimical to the egalitarian and universalistic ideas that underpin a genuine welfare state and that some of the policies so far adopted have reflected that, such as changes to labour legislation, a freeze in public expenditure, and the reform of the pension system. Others argue, also persuasively in my view, that the Workers' Party government itself never made a priority of redistribution, plunging the social protection system 'deeper into the logic of the market', ie the logic of financialisaton and privatisation through policies of tax credits and exemptions 'in favour of businesses and rich households, concentrating wealth and power against the grain of collective interest'.[63]

A thorough analysis of such arguments and developments goes well beyond the scope of this chapter. But it illustrates well, I hope, the complex role of ideas not only in the adoption of social policies through constitutions and ordinary legislation but also their actual implementation and effectiveness in the real world.

63 See Lena Lavinas, *The Takeover of Social Policy by Financialization. The Brazilian Paradox* (Palgrave Macmillan 2017) 175–176.

Chapter 3

Law and Social Policy in the People's Republic of China

From Communism to Marketisation

Albert H.Y. Chen

Introduction

In 'one of the most celebrated'[1] passages in the Chinese Confucian classics that were composed more than two millennia ago, an ideal society was portrayed as follows:

> When the Great Way was practiced, the world was shared by all alike. The worthy and the able were promoted to office and men practiced good faith and lived in affection. Therefore they did not regard as parents only their own parents, or as sons only their own sons. The aged found a fitting close to their lives, the robust their proper employment; the young were provided with an upbringing and the widow and widower, the orphaned and the sick, with proper care. Men had their tasks and women their hearths. . . . This was the age of Grand Unity.[2]

This ideal society is one in which 'the aged', 'the young', 'the widow and widower', 'the orphaned', and 'the sick' are all well taken care of by society. It is thus a caring society in which the welfare of the less fortunate members of society – those who are weak and vulnerable – is well provided for. Confucianism also stresses that the ruling elite should practise moral virtues and exercise power in the interests of the people.[3] There existed institutions and policies in imperial China to take care of victims of natural disasters and the

1 Wm. Theodore de Bary, Wing-tsit Chan, and Burton Watson (eds), *Sources of Chinese Tradition*, vol 1 (Columbia University Press 1960) 175.

2 Translated text in de Bary, Chan, and Watson (n 1) 176. This quotation is from the opening passage of the '*Liyun*' ('Evolution of Rites') chapter of *Liji* (the *Book of Rites*), one of the great books of Confucian classics. The *Book of Rites* is believed to have been complied by Confucian scholars more than two millennia ago in the Han dynasty.

3 For traditional Chinese Confucian notions of welfare, see Cecilia Chan and Nelson Chow, *More Welfare after Economic Reform? Welfare Development in the People's Republic of China* (Centre of Urban Planning and Environmental Management, University of Hong Kong 1992); Joe Cho-bun Leung and Richard C. Nann, *Authority and Benevolence: Social Welfare in China* (Chinese University Press

DOI: 10.4324/9781003242826-3

most unfortunate members of society.[4] Thus modern notions of social welfare and social security are not entirely foreign to traditional Chinese thought, even though the latter did not generate the concept of human rights or social rights secured by the Rule of Law.[5] The humanistic philosophy of Confucianism, which played as important a cultural and intellectual role in Chinese civilisation as Christianity played in the West, preaches the moral values and virtues of benevolence and righteousness. Confucian benevolence, like Christian love, is ultimately an expression of care and concern for the interests and well-being of fellow human beings.[6]

Chinese society has undergone revolutionary upheavals in modern times. As in the case of other non-Western civilisations, China has been confronted by the challenges of Western modernity. Since the late nineteenth century, Chinese thinkers and officials – while being proud of the glory and achievements of Chinese civilisation in the past – perceived China at that time as backward relative to the West and thus in desperate need of modernisation or catching up with the West. The project of modernisation and national salvation[7] was understood by many Chinese intellectuals and statesmen as including the construction of a modern nation-state with a constitution and a legal system that affirms and protects citizens' constitutional rights, including not only civil and political rights but also social and economic rights.[8]

This chapter is a study of some aspects of law and social policy in the People's Republic of China. It seeks to tell the story of how ideas, values, and constitutional and legal norms relating to social policy have evolved in modern China. The main focus will be on state policies, laws, and regulations relating to what is generally known in the Western world as social security, social welfare, or social protection, including social insurance and social assistance. The changing social policies relating to health and medical care, housing, and land will also be briefly mentioned for comparative purposes but not discussed in detail.

1995); T. Wing Lo and Joseph Cheng (eds), *Social Welfare Development in China: Constraints and Challenges* (Imprint 1996).

4 Nelson Chow, 'Western and Chinese Ideas of Social Welfare' (1987) 30 International Social Work 31; Aiqun Hu, *China's Social Insurance in the Twentieth Century: A Global Historical Perspective* (Brill 2016) chap 1.

5 See eg Michael C. Davis (ed), *Human Rights and Chinese Values* (Oxford University Press 1995).

6 However, Confucianism prioritises family and social relationships rather than universal love for all human beings. Thus, filial piety and care and concern for one's family members are key Confucian virtues. See generally Albert H.Y. Chen, 'The Rise of Rights: Some Comparative Civilizational Reflections' (1998) 25 Journal of Chinese Philosophy 5–30.

7 For the relevance of this project to social welfare thinking in modern China, see Shih-Jiunn Shi, 'Reviving the Dragon: Social Ideas and Social Policy Development in Modern China' (2017) 53(3) Issues and Studies (DOI: 10.1142/S1013251117500060).

8 See generally Randle R. Edwards, Louis Henkin, and Andrew J. Nathan, *Human Rights in Contemporary China* (Columbia University Press 1986); Yong Xia, *The Philosophy of Civil Rights in the Context of China* (Martinus Nijhoff 2011).

Apart from this introduction (part I), this chapter consists of the following parts. Parts II and III review the history of social policy in the post-imperial or republican period (1911–1949) of modern China, and then in the Maoist era of the People's Republic of China (PRC) that was established in 1949. Parts IV and V cover respectively the initial period (1978–2000) and later period (2001–the present) of the era of 'reform and opening'. Finally, part VI provides some concluding reflections.

The Development of Social Policy and Law in the Republican Era

Modern Western legal and political ideas were introduced into China in the late Qing dynasty, which came to an end with the Revolution of 1911.[9] The Qing Empire was transformed into a republic known as the Republic of China. A legal system modelled on Western legal systems – particularly the Continental European model – was in the course of construction. China underwent rapid social and economic change, particularly in the major cities, as industrialisation and urbanisation proceeded. Western ideas of social insurance and the state's responsibility for providing protection against the risks of modern industrial life were introduced and positively received in China.[10] Such ideas had begun to be practised in some European states in the late nineteenth century and became increasingly influential globally after the Russian Revolution of 1917 and the establishment of the International Labour Organisation (ILO) in 1919, of which the Republic of China was a member.[11] In 1930, a branch of the International Labour Office was established in Nanking.[12]

Both the Peking Government (sometimes known as the 'warlord government') of the Republic of China and the Nanking Government (established by the Chinese Nationalist Party or Kuomintang (KMT) in 1928 after the 'Northern Expedition' – a civil war against the 'warlords') enacted some laws in the domain of labour protection and social welfare. Major developments in this regard include the enactment of the Factory Law (1924) and the Law on Social Assistance (1943) (*shehui jiuji fa*, '*shehui juiji*' being translated as 'social assistance').[13]

9 See generally Immanuel C.Y. Hsu, *The Rise of Modern China*, 6th edn (Oxford University Press 2000).

10 Aiqun Hu (n 4) chs 3–4; Nara Dillon, *Radical Inequalities: China's Revolutionary Welfare State in Comparative Perspective* (Harvard University Asia Center 2015) chap 1.

11 For the influence of the ILO on Chinese labour and social law and policy in the Republican era, see Hu (n 4) chaps 3–4.

12 Li Qiong, 'A Preliminary Study of Social Insurance during the Period of the Republic of China' (2006) 1 Journal of Central China University of Science and Technology (Social Science Edition) (Huazhong kejidaxue xuebao shekeban) 82–86.

13 Pan Huaiming, *A Study of Social Security Legal System with Chinese Characteristics* (Zhongguo tese shehuibaozhang falüzhidu yanjiu) (Zhongguo caifu chubanshe) 71–72; Shen Jie, 'A Comparative Study of the Development Path of Social Security in China, Japan and Korea' (2013) 17 Social Security Studies (Shehui baozhang yanjiu) 45, 50–52 (in Chinese).

Article 45 of the Factory Law, which applied to factories using certain types of machinery and employing more than thirty workers, required employers to pay compensation when workers were injured or killed as a result of industrial accidents, and in cases of workers' illness to pay medical expenses and sickness allowance. The amendment of this law in 1932 introduced compensation for occupational diseases.[14] The Law on Social Assistance, drafted by a Chinese official educated in Germany, was the first piece of modern Chinese legislation that introduced fairly comprehensive provisions for the relief of poverty. Those entitled to assistance included the needy above the age of 60 or under 12, pregnant women, those without the capacity to work as a result of illness, injury, or disability, and victims of natural disasters. This law was conceptually significant because it established the people's right to social assistance, and the state's obligation to provide such assistance.[15]

In the period 1931–1941, the KMT Government also drafted bills for a Law on Compulsory Labour Insurance (*qiangzhi laogong baoxian fa*, '*laogong baoxian*' being translated as 'labour insurance')[16] and Principles of Social Insurance Law (*shehui baoxian fa yuanze*, '*shehui baoxian*' being translated as 'social insurance'), though they were never enacted as law.[17] During the Sino-Japanese War, the KMT Government in 1943 introduced regulations on a labour insurance scheme for workers in the salt industry. The regulations, as revised in 1945, established a system of compulsory insurance to which both employers and workers paid contributions into a government-managed fund. The fund would make payments to workers on occasions of industrial accidents, illness, marriage, and retirement.[18]

In this Republican era, some social welfare institutions were established, including some operated by foreign religious or charitable bodies.[19] One of the earliest legal instruments promulgated after the 1911 Revolution was a set of regulations enacted in 1915 on institutions providing work and training for the destitute. In 1928, the new KMT Government in Nanking adopted a set of regulations on state-run institutions for poverty relief, including orphanages and homes for the elderly, disabled, and babies.[20]

14 Li Xinjun, 'Legislation on Medical Insurance during the Period of the Nanking National Government (1927–1937)' (2011) 31(2) Journal of Shangrao Normal University (Shangrao shifan xueyan xuebao) 66–70.

15 Shen (n 13) 51–52.

16 Nelson W.S. Chow, *The Administration and Financing of Social Security in China* (Centre of Asian Studies, University of Hong Kong 1988) 18.

17 Pan (n 13) 72; Li (n 12).

18 Li (n 12). A similar compulsory insurance scheme was introduced in Chongqing, the wartime capital, under which both employers and employees paid contributions. The scheme applied to civil servants and to certain industrial undertakings employing more than thirty workers: see Li (n 12).

19 They were all nationalised after the PRC was established in 1949: see Chan and Chow (n 3) 22–23; Liu Jingjing, *A Study of Chinese Social Security System from a Constitutional Perspective* (Xianzheng shiyexia Zhongguo shehuibaozhang zhidu yanjiu) (Fudan daxue chubanshe 2013) 35.

20 Shen (n 13) 51.

By the 1930s, a significant body of scholarship on social assistance, social work, social policy, labour, and poverty issues had emerged.[21] Chinese scholars published books on '*shehui shiye*' (the Chinese translation of the term 'social work') and '*shehui jiuji*' (the Chinese translation of the term 'social assistance'). Books on '*shehui zhengce*' (social policy) were translated from Japanese and German into Chinese.[22] There was a considerable degree of consensus among scholars that China should introduce some form of social insurance, at least for workers who needed financial support at times of industrial accidents, sickness, unemployment, and old age.[23]

The more mature thinking in the Republican era on matters of labour protection and social welfare is reflected in the text of the Constitution of the Republic of China enacted in 1946 by a constituent assembly dominated by the KMT.[24] The KMT adhered to the ideology known as 'the Three People's Principles' developed by Dr Sun Yat-sen,[25] generally regarded as the founding father of the Republic of China and the paramount leader of the KMT before his death in 1925. Article 1 of this constitution declares that the Republic of China was founded on the basis of the Three People's Principles.

The three principles were the principles of nationalism, of people's rights, and people's livelihood. The third principle was influenced by socialism, and included ideas of equalisation of land rights and regulation of private capital. Apart from the three principles, it is also noteworthy that some of the draftsmen of the 1946 Constitution were influenced by contemporary European ideas of 'Sozialstaat', social insurance, welfare state, or social rights.[26] The rights provided for in the 1946 Constitution include the right to life and the right to work (Article 15). One section of the constitution – Section 4 of Chapter 13 (on 'basic State policies') is entitled '*shehui anquan*', which may be translated as 'social safety' or 'social security'. It (in Article 153) requires the state to make laws to protect workers and peasants, and to accord special protection to women labour and child labour. It (in Article 155) also provides that 'the State shall implement a social insurance (*shehui baoxian*) system in order to promote social welfare (*shehui fuli*)', and that 'the State shall provide assistance (*fuzhu*) and relief (*jiuji*) to the elderly, the weak, the disabled, those unable to earn an income and victims of disasters'.

21 Shen (n 13) 50.
22 Shen (n 13).
23 See the works cited at n 10.
24 This constitution is still largely in force in Taiwan today. See generally Tuan-sheng Ch'ien, *The Government and Politics of China 1912–1949* (Harvard University Press 1950).
25 Sheng Wang, *The Thought of Dr. Sun Yat-sen* (Li Ming Cultural Enterprise 1981); Audrey Wells, *The Political Thought of Sun Yat-sen: Development and Impact* (Palgrave 2001).
26 Su Yongqin (ed), *Branches of Constitutional Law* (Bumen xianfa) (Yuanzhao 2006) 284–287, 302–303.

China in the Republican era was unable to make significant social and economic progress because it was at first torn by warlord strife, and, even after the establishment of the relatively strong KMT Government in Nanking in 1928, China was not unified because there were areas under the control of the Chinese Communist Party (CCP). Later on, full-scale Japanese invasion resulted in the greater part of China being conquered by Japan.

After the CCP was founded in 1921, the Chinese Communists began to develop their own tradition of labour protection and social insurance.[27] For example, in 1922, they promulgated an outline of labour law which required employers to pay insurance premiums for their workers.[28] The Labour Law of the Chinese Soviet Republic established by the CCP in the Jiangxi province in 1931 contained one chapter on '*shehui baoxian*' (social insurance),[29] which required employers to pay, in addition to the worker's wage, an amount equivalent to 10 to 15 percent of the wage to a social insurance fund that would pay workers in the event of sickness, injury, maternity, incapacity, and unemployment. Shortly after the Second World War, the CCP took over Northeastern China, and promulgated in 1948 the Wartime Provisional Regulations on Labour Insurance (*laodong baoxian*) for Public Enterprises in the Northeast, requiring the public enterprises concerned to pay an amount equivalent to 3 percent of the workers' wages as labour insurance premium.[30]

The policy orientation of these CCP laws and regulations, including the idea that workers need not contribute any insurance premium, was largely shaped by Leninist and Stalinist theories and practice in the Soviet Union. 'While Bismarckian social insurance was basically financed by both employers and employees, Lenin thought that social insurance should be financed solely by the state and workers should not pay for their benefits'.[31] Lenin also believed that the insurance system should be administered by workers. In the 1930s, the state-funded insurance system for Soviet workers was administered by trade unions.[32] According to Soviet theory, the wage of workers included not only cash payment but also a 'social wage', which included social insurance, free medical service, housing, and free education for their children.[33]

27 Wang Wei, *A Study of the Chinese Social Security Legal System* (Zhongguo shehuibaozhang falüzhidu yanjiu) (Zhongyang minzu daxue chubanshe 2008) 20–23.

28 Chow (n 16) 17–18.

29 Shen (n 13) 52; Pan (n 13) 73–74.

30 Liu Cuixiao, *Legal History of Social Security in the People's Republic of China* (Zhonghua renmin gongheguo shehuibaozhang fazhi shi) (Shangwu yinshuguan 2014) 8; Wang (n 27) 22–23; Liu (n 19) 33; Pan (n 13) 75.

31 Aiqun Hu, 'Social Insurance Ideas in the People's Republic of China: A Historical and Transnational Analysis' (2016) 6(3) Transnational Social Review 297, 300. For the socialist concept of social insurance see also Ulrike Davy, Chapter 6 in this volume, p. 226.

32 Hu (n 31).

33 Li (n 12).

Social Policy and Law in the Maoist Era (1949–1977)

Introduction

The Civil War in the late 1940s resulted in the KMT's defeat and retreat to Taiwan, and the CCP establishing the PRC in 1949. In this and subsequent sections, we will examine the evolution of Chinese social policies in various domains such as social security and welfare, health care, housing and land, and the ideas, values, and goals that informed such policies. Differences in the dominant ideas, values, and goals underlying social policies in different periods of the PRC's history may be observed. Roughly speaking, three periods may be discerned in the history of the People's Republic of China: (1) the Maoist period, which ended soon after Mao's death in 1976; (2) the initial period of 'reform and opening' beginning in the late 1970s and continuing until the turn of the century; and (3) the later period of 'reform and opening' that can be considered to have begun at the 16th National Congress of the CCP in 2002 (at which Hu Jintao became the Party's General Secretary) and continuing up to the present.

Overview of the Maoist era

In the Maoist period, there was an attempt to put into practice socialist ideas of elimination of capitalist exploitation, introduction of the public ownership of the means of production, and some kind of egalitarianism, with all members of society contributing their labour to the collective good and being taken care of by their work units or agricultural collective organisations (such as communes). All economic production was nationalised in the urban areas and collectivised in the rural areas. There was in effect an integration of economic and social policies in the command economy of the socialist system.[34] The majority of the urban population worked in state organs or state-owned or collectively-owned economic enterprises which took care of the basic welfare needs of their workers in terms of social security, housing, medical care, and even the education of their children. In the rural areas, the elimination of privately owned land and the collectivisation of agriculture led to agricultural production being organised in communes, which also took care of the welfare needs of their members though at a minimum level.

It should be noted that neither the term 'social security' nor 'social welfare' (the Chinese translations of which are '*shehui baozhang*' and '*shehui fuli*' respectively) was used in the Chinese laws and official documents in the Maoist period. The Chinese terms actually used to describe relevant social policies would be mentioned in the discussion that follows.

34 Hatla Thelle, *Better to Rely on Ourselves: Changing Social Rights in Urban China since 1979* (Nias 2004) 66–67.

The Common Programme of 1949

A provisional constitution known as the Common Programme was promulgated at the time of the establishment of the PRC in 1949.[35] As far as labour and social security were concerned, the Common Programme provided in its chapter (Chapter 4) on 'economic policy' that collective contracts should be made between capital and workers (represented by trade unions) in private enterprises, working hours should be limited to eight to ten hours, minimum wages should be established by the government, a system of labour insurance (*laodong baoxian*) should be 'gradually introduced', and the interests of young workers and women workers should be specially protected. It should be noted that the Common Programme of 1949 envisaged the continued existence in China of the 'national bourgeoisie' (*minzu zichan jieji*) and capitalist enterprises run by them. However, by the mid-1950s, all private enterprises had been nationalised and the 'capitalist class' eliminated in China. At the same time, collectivisation of agriculture took place in rural China.

Special Compensation Schemes, Social Assistance, and Labour Insurance

The year 1950 saw the enactment of five sets of regulations for the purpose of conferring special compensation and benefits (known in Chinese as (*youfu* 优抚), hereafter called 'special compensation') on particular categories of needy people such as ex-servicemen and their family members, and family members of martyrs for the Revolution.[36] A rudimentary system of social protection began to emerge consisting of such special compensation schemes, as well as social assistance or relief (known in the Chinese literature as '*shehui jiuji*' or '*shehui jiuzhu*') for victims of natural disasters, the destitute, and the dis-located.[37]

Another major development took place in 1951, when the Labour Insurance Regulations (LIR) were enacted.[38] This is probably the most significant

35 The full title of this document is the Common Programme of the Chinese People's Political Consultative Conference (CPPCC), adopted on 29 Sept 1949. The Common Programme permitted the continued existence of the private sector of the economy. Such private sector was eliminated in the course of the 1950s during which the 'socialist transformation' of agriculture and capitalist industry and commerce took place.

36 Wang (n 27) 25–26; Liu (n 19) 36.

37 Liu (n 19) 35; Chan and Chow (n 3) 28–29. The Ministry of Civil Affairs administered social assistance and relief.

38 Chow (n 16) 19–23; Jinglian Wu, *Understanding and Interpreting Chinese Economic Reform* (Thomson 2005) 327; Linda Wong, 'Mending the Chinese Welfare Net: Tool for Social Harmony or Regime Stability?' in Joseph Y.S. Cheng (ed), *China: A New Stage of Development for an Emerging Superpower* (City University of Hong Kong Press 2012) 543 (chap 18) 551; Zuo Jing, *Rural Social Security System and Innovation in China* (Zhongguo nongcun shehuibaozhang falüzhidu chuangxin yanjiu) (Xiamen daxue chubanshe 2007) 15–16.

legal instrument adopted in the Maoist era in the domain of social insurance. The LIR established a system of employers' responsibility for the workers' health care and welfare in the event of injury in work, sickness, maternity, and retirement, partly through direct provision (of medical treatment, for example) and partly through a labour insurance (*laodong baoxian*) system. The regulations were originally applicable only to large enterprises (employing more than 100 workers) in certain industries, but subsequently extended to all enterprises in the urban areas.[39]

The regulations provided for payments to workers or their dependants in case of sickness, maternity and work-related injury, incapacity, and death; non-work-related injury, incapacity, and death (with less generous treatment than the case of work-related accidents); and pensions were payable for retired workers. (Special and more generous treatment was provided for exemplary or 'model' workers who had made 'special contribution' to the enterprise and 'war heroes' who had joined the enterprise, while those who had been sentenced to deprivation of their political rights were not eligible for benefits under the regulations.) A scheme similar to the LIR was subsequently set up for government officials, party cadres, and staff working in other institutional units of the state.[40]

The scheme established by the LIR drew on the relevant experience of the Soviet Union.[41] Insurance premiums were paid only by the enterprises; workers need not contribute. Enterprises were to contribute monthly to the

39 The levels or amounts of benefits enjoyed by workers in different types of enterprises were not the same. For example, workers in 'collective enterprises' (*jiti qiye*) were treated less generously than workers in state-owned enterprises. See Jane Duckett, 'Health and Social Policy' in Chris Ogden (ed), *Handbook of China's Governance and Domestic Politics* (Routledge 2013) 67 (chap 6) 68. Collective enterprises had diverse backgrounds. Unlike state-owned enterprises, they were not directly established and controlled by the government. 'Urban "big collectives" refer to enterprises established by local governments at the district level or above'. (Wu (n 38) 331) Collective enterprises also included, for examples, cooperatives (*hezuo she*) formed by individuals or collective bodies of people, and formerly private enterprises that had undergone 'socialist transformation'. Collective enterprises were not considered either state-owned enterprises or private enterprises. See Li Min, 'A Property Rights Analysis of Collective Enterprises in Cities and Towns' (Chengzhen jiti qiye de wuquan fenxi) (2013) 7(6) Journal of Central South University of Forestry and Technology (Social Science Edition) (Zhongnan linye kejidaxue xuebao shehuikexueban) 107.

40 'State sector workers enjoyed broad benefits including housing, education, health care, and pensions. Civil servants and Communist Party officials received even higher level of benefits': Mark W. Frazier, 'Welfare Policy Pathways Among Large Uneven Developers' in Scott Kennedy (ed), *Beyond the Middle Kingdom: Comparative Perspectives on China's Capitalist Transformations* (Stanford University Press 2011) 89 (chap 5) 93. For relevant regulations, see Wang (n 27) 24–25; Li Jianfei (ed), *Social Security Law* (Shehui baozhang fa), 3rd edn (Zhongguo renmin daxue chubanshe, 2008) 27. For example, old age pensions for cadres and civil servants were provided for in the Interim Provisions on the Retirement of Workers and Officials promulgated by the State Council in 1958: see Li Jianfei, *Labor Law and Social Security Law of China* (Beijing: Zhongguo renmin daxue chubanshe, 2014) 251.

41 Hu (n 31) 297; Dillon (n 10) chaps 3, 4; Chow (n 16) chaps 2, 3.

labour insurance fund 3 percent of the total wage bill of their workers, which was in addition to the wage to be paid. Borrowing from the Soviet model, trade unions led by the All-China Federation of Trade Unions participated in the administration of the insurance scheme, until the Cultural Revolution era during which no common insurance fund existed, and each enterprise became responsible for its own workers.[42]

It has been pointed out that the provisions that the LIR scheme made for workers and their dependants were so generous that it was questionable whether they were consistent with China's relatively low level of economic and social development at the time.[43] The planned economy assigned individuals to jobs in state-owned enterprises or other work units (or '*danwei*' in Chinese).[44] Workers enjoyed life-long employment (until retirement) in these enterprises or units, which provided to them welfare 'from cradle to grave',[45] not only in the contingencies covered by the LIR but also in matters such as housing, medical care, and children's education. The socioeconomic policy that the government adopted for urban residents could be described as 'high employment, low wage and high welfare', with everyone 'eating from the same big rice bowl'.[46]

At the time of the enactment of the LIR, there were still private enterprises and enterprises jointly owned by government and private entrepreneurs in China. However, by the mid-1950s, all enterprises and business had been nationalised, and the urban economy was operated entirely by state-owned or collectively-owned entities. As state-owned enterprises were fully financed by the state, the legal requirement that enterprises or employers should bear the full costs of their workers' insurance effectively meant that these costs were borne by the state. The situation of collectively owned enterprises was more complicated,[47] as they were not formally owned by the state but were more autonomous in their operation, though in practice they were under the control of local governments.

42 This policy was stated in the 'Opinions on the Reform of Several Systems in the Financial Work of State-owned Enterprises' issued by the Ministry of Finance in 1969: see Li, *Labour Law and Social Security Law* (n 40) 252.

43 Chow (n 16) 26.

44 Duckett (n 39) 68; Joe C. B. Leung and Yuebin Xu, *China's Social Welfare: The Third Turning* Point (Polity 2015) 22.

45 Linda Wong and Ka-ho Mok, 'The Reform and the Changing Social Context' in Linda Wong and Stewart MacPherson (eds), *Social Change and Social Policy in Contemporary China* (Avebury 1995) 1, 16; Norman Flynn, Ian Holliday, and Linda Wong, 'Introduction' in Linda Wong and Norman Flynn (eds), *The Market in Chinese Social Policy* (Palgrave 2001) 1, 3; Tony Saich, *Governance and Politics of China*, 3rd edn (Palgrave Macmillan 2011) 297.

46 Chan and Chow (n 3) 36, 43.

47 For collective enterprises, see n 39 above.

Health Care, Housing, and Land

All hospitals were nationalised after the establishment of the PRC in 1949. Throughout the Maoist era, all hospitals were part of the state sector and some large state-owned enterprises and government or military units operated their own hospitals for staff.[48] In the countryside, community-based schemes such as barefoot doctors were developed.[49]

After the Revolution, a new system of land ownership was introduced across the whole country.[50] This was the socialist public ownership of land, which took one of two forms, depending on whether the land was in the urban area or in the rural area. In the former, all land was owned by the state (such 'State ownership' is also known as 'ownership by the whole people'). In the latter, a form of public ownership known as 'collective ownership by the labouring masses' was introduced, under which a particular piece of land in a rural area would be 'collectively owned' by the peasants living in that area. As regards buildings in urban areas, in theory they could still be privately owned, but in practice most buildings, whether for residential, commercial, or industrial use, were nationalised in the 1950s. The system of land ownership just described was established in the Maoist era, and was subsequently codified in the 1982 Constitution of the PRC.[51]

In the Maoist era, most people living in urban areas were employed by state organs, state-owned enterprises, or other state-owned institutions. Housing accommodation was provided to workers or employees as a kind of welfare benefit by their work units.[52] A nominal rent would be charged, but entitlement to housing accommodation was regarded as part and parcel of employment which was in practice lifelong, and the housing accommodation could even be inherited by the next generation. Allocation of housing belonging to the work units was administered by the managers of the work units themselves.

In the rural areas, radical land reforms were introduced immediately after the Revolution. One of the first laws enacted after the PRC was established was the Land Reform Law 1950. There was massive redistribution of land; landowners and rich peasants were the targets of ruthless 'class struggles', and their land was confiscated and redistributed to poor peasants. In the course of the 1950s, full-scale collectivisation of agriculture was introduced. Private

48 Duckett (n 39) 68.

49 See n 62.

50 For the development of the system of land ownership and property law in the PRC, see generally Albert H.Y. Chen, 'The Law of Property and the Evolving System of Property Rights in China', in Guanghua Yu (ed), *The Development of the Chinese Legal System: Change and Challenges* (Routledge 2011), 81–112 (chap 4).

51 See Articles 6 and 10 of the 1982 Constitution.

52 Thelle (n 34) 144–149.

ownership by peasants was replaced by 'collective ownership by the laboring masses'. A three-tier system of ownership and management of rural land was established, with 'production teams' being led by 'production brigades' which were in turn under the 'people's communes'.[53]

Social Security for the Rural Population?

In contrast to China's urban workers, the rural population – which constituted 80 percent of China's population at the time of the establishment of the PRC – enjoyed little legal or formal protection of the kind provided by the LIR. The social policy of privileging the urban working class may be explained with reference to several factors.[54] First, the Marxist-Leninist ideology and the Soviet model, both followed by the CCP in the 1950s (although Mao began to depart from the Soviet model in the late 1950s), emphasised the role played by the urban working class in the socialist revolution, and considered the communist party to be the vanguard of the proletariat or workers.[55] Secondly, given the low level of economic development in China at the time, the scarcity of resources, and the limited capacity of the new CCP-led government, it would simply be impossible to provide a social insurance scheme that was universally applicable to all. Indeed, as mentioned earlier, the scheme established by the LIR was already very generous, and had already been expanded to cover most of the urban population. Thirdly, it has been pointed out that once the urban workers were incorporated into the scheme initially, the politics of scarcity or 'rationing' was such that the 'insiders' (those already eligible to enjoy benefits under the existing system) would resist expansion of the scheme to 'outsiders' and would seek to keep resources within the scheme.[56]

Another very important factor was the CCP's 'dualistic' strategy of China's economic development, which involved the 'surplus' being produced in the rural areas being transferred to the cities to support their economic and industrial growth.[57] Agricultural products of the rural area were sold in the cities at low prices fixed by the government. This meant a transfer by the exercise of political power of economic resources from the rural to the urban areas for the purpose of the nation's overall industrial development and modernisation. The enactment in 1958 of regulations on the household registration (*hukou* or

53 See generally Chen (n 50).

54 Chow (n 16) 22 ('state-run enterprise workers . . . formed the backbone of the communist regime'). See also Chan and Chow (n 3) 36.

55 Thus Article 1 of the 1954 Constitution of the PRC stated that the PRC was a people's democratic state led by the working class and based on the alliance of workers and peasants.

56 Dillon (n 10), especially 'Introduction' and 'Conclusion'.

57 Leung and Xu (n 44) 19; Saich (n 45) 298, 316; Xu Jiahui and Guo Xiangyu, *A Study of the Rural Social Security Legal System in China* (Zhongguo nongcun shehuibaozhang falüzhidu yanjiu) (Zhongguo nongye chubanshe 2013) 98–99.

huji) system institutionalised the differentiation between the urban and rural populations.[58] People living in China's rural areas could not freely migrate to the cities.[59]

The collectivisation of agriculture in the rural areas culminated in the establishment of 'people's communes' in 1958.[60] The welfare needs of the rural population were taken care of by their own family members[61] – thus demonstrating reliance on the Chinese tradition of the centrality of social relationships within the family, filial piety, and mutual support and solidarity among family members – and by the communes which were both economic and administrative organisations. For example, a cooperative medical scheme with features such as 'barefoot doctors' was established.[62] The 'cooperative' nature of the scheme meant that it was operated by the peasants in the communes without any state funding. For those without family members and unable to work to support themselves economically, a residual welfare system known as the 'Five Guarantees' (*wubao*) (social provision to the destitute of the five items of food, clothing, shelter, medical care, and burial expenses) was introduced.[63]

The differential treatment of the urban and rural populations in Maoist China demonstrates that there was no concept of equality of all the people or of citizens as far as social and economic rights were concerned. Actually, the Marxist-Leninist theory as adopted in Maoist China distinguished between different social classes, and urban workers and peasants were regarded as belonging to different classes. Thus Article 1 of the first constitution of the PRC, which will be further discussed later, provided that the PRC was a 'people's democratic State' led by the 'working class' and based on an 'alliance between workers and peasants'. Even among workers or members of the urban population, there was no theory or practice that they should be accorded equal treatment. It has been pointed out that practices during the Maoist era were characterised by 'hierarchism', which means that there was differential treatment as between

58 Leung and Xu (n 44) 23–24; Roger C.K. Chan, 'The Urban Migrants – the Challenge to Public Policy' in Wong and MacPherson (n 45) 140 (chap 7). The rigid system of household registration prohibited migration from the rural areas to cities until this policy was relaxed in 1984: see Wong and Mok (n 45) 3–4.

59 At the time the PRC was established, approximately 80 percent of the population were peasants in the rural areas: see Xu and Guo (n 57) 84. Subsequently, in the period 1990–2006, the urban population increased from 26.4 percent to 43.9 percent of China's total population: see Chak Kwan Chan, King Lun Ngok, and David Phillips, *Social Policy in China* (Policy Press 2008) 6.

60 Chan, Ngok, and Phillips (n 59) 28; Leung and Xu (n 44) 19.

61 Chan and Chow (n 3) 37 ('The importance of the family in the provision of care in the PRC'), 40 ('the welfare model of the PRC before the economic reform can be described as a hybrid socialist model, which stems from a State socialist concern of system maintenance, ideological commitment to socialist redistribution, and pragmatic adherence to the traditional family care').

62 Duckett (n 39) 68 ('barefoot doctors' were 'farmers trained in basic preventive health and sanitation measures who worked as paramedics in the villages').

63 Duckett (n 39) 68; Leung and Xu (n 44) 99.

officials and workers, and among workers there was differential treatment as between those working in state-owned enterprises and those in collectively-owned enterprises.[64]

Famine and Class Struggles

Any assessment of social welfare and security in Maoist China cannot be adequate without taking into account the experience of the victims of the great famine of 1958–1961[65] and the 'class struggles' that culminated in the 'Cultural Revolution' that began in 1966.[66] It was estimated that 36 to 45 million people starved to death during the great famine, partly caused by weather and partly by government policy errors. In the course of 'class struggles', millions of people were persecuted as 'class enemies' or 'counter-revolutionaries'; some were murdered and many subjected to cruel and unusual punishment.[67] The discussion of social welfare or security is entirely meaningless as far as these episodes of PRC history are concerned, when the social environment itself became destructive of a dignified human existence. Furthermore, according to the thinking prevalent in the Maoist era, whether a person should enjoy social protection depended on his or her political opinion; those who were enemies of socialism should not be given protection.[68] For example, the Labour Insurance Regulations expressly provided that they were not applicable to those who had been deprived of their political rights.[69]

The 1954 Constitution

The constitution that was – at least in theory – in force in the PRC during the Maoist era was the constitution enacted in 1954, which was the first constitution in the PRC's history.[70] Drafted under the influence of Stalin's 1936 Constitution,

64 Hu (n 31) 305.
65 See eg Jisheng Yang, *Tombstone: The Great Chinese Famine 1958–1962* (transl. by Stacy Mosher and Guo Jian; Farrar, Straus & Giroux, 2012).
66 See eg Frank Dikötter, *The Cultural Revolution* (Bloomsbury 2016).
67 Xingzhong Yu, 'Citizenship, Ideology, and the PRC Constitution' in Merle Goldman and Elizabeth J. Perry (eds), *Changing Meanings of Citizenship in Modern China* (Harvard University Press 2002) 288 (chap 11) 293 ('reactionary classes such as the bureaucratic class [of the former KMT regime] and the landlord class . . . do not enjoy the rights of the people'); Chan and Chow (n 3) 30 ('welfare relief was only given to a selected group of "deserving" citizens while political dissidents, people who do not comply with the rules, and politically labelled persons would not be given assistance. These people not only suffered from political prosecutions but were also deprived of their jobs, promotion prospects, financial subsidies, housing and welfare entitlements').
68 Shen (n 13) 53.
69 See Article 4 of the Regulations.
70 For the constitutional history of the PRC, see eg Albert H.Y. Chen, *An Introduction to the Legal System of the People's Republic of China*, 5th edn (LexisNexis 2018) chaps 3, 4, 11.

it provided for a state structure similar to that of the Soviet Union. As in the case of the USSR Constitution, the PRC Constitution (in Chapter 3, entitled 'the fundamental rights and duties of citizens') provided for various rights of citizens, including civil and political rights as well as economic, social, and cultural rights (such as the right to work (*laodong*, alternatively translated as 'labour') (Article 91) and the right to receive education (Article 94).

The constitutional provision in the 1954 Constitution that was most relevant to social welfare and security was Article 93, which provided that

> [L]aborers (*laodongzhe*) in the PRC have the right to receive material assistance (*wuzhi bangzhu*) in times of old age, sickness or loss of the capacity to work. The State shall organize social insurance (*shehui baoxian*), social assistance and relief (*shehui jiuji*), and medical and hygiene enterprise for the masses, and shall gradually expand these facilities so as to ensure that laborers will enjoy these rights.

Although the term of 'social insurance' (*shehui baoxian*) appeared in this provision, as it had appeared in the labour law of 1931 adopted by the Chinese Soviet Republic and the 1946 Constitution enacted by the KMT regime, this term was hardly used in the laws and official documents of the Maoist era, during which the term 'labour insurance' used in the LIR itself was the preferred term.

The reference to 'laborers' in Article 93 of the 1954 Constitution suggests that the right to receive social support and assistance at times of need was conceived of as being conferred on those who engaged in labour and thus made a contribution to society, rather than as flowing from or being attached to citizenship. This concern for the welfare rights and security of workers rather than citizens generally can be attributed to Marxist and Soviet ideology. In fact, it was doubtful whether all citizens as people of the nation enjoyed equal rights. Mao's concept of 'people's democratic dictatorship' – which was used to theorise the nature of the state in the PRC – involved the distinction between 'the people' (consisting mainly of the working class and the peasants) and 'the enemies' (class enemies), and the people – led by the CCP – exercising dictatorship over their enemies. The enemies or 'reactionary classes' were not supposed to enjoy any rights.

In the Maoist era, the 1954 Constitution and the system of socialist legality based on the Soviet model did not enjoy much authority and respect – particularly when compared with documents of party policy and speeches of party leaders – and were completely disregarded during the 'Cultural Revolution'. In 1975, the second constitution in the PRC's history was promulgated. This constitution, which codified the Maoist ideology of the 'Cultural Revolution' era, was short-lived and replaced soon after Mao's death by the 1978 Constitution.

Social Policy and Law in the Initial Period of the Era of 'Reform and Opening' (1978–2001)

Introduction

Mao's death in 1976 brought an end to the PRC's Cultural Revolution era of leftist excesses. Mao might have intended to build a genuine communist and egalitarian society in China, but the practical result was that millions were persecuted as class enemies and China was in a state of massive poverty and social stagnation. The time was ripe for a fundamental policy change or a paradigm shift. This materialised when Deng Xiaoping – who succeeded to consolidate power by 1978 as the paramount leader of the CCP – launched a new policy of 'reform and opening', which meant putting an end to 'class struggles' and focusing the CCP's and the nation's energy on economic development and modernisation.[71]

In this new era of 'reform and opening' that began in the late 1970s and has continued up to this day, the PRC achieved rapid and continuous economic growth so as to become the second largest economy in the world. Economic development has been accompanied by far-reaching social changes in the course of a great transition from the former socialist planned economy to what since the 1990s has been officially called a 'socialist market economy', with a vibrant private sector and large-scale markets for goods, services, land, capital, and labour. The challenges and risks of this transition, which inevitably involved some people losing out and others making gains, entailed the development of new social policies for the purpose of maintaining the CCP regime's political legitimacy and the stability of the changing society.[72]

Overview

In our discussion of this era of 'reform and opening', it is possible to draw a line between the initial period (1978–2001) and the later period (2002–the present) that began with the 16th National Congress of the CCP in 2002 at which Hu Jintao became CCP General Secretary.

In the initial period of 'reform and opening', priority was accorded to economic development rather than social and economic equality. It was considered that economic efficiency and growth could be achieved by letting market forces work. There was a gradual transition from the pre-existing socialist planned economy to a market economy in which market forces replaced bureaucratic control as the major means of coordination of economic activities. This involved

71 See generally Loren Brandt and Thomas G. Rawski (eds), *China's Great Economic Transformation* (Cambridge University Press 2008); Paul G. Clifford, *The China Paradox* (de Gruyter Press 2017).

72 See generally Bruce J. Dickson, *The Dictator's Dilemma: The Chinese Communist Party's Strategy for Survival* (Oxford University Press 2016); Stein Ringen, *The Perfect Dictatorship: China in the 21st Century* (Hong Kong University Press 2016).

a significant change in the role of the state, particularly a significantly reduced role of the state in the economic arena. For example, state-owned enterprises were required to compete in the market for survival instead of relying on state subsidies. Private and joint shareholding enterprises came into existence.

The transition from the planned economy to a market economy inevitably gave rise to social problems such as unemployment, loss of social security which had hitherto been provided by state-owned work units, and increasing social and economic inequality. In the initial period of 'reform and opening', the old mechanisms for social security were in the course of disintegration, while new mechanisms such as social safety nets had not yet been well developed. This was the case not only in the urban areas where state enterprise reform was being carried out, but also in the rural areas where the communes gave way to a considerable degree of privatised agricultural production under the household contract responsibility system.

The initial success of marketisation of the economy had a 'spillover' effect[73] on the provision of social services such as housing and medical care, in which a process of marketisation, commercialisation, or commodification took place in this initial period of 'reform and opening'.

In what can be called the later period of 'reform and opening' after the turn of the century, there was a growing recognition that the state should assume or re-assume responsibility for the provision of basic social or public goods, and such social goods should be made available universally to all citizens.[74] This can be interpreted as a response to growing discontent with the rising cost of housing and medical care, and increasing social and economic inequality, which had the potential of threatening social stability and diminishing the political legitimacy of the regime.[75]

In this section of the chapter, we will first consider matters of social security in the initial period of the era of 'reform and opening', and then turn to health care, housing, and land.

Gradual Emergence of a New System of Social Insurance and Social Assistance

From 1978 to the 1980s

At the constitutional level, the reform era was marked by the enactment of the new Constitution of 1982. This is the fourth constitution in PRC history: the 1954 Constitution had been replaced by the 1975 Constitution that reflected the Cultural Revolution ideology, which in turn was superseded by the 1978

73 Duckett (n 39) 73.

74 ibid 76.

75 See generally Dickson (n 72) chap 4.

Constitution that was enacted after Mao's death but before Deng assumed full control of the CCP. The 1982 Constitution restored some of the positive features of the 1954 Constitution (as distinguished from the 'leftist' features of the 1975 and 1978 Constitutions) and improved upon it. The chapter on 'the fundamental rights and duties' of citizens now occupies a more prominent place as Chapter 2 of the constitution instead of being Chapter 3 in the previous constitutions.

Article 5 of the 1982 Constitution, which finds no parallel in previous constitutions, expressly affirms the supremacy of the constitution over laws and regulations, requires all state organs and political parties to abide by the constitution and the laws, provides that 'no organisation or individual may have the privilege of being above the Constitution and the laws', and declares that 'the State shall defend the unity and dignity of the socialist legal system'.

As far as social policy is concerned, two articles in the 1982 Constitution are particularly relevant. Article 44 provides for a retirement system for the staff of state organs, enterprises, and institutional units to enable them to enjoy a post-retirement life. Article 45 is based on and improves upon Article 93 of the 1954 Constitution. It reads as follows:

> Citizens of the PRC have the right to receive material assistance from the State and society in times of old age, sickness or loss of the capacity to work. The State shall develop social insurance, social assistance and relief (*shehui jiuji*), and medical and hygiene enterprises as necessitated by citizens' enjoyment of these rights. The State and society shall secure the livelihood of disabled servicemen and provide special compensation and benefits to the family members of martyrs and of servicemen. The State and society shall provide assistance to the blind, the deaf, the mute, and other disabled citizens in their work, life and education.

A significant change of language relative to the corresponding provision in the 1954 Constitution is that the right to receive social support and assistance at times of need is now vested in 'citizens' and not just 'labourers'. It is noteworthy that there was not yet any direct mention of the term 'social security' in the 1982 Constitution.[76] As mentioned later in this chapter, the state's duty to 'develop a social security system that is commensurate with the nation's level of economic development' finally received constitutional recognition when Article 14 of the constitution was revised in 2004.

Economic reforms in the reform era began with the introduction of the 'household contract responsibility' system of agricultural production in the rural areas (superseding the previous practice of the communes organising

76 For details on the meaning of 'material assistance' see Ulrike Davy, Chapter 6 in this volume, p. 215.

production in a collective manner) and the reform of state-owned enterprises in the urban areas. Both reforms had important implications for the existing practice of social security.[77] In the countryside, the abolition of the communes and the de-collectivisation or de facto privatisation of agricultural production meant that families were left on their own and could hardly rely on the collective to meet their welfare needs.[78] In cities, where workers used to 'eat from the same big iron rice bowl', had enjoyed security of job tenure, and had their welfare needs well taken care of by their work units, enterprise reform in the direction of increased autonomy for enterprises, marketisation, and privatisation exposed them to the risks of unemployment and of their employers no longer catering for their welfare and security.[79]

From the legal point of view, the year 1986 marked the beginnings of a new environment for urban workers. In 1986, new Regulations on Labour Contracts were enacted, providing that newly recruited workers in state-owned enterprises would be employed on the basis of labour contracts and would no longer be guaranteed lifelong employment.[80] Departing from the approach adopted in the Labour Insurance Regulations of 1951, now *both workers and enterprises* were to make contributions to a pension fund to cater for workers' retirement. In the same year, a Law on Bankruptcy of Enterprises and provisional rules on insurance for workers from state-owned enterprises 'awaiting employment' were introduced.[81] The Bankruptcy Law allowed state-owned enterprises to close down and thus to terminate their workers' employment. The insurance rules for 'workers awaiting employment' (the term 'unemployed' was not yet used at this stage) implicitly recognised that unemployment would exist in the PRC, contrary to the former ideology that socialism would provide full employment for all so that all could engage in productive labour. It has been pointed out[82] that in this Chinese context, such unemployment insurance served some peculiar functions not served by such insurance in the West, such as facilitating labour mobility which had not previously existed and enabling state-owned enterprises to reform themselves by reducing their surplus labour.

The year 1986 also saw the beginning of the official recognition and promotion of the term and concept of '*shehui baozhang*' (which, as discussed later, is the Chinese translation of 'social security'), which had hardly been used in the past in the PRC. The Seventh Five-Year Plan for China's economic and social development expressly provided, among other matters, that China should seek

77 Chan, Ngok, and Phillips (n 59) chap 3 ('Social policy in the context of economic reforms').

78 Wu (n 38) 352.

79 Wong (n 38) 564.

80 Wu (n 38) 328; Wong and Mok (n 45) 6–7.

81 Chan, Ngok, and Phillips (n 59) 32; Wu (n 38) 349.

82 Chu, 'Politics of Welfare in China' in T. Wing Lo and Joseph Cheng (eds), *Social Welfare Development in China: Constraints and Challenges* (Imprint 1996) 51, 60; Flynn, Holliday, and Wong (n 45) 6.

to develop a 'socialist social security system with Chinese characteristics'.[83] The concept of '*shehui baozhang*' was understood to embrace social insurance (such as insurance for pension, illness, and unemployment), social assistance and relief (*shehui jiuji* or *shehui jiuzhu*), special compensation and benefits (*youfu*) (for ex-servicemen and martyrs' families as mentioned earlier), and social welfare (*shehui fuli*) services.[84]

The term '*shehui baozhang*' is clearly a Chinese translation of the term 'social security', as '*shehui baozhang*' is also used in the official Chinese translations of Article 22 of the Universal Declaration of Human Rights (1948) and Article 9 of the International Covenant on Economic, Social and Cultural Rights (1966), both of which provide for the right to social security. '*Shehui baozhang*' also appears in the official Chinese title of the ILO Social Security (Minimum Standards) Convention, 1952 (No. 102). For comparative purpose, it is noteworthy that as mentioned earlier, the Chinese term used in the 1946 Constitution of the Republic of China to express the concept of 'social security' was '*shehui anquan*', and the term '*shehui baozhang*' does not appear in that constitution. Neither does it appear in the 1954 Constitution or the 1982 Constitution of the PRC.

The 1990s

Major steps began to be taken in the 1990s towards the construction of a system of social insurance that includes pensions for the retired, payment of medical expenses for the sick, compensation for work accidents, subsidies for maternity, and payments to support the unemployed. Some of the insurance schemes, such as those for retirement pensions and medical expenses, required tripartite contributions from the state, enterprises, and workers, and involved the establishment of state-administered collective funds into which insurance premiums would be paid. Some schemes, such as those for work accidents and maternity, do not require contributions from employees. The coverage of the various schemes was usually limited initially (for example, being limited only to workers in state-owned enterprises),[85] and was gradually extended to cover more people (such as other urban employees, rural-to-urban migrant

83 Nelson Chow, 'Social Security Reform in China' in Wong and MacPherson (n 45) 27 (chap 2) 30–32.

84 See generally Zheng Gongcheng, *The Path of Social Security with Chinese Characteristics* (Lun Zhongguo tese de shehuibaozhang daolu) (Wuhan daxue chubanshe 1997) 146–149; Zheng Gongcheng (ed), *Commentary on and Guide to the Social Insurance Law of the PRC* (Zhonghua renmin gongheguo shehui baoxian fa shiyi yu shiyong zhiyin) (Zhongguo laodong shehuibaozhang chubanshe 2012) 389–390; the PRC's report on 'Implementation of the international Covenant on Economic, Social and Cultural Rights' submitted in 2003, UN Doc E/1990/5/Add.59, paras 83–95 ('the right to social security').

85 Saich (n 45) 297–298.

workers,[86] other urban residents who are not employees, and the rural population). In the course of the 1990s, an innovative social assistance scheme was developed providing for cash transfer (known as 'Minimum Livelihood Guarantee') to the needy. Some of the major developments in the domains of social insurance and social assistance and relief, including relevant developments at both the policy and legal levels, will be outlined below.[87]

In 1991, a major step forward in the construction of a social insurance system was taken when the government made a Decision on Pension Reform in Urban Enterprises.[88] The Decision made provisions for an insurance system for old age involving tripartite contributions from the state, enterprises, and workers, and the simultaneous introduction – probably under the influence of the World Bank – of 'individual accounts' and 'social pooling' in the operation of the insurance funds. This was a significant reform measure relative to the pension system that existed in pre-reform era, whose costs were entirely borne by state-owned enterprises with no requirement of payment of contributions by employees. The adoption of the principle of contributory insurance – involving shared responsibilities for the employee's welfare on the parts of the state, the employer, and the employee himself or herself – was thus a major development in the domain of social insurance in the PRC.

In 1993, the CCP at the Third Plenum of its 14th Central Committee made a landmark Decision on the Development of a Socialist Market Economy in the PRC, signalling the deepening of economic reforms in the direction of marketisation and privatisation.[89] In this Decision, 'social security' (*shehui baozhang*) was described as one of the five pillars of the developing socialist market economy, thus indicating the importance the CCP attached to the development of a system of social security. The year 1993 also saw the first experiment in 'Minimum Livelihood Guarantee' (MLG) in Shanghai – an innovative scheme of social assistance in the form of cash transfer to those who do not have income or resources that can sustain a minimum standard of living.[90] In the same year, revised rules were enacted on insurance for workers

86 Despite the household registration system introduced in 1958 as mentioned earlier, peasants from the rural areas were allowed since 1984 to move to cities to seek employment (Wong and Mok (n 45) 3–4). However, for many years since 1984, such migrant workers were not treated equally as people with urban household registration for the purpose of entitlement to various social benefits, simply because the former's '*huji*' (household registration) was still in the countryside: Chu (n 82) 58.

87 This chapter has not covered the important work of poverty alleviation (*fupin*) which has been successful in improving the standard of living of hundreds of millions. See Leung and Xu (n 44) 61–65, 103–104.

88 Wong (n 38) 552; Wu (n 38) 332; Chan, Ngok, and Phillips (n 59) 32.

89 Chan, Ngok, and Phillips (n 59) 34; Wu (n 38) 333–335.

90 Wong (n 38) 547; Tony Saich, *Providing Public Goods in Transitional China* (Palgrave Macmillan 2008) 55; Lutz Leisering, Tao Liu, and Tobias ten Brink, 'Synthesizing Disparate Ideas: How a Chinese Model of Social Assistance was Forged' (2017) 17(3) Global Social Policy 307.

from state-owned enterprises 'awaiting employment'. In 1994, this kind of insurance was finally renamed 'unemployment insurance'.[91]

In 1994, the first comprehensive labour law in the PRC's history was enacted. It contained, among others, provisions for minimum wage, work injuries, and insurance for workers. Rules on maternity insurance were enacted in the same year, providing for 'social pooling' of insurance premiums paid by enterprises.[92] The year 1994 also saw major developments in the domain of social security in the rural areas: The first official regulations on the 'Five Guarantees' (*wubao*) system (which originated in the 1950s as mentioned earlier) were enacted.[93] A decision was also taken to restore the cooperative medical scheme in the rural areas that had almost collapsed in the course of the 1980s.[94]

In 1996, the existing system of compensation for work accidents was regularised and improved by the enactment of new provisional measures on insurance for work injuries.[95] As in the case of maternity insurance, these rules provided for the 'social pooling' of insurance premiums paid by enterprises.

In 1997, the 15th National Congress of the CCP was held. On the subject of social security, the Party Congress adopted the policies of 'establishing a social security system, introducing pension and medical insurance systems based on the combination of social pooling and individual accounts, improving the systems of unemployment insurance and social assistance and relief (*shehui jiuji*), and providing basic social security'.[96] As regards pension insurance, a unified contributory insurance scheme was introduced in 1997 for all state-owned and collective enterprises in the urban areas.[97] The scheme was expanded in 1999 to cover private enterprises and foreign-investment enterprises, and further expanded in 2002 to cover the self-employed.[98] Municipal social insurance bureaus were set up to collect premiums and to pay pensions.[99] The growing importance of social security was evidenced by the establishment under the

91 Wu (n 38) 349; Wang (n 27) 29.

92 Institute of Law, Chinese Academy of Social Science (ed), *Thirty Years of Rule of Law in China 1978–2008)* (Zhongguo fazhi sanshi nian) (Shehui kexue wenxian chubanshe 2008) 396; Wang (n 27) 31.

93 Xu and Guo (n 57) 96.

94 Saich (n 45) 320.

95 Institute of Law (n 92) 396; Liu (n 19) 40.

96 Li Yuede, 'Developing and Improving the Social Security System' (in Chinese), in *Reader on the Constitution and Constitutional Amendment* (Xianfa he xianfa xiuzheng an fudao duben) (Zhongguo fazhi chubanshe 2004) 206, 211. As regards medical insurance, the State Council in 1998 promulgated a Decision on the Establishment of a Basic Medical Insurance System for Workers in Cities and Towns: see Zuo (n 38) 17.

97 Wong (n 38) 552; Institute of Law (n 92) 393.

98 Lihong Lin, 'The Rise of Rights and Protections for the Disadvantaged' in Dingjian Cai and Chenguang Wang (eds), *China's Journey Toward the Rule of Law: Legal Reform 1978–2008* (Brill 2010) 301 (chap 7) 307.

99 Saich (n 45) 312.

State Council of the Ministry of Labour and Social Security in 1998.[100] (The Ministry was renamed the Ministry of Human Resources and Social Security in 2008.[101] Social assistance such as the Minimum Livelihood Guarantee scheme or relief for victims of natural disasters falls under the responsibility of another ministry – the Ministry of Civil Affairs.)

Major advances in social security and welfare occurred at the turn of the century. The year 1999 saw the enactment of several important pieces of regulations, including the Regulations on Unemployment Insurance[102] (providing for contributions from both employers and employees in both the state-owned and private sectors of the economy and marking a more mature stage of development of the unemployment insurance that started in 1986), the Regulations on Minimum Livelihood Guarantee (MLG) for Urban Residents[103] (extending the MLG scheme that started in Shanghai in 1993 to all cities), and the Provisional Regulations on the Collection of Social Insurance Fees.[104] In 2000, a National Social Insurance Fund was established, together with a National Council for Social Security for the supervision of the fund.[105]

Among the aforementioned developments at the turn of the century, the enactment of the Regulations on Minimum Livelihood Guarantee (MLG) for Urban Residents was particularly significant, and represented a major breakthrough in the domain of social assistance in China. It has been pointed out that

> '[S]ocial cash transfers' (SCTs), defined as tax-financed regular noncontributory cash transfers to the poor for general subsistence . . . have spread in the Global South since the 1990s and have become a global consensual model.[106]

The MLG is the Chinese version of SCT. The Regulations on MLG provide that where the average income of members of a family falls below the relevant MLG level as determined by the local government, they have the right to material assistance in the form of MLG. The scheme is financed by the local government and administered by local government agencies under the Ministry of Civil Affairs. The regulations provide that disputes relating to entitlements to or payments of MLG are resolved either by petitions for administrative review or litigation in the courts.

100 ibid.

101 Lin (n 98) 329.

102 Wong (n 38) 554; Institute of Law (n 92) 394.

103 Wong (n 38) 549; Wu (n 38) 351 (pointing out that the scheme was funded by local governments which also determined the amounts payable under the scheme). For a study of the scheme, see generally Leisering, Liu, and ten Brink (n 90).

104 Zuo (n 38) 20.

105 Saich (n 45) 313; Wu (n 38) 342.

106 Leisering, Liu, and ten Brink (n 90) 308.

In the domain of medical insurance, a major step forward was taken in 1999, when a contributory insurance scheme was introduced for all employees in both the state sector and private sector in the urban areas.[107] Another noteworthy development was that the PRC signed the International Covenant on Economic, Social and Cultural Rights in 1997, and ratified it in 2001. The rights provided for in the Covenant include the right to social security. The PRC has since submitted three reports (in 2004, 2010, and 2019) under this Covenant to the Committee on Economic, Social, and Cultural Rights.[108]

At the annual session of the National People's Congress (NPC) (China's Parliament) in 2001, a report was presented by the NPC Standing Committee in which it was stated that China's socialist legal system consisted of seven main areas of law, one of which was 'social law' (*shehui fa*).[109] The recognition of social law, which in the PRC is usually taken to include as its core labour law and laws relating to social security, as one of the seven components of Chinese law gave a boost to legislative work and legal scholarship in this regard.

Health Care, Housing, and Land

In the era of 'reform and opening', the system of medical services and healthcare changed in the direction of commercialisation and reduced government funding for the healthcare system. The period 1979–1987 saw de facto privatisation of much of medical care. By 1989, the private practice of healthcare had been legalised.[110] In the 1980s and 1990s, government funding for healthcare declined as a share of the nation's total health spending.[111]

With reduced government funding for the system, healthcare providers charged rising fees for their services. Hospitals relied more and more on the sale of pharmaceutical drugs as a major source of their income in addition to fees paid by patients for medical services.[112] In the late 1990s, some public hospitals

107 Wong (n 38) 553; Saich (n 45) 316.

108 Initial report on 'Implementation of the International Covenant on Economic, Social and Cultural Rights', 27 June 2003, UN Doc E/1990/5/Add.59; (second) report on 'Implementation of the International Covenant on Economic, Social and Cultural Rights', 30 June 2010, UN Doc UN Doc E/C.12/CHN/2; third periodic report submitted by China under Articles 16 und 17 of the Covenant, 19 December 2019, UN Doc E/C.12/CHN/3. See also the White Paper of the Information Office of the PRC State Council on *China's Social Security and its Policy* (PRC Government Website: gov.cn, September 2004).

109 Lin (n 98) 306; Ye Jingyi and Yan Tian, 'A Study of the Status of Social Law' (in Chinese), in Chen Su (ed), *People's Livelihood and Social Law* (Minsheng baozhang yu shehuifa jianshe) (Shehui kexue wenxian chubanshe 2009) 3.

110 Saich (n 45) 320.

111 Duckett (n 39) 70; Dickson (n 72) 178.

112 Wong (n 38) 557.

began to be privatised.[113] By the year 2016, 57 percent of hospitals were operated by non-government agencies.[114]

As regards urban housing, the general policy orientation in the reform era was to move away from provision of housing by work units to commercialisation or marketisation of housing.[115] Existing tenants of accommodation owned by work units were encouraged to purchase their homes at a subsidised price.[116] At the same time, 'land use rights' in state-owned land in urban areas were sold to developers (who acquired such rights for periods as long as seventy years, and who could in turn sell such rights to purchasers of apartments in buildings built by developers on such land) for the purpose of residential development.[117] The policy was to develop a housing market in which people's residential needs could be satisfied.[118]

In the reform era, the most important policy change with regard to the rural area was the de-collectivisation and partial privatisation of agricultural production. A 'contract responsibility' (*chengbao* in Chinese) system of agricultural production was introduced, under which the rural collective would grant to each individual peasant household the *chengbao* operational right over a plot of collectively owned land. A contract would be entered into under which the peasant household would be granted the right to use and derive economic benefits from the land subject to certain payments to the collective. For ordinary farmland, the period of grant would be thirty years, with the possibility of renewal. At the same time, peasant households also have the right to apply for and to obtain a grant of the right to use a piece of collectively owned land for the purpose of building their residential houses. These forms of land rights enjoyed by peasants were considered to perform an important 'social security function'.[119]

Social Policy and Law in the Later Period of the Era of 'Reform and Opening' (2002–the Present)

Introduction

What we call the later period of the era of 'reform and opening' can be said to begin with the 16th National Congress of the CCP in 2002. This period corresponds to the terms of Hu Jintao and Xi Jinping as CCP General Secretaries

113 Duckett (n 39) 70.

114 Information Office of the State Council of the PRC, White Paper on 'Development of China's Public Health as an Essential Element of Human Rights', 29 Sept 2017, <http://english.www.gov.cn/archive/white_paper/2017/09/29/content_281475894089810.htm> accessed 28 February 2022.

115 ibid 124–134.

116 Liang Ruobing, 'China's New Public Housing Policy: The Case of Xiamen', in Zhao Litao and Lim Tin Seng (eds), *China's New Social Policy: Initiatives for a Harmonious Society* (World Scientific 2010) 93 (chap 5) 95.

117 Chen (n 50).

118 Duckett (n 39) 70.

119 ibid.

(Hu in 2002–2012, Xi in 2012–the present). In this period, the Party-State responded to the growing social and economic inequalities generated by marketisation of the economy by further developing and expanding social security for more and more people, and resuming a more active role in the provision of social services and public goods, including health care, housing, and education. The state operated under a dual incentive of enabling the wealth created by the economic reform to be more broadly and equitably shared among the people and to be used to improve their livelihood, and of maintaining social stability and hence the political legitimacy of the regime.

The concepts of the 'scientific concept of development' and 'harmonious society' developed by the Hu Jintao regime may be interpreted as an adjustment to or modification of the previous approach that economic development should be pursued at all costs, and a recognition that higher priority should now be accorded to the needs of lower-income groups and rural residents, particularly those in poor regions of the country.

Developments in Social Security After 2001

In 2002, a new cooperative medical insurance scheme was launched for China's rural areas.[120] Unlike the cooperative health care in the rural areas in the Maoist era, this scheme was subsidised by the central and local governments, with contributions from peasants who participated in the scheme on a voluntary basis.

In 2003, the State Council enacted the Regulations on Insurance for Work Injuries,[121] which consolidated the existing system of compensation for work accidents and expanded its coverage to include migrant workers and informally employed staff. Premiums were payable by employers in both the state sector and private sector of the economy; employees were not required to contribute.

The following year of 2004 was a milestone for the development of social security in the PRC. In this year, the Constitution of 1982 was amended for the fourth time.[122] Articles 14 and 33 were among the constitutional provisions affected by this amendment. Article 14, which is in Chapter 1 ('General Principles') of the constitution, deals with labour and the people's livelihood. The amendment introduced the following provision into Article 14: 'The State shall develop a social security system that is commensurate with the nation's level of economic development'. The term 'social security' (*shehui baozhang*) thus appeared for the first time in the Constitution of the PRC. Another article affected by the amendment was Article 33, the first article in Chapter 2 ('The Basic Rights and Duties of Citizens') of the constitution. The amendment

120 Wong (n 38) 556–557; Zuo (n 38) 24–25; Chan, Ngok, and Phillips (n 59) 39.

121 Liu (n 30) 183; Tao Liu and Lutz Leisering, 'Protecting Injured Workers: How Global Ideas of Industrial Accident Insurance Travelled to China' (2017) 2(1) Journal of Chinese Governance 106.

122 See generally *Reader on the Constitution and Constitutional Amendment* (n 96).

of 2004 introduced the following provision into this article: 'The State shall respect and protect human rights'. Although the 1982 Constitution had provided for various species of citizens' rights, this was the first time that the term 'human rights' (which had previously been foreign to the Marxist-Leninist-Maoist discourse in the PRC) was written into the PRC Constitution. A few months after the constitutional amendment of 2004, the Information Office of the State Council published a 'White Paper' on 'China's Social Security and its Policy', which described the achievements made in this field so far.[123]

In 2006, the State Council enacted new Regulations on the Five Guarantees Subsistence Programme for Rural Areas,[124] which built upon the existing system of the 'five guarantees' mentioned earlier, and provided funding support from local governments for this purpose.

In 2007, the medical insurance scheme for employees in the urban areas was extended to cover all urban residents, including students, the elderly, and others not engaged in employment.[125] In the same year, it was decided to extend the MLG scheme from the urban areas to the rural areas.[126] This was a major step forward in the provision of social assistance in the rural areas.

In 2009, the pension scheme for urban workers was expanded to cover migrant workers from the rural areas.[127] In the same year, it was decided to introduce pension insurance in the rural areas funded jointly by peasants, rural collective organisations, and government.[128]

The year 2010 was a milestone in the development of the law of social security in the PRC. In this year, the Law on Social Insurance (LSI) (*shehui baoxian fa*) was enacted by the NPC Standing Committee.[129] This was the first law (as distinguished from lower-level legal norms such as regulations enacted by the State Council or rules enacted by ministries of the State Council) in the legal history of the PRC that provides for social insurance in a systematic and comprehensive manner. Five species of social insurance are covered

123 See n 108 above; and Zhu Guobin, 'Right to Social Security: Assessing Chinese Practice Against International Standards' in Surya Deva (ed), *Socio-Economic Rights in Emerging Free Markets: Comparative Insights from India and China* (Routledge 2016) 312 (chap 14).

124 Liu (n 30) 353–354; the PRC's second report on 'Implementation of the International Covenant on Economic, Social and Cultural Rights' (n 108) 39–40.

125 Institute of Law (n 92) 394; He Wenjiong, 'China's Social Security: Development and Prospect' (2013) 17 Social Security Studies (Shehui baozhang yanjiu) 1, 2 (in Chinese).

126 Liu (n 30) 357; Wong (n 38) 550; Leisering, Liu, and ten Brink (n 90).

127 See the PRC's second report on 'Implementation of the International Covenant on Economic, Social and Cultural Rights' (n 108) 36. The regulations enacted in 2009 also provided for inter-provincial transfer and continuation of pension insurance.

128 Liu (n 19) 41; PRC's second report on 'Implementation of the International Covenant on Economic, Social and Cultural Rights' (n 108) 38.

129 For the background of the enactment of this Law, see Li Shishi and Xin Chunying (eds), *Scientific Legislation and Democratic Legislation* (Kexue lifa yu minzhu lifa) (Zhongguo minzhu fazhi chubanshe 2013) 195–214. For a commentary on the provisions of this Law, see Zheng (ed) (n 84).

by this law – basic pension insurance, basic medical insurance, work injury insurance, unemployment insurance, and maternity insurance. Although these species of social insurance had already been in existence before the enactment of this law, the law provides a framework for their further development, and empowers the State Council to make more detailed provisions for its implementation. The law also elaborates upon the constitutional provisions on social security and the right to material assistance, specifies clearly who should pay what amount of insurance premiums for which type of social insurance, and regulates the administrative operation of the schemes. The legal foundation for the right to social security in the PRC has thus been firmly established.

As regards pension insurance, the LSI provides that all employees in enterprises and their employers should contribute to centrally administered insurance funds which will receive government subsidies.[130] The insurance system is based on the combination of 'social pooling' and 'individual accounts'; the individual employee's contribution is paid into the 'individual accounts'. Self-employed persons may choose to participate in basic pension insurance by paying their own contributions into the fund. The LSI makes separate provisions for new systems of 'new rural social pension insurance' and 'urban residents social pension insurance' which are also based on contributions to central funds. In the former case, peasants may choose to participate by paying contributions themselves, with subsidies by the rural collectives and local government. In practice, the average level of benefits payable under these two systems is much lower than that under basic pension insurance. The government has enacted separate regulations on pension schemes which employees and their employers may voluntarily enter into as a supplement to the pension insurance provided by the LSI.[131]

As in the case of basic pension insurance, the LSI requires all employees and their employers to contribute to the central funds for basic medical insurance, and the self-employed may choose to participate in basic medical insurance. The LSI makes separate provisions for the 'new rural cooperative medical system' and 'basic medical insurance for urban residents'. For example, urban residents who are not employees may choose to participate by making contributions to the latter scheme which is partly subsidised by the government. Exemptions from payment of contributions are granted to the disabled and those receiving MLG payments.

As regards work injury insurance, the LSI provides that this is applicable to all employees, and re-affirms the principle that contributions to the central insurance funds are payable only by employers but not employees. Different levels

130 Civil servants and cadres are not subject to the LSI but are governed by a separate system.

131 Such regulations include those on 'enterprise annuities' (*qiye nianjin*) (for business enterprises) and 'occupational annuities' (*zhiye nianjin*) (for government and social institutions).

of premiums are applicable to different industries and occupations as the risks of work accidents vary.

As regards unemployment insurance, the LSI requires all employees to participate in the insurance scheme. Both employees and employers should make contributions to the central funds.

The last species of insurance provided for by the LSI is maternity insurance, which is applicable to all employees. Only employers are required to make contributions to the funds for maternity insurance.

Considerable progress was made in the implementation of the Law on Social Insurance after its enactment in 2010. In 2011, the pension scheme for urban employees was extended to cover urban residents who are not engaged in employment.[132] In 2012, complete coverage by pension insurance of both urban and rural populations was achieved.[133] In 2013, full coverage by basic medical insurance of the rural population was achieved.[134] In 2014, the pension schemes for urban areas and rural areas respectively were unified into one system.[135] However, the levels or amounts of benefits payable under different schemes and for different categories of people vary considerably.[136] Much remains to be done in raising such levels or amounts.

A major legislative development since the enactment of the Law on Social Insurance in 2010 was the promulgation by the State Council of the Provisional Measures on Social Assistance in 2014.[137] The Ministry of Civil Affairs is designated as the government organ with overall responsibility for social assistance ('*shehui jiuzhu*'). Eight species of social assistance are provided for in the Measures: Minimum Livelihood Guarantee (MLG);[138] support for the destitute ('destitute' being the English translation of '*tekun renyuan*', defined in the Measures to include elderly or disabled people or children under 16 who have no capacity to work, no means of livelihood and no family members who can provide financial support for their livelihood); relief for victims of natural disasters; medical relief; educational assistance; housing assistance; employment assistance; and temporary relief.

Some of these forms of social assistance are inter-related. For example, medical relief, educational assistance, and housing assistance are available to those

132 He (n 125) 3.

133 *White Paper on Progress in China's Human Rights in 2013* (Information Office of the State Council, May 2014), <http://english.www.gov.cn/archive/white_paper/2014/09/09/content_281474986284512.htm> accessed 28 February 2022, section 2.

134 ibid.

135 ibid.

136 He (n 125) 11.

137 For the Chinese text, see <www.gov.cn/zhengce/2014-02/28/content_2625652.htm> accessed 28 February 2022.

138 For a recent study of MLG from a socio-political perspective, see Jennifer Pan, *Welfare for Autocrats: How Social Assistance in China Cares for its Rulers* (Oxford University Press 2020).

receiving payments for MLG and those receiving assistance for the destitute. In 2015, the existing programme of 'Five Guarantees Subsistence' for rural areas was subsumed under the system of 'support for the destitute' in the rural areas.[139]

In October 2017, the 19th National Congress of the CCP was held, at which President Xi Jinping presented his report as Party General Secretary and put forward his comprehensive platform, vision, and strategies for China's 'socialist modernisation', collectively known as 'Xi's Thought on Chinese-style Socialism for the New Age'.[140] Xi's vision is that China would become a 'society of moderate prosperity' (*xiaokang*) by the year 2020; 'socialist modernisation' would be realised by the year 2035; and by 2050 China would become a 'modernised and strong socialist state that is wealthy, democratic, highly civilised, harmonious and beautiful'. Xi's report consisted of thirteen parts, and part 8 was on the improvement of people's livelihood and the strengthening of social governance. Part 8 consisted of seven sections, and section 3 was on 'the strengthening of the construction of the social security system'. Here Xi proposed the development of a 'multi-level social security system' that covers all the people, that is sustainable and that is operated by 'unified coordination' for both urban and rural areas. The objective was that all the people should participate in relevant social insurance schemes.

As regards pension insurance, Xi suggested that the ultimate goal would be to achieve 'national unified coordination' of the administration of pension insurance for urban workers and both urban and rural residents. This would enable the existing problems of uneven development of pension insurance schemes in different geographical areas to be overcome. As regards medical insurance, Xi proposed the improvement of unified basic medical insurance and serious illness insurance schemes for both urban and rural residents. He also proposed the further improvement of insurance schemes for unemployment and work injuries, the construction of a 'nationally unified social insurance public service platform', 'unified coordination of the social assistance system for both urban and rural areas', and further improvement of the system of 'minimum livelihood guarantee'.

The last major legal development that took place before this chapter was finalised (in January 2022) was the publication for public consultation of a draft of a Social Assistance Law in September 2020.[141] The draft law consists of eighty

139 Li Zhengang, 'A report on the analysis of the situation of the development of social assistance in urban and rural areas in 2018', in Li Peilin, Chen Guangjin, and Zheng Yi (eds), *Society of China Analysis and Forecast (2019)* (*Zhongguo shehui xingshi fenxi yu yuce*) (Shehui kexue wenxian chubanshe, 2019) 77, 82.

140 See 'Full text of Xi Jinping's report at 19th CPC National Congress' (18 Oct 2017), <www.chinadaily.com.cn/china/19thcpcnationalcongress/2017-11/04/content_34115212.htm> accessed 28 February 2022.

141 For the Chinese text, see <https://baike.baidu.com/item/%E4%B8%AD%E5%8D%8E%E4%BA%BA%E6%B0%91%E5%85%B1%E5%92%8C%E5%9B%BD%E7%A4%BE%E4%BC%9A%E6%95

articles divided into eight chapters, including general principles, categories of recipients of social assistance, the content or substance of social assistance, the procedure of social assistance, the participation of community bodies, supervision and management, legal liability, and supplementary provisions.

Article 1 of the draft law provides that this law is enacted to secure the basic livelihood of citizens, to ensure that citizens can share in the achievements of China's reform and development, and to promote social justice, social stability, and harmony. Article 2 provides that citizens have the right to apply for and receive social assistance in accordance with this law. According to Article 3, the state shall develop and improve the social assistance system, so that citizens may receive material assistance and services from the state and from society in circumstances where they are unable to maintain a basic livelihood by their own efforts. Local governments at various levels are required by this law to assume the primary responsibility for providing social assistance under the general leadership of the State Council.

The draft law provides for nine categories of recipients of social assistance: (1) families covered by Minimum Livelihood Guarantee; (2) the destitute; (3) low-income families; (4) poor families (determined on the basis of their income and their expenditure on essential items); (5) victims of natural disasters; (6) vagrants and beggars without means of livelihood; (7) families or persons facing temporary difficulties; (8) persons of unknown identity or unable to make payments who need emergency assistance; and (9) other families or persons with special difficulties as determined by the provincial authorities.

As regards the content or substance of social assistance, eleven types are specified in the draft law, including those provided for in the Provisional Measures on Social Assistance mentioned earlier, and the following additional types of assistance: illness emergency assistance; assistance for vagrants and beggars without any means of likelihood; and other forms of assistance as determined by the local government. Generally speaking, as provided in Article 27, the modes of assistance include cash payment, provision of physical products or goods, as well as provision of services.

Health Care, Housing, and Land

Health Care

As mentioned earlier, government funding for healthcare declined as a share of the nation's total health spending in the 1980s and 1990s.[142] The trend only began to change after the turn of the century. Government expenditure on

%91%E5%8A%A9%E6%B3%95/22861285?fr=aladdin> accessed 28 February 2022, or <www.creditsr.gov.cn/web/cont_8ca2194748304ae5ad2999376fbf7738.html> accessed 28 February 2022).

142 Duckett (n 39) 70; Dickson (n 72) 178.

healthcare as a share of the nation's total health care expenditure rose from 15 percent in the year 2000 to 20 percent in the year 2007 (the relevant percentage was 36 percent in 1980).[143] As a result of increased government funding for the healthcare system, people's out-of-pocket expenses as a share of the nation's total health expenditure decreased from 60 percent in 2001 to 34 percent in 2013. The latter figure was considered to be 'more in line with upper-middle-income countries'.[144]

In 2005, a think tank published a report suggesting that the medical reform of the past two decades, particularly the commercialisation of public hospitals, was a failure.[145] The government began to review actively its policy on medical and healthcare. After public consultation in 2008, a decision was taken in 2009 which renewed the state's commitment to public provision of medical and healthcare services after three decades of commercialisation.[146] An important policy document jointly issued by the State Council and the CCP that year reaffirmed the state's responsibility in ensuring that accessible and affordable medical and healthcare services would be provided to all.[147] Equal access by all to basic healthcare services was stipulated to be an important goal to be achieved. For this purpose, the government would increase its investment in the healthcare system. More community-based clinics providing primary care would be established in rural areas and townships, in addition to hospitals in counties and cities. While the market and the private sector would still have an important role to play in healthcare, the government would strengthen its regulation of the dispensation and pricing of pharmaceutical drugs as well as the pricing of basic medical services in hospitals. It would also ensure that the provision of medical and healthcare services by all providers would be on a non-profit basis.

Housing

The commercialisation of housing in the initial period of the reform era meant that lower-income groups found it increasingly difficult to afford their own housing, whether by rent or purchase. The government therefore decided to introduce a three-tier system of housing in the urban areas:[148] private housing sold at market price; 'economical and affordable housing' which was subsidised by the government; and low-rental public housing which was

143 Saich (n 45) 318.
144 Dickson (n 72) 178.
145 Wong (n 38) 558; Gu Xin, 'Towards Central Planning or Regulated Marketization? China Debates on the Direction of New Healthcare Reforms', in Zhao and Lim (n 116) 23 (chap 2) 29.
146 Duckett (n 39) 71.
147 Wong (n 38) 558.
148 Liang (n 116) 95; PRC's report on 'Implementation of the International Covenant on Economic, Social and Cultural Rights' submitted in 2003 (n 84) para 111.

heavily subsidised by the government. At first there was shortage of low-cost housing subsidised by the government. Since 2007, the central government imposed more stringent requirements on local governments to devote adequate financial resources to the construction of low-cost housing for lower-income groups.[149]

The general trend in housing policy thus paralleled that in medical care: In the Maoist era, provisions of housing or medical care were made by work units owned by the state; in the initial period of the reform era, there was a strong movement towards commercialisation and marketisation; in the later period of the reform era, the state assumed more responsibilities than in the earlier period of the reform era to ensure that the interest of lower-income groups would be taken care of.

Land

At the same time as making provisions for the grant of the right to use state-owned land in urban areas and the right to use collectively owned land in rural areas, the constitution and the laws also provide for the possibility of requisition or expropriation of such land-use rights by the state.[150] Such expropriation may be imposed for public interest subject to certain procedural requirements and payment of compensation. In 2004, Article 10(3) of the constitution was amended to provide expressly for compensation for requisition or expropriation of land. This was a significant development.

The expropriation of urban and agricultural land involved eviction of existing residents and has been a major source of conflict between the authorities and the people in the reform era. Critics point out that residents' housing and land rights were often violated and sacrificed for the sake of economic development. Such 'forced eviction . . . and land-grabs show the developmental-welfarist argument of the Party-State at full play, as it is in these contexts that the authorities tend to demand individual "sacrifice" for the greater good'.[151] It has been pointed out that 'some 120 million people were affected by rural expropriations as of 2012', and large-scale 'urban takings' have also taken place.[152] 'Because it uses pressure, threats and violence that remain hidden and suppressed, it is hard to assess the scope of rights violations that occur'.[153]

149 Liang (n 116) 101.

150 See Article 10(3) of the 1982 Constitution, which was amended in 2004 to provide expressly for compensation for requisition or expropriation of land.

151 Eva Pils, *Human Rights in China* (Polity 2018) 100.

152 ibid 101.

153 ibid 102.

Central and Local Governments

A salient feature of Chinese social policy concerns the complex relationship between the central government in Beijing and different levels of local governments in the provinces, cities, counties, and townships. In the reform era, there has been considerable delegation of power from the central to local governments, including the power to extract financial resources (by taxation) from the community and to engage in experiments and innovations in the domain of social welfare and security. For a long time in the reform era, there was no model or practice as regards particular matters of social welfare and security that was uniformly applicable throughout the country. Instead, different schemes and practices existed in different localities at the same time.[154] In the course of time, the accumulation of local experience has enabled policy-makers at the national level to devise and introduce for the whole nation policies and schemes that have proved to be successful and effective in some localities. Even after such nation-wide policies, schemes and legislation have been promulgated, local authorities often retain considerable power and discretion in their implementation. For example, the levels of monetary benefits under various insurance and welfare schemes can vary in different regions.[155]

The Urban-Rural Divide

Another salient feature of the development of social policy in the PRC has been the differential treatment of the urban and rural populations, with the former being privileged both in the Maoist period and the reform period. Given the scarcity of resources in this poor and developing country, the policy of the Party-State has been to accord priority to urban residents. Even among urban residents, there has been a long-standing differential treatment of different categories of urban residents, with the workers in state-owned enterprises and the staff of state organs and state institutional units being privileged. For example, in the development of social insurance, workers in state-owned enterprises were the first to enjoy the benefits of the relevant schemes, which were gradually extended in the course of time to cover employees of other enterprises such as private and foreign-investment enterprises. Rural-to-urban migrant workers have long suffered from discrimination (in terms of the provision of social services and security) and have been under-privileged relative to other urban residents.[156] The household registration system introduced in the 1950s that contributed to differentiation of treatment on the basis of the location of

154 Zheng, *The Path of Social Security* (n 84) 380.
155 Lo and Cheng (n 3) 63.
156 Xu and Guo (n 57) 99.

one's household registration has been operational for decades.[157] It was only in the later period of the era of 'reform and opening' that the social security provisions originally enjoyed only by urban residents were gradually extended to the rural population.

Conclusion

From Communism to Market Reform

The most important factor that has shaped the changing social policies in the history of the PRC has been the economic system and the strategy of economic development, which in turn have been shaped by the Party-State's ideology and goals. In the Maoist period, industrial production by urban state-owned enterprises was promoted and accorded priority, and collectivised agriculture was practised in the communes in the rural areas. The social welfare and security of the urban working class and state and party cadres were well taken care of by the state directly. Rural communities largely took care of themselves; limited schemes were introduced such as cooperative medicine for the sick and residual welfare in the form of the 'Five Guarantees' for the destitute.

In the post-Mao era of economic reforms in the direction of marketisation and privatisation, state-owned enterprises were gradually relieved of their welfare burdens, the state sector of the economy was much reduced in size, and the rural communes were abolished. The former systems of welfare provisions by state-owned enterprises and communes gradually declined or even disintegrated. In order to maintain social and political stability, promote economic development and to bolster the legitimacy of the regime, it was necessary to introduce substitute mechanisms to cater for the welfare needs of the urban and rural populations. A new social welfare system was needed 'to manage the social risks and failures of the market system'.[158] After some initial explorations in the 1980s, the Party-State decided to develop a system of social security based on the concept of social insurance, with the state, employers, workers, peasants, and other citizens sharing the cost of insurance for old age pensions and medical expenses. Social insurance also covers work accidents, maternity, and unemployment. At the same time, the state would provide social assistance and relief for the particularly needy and destitute through schemes such as Minimum Livelihood Guarantee (MLG) for both urban and rural residents and the 'Five Guarantees' for rural residents. This new system of social welfare and security had begun to evolve in a piecemeal, experimental, and gradual manner since the mid-1980s, and only reached a more mature stage of development

157 Thus, a significant trend in recent reforms has been 'to de-link social services and welfare benefits from *hukou* status': Saich (n 45) 324.

158 Wong (n 38) 543.

and became more comprehensive in its coverage in the second decade of the twenty-first century.

Developments in social assistance have been closely linked to the Chinese government's efforts in poverty alleviation in the last few decades. On 25 February 2021, in one of the events organised to mark the 100th anniversary of the founding of the Chinese Communist Party, Xi Jinping declared that by this time China had completed the task of eliminating 'extreme poverty'.[159] It was pointed out that in the case of China, the poverty eradication target in the United Nations' 2030 Agenda for Sustainable Development had been achieved ten years ahead of schedule. Further details and figures were provided in the White Paper on 'Poverty Alleviation: China's Experience and Contribution' published by the Information Office of the State Council on 6 April 2021.[160] It states that China has fought a decisive battle against poverty that is unprecedented in scale and intensity, and has benefitted the largest number of people in human history. Since the era of 'reform and opening' began in the late 1970s, a total of 770 million rural residents living below the poverty line have been lifted out of poverty. This figure includes 122 million people living below the poverty line in the year 2011 who were lifted out of poverty by 2021. The poverty line in 2011 had been set at RMB 2,300 per year. The average per capita annual disposable income of the rural population in poor areas has increased from RMB 6,079 in 2013 to RMB 12,588 in 2020. The White Paper also mentioned that the baseline for applying the Minimum Livelihood Guarantee (MLG) among the rural population was RMB 2,068 per year per person in 2012, and has been raised to RMB 5,962 by 2020.

Foreign Models and Influence

It is noteworthy that most of the policies and practices adopted by the PRC during both the Maoist era and the reform era were hardly original and involved much borrowing from foreign models and experience. For example, the labour insurance scheme introduced in China's urban areas in the 1950s was largely modelled on that in the Soviet Union. Indeed, the 1950s were a period in which the PRC adopted a Soviet-style constitutional structure and borrowed extensively from the Soviet Union in developing its economic system and legal system.

In the reform era, the PRC began to borrow from Western industrial nations with capitalist market economies. This is not surprising, as the overall trend of economic reform in the post-Mao era has been to achieve a transition from

159 'Xi declares "complete victory" in eradicating absolute poverty in China', 26 February 2021, <www.xinhuanet.com/english/2021-02/26/c_139767705.htm> accessed 28 February 2022.

160 <http://english.www.gov.cn/archive/whitepaper/202104/06/content_WS606bc77ec6d0719374afc1b9.html> accessed 28 February 2022.

a planned economy to a market economy, so that China's economic system would resemble more closely that in capitalist countries. As was the case in these countries, the PRC came to experience the need to provide a social safety net to guard against the risks that the market poses for the welfare and security of the people. The systems of social welfare and security in industrialised market economies thus became the points of reference for Chinese reformers seeking to develop a social welfare and security system that can meet the needs of the Chinese people at this stage of the nation's development. It is interesting to note in this regard that the Chinese scholarship on social welfare and security law abounds with references to relevant Western experience, particularly Bismarck's initiatives in the 1880s to introduce labour and social insurance legislation in Germany, the German concept of social law (*Sozialrecht*), and the development of social security policies and laws in the USA and Britain.

The Role of Law

In the legal system of the PRC, there exist multiple levels of legal norms. At the highest level stands the constitution. Next come the laws (*falü*) enacted by the National People's Congress (NPC) or the NPC Standing Committee (under the 1982 Constitution). At the next lower level are the regulations enacted by the State Council, followed by the rules enacted by the ministries of the State Council. Provinces and municipalities may also enact local regulations and rules. There is thus a complex web of laws, regulations, and rules in the PRC legal system.

In the Maoist era, the Labour Insurance Regulations 1951 were the major legal enactment in the domain of social security. There was no law (in the sense of law enacted by the NPC) in the domain of social welfare and security in the Maoist era, but this is not surprising as few laws were made in this era, and there was not even a criminal code during this era.

In the reform era, the Party-State devoted considerable efforts to the construction of a 'socialist legal system with Chinese characteristics'. In addition to lower-level norms such as regulations and rules, many laws were enacted by the NPC or NPC Standing Committee. However, when compared with the enactment of laws in domains such as criminal law, civil law, economic law, administrative law, and labour law, the law of social security was a late developer. As mentioned earlier, the law in this domain – the Social Insurance Law – was only enacted by the NPC Standing Committee in 2010. In the reform era, many developments in social welfare and security were initiated by policy documents or legal norms at lower levels than laws. Many relevant legal norms were at levels even lower than that of regulations enacted by the State Council. The first regulations enacted by the State Council in the reform era on matters of social insurance were the Regulations on Unemployment Insurance and the Regulations on Insurance for Work Injuries, and they were only enacted in 1999 and 2003 respectively.

The Judicial Role

As regards the role of the judiciary in developing the law of social welfare and security, it should be noted that the PRC does not have any constitutional court, and the ordinary courts do not have a role to play in interpreting the constitution and developing a jurisprudence of constitutional rights. The constitutional provisions on rights provide guidance to the government (headed by the State Council) and the legislature (ie the NPC and its Standing Committee) on matters of policy and law-making, but cannot be enforced by any court as against the government or the legislature. But as in other legal systems, PRC courts do have an important role to play in applying the law to concrete cases litigated before the courts.

Comparative Reflections

The PRC has come a long way since Mao Zedong declared the establishment of this new communist republic at the Gate of Heavenly Peace on 1 October 1949. In the domain of social policy, as in most other policy domains in the course of PRC history, the story has been one of trial and error, and also progress being achieved if a broad historical perspective is to be adopted. In the Maoist era, social welfare and security were relatively well provided for in the case of the urban working class and cadres of the Party-State, and a residual welfare system also existed in the rural areas where the 'people's communes' could take care of the needy. The infrastructural support for welfare and security of the Maoist era gradually disintegrated in the reform era with the rise of the market, the decline of state-owned enterprises, and the abolition of the communes. In order to maintain social and political stability and bolster regime legitimacy, the Chinese reformers developed a new system of social security based on the concept of social insurance, as supplemented by schemes of social assistance and relief for the particularly needy, weak, and vulnerable.

These developments in the PRC may be usefully compared and contrasted with East Asian developmental states such as Taiwan and South Korea, with Eastern European countries that have moved from communism to post-communism, and with other major developing countries such as India and Indonesia.[161] In East Asian developmental states, social welfare and security provisions were generally inadequate during their authoritarian eras of rapid economic growth,[162] but improved significantly after democratisation.[163] In

161 See generally Mark W. Frazier, 'Welfare Policy Pathways Among Large Uneven Developers', in Scott Kennedy (ed), *Beyond the Middle Kingdom: Comparative Perspective on China's Capitalist Transformation* (Stanford University Press 2011) 89–109 (chap 5).

162 Saich (n 90) 10–12; Leung and Nann (n 3) 165.

163 An example is provided by the case of Taiwan. See Su Yongqin (ed), *Departmental Constitutions* (Bumen xianfa) (Yuanzhao chubanshe 2005), part II, section 2 (social constitution).

post-communist states, the transition from communism to the market was usually accompanied by a reduction of social welfare and security.[164] The PRC's trajectory of social welfare and security is thus quite different from these cases. As regards other developing countries, the PRC's performance in the domain of social welfare and security seems to compare favourably with cases such as India and Indonesia.

However, when compared with India with its strong record of public interest litigation and an activist Supreme Court exercising the power of constitutional interpretation and review, in the PRC the role of the constitution and the judiciary in shaping developments in social welfare and security is apparently weak and minimal. In the Maoist era, the PRC did not have an effective constitutional and legal system. The reform era has seen great strides in the development of a 'socialist legal system with Chinese characteristics'. Nevertheless, legislative developments in the domain of social welfare and security have lagged behind developments in other major areas of law. At the constitutional level, the idea of citizens' right (as distinguished from labourers' right) to social assistance received recognition for the first time in the Constitution of 1982, which was amended in 2004 to call for the development of a social security system. These constitutional provisions operate largely as what the Indian Constitution calls 'directive principles of state policy'. While Chinese courts play no role in interpreting and enforcing the constitution, the enactment of the Social Insurance Law in 2010 breeds some optimism that social security in the PRC will finally find a firm legal foundation, and that the enjoyment by the Chinese people of social welfare and security benefits will no longer be merely a matter of government discretion or favours bestowed by the ruler on his subjects, but a matter of the basic rights of the citizens of a constitutional state based on the Rule of Law, or, in the words of the Chinese constitutional amendment of 1999, a 'socialist Rechtsstaat' (*shehuizhuyi fazhiguojia*).

164 'Among nations with comprehensive social security programmes, socialist [communist] countries usually have the most elaborate systems and the highest expenditure on social security as a percentage of their Gross National Product': Chow (n 16) 8.

Chapter 4

Law and Social Policy in India

From Growth-Based Welfare to Welfare Entitlements

Sarbani Sen

Introduction

The object of this chapter is to provide some perspectives on law and social policies in India over certain critical historical periods, ie, the British period (nineteenth century to 1947), the period of the drafting of the Indian Constitution (1947–1949), the 1950s and '60s, the 1970s and '80s, and the post-1990s. The overall aim is to examine the political and social context for the emergence of ideas and values underlying constitutional provisions for social welfare, the formulation of social rights, judicial decisions, and pertinent social security laws that shaped social policies in India.

Colonial India: The British Approach to Policies of Social Welfare

The Political and Economic Context

Unlike the 'settlor' imperial Mughal rulers, British rule in India was characterised by an 'extractive/exploitative' impulse. Colonial governance was founded on a theory of indivisible sovereignty with a monopoly of military control and authority over revenue collection. With the transfer of power to the British Crown-in-Parliament after 1857, Queen Victoria's Proclamation of 1858 seemed to point to a new justification for British rule in India, namely to

> stimulate the peaceful industry of India, to promote works of public utility and improvement, and to administer the government for the benefit therein. In their prosperity will be our strength, in their contentment our security, and in their gratitude our best reward.[1]

Yet, the logic of imperialism and the facilitation of British interests continued to dictate India's administrative and legal systems.

1 Ramsay Muir, *The Making of British India 1756–1858* (Manchester University Press 1915) 384.

DOI: 10.4324/9781003242826-4

Rule by a Colonising Minority

Political debates in Britain in the nineteenth century on the imperial role in India was characterised by the Evangelical belief in the Gospels on the one hand, and the Radicals' or Utilitarians' belief in reason, the superiority of Western civilisation, and the possibility of indefinite progress on the other. Static and decaying civilisations such as India's could only progress through the introduction of Western enlightenment and rational thinking. Indian social customs were denounced. Governors-General such as Bentinck[2] engaged in social reform aimed to plant Western ideas and institutions in India, in particular through the promotion of a modern Indian educational system. After the 1857 Mutiny, the Westernising policy took the form of the British playing an 'enabling role', primarily through public works such as roads and railways or irrigation systems to reduce famines. British political attitude was of prolonged trusteeship towards a ward in court in relation to the Indian people. From the nationalist perspective however, British economic and social policies and its administrative and legal structures were the primary causes of the country's backwardness and poverty. For the nationalist movement, the British Government of India was an oppressive government operating an unjust legal system as an instrument for furthering mainly British interests and creating further divisions and social inequalities.

British administration in India remained largely centralised, unrepresentative, and irresponsible. The Government of India Act of 1858 transferred power to the British Crown from the East India Company. Such powers were exercised through the governor-general-in council. The governors-general ruled through their nominated councils. New legislation in 1861 allowed non-official members of a legislative council to be nominated Indian members.[3] The Morley-Minto Reforms of 1909 introduced the principle of elected legislative representatives at the centre and provinces through limited franchise.[4] But the impact of such members on policy making and governance remained marginal. The Government of India Acts of 1919 and 1935 introduced a limited federal structure with limited devolution of authority to the provinces. Control over key areas of administration remained with the governor-general. The limited franchise that was finally extended to Indians by the Morley-Minto Reforms of 1909 and the Montague Chelmsford Reforms of 1919 was divided among several of the communal identities the British had created within Indian society – there were seats reserved for Hindus, Muslims, Sikhs etc. This electoral practice was continued in the provisions of the Government of India Act of 1935.[5]

2 Governor-General of India from 1824 through 1835.

3 The Indian Councils Act of 1892 allowed such councillors to ask questions and criticise the government's budget.

4 Such elected legislative councillors could question the government and debate the annual budget and introduce legislative proposals. Such proposals could be subject to an executive veto.

5 Partha Chatterjee and Gyanendra Pandey (eds), *Subaltern Studies: Writings on South Asian History and Society*, vol 7 (Oxford University Press 1992).

Imperial Policies of Economic Exploitation

Economic historians have examined how early British rule discouraged indigenous manufacturing in order to make India primarily a supplier of raw materials for British industries. There were prohibitive tariffs on Indian goods entering England while English goods were admitted into India with nominal or no duties. In the agricultural sector, the land tax was heavy and uncertain, and the British administration intercepted the incomes and gains of the tillers and added to its land revenue demands at each recurring settlement, leaving the cultivators poor. Proceeds of taxation were withdrawn from India and were not returned to the cultivators in the form of public goods and services. Indian revenues flowed out of the country as 'home charges' or were spent on the British administration.[6] The unrepresentative nature of British rule was seen as the root cause for such policies – Indian agriculture, landed interests, their trades, and industries – were not represented.[7]

Policies of Social Welfare

In view of overarching imperial imperatives dominating British social and economic policies, a comprehensive system of social insurance did not exist in India until 1945. Traditionally, the family or the home was the only form of social security during periods of sickness, unemployment, or old age, other than charity.[8] Mendicants were partly made up of disabled or unemployed workers who had lost touch with the countryside. But the introduction of Western civilisation based on individualism and the play of modern economic forces undermined the joint family system and the traditions of charity. Moreover, there was also the rising cost of living, a materialistic attitude, growing pressure of population on the land, and increased fragmentation of the holdings which reduced rural standards of living.

The schemes that emerged during the British period after World War I and the formation of the International Labour Organisation (ILO) were built on a thin notion of state responsibility towards the welfare of the people and were primarily for the purpose of securing political stability and legitimacy for the rule, stimulating productivity, and improving industrial relations. A certain notion of improving the conditions of industrial labour and taking care of vulnerable groups did emerge, but not as a primary duty of the state. Restricted public financial resources, the severity of foreign competition, which made Indian industrialists unwilling to provide social insurance for their workers, and

6 Romesh Dutt, *The Economic History of India Under Early British Rule*, vol 1 (Kegan Paul, Trench, Trübner 1902) v – xxiv.

7 ibid.

8 A.N. Agarwala, 'Problems of Social Security for Industrial Workers in India' (1945) 51 International Labour Review 1, 2–4.

poverty, illiteracy, and lack of organisation of the workers were contributing factors. Hence, British policies primarily took the form of statutory regulation and protection of Indian industrial labour.[9] The policies did not involve the establishment of state financed schemes from which benefits were dispensed in cases of emergency according to a determined schedule and on a uniform basis.

Social Policy Instruments

Employment Injuries

The ILO passed a convention on employment injuries in 1921 and asked its members to ratify it. The Government of India did not ratify that convention, but the recommendations of a committee appointed by the Indian Legislative Assembly in 1922 led to the Workmen's Compensation Act of 1923.

The Workmen's Compensation Act was based on the principle of occupational risk where liability resulted not on any act or omission of the employer, but upon the existence of the relationship which the employee bore to the employment because of and in the course of which the employee was injured. Liability for paying compensation rested with the employer irrespective of fault. The loss of earning power consequent upon an industrial accident was deemed a loss arising out of the business and that had to be borne by the employer. However, the act did not provide for effective guarantees for such payments as, for instance, an obligatory insurance at the cost of the employer in case of inability to make payments.

The Workmen's Compensation Act covered employment injuries, that is, injuries arising out of and in the course of employment (including temporary disablement; permanent partial disablement; permanent total disablement and death) and contracted occupational diseases listed in the act. The act imposed on the employer the obligation to provide compensation to the worker.[10] But the protection granted by the act left many gaps: Protection was confined to certain employments based on size; to certain injuries based on duration; and

9 Such statutes included the Indian Mines Act 1923; the Indian Boilers' Act 1923; the Indian Trade Union Act 1926; the Payment of Wages Act 1936; and a series of labour laws passed by the Indian provinces.

10 Under the Workmen's Compensation Act, benefits for permanent total disablement were paid as lump sums according to a schedule in the act. Permanent partial disablement benefits were calculated on the basis of wages and the percentage of the loss of earning capacity resulting from the injury (as specified in the act). N. Hasan, *The Social Security System of India* (S. Chand & Co. Ltd. 1972) 70–74. In cases of temporary total disablement, where the workmen were wholly incapacitated from work he was capable of performing before the injury, the amount of compensation equalled their full wages in the case of the lowest income group and about 20 percent of the wages in case of the highest income group payable in half monthly instalments till the time of recovery. P.C. Srivastava, *Social Security in India* (Lokbharti Publications 1964) 216. In the case of permanent disablement and death, compensation took the form of a lump sum payment.

to certain workers based on the amount of their wages and the nature of their work. The rates of compensation were low. With regard to injuries causing death, lawmakers had opted for lump sum payments to avoid (regular) pension payments. The Workmen's Compensation Act did not make any provision for medical treatment of disabled workers or for their physical/vocational rehabilitation.

Maternity Benefits

The draft Convention concerning employment of women before and after childbirth, adopted by the ILO in 1919, was not ratified by the Government of India. Still, maternity benefit legislation was adopted by some provinces under which the employer was liable to pay maternity benefit to women workers for a specified period. No portion of the cost of the benefits was met by the state, and there was no common fund created out of tripartite contributions. The schemes placed the entire burden of paying benefits and providing medical facilities on the employer alone.

The state legislations provided different benefits and prescribed varying qualifying conditions. Though the legislations did not lay down a maximum salary limit for coverage of the beneficiary, almost all state legislations laid down minimum service conditions for eligibility to benefits under the schemes. The schemes made provision for monetary as well as non-monetary benefits (eg, maternity leave), and for additional benefits such as food concessions during the pre- and post-natal periods, free medical aid during confinement or payment of a medical bonus if no medical care was provided for otherwise. There were no administrative structures to administer the schemes – the administration was largely left to factory inspectorates in all the states.[11]

Sickness Insurance

TENTATIVE APPROACHES

The ILO's tenth session in 1927 considered the question of compulsory sickness insurance. The International Labour Conference accepted that such schemes provided the best means of 'constantly and systematically applying provident measures to obviate or make good any loss of the workers' productive efficiency'. The Government of India approved the ILO's view in the Indian Legislative Assembly in March 1928 but concluded that any such comprehensive scheme was not practicable under existing conditions. Faced with problems of

11 Hasan (n 10) 100–104. The Mines Maternity Benefits Act 1941 was passed to regulate conditions of work of women employees and to safeguard the health of pregnant employees.

migratory labour, shortage of medical personnel for certification and the costs involved, neither were provincial governments encouraging in their response.[12]

Nonetheless, in the 1930s and early 1940s, committees and labour conferences kept the idea of introducing a sickness insurance in India alive. The Royal Commission on Labour stated in 1931 that there was a need for Indian workers of some form of sickness insurance since the incidence of sickness was substantially higher than in Western countries, the medical facilities were much less adequate, and the wages generally paid make it impossible for most workers to get through more than a very short period of illness without borrowing.[13] In 1934, the Bombay Textile Labour Inquiry Committee recommended that a compulsory and contributory sickness insurance scheme (including both cash and medical benefits) should be started in the cotton textile centres of the province, in which the employers, workmen, and the state were expected to contribute.[14] In the early 1940s, the first three Labour Ministers' Conferences were in favour of introducing a sickness insurance scheme, and so were the All India Organisation of Industrial Employers' and the Employers' Federation of India.[15] In 1942, the Labour Department of the Government of India came up with a tentative proposal (covering certain industries) that was inspired by developments in Great Britain (Beveridge), the United States, and Canada. The time was ripe for politics to seriously consider establishing a scheme of sickness insurance, and possibly even more comprehensive measures of social security, following the change in the ILO's focus on comprehensive schemes of social security rather than protection against individual contingencies.[16]

THE ADARKAR REPORT

Early in 1943 the Government of India appointed a commission under the chairmanship of B.P. Adarkar tasked to frame a scheme of sickness insurance for industrial workers. The commission's report of 1944 conceived of a scheme of social insurance as the nucleus of a comprehensive social insurance scheme including maternity benefits and employment injuries. The scheme was to be compulsory,

12 Hasan (n 10) 41.
13 ibid 42.
14 ibid 42–43.
15 ibid 43.
16 Pursuant to a resolution of the Tripartite Labour Conference of September 1943, a Labour Investigation Committee was appointed by the Government of India in 1944 (Rege Committee) whose report was to be the basis for framing a Beveridge Plan for India. A Health Survey and Development Committee was also appointed to make a comprehensive survey of health conditions to recommend a plan for future development. Hasan (n 10) 44, 88. For the ILO's turn toward 'social security' see International Labour Office, *Approaches to Social Security. An International Survey* (International Labour Office 1942); International Labour Office, *Social Security: Principles, and Problems Arising Out of the War* (International Labour Office 1944); Ulrike Davy, Chapter 6 in this volume, p. 207.

and it had to be contributory – along with employers and workers, the state should also share a definite proportion of the cost of the scheme. Thus, for the first time, there was an emphasis on the need for state subsidy. The ILO experts appointed by the government to review the scheme endorsed Adarkar's views. The Adarkar report and the ILO suggestions emerged as the Employees' State Insurance Act of 1948 initiating the start of social insurance coverage for industrial workers in India.[17]

THE EMPLOYEES' STATE INSURANCE ACT OF 1948

The Employees' State Insurance Act of 1948 applied to all factories nationwide. The definition of 'factory', however, narrowed the scope of the act.[18] The scheme covered all employees in the covered establishments whether they were engaged in manual or clerical work but whose monthly wages did not exceed Rs 500. Thus, it was intended to cover all categories of low-income group employees and not just industrial workers.

The scheme provided protection of income as well as medical services in case of 'sickness' – a condition which required medical treatment and necessitated abstention from work. The act also covered maternity/confinement, and employment injuries covering both industrial accidents (which could result in total or partial disablement or death) and occupational diseases arising in the course of the worker's employment.[19] Accordingly, the act introduced sickness benefits, maternity benefits, disablement benefits (including benefits for dependents), and medical services.

Both employers and employees were required to make cash contributions towards the cost of benefits. Employers would pay at double the rates of the contributions made on behalf of the employees. The employer liability principle was at the basis of employer contributions; the act held employers liable to compensate the loss of earnings of the employees up to a certain extent. The central or state governments made no contributions, but they subsidised the scheme by meeting a part of the cost of the administration and the medical services respectively.[20] Availability of medical services was not conditional on contributions. The provision of medical services was the responsibility of the state governments, which determined the scale of the benefits. The Employees' State Insurance Corporation (ESI Corporation) had to defray an agreed share of expenses

17 Srivastava (n 10) 89–91. For a more detailed analysis of the Adarkar Report see Hasan (n 10) 45–58.

18 According to the act, factory meant those premises in which a manufacturing process was being carried on with the aid of power with not less than twenty workers during the preceding 12 months. Seasonal factories, perennial factories employing less than twenty workers, and establishments which did not use power were excluded.

19 Hasan (n 10) 156–158.

20 Srivastava (n 10) 101–103.

incurred by the state government.[21] The administration of the fund (consisting of contributions and grants by the governments) was vested in the Employees' State Insurance Corporation which was set up by the central government in 1948.[22]

Unemployment Insurance

Against the background of workers' unrest, the Bombay Strike Enquiry Committee, appointed in 1928, proposed that millowners be made responsible for alleviating the distress caused by unemployment arising from schemes aimed to improve industrial efficiency. This was to be done through a voluntary gratuity scheme, namely the establishment of a 'Out-of-Work Donation Fund' from which gratuities amounting to four to six weeks' wages would be granted to discharged workers to enable them to maintain themselves during the time that they were looking for other employment. No action was taken on that proposal.[23]

In 1931, the Royal Commission on Labour also went into the problem of unemployment insurance. Similar to the Bombay Strike Enquiry Committee the commission held that 'where any comprehensive scheme of reduction [of employment] is contemplated in an industry, the introduction of a joint scheme [based on contributions from employers and workers] . . . should be considered'.[24] But the commission's report stated that it could not regard any national system of insurance with which it was familiar as feasible at that time in India and that in the present situation the village home afforded the industrial worker his best available security in times of unemployment or sickness. The report concluded, 'The fullest insurance against unemployment . . . would be provided by the growth of Indian industry'.[25]

Unemployment Relief

The Industrial Disputes Act of 1947 (as amended in 1953) made provision for a form of unemployment relief. Under the 1953 amendment, employers of certain categories of establishments were liable to pay compensation to workers

21 The state's share was one quarter of the cost of such services to the insured persons. The ESI Corporation with the approval of the state government could establish hospitals, dispensaries, and other medical and surgical services as the ESI Corporation thought necessary.

22 The ESI Corporation was an autonomous body and functioned under the control of the central government. The ESI Corporation was composed of representatives of various interests such as the central and state governments, the medical profession, employers, and employees.

23 Agarwala (n 8) 5.

24 Royal Commission on Labour in India, *Report of the Royal Commission on Labour in India* (Government of India 1931) 35.

25 ibid 34. Two Indian members of the Commission pointed out that industrial life tended to break down the family system and in the absence of provident funds for industrial workers, the government ought to encourage employers by financial grants or otherwise, to start such schemes for their employees. Agarwala (n 8) 7.

(with some exclusions) who were laid off or retrenched (lump sum). Such payment was conditional on the length of service. The workers concerned were not required to pay any contributions nor was any state authority. The sole responsibility for contributions was of the employers, though conditions of unemployment often arose on account of factors beyond the control of individual employers and were caused by governmental labour policies. The scheme was essentially about improving industrial relations. No machinery was set up to secure re-employment.

Inadequacies of British Social Welfare

Though the schemes established in the 1920s and 1930s were created through central legislation, there were almost no provisions for financial contributions by the state nor were benefits tax based. Contributions were primarily by the employers and employees and intended to meet certain contingencies such as sickness, unemployment, or maternity. A comprehensive framework for a national social insurance structure did not emerge. The schemes primarily targeted industrial workers, and not peasants, the informal sector, lower castes, or poor migrant labour. Entitlement to benefits was conditional on minimum service conditions, scale of wages, and rate of contributions. Inadequate statistical data and unwillingness on the part of the central and provincial governments to bear an additional financial burden often caused schemes to fail. Lack of economic progress and increase of national dividend and per capita income made it difficult for the state to accumulate tax revenues in order to finance social insurance plans. Trained personnel were scarce, and the workers' ignorance and illiteracy made it difficult for them to know of their rights and procedures for paying contributions and drawing benefits under existing statutory provisions.[26]

The Nationalist Debate: The Indian Approach to Social Welfare

Ideational Background

Synergistic links both in form and substance between the nationalist discourse against British rule and drafting the constitution are evident in the Constituent Assembly serving as a symbol of the sovereign body of the Indian people, a culmination of prior forms of popular political mobilisation and assertion of their sovereignty against British authority.[27] Substantively, the task before the Constituent

26 Agarwala (n 8) 13–16.

27 Sarbani Sen, *The Constitution of India. Popular Sovereignty and Democratic Transformations* (Oxford University Press 2007) Part Two.

Assembly was a complex one. There were shifts of emphasis in Congress ideology as it progressed from early Moderate thought to the Gandhian and Nehruvian periods.[28] Alternate or radical views also emerged that challenged accepted viewpoints and opted for different forms of political organisation and processes of social transformation.[29] However, the predominant focus that emerged during the working of the Constituent Assembly was building a modern nation state, with representative and responsible forms of governance, and to secure the liberties of the people against arbitrary government. There were also references to state responsibility for promoting economic progress and social transformation to create a more just and equitable society.

Nationalist thinking during the colonial period included two parallel strands of thought, the political and the social. Nationalist demands for political reforms and civil liberties from the British government also included the idea that the state had a positive obligation to provide its people with certain economic and social conditions.[30] For instance, the Commonwealth of India Bill of 1925 contained a provision that all persons were to have free elementary education. The Nehru Report of 1928 contained provisions for a living wage for industrial workers, and protection against the economic consequences of old age, sickness, and unemployment. Labour was to be freed from conditions of serfdom. There was to be protection for women workers such as maternity leave.[31]

28 For understanding the formation, structure, and processes of decision making in the Constituent Assembly see Granville Austin, *The Indian Constitution: Cornerstone of a Nation* (Clarendon Press 1966) 8–25.

29 For instance, while the Constituent Assembly was in session, in March 1948, tensions emerged between the Socialist Party of India and the Indian National Congress. The Socialist Party argued that the Draft Constitution 'fell short of economic and equalitarian ideas' that were integral to the freedom movement. The Socialist Party's own 1948 draft included an 'Economic Rights' section: Private property and private enterprise would be subject to 'general interest of the republic and its toiling masses'. There was also a section on 'Directive Principles of State Policy' to establish a socialist order. However, Ambedkar made it clear that the Directive Principles were not meant to create a socialistic economy – the decision was left for future parliaments to take. See the Socialist Party's Draft Constitution of the Indian Republic, <www.constitutionofindia.net/historical_constitutions/draft_constitution_of_the_republic_of_india__socialist_party__1948__1st%20January%201948> accessed 28 February 2022. See also the Gandhian alternative to nation building, <www.constitutionofindia.net/historical_constitutions/gandhian_constitution_for_free_india__shriman_narayan_agarwal__1946__2nd%20April%201945> accessed 28 February 2022; the drafts presented by M.N. Roy incorporating radical socialist ideas, <www.constitutionofindia.net/historical_constitutions/constitution_of_free_india___a_draft__m_n__roy__1944__1st%20January%201944>; and Ambedkar's draft on 'States and Minorities' <www.constitutionofindia.net/historical_constitutions/states_and_minorities__dr__b_r__ambedkar__1945__1st%20January%201945> accessed 28 February 2022. This draft was presented to the Fundamental Rights Sub-Committee based on an earlier draft called 'Political demands of the Scheduled Castes', <see www.constitutionofindia.net/historical_constitutions/political_demands_of_scheduled_castes__scheduled_castes_federation_1944__23rd%20September%201944> accessed 28 February 2022.

30 Austin (n 28) chap 2.

31 ibid 54–55.

The Congress session held in Karachi in March 1931 adopted the Resolution on Fundamental Rights and Duties and Economic Programme, which was a declaration of rights and also a socialist manifesto.[32] The Resolution was based on ideas influenced by Nehru such as the provisions concerning the welfare of the workers and of the people generally and the placing of the primary responsibility for social welfare on the state.[33] The provisions – which became a precedent of the Directive Principles – stated that '[in] order to end the exploitation of the masses, political freedom must include the real economic freedom of the starving millions'. The state was to safeguard 'the interests of industrial workers' with 'suitable legislation' for a living wage, healthy conditions of work, limited hours of work, and protection from 'the economic consequences of old age, sickness, and unemployment'. Women and children were also to be granted protection through special benefits. The state was to 'own or control key industries and services'.[34]

Nehru influenced the Assembly's thinking that economic progress could only be achieved through planning by a centralised state authority to introduce modern agricultural methods, transport, power generation, and industrial development. By 1947, the idea of state responsibility for social welfare was an accepted principle. Nehru and other socialists were influenced by the ideas of Karl Marx, T.H. Green, Harold Laski, and Sidney and Beatrice Webb. It was widely assumed that 'political equality . . . is never real unless it is accompanied by . . . economic equality'[35] and that 'true individual freedom cannot exist without economic security . . . necessitous men are not free'.[36] Assembly members understood that 'the utility of a state has to be judged from its effect on the common man's welfare'.[37] That consensus notwithstanding, the nationalist discourse faced vexing questions about whether to prioritise the political or social revolution; if the state should be committed to socialist objectives in the constitution; and whether to hold the government judicially accountable for realising certain social and economic rights. During the drafting, the approach that prevailed was that while political independence had to be prioritised, this was not an end in itself but a 'means to an end' which was the 'raising of the people . . . to higher levels and hence the general advancement of humanity'.[38]

32 Indian National Congress, *Resolutions on Economic Policy and Programme, 1924–54* (All India Congress Committee 1954) 6.

33 Austin (n 28) 57.

34 ibid.

35 Harold J. Laski, *Grammar of Politics* (George Allen & Unwin Ltd 1925) 162.

36 A quote attributed to Franklin Roosevelt by K.T. Shah in a letter to Prasad dated 15 February 1947. Prasad papers, File 4-C/47, quoted in Austin (n 28) 60.

37 H.V. Kamath in the Constituent Assembly, Constituent Assembly Debates, vol 7, 5 November 1948, 7.49.69; also quoted in Austin (n 28) 60.

38 Jawaharlal Nehru, *The Unity of India. Collected Writings 1837–1940* (Lindsay Drummond 1948) 11.

K. Santhanam, a prominent member of the Constituent Assembly, spoke of three revolutions – the political revolution would end with independence; the social revolution was to 'to get (India) out of the medievalism based on birth, religion, custom, and community and reconstruct her social structure on modern foundations of law, individual merit and secular education'. The third revolution was an economic one: 'The transition from primitive rural economy to scientific and planned agriculture and industry'.[39] Nehru anticipated that the three revolutions were interrelated: A modern nation state that could provide for social welfare required certain preconditions, namely, a stable and united political community based on popular consent, economic development, and social restructuring. In his Objectives Resolution, Nehru stated, 'I stand for Socialism and, I hope, India will stand for Socialism. . . . What form of Socialism . . . is another matter for your consideration'.[40] However, Nehru was clear that such a state would seek to secure to 'all the people of India justice, social, economic and political; equality of status, of opportunity, and before the law'. Nehru's pragmatic approach prevailed in the Assembly and a democratic constitution with a socialist bias was crafted, so as to allow for such social welfare measures as the citizens desired or their needs demanded, to be enacted through their elected representatives in government.[41]

Drafting the Constitution

The core of the constitution's commitment to social welfare lies in some Fundamental Rights provisions of Part III and in the Directive Principles of Part IV.[42] Although the Fundamental Rights primarily protect individuals and minority groups from arbitrary state action, three of the Fundamental Rights are also designed to protect individuals against social discrimination and prejudice. Article 17 abolishes untouchability. The anti-discrimination provisions – Article 15(1) and (2), Article 16(2) – protect citizens from being discriminated against on certain grounds (religion, race, caste, sex, place of birth) in the use of commercial and other public spaces and employment in state services. Article 23 prohibits forced labour. However, the Directive Principles in Part IV are the clearest illustrations of the Constituent Assembly's thinking on social welfare, containing ideas of social security and the welfare state, of justice, modernisation, development, and socio-economic reform.[43] The Directive Principles

39 K. Santhanam, in the Magazine section of The Hindustan Times, New Delhi, 8 September 1946.

40 Resolution on Aims and Objects, moved by Jawaharlal Nehru in the first session of the Constituent Assembly, Constituent Assembly Debates, vol 1, 13 December 1946, 1.5.1.

41 Socialist ideologies in the Constituent Assembly ranged from Marxism to Gandhian Socialism.

42 Item 23 of the Concurrent List in the Seventh Schedule contains the words 'social security and social insurance' on which both the central and state governments can legislate.

43 For details on the drafting of these provisions in the Constituent Assembly, see B. Shiva Rao, *The Framing of India's Constitution: A Study* (Indian Institute of Public Administration 1968) chaps 7 and 8; Austin (n 28) chaps 3 and 4.

refer to ideas of making the state responsible for the welfare of its citizens, to the rights adopted by the All Parties Conference of 1928, and the Karachi Resolution of 1931.[44]

The constitution-makers agreed that the values in Part IV were to be 'fundamental in the governance of the country' and 'in making laws'. The overarching ideology of the Principles appears to be the creation of a just social order. The principle of justice – social, economic, and political – was to inform all institutions of national life, as stated in Article 38(1) of the constitution. The title of Article 38 affirmed that the welfare of the people could only be promoted within such a social order. The concept of 'welfare' that emerges from the Principles includes the state directing its policies to securing adequate means of livelihood; the right to work; a living wage; decent conditions of work; maternity relief; and securing the health of workers, women, and children. There are references to measures to be taken by the state to provide free education to children up to the age of fourteen years,[45] and public assistance in cases of unemployment, old age, sickness, disablement, and in other cases of undeserved want. The state is also to secure adequate nutrition and improvement of public health and promote with special care the educational and economic interests of the lower castes and of weaker sections of the people (Article 39).

The Principles addressed India's historic legacy of multiple and mutually reinforcing inequalities:[46] Social 'inequalities' (gender and caste) and economic inequalities (of income, ownership, and control of material resources and means of production), which often produced inequalities of access to education, to adequate nutrition, to health services. The Principles also categorised vulnerable sections based on specific characteristics such as old age, disability, and sickness. The role of the state – as envisioned by the Principles – was to 'enable' rather than 'provide', though in certain cases the state was directed to undertake suitable policies or economic organisation to reach specific goals such as adequate means of livelihood for citizens; a living wage for workers, both industrial and agricultural; equal pay for men and women; to secure the health of all workers; education; public assistance in certain cases; decent conditions of work; and to ameliorate the educational and economic interests of the Scheduled Castes and Tribes. However, Article 41 of the constitution established that state responsibilities had to be undertaken 'within the limits of its [the state's] economic capacity and development'.

44 See p. 88, 95 in this chapter.

45 Ambedkar explained that the clause that every child shall be kept in an educational institution until 14 years was because child labour in factories, mines, or hazardous occupations under 14 years was abolished under Article 24 of the constitution.

46 See Jean Drèze and Amartya Sen, *An Uncertain Glory. India and its Contradictions* (Princeton University Press 2013) chap 8.

Justiciability of the Directive Principles

The issue of whether the Directive Principles should be made justiciable, ie enforceable in a court of law, was contested ground. Constituent Assembly members such as Munshi, Ambedkar, and Shah would have made the Directives justiciable. Shah, a doctrinaire socialist, believed that there must be a time period within which the Directives had to be made justiciable; otherwise, they would be mere 'pious wishes'.[47] B.N. Rau, however, preferred 'to set out the positive rights merely as moral precepts for the authorities concerned'.[48] Rau included in his 'Constitutional Precedents' the Irish example of distinguishing between justiciable and non-justiciable rights. His defence was that '[m]any modern constitutions do contain moral precepts of this kind', and 'nor can it be denied that they may have an educative value'.[49] Rau believed that it may occasionally be necessary for the state to invade private rights (justiciable and thus protected) in the discharge of one of its fundamental duties. That is why Rau suggested in his Draft Constitution that no law made by the state in pursuance of its policies under the Directive Principles could be invalidated for contravening the Fundamental Rights.[50] However, the Drafting Committee did not include this suggestion in their draft provisions.

At the first meeting of the Fundamental Rights Sub-Committee in 1947, Alladi Krishnaswami Ayyar saw no use in laying down unenforceable precepts in the constitution. Ambedkar and Masani had similar views. Munshi's and Ambedkar's drafts of Fundamental Rights included the right to work and for every citizen to have free primary education (Munshi).[51] But while drafting the negative rights provisions, the Fundamental Rights Sub-Committee realised that some were more susceptible to court enforcement than others and that there was a need for non-justiciable rights.[52] Anticipating further criticism that these Principles should be viewed as fundamental to the ordered progress of the state, the Sub-Committee in finalising its report redrafted the opening clause: 'While these principles shall not be cognisable by any court they are nevertheless fundamental

47 Shah's minute, dated 20th April, 1947, quoted in Austin (n 28) 79 footnote 19.

48 Rau, Constitutional Precedents, Third Series (Government of India Press 1946), 10–24, quoted in Austin (n 28) 77 footnote 10. Justiciable rights meant that the rights could be judicially enforced. The Directive Principles cannot be enforced by any court, see Article 37.

49 B.N. Rau, *India's Constitution in the Making* (Orient Longman 1960) 364–365, quoted in Austin (n 28) 77 footnote 12. See also B. Shiva Rao, *The Framing of India's Constitution. Select Documents*, vol 1 (The Indian Institute of Public Administration 1966) 165.

50 B. Shiva Rao, *The Framing of India's Constitution. Select Documents*, vol 3 (The Indian Institute of Public Administration 1967) 222, 226–227.

51 Rao B. Shiva Rao, *The Framing of India's Constitution. Select Documents*, vol 2 (The Indian Institute of Public Administration 1967) 69; Ambedkar's draft, article II (II) (4) and explanatory notes thereon, ibid 89–90, 99.

52 Alladi Krishnaswami Ayyar supported this position in a note submitted on 14 March 1947 in which he stressed the distinction between justiciable rights and rights which were 'merely intended as a guide and directing objectives to state policy'. Rao (n 51) 67.

in the governance of the country and their application in the making of laws shall be the duty of the state'.

As foreseen, there were Constituent Assembly demands for greater enforceability of Part IV. One member said,

> I think it is the primary duty of government to remove hunger and render social justice to every citizen and to secure social security. . . . The teeming millions do not find any hope that the Union Constitution . . . will ensure them a minimum standard of living and a minimum standard of public health.[53]

But majority opinion was that the Principles should be kept general, leaving 'enough room for people of different ways of thinking' towards social change.[54] Introducing the draft constitution in the Assembly in November 1948, Ambedkar said that though the Directive Principles had no legal force behind them, he was not prepared to conclude that they were 'useless'. Synthesising democratic values with those of social transformation, he said,

> The draft constitution as framed only provides a machinery for the government of the country. It is not a contrivance to install any particular party in power. . . . Who should be in power is left to be determined by the people. . . . But whoever captures power will not be free to do what he likes with it. In the exercise of it, he will have to respect these Instruments of Instructions which are called the Directive Principles. . . . He may not have to answer for their breach in a court of law. But he will certainly have to answer for them before the electorate at election time.[55]

Equality

Members such as Alladi Krishnaswami Ayyar discussed the problem of the concept of equality being an obstacle to social welfare laws classifying men and women employees or laws demanding differential treatment of vulnerable groups such as backward classes, or Scheduled Castes and Tribes. Ayyar preferred using the phrase that 'no person should be denied the equal protection of the law'. But 'equality before the law' and 'equal protection of the laws' were both added to Article 14 of the constitution.

The principle of equality under Article 14 does not require identical treatment by the state but allows for 'reasonable classifications' where

53 B. Das in the Constituent Assembly, Constituent Assembly Debates, vol 5, 30 August 1947, 5.46.29.
54 Austin (n 28) 83.
55 Constituent Assembly Debates, vol 7, 4 November 1948, 7.48.243.

unequal categories can be treated differently.[56] The initial constitutional draft permitted the state to make 'special provisions' for groups such as women and children. These categories are only illustrative. The state can also make special provisions for those not specifically mentioned, where there is 'reasonable classification' under Article 14. The original text also explicitly contained further principles of positive discrimination. For instance, under Article 16(4) the state was explicitly allowed to make reservation of appointments or posts in state services in favour of 'any backward class of citizens' not adequately represented in services under the state.[57] Subsequent amendments created further categories of Scheduled Castes and Tribes and socially and educationally backward communities for admission to state sponsored educational institutions.[58] Subsequent case law has expounded on these categories.[59]

The Supreme Court of India has interpreted the idea of equality under the constitution to mean 'substantive equality'.[60] The underlying premise is that social justice is not constitutionally limited by values of formal equality or efficiency but is a 'seamless web' of harmonious values. This premise influenced later judicial interpretation that Article 16(4) is merely an 'illustration' of

56 The principles of 'reasonable classification' embedded in Article 14 was expressed in early Supreme Court. See *State of West Bengal v Anwar Ali Sarkar*, AIR 1952 SC 75; *Kathi Raning Rawat v State of Saurastra*, AIR 1952 SC 123.

57 During constitution-making, the Sapru Committee Report of 1945 tabled the question of marginalised groups such as the Scheduled Castes and suggested that discriminatory social customs should be eliminated. All citizens were to have the right to education, regardless of caste distinctions in any educational institution maintained or aided by the state. There could be no discrimination on grounds of religion, caste, or creed in public employment or for access to public spaces and facilities. There would be no form of forced labour. The Sapru Committee Report suggested further that the Constituent Assembly should consider schemes for the uplift of lower castes and make special provisions for their education and protection. For the Sapru Committee Report of 1945, see <www.constitutionofindia.net/historical_constitutions/sapru_committee_report__sir_tej_bahadur_sapru__1945__1st%20December%201945> accessed 28 February 2022. Article 16(4) is one of the outcomes of the considerations taking place in the Constituent Assembly.

58 The Constitution (First Amendment) Act, 1951 and the Constitution (93rd Amendment) Act, 2005.

59 Later cases, such as *Indra Sawhney v Union of India*, AIR 1993 SC 477; *Ashoka Kumar Thakur v Union of India* (2008) 6 SCC 1; *M. Nagaraj v Union of India* (2006) 8 SCC 212, have laid down the principles for determining 'socially and educationally backward', and 'other backward' classes as well as the 'extent' of reservations that is constitutionally valid. For a detailed analysis of 'reservations' see Vinay Sitapati, 'Reservations' in Sujit Choudhry, Madhav Khosla and Pratap Bhanu Mehta (eds), *Oxford Handbook of the Indian Constitution* (Oxford University Press 2016) 720.

60 In *State of Kerala & Anr v N.M. Thomas*, Ray CJ's majority opinion states that the 'question of unequal treatment does not really arise between persons governed by different conditions and different sets of circumstances'. *State of Kerala & Anr v N.M. Thomas*, AIR 1976 SC 490. This perspective has been upheld in later cases. See also Gautam Bhatia, 'Equality under the Indian Constitution' in Ulrike Davy and Antje Flüchter (eds), Imagining Unequals, Imagining Equals. Concepts of Equality in History and Law (Bielefeld University Press 2022) 231.

Article 16(1), or that Article 15(3) only reiterates the principles of Article 15(1) of the constitution.[61]

Social Policy in the 1950s and 1960s

The Political and Social Context

The constitution-makers envisioned a Westminster-style parliamentary democracy where executive and legislative acts were subject to the constitution and judicial review.[62] Granville Austin states: 'Thus began the enterprise of nation building, economic development and social change to which the Congress party had so long been dedicated'.[63]

However, soon conflicts emerged between the demands of the social revolution (achieving social justice and an equitable society based on the state undertaking primary responsibility for meeting the basic needs of vulnerable groups) on the one hand and the Fundamental Rights and democratic values in the constitution on the other. As the government enacted measures to address problems of traditional social hierarchies (the local caste hierarchy closely paralleled the distribution of land ownership in the village economy and was reflected in the allocation of political authority),[64] a largely agricultural economy, and widespread poverty tensions arose in balancing individual rights and collective interests. The tensions were mirrored in institutional struggles between the executive's role in social reform and the legitimacy of judicial intervention in 'ordering the life of a progressive people'.[65] The First Amendment to the Constitution of 1951, for instance, was a response to the need to balance the individual right to equality against group rights of 'backward' communities to gain access to state sponsored education.[66]

In the 1950s and 1960s, constitutional references to the state's duties to secure social welfare in the Directive Principles and other constitutional provisions did

61 Article 15 of the constitution is the 'non-discrimination' provision of the Indian Constitution and prevents the state from discriminating against citizens on the prohibited grounds specified in clause (1), such as religion, race, caste, sex, place of birth. Article 16(1) and (2) of the constitution embody the principle of 'equality of opportunity' for all citizens in matters relating to employment or appointment to any office under the state and lists the prohibited grounds of discrimination (religion, race, caste, sex, descent, place of birth, residence).

62 In the Indian model, the president is a constitutional head, with the prime minister as the leader of the majority party in Parliament heading the government through the Cabinet of Ministers. There is a federal devolution of authority between the central and state governments.

63 Granville Austin, *Working a Democratic Constitution. The Indian Experience* (Oxford University Press 1999) 13.

64 Francine R. Frankel, *India's Political Economy, 1947–1977. The Gradual Revolution* (Princeton University Press 1978) 8.

65 Attorney General M.C. Setalvad on 26 January 1950, quoted in Austin (n 63) 123.

66 See p. 90, 92, 103 in this chapter.

not result in the emergence of a comprehensive framework of social insurance or social assistance schemes. Economic planning dominated politics.

Economic Planning

The nationalist critique of India's economic decline under colonialism resulted in a post-independence focus on 'nation building' and on increasing economic growth. Economic development was considered an essential prerequisite for the state to engage in social welfare measures.[67] Policies for growth and development were characterised in broadly reformist and socialist terms during the Nehru years. These policies also reflected Gandhi's teachings that had influenced the 1931 Karachi resolution. The resolution contained the first reference to the need to 'end . . . the exploitation of the masses . . . and real economic freedom for the starving millions'.[68] Gandhi's approach to political organisation and social planning was based on his critical analysis of modern industrial society.[69] For Gandhi, only village reconstruction would eliminate the problems of untouchability, illiteracy, and disease. Therefore, Gandhi deemed it necessary to revive traditional handicrafts, cooperative ownership and cultivation of land, and the concept of trusteeship. Congress workers were to engage in a 'Constructive Programme' for 'village uplift', meaning better health, increasing rural income through the revival of village industries, and providing basic education.

Gandhian thinking created an interest in the normative aspects of economic modernisation. In his 'Discovery of India', Nehru stated that modern industrial society was based largely on the absence of social values.[70] Moreover, Nehru wanted to approach the multiple goals of India's development through an incremental and non-violent approach from within India's democratic system. The Gandhian critique also caused an interest in exploring alternative approaches to economic growth than a purely Western capitalist approach. The interest in a Soviet pattern of economic planning as a 'scientific' approach to

67 Agarwala (n 8) 14–15.

68 Indian National Congress (n 32) 6.

69 Gandhi characterised modern industrial society as one based on class violence, a state-centred political culture, and militarism, though his critique of modern industrial society was distinct from the typical Marxian analysis of the capitalist mode of production based on the labour theory of value and exploitation. M.K. Gandhi, *Panchayati Raj* (compiled by R.K. Prabhu, Navajivan Publishing House 1959); M.K. Gandhi, *Sarvodaya* (edited by Bharatan Kumarappa, Navajivan Publishing House 1954).

70 Jawaharlal Nehru, *The Discovery of India* (The Signet Press 1946) 678, deploring the excessive individualism of the West and finding that 'the competitive and acquisitive characteristics of modern capitalist society, and enthronement of wealth, and the continuous strain and lack of security for many' had afflicted entire populations with neurotic anxieties even in the midst of great material abundance.

problems of resource allocation and investment, for instance, has been viewed as a consequence of Gandhian thinking.[71]

The policies of the 1950s and 1960s also embodied values of state responsibility for nation building, for social transformation through legal means, and 'for modernisation' to increase productivity and build a new nation. State responsibility required state ownership and regulation of land and other means of production. The 1947 Jaipur meeting of the All India Congress Committee reiterated that the state would be responsible for starting new enterprises in all key industries; existing industries in the field would be transferred from private to public ownership after a period of five years.[72] This strategy was expected to lay the foundations of a self-reliant economy and solve the problem of unemployment. Economic planning was to be spearheaded by a Planning Commission.[73] According to a 1955 Congress resolution, state control and interventions in economic planning would mean 'the establishment of a socialistic pattern of society where the means of production are under social ownership and control, . . . and there is equitable distribution of the national wealth'.[74]

Social and economic policies of the Planning Commission and the Congress party largely conformed to long-standing values of equality and social justice which became the means and the goal of [India's] development and the entire planning effort.[75] The Directive Principles also influenced state social policy.[76] The Cabinet resolution establishing the Planning Commission in March 1950 specified three principles of economic planning: For one, all citizens would equally have a right to an adequate means of livelihood. For another, the operation of the economic system would not result in a concentration of wealth and means of production. Finally, the ownership and

71 In 1953, Shriman Narayan, as the general secretary of the All India Congress Committee, claimed that there was 'no fundamental difference between the ideologies of the Congress, Socialism and Sarvodaya'. Quoted in Francine R. Frankel, *India's Political Economy, 1947–2004*, 2nd edn (Oxford University Press 2005) 106. However, Jean Drèze and Amartya Sen have written that India's economic planning in the Nehru years was not Soviet-style planning with extensive nationalisation of industries. According to Drèze and Sen, India was attempting a sort of state-led development strategy where most of the economy (with the exception of what were seen as 'essential services') were in the hands of the private sector. Drèze and Sen (n 46) 25.

72 This was decided by the Committee on Objectives and Economic Program. See Indian National Congress (n 32) 32; Frankel (n 64) 77. See also the Resolution on Industrial Policy, 6 April 1948, quoted in Frankel (n 71) 77.

73 In January 1950, the Working Committee of the Congress agreed to a resolution calling for the creation of a Planning Commission. Frankel (n 71) 84–85.

74 Jawaharlal Nehru, 'Planning and Development', speech delivered to the National Development Council, 9 November 1954, quoted in Frankel (n 71) 117.

75 Planning Commission, Government of India, *The New India: Progress through Democracy* (Macmillan Company 1958) 34.

76 Tarlok Singh, *India: Towards an Integrated Society: Reflections on Planning, Social Policy, and Rural Institutions* (Orient Longmans 1969) 253–254.

control of the material resources of the country would be distributed so as to subserve the common good.[77] The First Five Year Plan, December 1952, also reiterated,

> [the socio economic] framework has itself to be remoulded so as to enable it to accommodate progressively . . . the demands for the right to work, the right to adequate income, the right to education and to a measure of insurance against old age, sickness and other disabilities. The Directive Principles of State Policy . . . make it clear that for the attainment of these ends, ownership and control of the material resources of the country should be so distributed as best to subserve the common good.[78]

While the Plans did not outline comprehensive government schemes of social assistance or social insurance, they did make financial outlays to improve infrastructure for health, education, and nutrition; to improve the conditions of backward classes; for social welfare schemes for women and children, and physically and mentally disabled groups. Under the First Five Year Plan, the Central Government set up a Central Social Welfare Board with the object of assisting voluntary agencies for organising welfare programmes for women, children, and handicapped groups.[79]

Social Policy Instruments

During the Nehru years, it would appear that state action to formulate social schemes which were tax-financed and means-tested became secondary to the predominant urge to build a political nation state and to achieve economic growth. State action to achieve social goals took the form of giving effect to constitutional provisions for special care for vulnerable groups. Certain statutory provisions were also formulated for the benefit of employed women. Additionally, a legal framework was enacted for provident funds schemes for employees or their beneficiaries on retirement, superannuation, and disability, along with pension and life insurance schemes. However, there was no state financing of such schemes.

77 Resolution (Planning) published by the Cabinet Secretariat in the Gazette of India Extraordinary, 15 March 1950.

78 For the First Five Year Plan, see <https://niti.gov.in/planningcommission.gov.in/docs/plans/planrel/fiveyr/1st/1planch1.html> accessed 28 February 2022.

79 The Second Plan also provided for funding to the 'people's sector', to assist voluntary social welfare organisations at the instance of a social welfare board. For the Second Five Year Plan see < https://niti.gov.in/planningcommission.gov.in/docs/plans/planrel/fiveyr/welcome.html> accessed 28 February 2022.

Special Care for Vulnerable Groups

The original text of the Constitution of India contained various provisions for compensatory treatment of disadvantaged citizens, based on categories such as caste, sex, or age.[80] There are also general anti-discrimination clauses under the 'Fundamental Rights' in Part III of the constitution: Articles 15 and 16 prohibit discrimination on certain grounds, such as religion, race, caste, sex, and place of birth, among others. Article 29(2) says that no citizen shall be denied admission into any government-supported educational institution on similar grounds.

The seeming contradiction between the 'special care' provisions allowing for preferential treatment and the general non-discrimination provisions was first raised before the Supreme Court of India in *State of Madras v Srimathi Champakam Dorairajan*.[81] In that case, the Madras Communal General Order which reserved seats in medical colleges for backward communities in accordance with Article 46 of the constitution, contained in Part IV (Directive Principles), was found by the Madras High Court (upheld in the Supreme Court) to be in violation of Article 29(2) of the constitution. The Supreme Court held that the Directive Principles could not override the Fundamental Rights which were sacrosanct and not liable to be overturned by legislation or an executive act.[82]

The potential danger presented by decisions such as *State of Madras v Srimathi Champakam Dorairajan* to the constitution's 'special care' provisions led to the First Amendment to the Constitution of 1951 which added clause 4 to Article 15. The newly inserted clause stated that nothing in Article 15 or in Article 29(2) of Part III of the constitution would prevent the state from making special provisions for the advancement of any socially and educationally backward classes of citizens or Scheduled Castes and Tribes listed by presidential notification under Articles 341 and 342 of the constitution. The term 'Scheduled Castes' referred to lower castes and 'untouchables' in the Indian social hierarchy with a historical legacy of discrimination.[83] The term 'Scheduled Tribes' referred to 'adivasi' (original inhabitants) or tribal communities who faced loss of lands and changes to their traditional ways of life from modernisation and

80 Part XVI of the original text of the Constitution of India contained thirteen articles providing for reservation of seats in legislatures for Scheduled Castes and Tribes. Article 15(3) allowed (and allows) the state to make special provisions for women and children. Article 16(4) empowered (and empowers) the state to reserve posts (in state services) in favour of 'any backward class of citizens' not adequately represented in such services.

81 AIR 1951 SC 226.

82 ibid. The Supreme Court also struck down other communal quotas – for example, in *Venkataramana v State of Tamil Nadu*, AIR 1966 SC 1089, quotas for government posts.

83 The caste system is generally considered to be *sui generis* to the Hindu social structure and characterised by restrictions on marriages outside the caste, exchanging food, and pursuing certain occupations.

economic development. Subsequent case law has created identifying criteria for determining 'social and educational' backwardness.[84]

Benefits for Women

The Maternity Benefits Fund Act of 1961 was passed by the Indian parliament to regulate the employment of women in certain establishments before and after childbirth and to provide for maternity and other benefits. The Act applied to every factory, mine, or plantation not covered by the Employees' State Insurance Act of 1948.[85]

Under the act, every woman was entitled to, and her employer was liable for, the payment of maternity benefit at the rate of the average daily wage for the period of her actual absence.[86] The maximum period for such benefit was (originally) twelve weeks of which not more than six weeks was to precede the date of her expected delivery. Such employees were also entitled to receive from her employer a medical bonus of (originally) Rs 25, if no pre-natal confinement and post-natal care was provided by the employer free of charge. The appropriate government was authorised to appoint inspectors to secure the enforcement of the act.

Provident Funds

The need for old age provisions for industrial workers was referred to in the 1931 report of the Royal Commission on Labour and in 1946 by the Rege Committee (established in 1944); both reports pointed out that a worker who had toiled for a long period in a factory could become destitute in his old age.[87] In 1947, the question was reviewed at the Asian Regional Conference of the International Labour Organisation and its recommendations were discussed at the tenth session of the Indian Labour Conference in 1948.[88] The enactment

84 See p. 103 in this chapter.

85 The Maternity Benefits Fund Act of 1961 has been amended a number of times, also to extend the scope of the act. In the 2017 amendment, maternity benefit was increased from twelve weeks to twenty-six weeks for two surviving children (of which not more than eight weeks shall precede the date of expected delivery and eighteen weeks after delivery) and remained twelve weeks for more than two children. The amendment also facilitated 'work from home' and made the provision of crèche facilities mandatory in establishments having fifty or more employees.

86 Section 5 of the Maternity Benefits Fund Act of 1961 defined average daily wage to mean the average of the woman's wages payable to her for the days on which she worked during the period of three calendar months immediately preceding the date from which she absented herself on account of maternity, or ten rupees, whichever was the highest.

87 Royal Commission on Labour in India (n 24) 269; Labour Investigation Committee, *Report on An Enquiry into Conditions of Labour in the Principal Municipalities in India* (Government of India 1946) 29; Srivastata (n 10) 69.

88 Preparatory Asian Regional Conference of the International Labour Organisation. *Record of Proceedings* (International Labour Office 1948) 275; Srivastata (n 10) 304.

of the Employees' State Insurance Act of 1948[89] made the need to address this issue even more pressing.

The Employees' Provident Funds Act of 1952 provided for retirement benefits in the form of provident funds for employees in factories and other establishments.[90] Originally, the Employees' Provident Funds Act was applicable to every establishment or factory which employed fifty or more persons.[91] Under the Employees' Provident Fund Scheme authorised by the act, a provident fund was (and is) instituted for each employee covered by the act. Contributions to the (individual) fund account were (and are) mandatory, for employees as well as for employers. The total amount of the contributions made by the employee and the employer plus interest constituted the maximum benefit an employee could receive under the scheme, once the qualifying conditions for entitlement were fulfilled (entitlement to the full amount required a period of membership of more than twenty years and retirement from services after reaching the retirement age). Shorter periods of membership led to a reduction of the contributions made by the employer, according to a defined scale.[92] The administration of the Employees' Provident Fund Scheme was (and is) in the hands of a Central Board of Trustees, a tripartite body consisting of representatives of the central government, the state governments and all-India employers' and employees' organisations.

The Employees' Provident Funds Act did make provision for old age, at least to some extent, and for certain categories of employees. But the benefit took the form of a lump sum, ie a one-time payment, and that lump sum remained meagre in case of short periods of membership, or – for dependents – in case of premature death.

Social policy in India in the 1970s and 1980s

The Political and Social Context

After Nehru, the government's economic policies initially retreated from socialist values and goals.[93] Subsequently, ideological factionalism developed between those with a vested interest in the status quo and those committed to

89 See p. 84 in this chapter.

90 The Employees' Provident Fund Act of 1952 was amended a number of times to increase its coverage and to put its provisions on a sounder footing.

91 Today, the act applies to factories/establishments employing twenty or more persons. Hence, smaller factories/establishments were and are excluded from the act.

92 Srivastata (n 10) 314.

93 Lal Bahadur Shastri, Nehru's successor, faced opposition to social reforms from the states. The World Bank argued that India's public sector programmes were too ambitious; and that Indian private enterprise and foreign private capital should have a larger role in industrial development. The Annual Plans between 1966–1969 relied more on the private sector, and there were a series of measures to relax controls under the Industrial (Development and Regulation) Act of 1951.

more radical socialist values. Promises given by the Congress to provide basic individual needs such as food, clothing, housing, education, and health could not be met. The democratic political framework failed to provide effective organisational devices for removing the problems of poverty or achieving the values of a just and equitable society.

Against the background of economic failures and the decline of Congress' popularity in the 1967 elections, the Congress party split, and Indira Gandhi won the 1971 elections with her new Congress party. But despite the formation of Congress majority governments at the centre and in the states, constitutional amendments that tried to prevent any legal obstruction to reform, and despite popular endorsement of 'Garibi Hatao' (remove poverty), the national leadership was unable to carry out social change through peaceful and parliamentary means. The political consensus that provided the foundation of a stable democratic government was destroyed. Following the adverse Allahabad High Court ruling against her election,[94] Indira Gandhi declared an emergency in June 1975 ostensibly in view of '[a]ttacks . . . intended to subvert the government's progressive programmes and to dislodge it'.[95] But the declaration of emergency resulted in a resurgence of the values of basic civil liberties and a turn to law and constitutionalism to grant the judiciary a 'new historical basis of legitimation'.[96] The Supreme Court's jurisprudence around Public Interest Litigation and new legislation to expand social welfare was prompted by the emergence of new social groups, such as civil rights activists, women's organisations, and non-party organisations, who created new political coalitions and social alliances.[97]

Social Goals and Political Conflicts

In 1967, the radical wing of the Congress drafted a Ten Point Programme to accelerate the attainment of a socialist society.[98] But contestations continued with those who favoured an incremental approach towards social justice. The

94 *The State of Uttar Pradesh v Raj Narain*, 1975 AIR 865. The Supreme Court ultimately upheld Indira Gandhi's election.

95 Austin (n 63) 307.

96 Sanjay Ruparelia, 'Contesting the Right to Law – Courts and Constitutionalism in India and China' in Prasenjit Duara and Elizabeth J. Perry (eds), *Beyond Regimes. China and India Compared* (Harvard University Asia Center 2018) 99, 109.

97 ibid 108.

98 The Ten Point Programme included a national policy of public distribution of food grains particularly to vulnerable sections of the population; the development of consumer cooperatives for supply of essential commodities at fair prices; and steps towards provision of minimum needs to the entire community. These goals required greater state regulation of key sectors of the economy and restricting concentration of economic power. See Austin (n 63) 175. The ideas of the programme were reiterated in 1969 in the economic regulation passed by the Bangalore session of the Congress Parliamentary party and the 'Note on Economic Policies' prepared by the Congress Forum for Socialist Action. ibid 177.

Planning Commission's 'Towards self-reliance, Approach to the Fifth Five Year Plan', released in 1972, reiterated that the basic premise of the Five Year Plans was 'development along socialist lines to secure rapid economic growth and expansion of employment, . . . and creation of the values of a free and equal society'.[99]

Proponents of social change also perceived a conflict between the values in the Directive Principles in Part IV and the Fundamental Rights in Part III of the constitution, which culminated in the 24th and 25th amendments to the Constitution of India. The Congress Forum suggested ending judicial review of laws that were 'in consonance' with the Directive Principles.[100] The Attorney General told a seminar organised by the Congress Forum and the Congress Parliamentary party in 1971 that the constitution should be amended to ensure Indians' economic liberties, which were 'more fundamental than the Fundamental Rights'. The report of the seminar stated that the Fundamental Rights in Articles 14, 19 and 31 'must be withdrawn . . . Without these changes our commitment to establish a socialist society shall remain a dead letter'.[101] Against these political conflicts, the 24th and the 25th amendments were meant to curb the range of judicial review, in particular the powers of the Supreme Court of India.

Social Policy Instruments

Key Constitutional Amendments

The 1971 electoral win for the Congress party took place based on slogans of a renewed commitment to economic and social reforms, of a programme of 'Garibi Hatao' (remove poverty), and of references to socialism along with democracy. The 24th and 25th amendments were introduced in Parliament in 1971.

The 24th Amendment modified Articles 13 and 368 of the constitution to authorise parliament to freely amend the Fundamental Rights.[102] Hence, constitutional amendments purporting to achieve social goals could no longer be judicially challenged for violating Fundamental Rights. Among other provisions, the 25th Amendment inserted Article 31C into the constitution, holding

99 Planning Commission, *Towards Self-Reliance, Approach to the Fifth Five Year Plan* (Government of India 1972).

100 Socialist India, 8 May 1971, 20.

101 Austin (n 63) 241–242.

102 The 24th Amendment asserted the constituent power of parliament under Article 368 of the Constitution, ie the power to change the constitution, and added: 'Nothing in Article 13 [declaring that all laws must conform with the Fundamental Rights] shall apply to any amendment made under [Article 368]'. The amendment overturned the Supreme Court decision in *I.C. Golaknath v State of Punjab,* AIR 1967 SC 1643.

that laws securing certain Directive Principles under Article 39 would not be deemed to be void on the ground that they violated certain Fundamental Rights (such as equality or property). The amendment clearly intended that laws purporting to give effect to certain social values expressed in the Directive Principles could not be invalidated by courts because of a violation of Fundamental Rights. The amendments expressed the political intention to 'subordinate the rights of individuals [as expressed in the Fundamental Rights under Articles 14, 19 and 31] to the urgent needs of society' as expressed in the Directive Principles.[103] Thus, an entire category of legislation was placed beyond the reach of judicial review.[104]

The 42nd Amendment Act of 1976 also aimed to protect social reform legislation from judicial scrutiny. The amendment added the word 'socialist' to the Preamble of the constitution and – in order to give primacy to the Directive Principles over the Fundamental Rights – extended the number of Directive Principles that lawmakers could allude to in order to make a law exempt from judicial review under Article 31C of the constitution.[105] The government argued that it was necessary 'to make the directive principles more comprehensive and give them precedence over those fundamental rights which have been allowed to be relied upon to frustrate socio-economic reforms for implementing the directive principles'.[106] Eventually, certain sections of the 42nd Amendment were declared unconstitutional by the Supreme Court in *Minerva Mills Ltd v Union of India*.[107]

Reformulation of the Reservations Policy

The First Amendment of 1951 empowered the state under Article 15(4) of the constitution to formulate special measures for socially and educationally backward classes of citizens. Such measures included, *inter alia*, reserving quotas in educational institutions for pupils or students belonging to such categories. Article 16(4) of the constitution allows (and allowed so from the beginning) the state to reserve posts in state services for backward classes of citizens who, in the opinion of the state, were not adequately represented in such services.

103 Austin (n 63) 254.

104 The 25th Amendment was, in principle, upheld by the Supreme Court in *Kesavananda Bharati Sripadagalvaru v State of Kerala* (1973) 4 SCC 225. However, the Supreme Court struck down a part of Article 31C which read 'and no law containing a declaration that it is for giving effect to such policy shall be called in question in any court on the ground that it does not give effect to such policy'.

105 Under the 42nd Amendment, lawmakers could allude to 'all or any of the principles laid down in Part IV [of the constitution]', not just a limited number of principles mentioned in Article 39 of the constitution.

106 Statement of Objects and Reasons, the Constitution (42nd Amendment) Act of 1976, <legislative.gov.in/constitution-forty-second-amendment-act-1976> accessed 28 February 2022.

107 *Minerva Mills Ltd v Union of India*, 1981 SCR (1) 206, 263. Section 4 (Justice Bhagwati dissenting) and Section 55 of the 42nd Amendment Act were declared unconstitutional by the majority decision.

Judicial decisions have varied in determining the beneficiaries of these clauses and also in determining the extent of reservations in educational institutions and state employment permissible under these clauses. The constitution helps in identifying Scheduled Castes and Scheduled Tribes. For both such groups, Article 366 refers to enumerations made by public notification under Articles 341 and 342 respectively. However, there is no constitutional definition of what constitutes 'backward classes'. Article 340 leaves the task of investigating the conditions of socially and educationally backward classes to commissions appointed by the president. The president has exercised his power under Article 340 only twice, once – in 1953 – to appoint the Kaka Kalelkar Commission, and again – in 1978 – to appoint the Mandal Commission. Both commissions presented a report suggesting criteria for defining the 'socially and educationally backward classes' and recommendations with a view to the advancement of these classes.[108] The commissions took caste as the dominant factor in determining backwardness, but no universally agreed formula was found. Thus, these issues became subject to review by the Supreme Court, most famously in *Indra Sawhney v Union of India.* The case of *Indra Sawhney v Union of India* challenged a Government Order implementing the 1980 Mandal Commission report.[109] The judgement of the Supreme Court in the case laid down important determining principles on some of the contested issues regarding reservation clauses.[110]

So far, affirmative action has primarily taken the form of numerical quotas for admission to state-sponsored educational institutions and to posts in the

108 *Report of the Backward Classes Commission* (Government of India 1955); *Report of the Backward Classes Commission, Parts 1 and 2* (Government of India 1980). The Mandal Commission evolved eleven 'indicators' or 'criteria' for determining social and educational backwardness. These eleven 'indicators' were grouped under three broad heads, ie social, educational, and economic.

109 AIR 1993 SC 477. The National Front government of V.P. Singh tried to implement the Mandal Commission recommendations by passing an Office Memorandum of August 1990 to reserve 27 percent of vacancies in civil posts and services under the government of India for socially and educationally backward communities.

110 In *Indra Sawhney v Union of India*, the Supreme Court held that caste represented an existing, identifiable social group and could be a starting point for identifying vulnerable groups. The economic criterion alone could not be the basis of backwardness. Within socially and educationally backward groups, further classification between the 'backward' and 'more backward' was deemed permissible, and the so-called 'creamy layer' had to be excluded. While in Article 16(4) the emphasis was on social backwardness, in Article 15(4) it was on both social and educational backwardness. The court further ruled that once a caste satisfied the criteria of backwardness, it would become a backward class for the purpose of Article 16(4), if, additionally, it was underrepresented in state services. Later, in *Ashoka Kumar Thakur v Union of India* (2008) 6 SCC 1, the Supreme Court said that 'backwardness' could be identified on caste and occupation/income/property holdings for the next ten years, after which only economic criteria should prevail. The removal of the 'creamy layer' to determine the existence of a 'backward class' under Article 16(4) as per *Indra Sawhney*, will apply equally well with regard to identifying a socially and educationally backward class in Article 15(5) of the constitution.

service of the state, both entry-level positions as well as promotions.[111] In the context of access to state employment, the state also used to set lower evaluation standards or relax qualifying marks in examinations. In *Indra Sawhney v Union of India*, the Supreme Court rejected the practice of relaxing entry criteria for the context of promotion to higher positions, arguing that such relaxation would compromise the efficiency of administration.[112] In *Indra Sawhney v Union of India*, the Supreme Court further held that the extent of reservations to posts in state employment must not exceed 50 percent of the posts in a cadre or service barring extraordinary situations. The mandated 50 percent quota obviously incorporates the idea of balancing equality rights of the general community and administrative efficiency with the need for achieving social justice.[113]

The reservations policy in India has raised various definitional and conceptual issues. First, with reference to the question of more affluent sections within each caste disproportionately monopolising benefits, judicial decisions and scholarly debate have suggested excluding wealthy individuals within these groups ('creamy layer') from benefits, and to create sub-quotas for especially disadvantaged groups within the quota.[114] There are also questions about additional 'reasonable classifications' that the state can make for granting such benefits.[115]

Second, the question of whether the state can require the private sector to adopt such policies has eventually been addressed by the Constitution (93rd Amendment) Act of 2005 which added Article 15(5), enabling the state to

111 Article 16(4A) of the constitution, inserted by Constitution (77th Amendment) Act of 1995, states that there can be reservation to posts in state services 'in matters of promotion' for Scheduled Castes and Scheduled Tribes only. *M. Nagaraj v Union of India* (2006) 8 SCC 212 validated the amendment.

112 The Constitution (82nd Amendment) Act of 2000 inserted a proviso to Article 335 (overriding the Supreme Court's decision in *Indra Sawhney v Union of India*) that the state may make provision for relaxation in qualifying marks or lowering the standards of evaluation for reservation in matters of promotion to state services or posts. The amendment was upheld in *M. Nagaraj v Union of India* (2006) 8 SCC 212.

113 The Constitution (103rd Amendment) Act of 2019 has overridden two principles laid down in *Indra Sawhney v Union of India*, namely, for one, that economic backwardness could not be the sole criterion for reservation, since reservation only provided a right of access to resources for backward and underrepresented classes and was not an anti-poverty programme; and for another, that there should be a 50 percent cap for reservations to posts in state services. The Amendment introduced Article 15(6) and Article 16(6) into the constitution. Article 15(6) allows for reservations for 'economically weaker sections of citizens' other than the classes mentioned in Articles 15(4) and 15(5) (that is, other than the Scheduled Castes and Tribes and socially and educationally backward classes). Article 16(6) does the same for public employment. The quantum of reservation is fixed at 10 percent over and above the existing reservation for scheduled castes and tribes and backward classes. An Explanation inserted in Article 15 states that 'economic weakness' shall be decided on the basis of 'family income' and other 'indicators of economic disadvantage'.

114 Sitapati (n 59) 724.

115 Reservations for women are constitutionally permitted. Reservations for religious groups, such as Muslims, remain constitutionally contested.

mandate reservations in private educational institutions, effectively overriding the judgement in *P.A. Inamdar v State of Maharastra*.[116] The Right of Children to Free and Compulsory Education Act of 2009 also mandates 25 percent reservations for disadvantaged groups in private schools unaided by the state.[117]

Third, the reservations clauses are often regarded as expressions of the value of 'substantive equality' in Article 14 of the constitution (right to equality). According to that interpretation, differential treatment is permitted, if differential treatment meets the test of 'reasonable classification'. The differential treatment implicit in the provisions allowing for reservations does not burden the groups addressed in those provisions. Differential treatment is meant to advance their interests. A deeper value underlying such tests is based on the Dworkinian distinction between the right to equal treatment and the right to treatment as an equal, that is, a right to equal respect and concern. The clauses allowing for preferential treatment also promote the Directive Principles in Articles 46 and 38.[118] The clauses also harmonise the competing constitutional values of equality (Articles 14, 15[1], and 16[1]), of social justice (Articles 15[4], 16[4], and 46), and efficiency in governance (Article 335).[119] The differential treatment that is implied in reservation schemes has been validated by the constitution itself.

Gratuity Payments

A gratuity is a one-time payment to the employee, made by the employer as a *quid pro quo* for a certain period of services. Initially, as a practice, the making of such payments evolved in the 1950s and 1960s on a voluntary basis. Soon, however, labour tribunals and the Supreme Court assumed that employees were entitled to receive such a payment in case of retirement or incapacity.[120] Bolstered by that judicial approach, gratuities became a form of retirement benefit received as of right, either in place of or in addition to provident fund

116 *P.A. Inamdar v State of Maharastra* (2005) 6 SCC 537. However, Article 15(5) of the constitution (as amended) does not apply to minority educational institutions, which are protected by Article 30(1) of the constitution. Article 15(5) was validated by the Supreme Court in *Pramati Educational and Cultural Trust v Union of India* (2014) 8 SCC 1. The enabling Article 21A of the constitution – especially its application to private unaided educational institutions – was also upheld in this decision.

117 The validity of the mandate was upheld in *Society for Unaided Private Schools of Rajasthan v Union of India* (2012) 6 SCC 102. However, the court excluded unaided minority schools from the mandate imposed by the Right to Education Act. In *Pramati Educational and Cultural Trust v Union of India* (2014) 8 SCC 1 both aided as well as unaided minority institutions were exempted from providing reservations.

118 M.P. Singh, 'Are articles 15(4) and 16(4) Fundamental Rights?' (1994) 3 Supreme Court Cases (Journal Section) 34–41.

119 Sitapati (n 59) 746.

120 Suresh C. Srivastata, 'Gratuity: The Approaches of Indian Judiciary' (1972) 7 Indian Journal of Industrial Relations 331.

payments. Gratuities bridged the gap in coverage left open by the Employees' Provident Fund Act or supplemented inadequate payments made from the provident funds.

In 1972, gratuities became mandatory by statutory law. The Payment of Gratuity Act of 1972 covered (and still covers) every factory, mine, oilfield, plantation, port, and railway company as well as every shop or establishment, in which ten or more persons are employed, which is quite a comprehensive range of applicability.[121] The act continues to provide for a scheme for payment of gratuity to employees upon their superannuation, retirement, resignation, and death or disablement due to accident or disease. Gratuity was payable to an employee on the termination of the employment after the employee had rendered continuous service for not less than five years, except in case of death or disablement. As a principle, the amount of payment equalled fifteen days' wages at the rate of wages last drawn by the employee. An amendment to the act made in 1987 obliged all employers in the private sector to obtain an insurance for the liability for making a gratuity payment from the Life Insurance Corporation or another prescribed insurer. By way of compulsory insurance, gratuities became a more reliable form of payment which employees could expect at the end of their employment.

Supreme Court's Jurisprudence

The Supreme Court's Involvement in Social Policies

The idea of a necessary dissonance between the Directive Principles (Part IV of the constitution) and the Fundamental Rights (Part III of the constitution) that had been propagated by the government[122] was judicially resolved when the Supreme Court in *Minerva Mills Ltd v Union of India* drew upon the basic structure doctrine of *Kesavananda Bharati Sripadagalvaru v State of Kerala* to declare Section 4 of the 42nd Amendment to the constitution invalid and beyond the amending power of parliament 'since it [damaged] the basic or essential features of the constitution . . . by the total exclusion of challenge to any law' meant to implement the Directive Principles at the expense of the Fundamental Rights in Articles 14 and 19 of the constitution. The court affirmed that the balance between Parts III and IV could not be destroyed.[123]

121 The Payment of Gratuity Act of 1972 sought to achieve two major objectives – establish uniformity in payment of gratuity to employees nationally, and to avoid differential treatment of employees in different branches of a single establishment.

122 See p. 102 in this chapter.

123 *Minerva Mills Ltd v Union of India*, 1981 SCR (1) 206, 263. The court held that the implication of the basic structure doctrine was that the clauses of Article 368 of the constitution that gave unconstrained amending power to Parliament were unconstitutional.

From the early 1980s onward, the Supreme Court's jurisprudence developed substantive norms to conceptualise poverty and hunger as a denial or violation of an expanded fundamental 'right to life' under Article 21.[124] *Maneka Gandhi v Union of India* was the breakthrough judgement for an open textured and expansive concept of 'life' and 'personal liberty' under Article 21 of the constitution.[125] Since Part IV of the constitution was deemed aspirational and non-justiciable, locating and explicating social and economic rights was done at a more implicit and interpretative level under Article 21. In developing a new rights-based constitutionalism for advancing social welfare, the court defined the right to life as 'the right to live with human dignity and all that goes with it, namely, the bare necessaries of life such as adequate nutrition'.[126] Under the umbrella of the 'bare necessities of life' the Supreme Court assembled a variety of rights such as the right to food, the right to education, and the right to health in Article 21.[127]

The development of the Supreme Court's jurisdiction to hear 'public interest litigation' created procedural innovations so that disadvantaged groups could access the legal/political process, mobilise, and voice their needs. Justice Bhagwati said that

> Anglo Saxon law . . . was developed and has evolved . . . essentially . . . to deal with situations involving the private right/duty pattern. It cannot possibly meet the challenge raised by . . . new concerns for the social rights and collective claims of the underprivileged.[128]

Enforcing orders by the Supreme Court required the cooperation of state agencies, since the orders were not self-executing and could not create new law. Relief in such cases merely ensured that the government carried out its obligations under the law.[129]

124 Illustrative cases are *Olga Tellis v Bombay Municipal Corporation*, AIR 1986 SC 180 (right to livelihood); *Bandhua Mukti Morcha v Union of India* (1997) 10 SCC 549 (right to minimum wages and abolition of forced labour); *Unni Krishnan v State of Andhra Pradesh*, AIR 1993 SC 217 (right to education); *Kishen Pattnayak v State of Orissa*, AIR 1989 SC 677, and *Peoples' Union for Civil Liberties v Union of India*, AIR 1982 SC 1473 (right to food).

125 *Maneka Gandhi v Union of India*, AIR 1978 SC 597.

126 *Francis Coralie Mullin v Administrator, Union Territory of Delhi*, 1981 AIR 746.

127 See also Varun Gauri and Daniel M. Brinks (eds), *Courting Social Justice. Judicial Enforcement of Social and Economic Rights in the Developing World* (Cambridge University Press 2008) exploring the judiciary's enforcement of health and education rights in developing countries.

128 P.N. Bhagwati, 'Judicial Activism and Public Interest Litigation' (1985) 23 Columbia Journal of Transnational Law 561, 570. The expansion of the rule of locus standi; epistolary jurisdiction; appointment of commissions for data gathering and monitoring enforcement of court orders; and crafting innovative remedial measures drawing on its powers under Article 32 of the constitution are instances of such innovations.

129 Demands for welfare rights and socio-economic entitlements through law, constitutionalism, and democracy have led to issues of transparency and accountability in government and identification numbers for citizens as beneficiaries to enable targeted cash transfers to the deserving poor. Ruparelia (n 96) 119.

The Right to Livelihood

The case underlying the judgement of the Supreme Court in *Olga Tellis v Bombay Municipal Corporation* related to the measures taken by the Bombay government to evict pavement dwellers who lived on pavements and slums in the city of Bombay and to deport them to their places of origin or to places outside the city. The court found that the main reason for the emergence and growth of squatter-settlements in cities like Bombay was the availability of job opportunities which were lacking in the rural sector. Such settlements allowed easier access to places of work.

The Supreme Court held that the right to life included the right to livelihood. The actual deprivation of life (through imposition of the death penalty, for instance) was but one aspect of the right. According to the court, no person could live without the means of living, that is, the means of livelihood. Depriving a person of the means of livelihood would not only denude 'life' of its effective content and meaningfulness but it would make life impossible to live. Article 39(a) and Article 41 of the constitution, so the court further held, required the state to secure to the citizens an adequate means of livelihood and the right to work. The court conceded that the state may not by affirmative action be compelled to provide adequate means of livelihood or work to the citizens. However, the court asserted that any person who was deprived of his right to livelihood, except according to just and fair procedure established by law, could challenge the deprivation as offending the right to life under Article 21. In this case, it was apparent that the dwellers' eviction from pavements and slums would lead to a deprivation of their means of livelihood. However, the court found that the right was not an absolute right and could be restricted in accordance with reasonable legal procedure.

The Right to Food

A petition brought in July 2001 on behalf of the poor in Rajasthan who had not been receiving the required employment and food relief mandated by the Rajasthan Famine Code of 1962 prompted the Supreme Court's judgement in *People's Union for Civil Liberties (PUCL) v Union of India.*[130] The petition was in response to the failure of the central and state governments to address acute hunger and starvation deaths at a time when India was producing a grain surplus. The petition wanted a constitutional right to food to be enforced under Article 21 of the constitution.

The Supreme Court stated that there was a state obligation to ensure 'that the poor and destitute and the weaker sections of society [did] not suffer from hunger or starvation'. The court passed a series of interim orders for public distribution of food grains to families and persons falling below the

130 Writ Petition (Civil) No 196 of 2001.

government-designated poverty line. The orders ranged from converting food security schemes into entitlements to increasing their coverage and putting in place mechanisms for effective monitoring and implementation. The order of 28 November 2001 especially, critically and expansively transformed the *PUCL* case by identifying which food schemes were to be considered legal entitlements under the constitutional right to food and determining in detail how those government schemes were to be implemented. Such orders have sought to define gradually, but in increasing detail, India's constitutional right to food and to hold the state accountable for instances of its violation.[131]

The Right to Education

In *Unni Krishnan v State of Andhra Pradesh*, the question before the Supreme Court was whether a citizen had the right to education for a medical, engineering, or other professional degree.[132] Referring to an earlier case, *Mohini Jain v State of Karnataka*,[133] the Supreme Court held that 'the right to education flows directly from the right to life'. According to the court, education – generally – had a fundamental significance in the life of an individual and the nation. Education brought enlightenment and dignity to an individual and transfigured human personality through a synthetic process of development of the body and enrichment of the mind. However, the question was about the content of such a right and how much and what level of education was necessary to make life meaningful. Answering that question, the Supreme Court contended that the right had to be construed in the light of the Directive Principles and the state had to provide for free education for every child up to 14 years. For children older than 14 years, the right to education was circumscribed by the limits of the economic capacity of the state and its development.

The state obligation encapsulated in the right to education could, so the Supreme Court held, be discharged by either establishing state institutions or by aiding, recognising and/or granting affiliation to private educational institutions. Higher education weighed heavily on national economic resources, so the state's obligation was not absolute and immediate. but relative and progressive. The state had to take steps to the maximum of its available resources to progressively achieve the full realisation of the right.[134]

131 The *PUCL* order of 28 November 2001 acted as a catalyst for the Right to Food and Work Campaign for Dignity and Survival and led to the National Food Security Act of 2013.

132 *Unni Krishnan v State of Andhra Pradesh*, AIR 1993 SC 217.

133 *Mohini Jain v State of Karnataka* (1992) 3 SCC 666.

134 The Right to Education Act of 2009 emerged from the Supreme Court judgement in *Unni Krishnan v State of Andhra Pradesh*. A constitutional amendment secured the right to education as a Fundamental Right in Article 21A. The Constitution (86th Amendment) Act of 2002. In *Society for Unaided Private Schools of Rajasthan v Union of India*, Kapadia CJ upheld the constitutional validity of the act so far as it applied to private non-minority schools and minority schools aided by the state.

Right to Adequate Medical Services

In *Paschim Banga Khet Mazdoor Samity v State of West Bengal*, a petitioner who had suffered serious head injuries and brain haemorrhage in an accident complained against medical authorities at various state-run hospitals in Calcutta who refused to admit him for emergency treatment.[135] The Supreme Court held that the constitution embodied the idea of a welfare state at the federal and state levels, with a primary government duty to secure general welfare by providing adequate medical facilities for its citizens. According to the court, Article 21 of the constitution imposed an obligation on the state to preserve and safeguard the right to life of every person. The court added that the state could not avoid its constitutional obligation to provide adequate medical services on account of financial constraints. The court insisted that a time-bound plan for providing these services had to be chalked out for ensuring availability of proper medical services. In particular, government hospitals and its medical officers had a duty to extend medical assistance for preserving human life. Failure on the part of a government hospital to provide timely medical treatment to a person in need of such treatment would result in violation of the right to life guaranteed under Article 21.

Politics of Public Interest Litigation

Public Interest Litigation interventions are seen as creating opportunities for Indian citizens to demand more social programs from the state, since many citizens may either not be aware of their rights or may be denied redressal through the political process. The Supreme Court's orders can create and enforce justiciable entitlements against the state by triggering legislative reform, and ensuring that existing state welfare programs are properly implemented. The Right the Education Act of 2009 and the National Food Security Act of 2013, for instance, are illustrations of the involvement of the Supreme Court in India's social policies.[136]

India since the 1990s

The Political and Social Context

The dominant role of the public sector in industrial development characterised Nehru's legacy and was associated with the goals of a self-reliant economy and a socialist pattern of society. But this vision was achieved at significant economic

135 *Paschim Banga Khet Mazdoor Samity v State of West Bengal* (1996) 4 SCC 37.

136 For a critique of the Public Interest Litigation movement see Madhav Khosla, 'Making Social Rights Conditional: Lessons from India' (2010) 8 International Journal of Constitutional Law 739; Arun K. Thiruvengadam, 'Revisiting *The Role of the Judiciary in Plural Societies (1987)*. A Quarter-Century Retrospective on Public Interest Litigation in India and the Global South' in Sunil Khilnani, Vikram Raghavan and Arun Thiruvengadam (eds), *Comparative Constitutionalism in South Asia* (Oxford University Press 2012) 341; Ruparelia (n 96) 115.

costs.[137] To address the problems of the Indian economy significant economic reforms occurred in the 1990s, which marked a departure from the approach to economic planning and development that had characterised the Nehru and Indira Gandhi periods. These reforms in the 1990s were the culmination of a prior period of contestations within the Congress party between the left wing and older congressmen who wished to continue Nehru's policy of self-reliance and Indira Gandhi's pro poor programme and those who wished to reform such policies. These contestations continued during the Janata party regime (1977–1980) and when the Congress won an electoral victory in 1980. Rajiv Gandhi (1985–1989) resorted to piecemeal changes, but still insisted that his government would continue the traditional approach of a mixed economy in which the public sector would control the 'commanding heights'. In 1985, the All India Congress Committee resolution also restated the Congress' commitment to the goal of achieving socialism.[138]

However, in May 1987, the Planning Commission circulated the text of a 'new industrial policy', proposing a package of incentives to the private sector for modernising certain basic industries.[139] This new policy constituted a break with past state policies favouring the public sector and the goal of economic self-reliance. The V.P. Singh government (1989–1990) which came to power after the Congress electoral defeat in 1989, attempted to adopt economic reforms (though without success) and the interim budget for 1991/1992 of Prime Minister Chandra Shekar's government (1990–1991) stated that in view of accumulated internal and external debt, only a comprehensive package of macro-economic adjustment would be a sustainable solution to the fiscal crisis in the next budget planned for May 1991.[140]

It was the economic reforms of the early 1990s led by Manmohan Singh, the finance minister under the Narasimha Rao government (1991–1996) and later prime minister of a Congress-led multi-party coalition government, the United Progressive Alliance (UPA 2004–2014), that finally led to increased economic progress. It has been noted: 'The robustness of high growth in India is undoubtedly connected with the economic reforms of the 1990s, which have built a solid foundation for continuing economic growth'.[141]

When the UPA won power in 2004, it not only prioritised rapid economic growth led by private investment, but also developed a narrative of 'inclusive development' that was for the common man. This approach, coupled with the left parties' alliance at the centre, influenced government policies that focussed

137 Public sector undertakings were characterised by a chronic shortfall of profits and inefficiencies. When Rajiv Gandhi became prime minister in 1984, both internal and external financial shortages showed signs of worsening.

138 Frankel (n 71) 586.

139 ibid 587.

140 ibid 589.

141 Drèze and Sen (n 46) 19.

on greater investments in providing social services, and enactment of legislation for a right to work, education, and the right to food during its two terms (2004–2009 and 2009–2014). It was under the UPA regime that a new welfare framework emerged based on rights legislation, though the foundation for the new 'entitlements' regime was the Supreme Court's jurisprudence in the 1980s and 1990s, expanding the interpretation of the right to life mentioned in Article 21 of the constitution.[142] Yet, the failures with respect to implementation that characterised the UPA's 'entitlements' regime encouraged parties such as the Bharatiya Janata Party (BJP) to express an alternative path to welfare when it came to power in 2014. The BJP's approach focussed on technology and direct cash transfers to redress failures in state capacity and to minimise its role. 'Aadhaar' and financial inclusion (through Aadhaar) were the key components.[143]

Economic Liberalisation and Rights-Based Welfare

The economic reforms of the early 1990s stimulated rapid growth, diversification, and technological change. But while aggregate economic prosperity increased public revenues, old social and sectoral inequalities were exacerbated. New vulnerabilities were created in the informal sector because of failings in the pattern of growth, distribution, and reform.[144] The political process in India, until the early 2000s, was relatively unresponsive to popular demands for improved social and economic welfare and accountability for improved delivery. Citizens were not empowered to place claims on the state and demand accountability for their implementation.[145]

The interaction between civil society activism and judicial interventions which evolved due to the state's failure to provide adequate social services to citizens, led to the emergence of enforceable social and economic rights through judicial interpretation that read Parts III and IV of the constitution together.[146] This development laid the foundation for legalisation of basic social 'entitlements' through rights-based legislation. Existing schemes from the pre-1990s period offered minimal protection, thus leaving room for an 'informal security regime' in which most citizens had to rely on supplemental informal

142 See p. 108 in this chapter.

143 Aadhaar enrolment occurred through the triple agenda of 'Jan-Dhan, Aadhaar, Mobile'. Direct transfer of benefits through technology was aimed at addressing issues of administrative failures in implementing welfare policies. See Yamini Aiyar, 'Maximum Schemes, Minimum Welfare' in Niraja Gopal Jayal (ed), *Re-forming India the Nation Today* (Viking 2019) 157, 160. For more details on 'Direct Cash Tansfers' see p. 121 in this chapter.

144 Amongst others, see Atul Kohli, *Poverty Amid Plenty in the New India* (Cambridge University Press 2012).

145 Yamini Aiyar and Michael Walton, *Rights, Accountability and Citizenship: Examining India's Emerging Welfare State* (Centre for Policy Research 2014).

146 See p. 107 in this chapter.

networks. The new rights-based welfare state changed the legal status of many people, providing formal social security for the first time.

The new rights-based welfare state has been viewed by some as part of a broader project of 'state building', in response to inefficiencies and corruption in social provisioning.[147] For others, the 'entitlements' regime embodied both the aspiration of delivering substantive social services and a deepening sense of 'citizenship'. It has been argued that if inclusion – civic, political, social, economic, and cultural – was the condition of full citizenship, then the public provision of welfare – whether through social and economic rights or through redistributive policies adopted by such regimes – can be a plausible way of creating such inclusivity and the emergence of the concept of 'social citizenship'.[148]

One important feature of the new rights-based welfare regime was the issue of institutional transparency and accountability. Mechanisms embedded in the legislated rights, such as social audits, grievance redressal systems, participatory planning, and the right to information, were the tools for building state capacity and accountability, since critics pointed out that a weak state infrastructure could impede implementation of such rights. Arguably, these mechanisms can also be viewed as creating opportunities for greater direct interactions between citizens and the state and could also reduce power asymmetries between them.

The basis, level, and scope of welfare entitlements varied. Different legislative acts recognised the rights of individuals as well as communities such as poor rural households. There was also a push towards 'universalism'. For instance, social policy instruments targeted not just industrial workers in the formal sector but the informal labour force in general. Additionally, instead of creating specific categories of beneficiaries as was done earlier (women, children, the elderly, mothers, people with disabilities, all living in poverty),[149]

147 The Right to Information Act of 2005 mandated all government agencies to release information regarding their activities to individual citizens upon request in a timely manner. The purpose of the 'Aadhaar' card was to give every resident of the country a Unique Identification Number (UID), to make sure entitlements reached their intended beneficiaries through direct cash transfers, beginning with pensions, scholarships, and maternity benefits. But critics feel that rights campaigns left untouched issues of inequalities of resources, of restructuring existing power structures, and of unequal social relations. See Neera Chandhoke, 'Democracy and wellbeing in India' in Yusuf Bangura (ed), *Democracy and Social Policy* (Palgrave Macmillan 2007) 164. For an analysis of the efficacy of rights legislation to provide for effective delivery of social services and for state transformation, see Aiyar and Walton (n 145).

148 Niraja Gopal Jayal, *Citizenship and its Discontents: An Indian History* (Harvard University Press 2013) chap 6. Jayal also posits a tension between the normative sense of substantive citizenship, in terms of which social provision can be seen as a moral imperative because substantive citizenship is incomplete in the presence of deep social inequality, and the policy sense, where redistributive taxation necessary for enforcing social rights can be viewed as diminishing the sense of a united civic community.

149 See p. 97 in this chapter.

new legislation created a universal right to primary education for all children between the ages of 6 and 14; insurance cover for rural and urban poor people was introduced, independent of employment status; and schemes such as the Rural Health Mission launched in 2005 envisaged creating universal access to equitable, affordable, and quality health care services.

Another important feature of the social policies is the focus on need: The state-funded social assistance schemes introduced in the 1990s were not based on principles of 'reciprocity' like the insurance schemes of the 1950s through the 1970s, but on covering basic needs. Benefits were not conditional on an individual's employment status and sector of work, but on status based on indicators such as poverty, geographical location, or familial relationship. Characteristic values underlying the new regime were social equity and human dignity; enlargement and enforcement of state responsibility for social welfare; state building; and creating legitimacy and modernisation.

After their 2014 electoral victory, the National Democratic Alliance (NDA) government under Narendra Modi adopted a narrative of welfare that it used to distinguish their welfare programs from the earlier UPA-led welfare schemes.[150] Though initially it was thought that the NDA would have a pro-market approach that would prioritise economic growth and roll back UPA-initiated welfare schemes, the NDA has actually adopted their own welfare agenda. The NDA government has done so by emphasising ideas such as 'maximum governance, minimum government' to reduce 'mindless populism' in favour of 'fiscal prudence',[151] and a political rhetoric of 'empowerment' as opposed to 'entitlement'. For example, in May 2015, while launching new social insurance schemes, Prime Minister Modi stated: 'Poor people don't need help. We have to change our thinking, . . . [and] way of functioning, the poor people need to be empowered . . . if they are empowered then they would be all geared up to fight poverty on their own strength'.[152]

However, the idea of 'empowerment' was never fully articulated. The NDA approach has also been criticised for its inner contradictions because despite the NDA's attempt to distinguish its approach from the UPA's welfare schemes, this approach has remained close to the earlier 'entitlements' vision. For instance, the BJP manifesto promised to expand education expenditure and ensure universal health coverage and to better implement the UPA's rights legislation. Moreover, on coming to power, the NDA's focus was not on dismantling the UPA 'entitlements' welfare system. Allocations in centrally sponsored schemes were only changed marginally. Under the NDA, the focus has been on improving existing delivery systems.[153]

150 Aiyar (n 143) 158.

151 This was stated by former Finance Minister Arun Jaitley during the preparation of his first budget, tabled in July 2014, quoted in Aiyar (n 143) 158.

152 Quoted ibid 160.

153 Aiyar (n 143).

Social Policy Instruments

Food Subsidies

Food subsidies help cope with the risks of hunger and malnutrition and historically, one of the key government responses was the distribution of food grains through the government controlled Public Distribution System. Established after World War II, it aimed to increase domestic agricultural production and improve food security.[154] Most of the food subsidy in India is now channelled to beneficiaries through the Targeted Public Distribution System to better target lower socio-economic groups. In December 2000 (expanded in 2003–2006), the Antyodaya Anna Yojana ('grain scheme for the downtrodden') further broadened the public distribution system. This expansion also included provision of food and goods to senior citizens and pensioners over 60 years, widows, the diseased, and infirm.

These measures to strengthen the Public Distribution System were reinforced through the introduction of the National Food Security Act of 2013, which provides subsidised food grains to 50 percent of the urban and 75 percent of the rural population. Monetary and nutritional support is mandated to pregnant and lactating women, and through the Integrated Child Development Services and Mid-Day Meal Schemes, malnourished children and those aged 6 months to 14 years were also covered. The National Food Security Act gave a legal standing to India's food safety network in accordance with the right to health and food under Article 21 of the constitution.[155] The act contains measures to prevent corruption, diversion, and leakages through better partnerships between the central and state governments.

Guarantee of Work

The National Rural Employment Guarantee Act of 2005 aims at enhancing the livelihood security of the rural population by guaranteeing 100 days of wage employment in a financial year to a rural household whose members volunteer to do unskilled manual work on community and infrastructure development projects. The act combines income transfers with initiatives intended to build capabilities of those below the poverty line by creating durable assets and

154 To facilitate distribution, the Food Corporation of India acts as a central nodal agency responsible for the procurement of food grains from farmers at a price that is often higher than market price. The individual state governments then procure the food grains at a subsidised price from the Food Corporation. These goods are then distributed to consumers via fair price or ration shops.

155 Neetu Abey George and Fiona H. McKay, 'The Public Distribution System and Food Security in India' (2019) 16(17) International Journal of Environmental Research and Public Health 3221. Under the National Food Security Act, 75 percent of the rural and 50 percent of the urban population are entitled to 5 kg food grains per month. Antyodaya Anna Yojana households are entitled to more.

strengthening the livelihood resource base of the rural poor. The act can be seen as a conditional cash transfer programme (cash for work). Adult members of a rural household may apply for such employment.[156] If employment is not provided within fifteen days, a daily unemployment allowance in cash has to be paid. At least one-third of persons to whom work is allotted have to be women. Wages are to be paid according to minimum wages for agricultural labourers in the state as prescribed under the Minimum Wages Act of 1948. Funding is shared between the central and state governments.

Social Assistance

The National Social Assistance Programme (NSAP) of 1995 was the first major social security programme begun in the post-liberalization era.[157] The general eligibility criterion is people living below the poverty line (BPL) though each component has further specific criteria. The programme provides immediate relief to the poor in case of vulnerabilities such as old age and widowhood, chronic need arising from conditions of disability, and contingencies such as death of the family's breadwinner. The types of benefits offered are cash and food. As there is no *quid pro quo*, this is an unconditional cash transfer program.

The National Social Assistance Programme seeks to comply with Article 41 of the Directive Principles and item 23 ('social security') in the Concurrent List. The programme is a fully funded centrally sponsored scheme. The NSAP schemes are mainly implemented by the Social Welfare departments of states and Union Territories in accordance with the general conditions applicable to all components of the National Social Assistance Programme as well as specific conditions applicable to each component.

Conditional Cash Transfers

The Janani Suraksha Yojana (JSY) targets reducing maternal and infant mortality by offering women cash rewards for delivering in public health centres, in accredited private health facilities, or at home with medical care. Sponsored by the central government, it integrates cash assistance with delivery and post-delivery care. Additionally, Accredited Social Health Activists (ASHAs) – women trained to liaise between pregnant females and public health facilities – are also given cash for encouraging women to deliver in hospitals.[158] The Indira Gandhi Matritva Sahyog Yojana (IGMSY) and the National Maternity Benefit

156 Such a household has to apply for registration to the local Gram Panchayat. After registration, a Job Card is issued to the household as a whole.

157 Government of India, Ministry of Rural Development, *National Social Assistance Programme (NSAP)*, <www.nsap.nic.in/nsap/NSAP-%20About%20us.pdf> accessed 28 February 2022.

158 Government of India, Ministry of Health & Family Welfare, <https://nhm.gov.in/index1.php?lang=1&level=3&lid=309&sublinkid=841> accessed 28 February 2022.

Scheme (NMBS) serve similar goals. The schemes provide cash benefits to pregnant women and women who have given birth if the women comply with health-related requirements.

Social Insurance for the Poor

Aam Aadmi Bima Yojana (AABY), launched in 2007, provides life insurance cover to the (rural and urban) poor, identified as those living below or marginally above the poverty line. The purpose of AABY is to prepare families in advance for the death or disability of the head of the family or another earning member of the household, between 18 and 59 years of age. The central government pays half of the insurance premium on behalf of beneficiaries and the other half is paid by the state government concerned, by a nodal agency, or by the member himself. Sums are paid to the nominees on their claims being presented to the relevant administrative agency.[159]

The Rashtriya Swasthya Bima Yojana (RSBY), launched in 2008, is a health insurance scheme covering unorganised sector workers in the below-the-poverty-line category and their family members (a family unit of five). The scheme provides health insurance cover of up to Rs 30,000 in hospitalization costs for five members of such families in public or private facilities. Beneficiaries are asked to pay only a nominal registration fee and the cost of the annual premium is shared by central and state governments while states are responsible for administrative costs.[160]

The NDA government under Narendra Modi added further schemes coined 'government sponsored socially oriented insurance schemes'. One important scheme is the Pradhan Mantri Jeevan Jyoti Bima Yojana (PMJJBY), available to all people between 18 and 50 years having a bank account and giving their consent to join, not just poor people in urban or rural areas. The risk covered by the insurance is death of the insured, due to any reason, at a relatively low premium (Rs 330 per annum). The scheme is primarily offered by the Life Insurance Corporation. Another important scheme is the Pradhan Mantri Suraksha Bima Yojana (PMSBY), available to people between 18 and 70 years, covering accidental death and full or partial disability at a premium of Rs 12 per annum. The scheme is primarily offered by the Public Sector General Insurance Companies.

159 Government of India, Life Insurance Corporation of India, *Annual Report 2012–13*, 60.

160 State governments engage in a competitive public bidding and select a public/private insurance company to provide health insurance in the state. The selected insurance company and district level officials are responsible for enrolment of such families and issuance of smart cards. A central list of enrolled households is the basis of financial transfers from the central to the state governments. Government of India, Ministry of Labour and Employment, *Annual Report 2012–13*, 3.

National Health Policy

India's national health policy comprises two important strands, which evolved over the last fifteen years. Earlier schemes envisioned delivery of medical services primarily through public providers. More recent schemes promote state-financed delivery of medical services through private providers. In that case, financing is based on state-purchased social insurance schemes.

A first significant step in promoting centrally sponsored national health services was the National Rural Health Mission (NRHM), launched in 2005 under the Congress-led UPA central government and intended to give financial support to schemes run by the states, who are – under the constitution – exclusively tasked with regulating and providing 'health care'. The (temporary) programme envisaged creating universal access to equitable, affordable, and quality health care services, since it was found that the rural public health care system in many states imposed an unfair financial burden on women, scheduled castes and tribes, and poor households. The key features included making the public health delivery system fully functional and accountable to the community, de-centralisation, rigorous monitoring and evaluation of standards, and flexible financing. Within broad national parameters and priorities, states had the flexibility to plan and implement state specific action plans, though the fund flow to the states was centrally prescribed. In 2013, the central government launched the National Urban Health Mission (NUHM) and created the National Health Mission as an umbrella for both the NRHM and NUHM.

In 2018, the NDA government launched a new programme called National Health Protection Scheme (NHPS) or the Ayushman Bharat Yojana (also known as Modi-care).[161] The aim was again to improve access, quality, and affordability of medical services, in particular for the poor. The programme created Health & Wellness Centres (HWCs) to deliver comprehensive primary health care, universal and free to users, with a focus on wellness and the delivery of an expanded range of services closer to the community. The services extend beyond maternal and child health care services and include care-giving for non-communicable diseases, palliative and rehabilitative care, mental health care, free essential drugs, and diagnostic services. In order to finance secondary and tertiary care by way of hospitalisation, the government relied on the mechanism of a state-financed (social) insurance, such as RSBY, providing coverage of up to Rs 5 lakh (about 7,800 US$, compared to Rs 30,000 under the RSBY) to roughly 100 million poor families or 500 million beneficiaries, identified through a socio-economic caste census (about 40 percent of India's

161 Government of India, *Ministry of Health and Family Welfare, National Health Policy 2017* (Government of India 2017); Shalendra D. Sharma, 'Health Care for India's 500 Million: The Promise of the National Health Protection Scheme' (2018) 18 Harvard Public Health Review 1; Shailender Kumar Hooda, 'Health System in Transition in India. Journey from State Provisioning to Privatization' (2020) 11 World Review of Political Economy 506.

population). Beneficiaries receive an insurance card linked to the Aadhar card that gives access to services from enlisted hospitals without any payment upfront. If the programme lives up to political expectations, it is indeed 'the world's largest government-funded health care programme', as proclaimed by the NDA government.

Social Security for Unorganised Workers

The Unorganised Workers Social Security Act of 2008 (UWSSA) was to provide for social security of unorganised workers on par with the organised sector. The act aimed to cover disparities between the unorganised and the organised workers with respect to minimum wages, social security benefits, and proper working conditions. The act was a contrast to most labour laws in India which are not universal and are applicable for particular types of work, employment relationships, sizes, and establishment.

The UWSSA incorporated existing social security schemes, such as schemes provided by the National Social Assistance Programme (benefits for the elderly, benefits for families), the Janani Suraksa Yojana (medical care for women prior to and after delivery), and various social insurance schemes for the poor (Aam Aadmi Yojana; Rashtriya Swasthya Bima Yojana).[162] But the central government had the discretion to formulate other suitable welfare schemes – for life insurance and disability cover; health and maternity benefits; and old age protection. The state governments were given the discretion to determine schemes regarding provident funds; employment injury benefits; housing; old age homes etc. Such schemes would be funded by the central government; jointly by the central and state governments; or partly funded through contributions from the beneficiaries of the scheme or employers. The central government was to constitute a National Social Security Board (consisting of the Union Minister of Labour and Employment, representatives of the unorganised sector workers, and employers) to recommend suitable schemes for different sections of unorganised workers, as would the states.[163]

After the NDA government came to power, an additional scheme was introduced at the central level in 2015, the Atal Pension Yojana (APY).[164] The APY is a co-contributory pension scheme to encourage workers in unorganised sector to voluntarily save for their retirement. Although the APY is primarily focused on workers in the unorganised sector, all citizens of the country between 18 and 40 years can join through their bank accounts. A minimum

162 See p. 118 in this chapter.

163 For an analysis of the working of the act see Tina Dutta and Parthapratim Pal, 'Politics Overpowering Welfare: Unorganised Workers' Social Security Act 2008' (2012) 47 Economic & Political Weekly 26.

164 For details of Atal Pension Yojana see <https://npscra.nsdl.co.in/nsdl/scheme-details/APY_Brochure.pdf> accessed 28 February 2022.

pension is guaranteed by the central government to the subscriber at the age of 60 years, with a minimum monthly contribution. The central government participates in the making of contributions.

Social Security

The Code on Social Security of 2020 (the 'Code') was passed by Parliament in September 2020. The Code merges existing labour laws such as the Employees' Compensation Act of 1923, the Employees' State Insurance Act of 1948, the Employees' Provident Funds and Miscellaneous Provisions Act of 1952, the Maternity Benefit Act of 1961, the Payment of Gratuity Act of 1972, and the Unorganised Workers Social Security Act of 2008. The state governments' primary responsibility for the formulation and implementation of social security schemes for unorganised sector workers has been reformulated into different jurisdictions for both central and state governments to formulate such schemes.

While the enactment of the Code seems a big step in Indian social policies, the Code has – in fact – not interwoven different social security schemes into one synchronised social security legislation. Rather, the Code appears as a collection of existing legislations without meaningful integration: There still exist centrally sponsored funds for unorganised sector workers' social security which are outside the purview of the Code. Hence, there is a proliferation of organisational structures which is not based on the principle of pooling of resources and risk profiles. Creating an administrative duality between central and state government social security measures with multiple funds and schemes could add to fragmentation of the social security regimes. Additionally, the Code and the rules make no mention of how and when existing social security schemes for unorganised workers will be funded.[165] There is also no arrangement for interstate coordination in the case of certain mobile segments of unorganised workers such as those in the building and construction sectors who tend to move across state borders. In short, the title of the act notwithstanding, the Code does not advance the universalisation of social security in India.

Direct Benefit Transfer

Direct Benefit Transfer (DBT) is the name of a programme or a method that echoes a more general trend to use information technology (also) for social policy purposes. The idea of 'direct benefit transfer' was widely discussed around

165 The National Social Security Fund (NSSF, created in 2010 under the Unorganised Workers Social Security Act of 2008, now merged with the Code) was to be used for schemes formulated for the welfare of unorganised sector workers as recommended by a committee. The funds were to be transferred from the Consolidated Fund of India to the NSSF. Santosh Mehrotra and Kingshuk Sarkar, 'Social Security Code, 2020 and Rules. A critique' (2021) 56(12) Economic and Political Weekly.

2010, and eventually picked up by the UPA government.[166] The NDA government under Modi expanded and strengthened the idea, in particular during the COVID-19 pandemic.[167] At its heart, the method is based on a technology platform, combining three elements, namely Jan Dhan Yojana (a bank account for each household in India), a unique 12-digital identification number carrying biometrical data (Aadhaar), and mobiles (for notifications of bank transfers, for making payments from bank account, ie making use of digital money, and for all sorts of communications). Hence, the technology platform is called the JAM trinity, a term invented by the NDA government.

When the UPA government launched the of idea of direct cash payments, the programme was meant to substitute in-kind benefits for cash benefits, to abolish price subsidies (for food, electricity, water, fertilisers), and – regarding existing cash benefits – to alter the mode of making payments from relying on intermediaries (postal services, panchayat offices) to directly addressing beneficiaries. In the context of social policy, the main target was the Public Distribution System that provides food grains to the poor through a system of specified low-price shops. The system is India's largest poverty-reduction programme, but also known for enormous leakages. Huge amounts of food grains meant to reach below-the-poverty-line families are sold (profitably) on the open market (rice mafia), and there is also the problem of fake card attesting eligibility.[168] Hence, the overall goal was to combat corruption and to rationalise anti-poverty schemes and thus save money. In 2019, the method of Direct Benefit Transfer also extended to the wages payable under the National Rural Employment Guarantee Act and the National Social Assistance Programme.[169] In the latter context, the method primarily serves targeting, in other words, making sure that the benefits only reach eligible beneficiaries.

166 See Government of India, Economic Survey 2013–2014 (Government of India) 94, <www.indiabudget.gov.in/budget2014-2015/es2013-14/echap-05.pdf> accessed 28 February 2022.

167 The first Economic Survey under the NDA government announced the intention to continue the push towards extension of the programme, contending that – as of early 2015 – 757 million Indians had been bio-identified and 139 million bank accounts had been created. Government of India, *Economic Survey 2014–15*, vol 1 (Government of India 2015) 9, <www.indiabudget.gov.in/budget2015-2016/es2014-15/echapter-vol1.pdf> accessed 28 February 2022. In 2021 and at the height of the pandemic, the NDA government stated that – because of Direct Benefit Transfer – 'the country could transfer money in crores of accounts through a click of button during the pandemic time'. Government of India, *Economic Survey 2020–21*, vol 2 (Government of India 2021) 37, <www.indiabudget.gov.in/budget2021-22/economicsurvey/index.php> accessed 28 February 2022.

168 See eg Himanshu and Abhijit Sen, 'In-Kind Food Transfers – I: Impact on Poverty' (2013) 48(45/46) Economic & Political Weekly 46; Silvia Masiero, 'Will the JAM Trinity Dismantle the PDS?' (2015) 50(45) Economic & Political Weekly 21.

169 Government of India, *Economic Survey 2018–19*, vol 1 (Government of India 2019) 3, <www.indiabudget.gov.in/budget2019-20/economicsurvey/index.php> accessed 28 February 2022.

Even though about 90 percent of India's residents by now have their Aadhaar cards carrying their unique 12-digit Aadhaar number, and the government strongly favours the method of direct benefit transfers, it seems unclear whether the efforts made have led to the success that the government was hoping for. The programme has been criticised from early on, and not only from the point of view of the right to privacy.[170] For one, having a bank account makes sense only when used but it seems that many accounts remain empty, for a number of reasons (lack of access to technologies; lack of availability of technologies; preference for cash to make ends meet). For another, the National Food Security Act is still implemented primarily through the Public Distribution System for in-kind benefits. While the UPA and NDA governments wished to transfer food subsidies to bank accounts of the beneficiaries who were then expected to buy food grains from the open market, by 2019, only very few localities made use of the cash transfer mode.[171] Finally, and more fundamentally, the replacement of in-kind benefits (food grains) creates new vulnerabilities, for instance, due to inflation, or power inequalities in household relations that disadvantage women and female children.[172] In short, the implementation of the programme has not (yet) met the goals set by the various governments involved.

Conclusions

The emergence of social policies in Europe was the result of the acknowledgement of a political responsibility for the welfare of citizens and constituted the compatibility of capitalism and democracy. However, its legitimating reasons, specific goals, and institutional realisations varied.[173] This chapter considers the

170 See eg Jayati Ghosh, 'Cash Transfers as the Silver Bullet for Poverty Reduction. A Skeptical Note' (2011) 46(21) Economic & Political Weekly 67; Peter Svedberg, 'Reforming or Replacing the Public Distribution System with Cash Transfers?' (2012) 47(7) Economic & Political Weekly 53; R.K.A. Subrahmanya, 'Social Protection of the Workers in the Unorganized Sector' (2013) 48 Indian Journal of Industrial Relations 460; Dipa Sinha, 'Cash for Food. A Misplaced Idea' (2015) 50(16) Economic & Political Weekly 17. Speaking out in favour of direct cash benefits eg Devesh Kapur, Partha Mukhopadhyay and Arvind Subramanian, 'The Case for Direct Cash Transfers to the Poor' (2008) 43(15) Economic & Political Weekly 37; Devesh Kapur, Partha Mukhopadhyay and Arvind Subramanian, 'More on Direct Cash Transfers' (2008) 43(47) Economic & Political Weekly 85.

171 Government of India, *Economic Survey 2019–20*, vol 2 (Government of India 2020) 211, <www.indiabudget.gov.in/budget2020-21/economicsurvey/index.php> accessed 28 February 2022.

172 See the ethnographic account by Emilija Zabiliūte, ' "Cards Are for Showing Off". Aesthetics of Cashlessness and Intermediation among the Urban Poor in Delhi' in Atreyee Sen, Johan Lindquist and Marie Kolling (eds), *Who's Cashing In? Contemporary Perspectives on New Monies and Global Cashlessness* (Berghahn Books 2020) 73.

173 Franz-Xaver Kaufmann, *European Foundation of the Welfare State* (Berghahn Books 2012) 20, 42. The underlying assumption is that the welfare state is a kind of consensual definition of a society's 'legal and therefore formal and explicit responsibility for the basic well-being of all of its members'. Harry K. Girvetz, 'Welfare State' in David L. Sills (ed), *International Encyclopedia of the Social Sciences*, vol 16 (The Macmillan Company & The Free Press 1968) 512.

development of social policies in India by focusing on the political, social, and economic circumstances in which the policies were made, by examining state responses (primarily through constitutional amendments, statutory law, government regulations, and judgements), and by elaborating on the ideas and values informing such action and the content of the law.

It is only since the economic reforms of the 1990s that a tenuous social security regime started to emerge in India. The chapter traces this delayed emergence back to the British period. During this period, despite periodic studies by investigative committees appointed by the Indian legislative assembly, Royal commissions, ministerial conferences, ILO reports, and precedents such as the Beveridge Report of 1942, a comprehensive system of national social welfare did not emerge. The unrepresentative and unjust administrative and legal framework primarily furthered imperial interests rather than the welfare of the Indian people. Lack of economic development, restricted public financial resources, poverty, illiteracy, and lack of organisation of workers and other vulnerable groups were factors responsible for the failure of a national welfare regime to emerge. Though schemes such as the centrally legislated Workmen's Compensation Act (1923), the Employees' State Insurance Act (1948), or provincial maternity benefits laws emerged, there were almost no provisions for financial contributions by the state nor were benefits tax-based. Contributions were made primarily by the employers and employees and intended to meet certain contingencies such as sickness, unemployment, or maternity. The schemes primarily targeted industrial workers. Inadequate statistical data and the unwillingness on the part of the central and provincial governments to bear an additional financial burden often caused schemes to fail.

The nationalist discourse and attempts at constitutional drafting that emerged during the colonial period such as the Commonwealth of India Bill (1925), the Nehru report (1923), and the Karachi Resolution (1931) did respond to widespread social and economic hardships. Different perspectives (ranging from communist thinking to Gandhian and Nehruvian thought) emerged on state-society relations. But the idea of an adequate system of social welfare did not play an important role in such debates, which primarily concentrated on the political revolution and the idea of securing political independence from British rule.

Similarly, during the period of drafting the constitution, the dominant focus was on building a modern nation state, with representative and responsible forms of government rather than creating a national welfare regime. However, there was also thinking by Nehru and the Congress socialists on state responsibility for promoting economic progress and social transformation, influenced by the ideas of Marx, T.H. Green, Laski, and the Webbs. Nehru's pragmatic approach – a state-sponsored welfare regime required certain preconditions such as a stable and united political community based on a representative and responsible form of government, social restructuring, and economic progress – ultimately prevailed. The constitution created the foundations of a democratic constitution with a socialist bias. The possibility of social welfare measures was left open to future politics and democratic processes. Consequently, state responsibilities for the welfare of citizens were not inserted as citizens' entitlements against the state. Rather, they took the form of guidelines for state action in the Directive Principles. The concept of 'welfare' that emerges from the Principles included the state directing its policies to securing 'adequate means of livelihood', the right to work, a living wage, decent conditions of work, maternity relief, securing the health of workers, women, and children, and free education to children. Most of the Principles required the state to 'endeavour' to reach these goals. Article 41 mentioned that there can be 'limits of its [the state's] economic capacity and development' when attempting to reach these goals.

The ratification of the constitution saw the emergence of a liberal democratic constitutional system. But creating a formal social welfare system was again – and for many decades – subordinated to the enterprise of nation building, economic growth and development, as a necessary precondition to the emergence of a national welfare state. Along with socialist ideas, Gandhian thinking, and his critique of modern industrialised societies influenced policy makers. Up to the 1970s, the Nehruvian approach to economic development tried to find an alternative to a capitalist mode in the form of a 'scientific' Soviet style state planning, and an incremental and non-violent method for economic and social progress. This approach focused on principles of state responsibility for nation building and economic planning, and social restructuring through legal means in order to lay the foundations of a socialist pattern of society. Such a society would be characterised by state ownership of the means of production and equitable distribution of wealth. A primary influence on state social policy were the Directive Principles in Part IV. Even though no social welfare measures that were state-sponsored or tax-financed emerged during this period, certain social welfare goals were enunciated in the Five Year Plans. 'Special care' provisions in the constitution for backward classes were strengthened, and certain statutory provisions were enacted for the granting of some social benefits to industrial labour.

However, by the 1970s, promises given by the Congress government to provide basic needs such as food, housing, education, and health care could not be met. Such failures created ideological conflict within the Congress party. The party split and the re-election of Indira Gandhi's Congress faction in the 1971 elections on the strength of political slogans such as 'Garibi Hatao' saw a more authoritarian trend in politics and the passage of key constitutional amendments such as the 24th and 25th amendments (1971) and the 42nd amendment (1976). These changes sought to protect social reforms legislation purporting to give effect to the Directive Principles from judicial scrutiny on grounds of violation of the Fundamental Rights.

The conflict between such legislation intending to give effect to certain Directive Principles and Fundamental Rights was eventually resolved by the Supreme Court through decisions such as *Kesavananda Bharati* and *Minerva*

Mills making a harmonious balance between Parts III and IV a part of the basic structure of the constitution. Moreover, the court was also willing to read Directive Principles into Fundamental Rights, most notably the 'right to life' under Article 21 of the constitution. Hence, it was the Supreme Court who took the first step toward welfare entitlements, allowing civil society groups to voice their discontent and raise various demands under the 'right to life' (public interest litigation).

The economic crisis of the early 1990s facilitated the passage of economic reforms under Manmohan Singh that paved the way for faster economic growth. The economic progress caused the Congress-led UPA coalition government (2004–2014) to not only prioritise rapid economic growth, but to develop a goal of 'inclusive development' for all citizens. There was no longer an excuse of lack of resources for not enacting a state-sponsored welfare regime. The court's activist jurisprudence from the 1980s and 1990s had laid the foundation for the emergence of an 'entitlements' approach to welfare during the UPA regime, prompting legislation on the right to food, on primary education, and on the right to earn a living. The 'entitlements' approach created a social security regime based on formal rights to state-sponsored and tax-financed benefits which changed the status of citizens vis-à-vis the state and the deepening of a sense of 'social citizenship' based on political, social, and economic inclusivity. Processes within welfare legislation such as social audits, grievance redressal systems, participatory planning, and the right to information, attempted to build state capacity, transparency, and accountability, which also empowered citizens against the state.

For the first time, the universalisation of benefits securing basic needs became a political goal. In contrast to the social welfare measures taken by the government in the periods of the 1950s and 1970s, welfare entitlements under the UPA were state-sponsored and tax-financed, and not primarily based on contributions by employers and employees. Both conditional and unconditional schemes emerged as well as social assistance programmes to provide immediate relief to the poor living below the poverty line in case of certain vulnerabilities. Additionally, the UPA's welfare policies were not based on the principle of 'reciprocity' like the schemes that characterised the earlier periods but on 'need'.

The NDA's welfare approach has tried to distinguish itself from the UPA regime. The NDA approach emphasised minimising state involvement in promoting welfare and used the rhetoric of 'empowerment' as opposed to 'entitlements'. However, despite the new rhetoric, the NDA's approach remains close to the UPA's 'entitlements' vision. The NDA did not attempt to dismantle the welfare regime put in place under the UPA government. Instead, the NDA government focused on improving existing delivery systems, favouring 'direct benefit transfers' over in-kind benefits (food grains), with mixed results at best. Apart from emphasising delivery, the NDA government continued the push towards universalisation, in particular in the field of low premium social insurance schemes and medical care services. In 2020, the NDA government, in an attempt to streamline the administrative framework for implementing welfare provisions and to consolidate existing labour laws and social legislation, enacted the Social Security Code, a political move that assembled all important statutes enacted since independence within a single framework titled 'social security', a term that had not been used by lawmakers earlier.

Thus, the UPA and NDA governments have seen the emergence of a legal and constitutional framework of welfare entitlements which citizens can enforce against the state, and which now marks a significant progress towards the creation of a comprehensive and universal state-sponsored welfare regime which was delayed in the periods of the 1950s and 1970s. But weak state capacity and delivery systems and the lack of a coherent and consistent vision of the ruling parties for such a welfare regime has adversely affected an effective implementation of this new welfare regime's ultimate goals.

Chapter 5

Law and Social Policy in South Africa

From Untold Suffering and Injustice to a Future Based on Human Rights

Letlhokwa George Mpedi

Introduction

The object of Chapter 5 is to provide some perspectives on law and social policies in South Africa over three critical political phases in the history of that country, ie, the Union of South Africa (1910 to 1961), the Republic of South Africa (1961 to 1994), and the post-apartheid Republic of South Africa (1994 to date). The overall aim is to examine the ideas underlying social rights and values in South Africa. To achieve these objectives, the paper first reviews the prevalent approaches to law and social policies by the Union of South Africa government and the pertinent social questions (eg, land question, race problem, and poor White problem) it sought to address. It then proceeds with an analysis of the laws and social policies promulgated during the Republic of South Africa period and their influence on the apartheid system and associated legacies. This section of the chapter is followed by a discussion on laws and social policies in the post-apartheid South Africa with a particular emphasis on the role of, *inter alia*, constitutional values, social rights, courts, and pertinent social security laws in shaping social policies in South Africa.

Union of South Africa (1910 to 1961)

The Formation of the Union of South Africa

The Union of South Africa (*Unie van Suid-Afrika* in Afrikaans) (hereinafter the Union) came into existence on 31 May 1910[1] pursuant to the Union of South Africa Act of 1909,[2] which amalgamated the British territories (Cape of

1 See, for further reading on the Union of South Africa, Robert H. Brand, *The Union of South Africa* (Oxford at the Clarendon Press 1909).

2 The Union of South Africa Act was passed through both Houses of the Imperial Parliament exactly as it was forwarded after the South African Convention was held. The act was assented to by King Edward VII on 20 September 1909; and a Royal Proclamation of 2 December 1909 declared the date of the establishment of Union of South Africa to be 31 May 1910.

DOI: 10.4324/9781003242826-5

Good Hope and Natal) and the two Boer Republics (namely, Orange River Colony and Transvaal).[3] The political unification of the four colonies came out of a National Convention, which took place on 12 October 1908 and concluded its work on 11 May 1909.[4] Only White leaders attended the National Convention.[5] In the main, the British and the Boers were looking only after their own interests. For instance, the engagements that led to the drafting of the Union of South Africa Act and the formation of the Union of South Africa excluded Blacks (ie Africans, Coloureds [*Kleurlinge* in Afrikaans][6] and Indians).[7] This led to protest action by the aforementioned group.[8]

The government structure of the Union of South Africa was analogous to that found in other British Dominions. Accordingly, a governor-general represented the Monarch. Section 8 of the Union of South Africa Act provided

3 Section 4 of the Union of South Africa Act of 1909.

4 Gail Nattrass, *A Short History of South Africa* (Jonathan Ball Publishers 2017) 137.

5 ibid.

6 The Encyclopaedia Britannica (Encyclopaedia Britannica, 'Coloured people' – accessed at www.britannica.com/topic/Coloured [28 February 2022]) defines a Coloured person as follows: 'Coloured, formerly Cape Coloured, a person of mixed European ("White") and African ("Black") or Asian ancestry, as officially defined by the South African government from 1950 to 1991. Individuals assigned to this classification originated primarily from 18th- and 19th-century unions between men of higher and women of lower social groups: for instance, between White men and slave women or between slave men and Khoekhoe [Khoikhoi] or San women. The slaves were from Madagascar, the Malayan archipelago, Sri Lanka, and India. In early 20th-century South Africa, the word "Coloured" was a social category rather than a legal designation and typically indicated a status intermediate between those who were identified as "White" and those who were identified as "Black". The classification was largely arbitrary, based on family background and cultural practices as well as physical features. Most South Africans who identified themselves as Coloured spoke Afrikaans and English, were Christians, lived in a European manner, and affiliated with Whites. Many lived in Cape Town, its suburbs, and rural areas of Western Cape Province. Significant numbers also lived in Port Elizabeth and elsewhere in Eastern Cape province and in Northern Cape province. In Cape Town and Port Elizabeth, they represented the middle and working classes and were employed as teachers, clerks, shopkeepers, artisans, and other skilled workers. Those living outside the towns were mostly labourers on White-owned farms. A Muslim minority, the so-called Cape Malays, lived mostly in separate communities and married among themselves for religious reasons. Until World War II there was considerable intermarriage between lighter-skinned Coloureds and Whites, and many individuals were absorbed into the White community. Severe apartheid laws established in 1948, however, immediately subjected Coloured individuals to a rigid separation of occupational opportunities, the abolition of voting rights in Cape Province, and laws that prohibited (until 1985) intermarriage and sexual relations with other groups. In the 1950s a further series of laws disenfranchised many Coloured individuals, confiscated their land, and forced them to relocate to less desirable areas. The designation "Coloured" and all restrictions based upon it were abolished in the 1990s as the apartheid system was dismantled and the legal classification system was abandoned'. See, for further reading on the Coloured people, Len Bloom, 'The coloured people of South Africa' (1960) 28 Phylon 139.

7 'The formation of the SANNC/ANC', <www.sahistory.org.za/article/formation-sanncanc> accessed 28 February 2022.

8 ibid.

that: 'The Executive Government of the Union is vested in the King, and shall be administered by His Majesty in person or by a governor-general as His representative'. The legislative power of the Union vested in the Parliament of the Union.[9] The Parliament of the Union had the power to enact laws for 'the peace, order and good government'.[10] English and Dutch languages were the official languages of the Union of South Africa.[11] This represented the two languages spoken by the two European groups in the Union.[12] Accordingly, they were treated on a footing of equality and possessed and enjoyed equal freedom, rights, and privileges. According to Section 137 of the Union of South Africa Act, 'all records, journals, and proceedings of Parliament shall be kept in both languages, and all Bills, Acts, and notices of general public importance or interest issued by the Government of the Union shall be in both languages'. This discriminated against native languages and rendered laws and policies inaccessible to the vast Black majority of the population of the Union.

Key Social Questions

The Land Question

The Union of South Africa legalised land dispossession through the Natives Land Act 27 of 1913.[13] This law criminalised the purchase or hire by Natives of land owned by non-Natives. It resulted in a meagre 7 percent of the land allocated to Africans, as the so-called Native reserves, while the rest of arable land was reserved for Whites.[14] It disempowered and drove the Natives straight into further destitution. The Natives Land Act was a key component of 'a series of laws [enacted] to deprive the African of his dependent means of subsistence, his cattle and his land, and to strip him of every possession except his labour power'.[15] It is over a century since this legislation has come into effect. However, its effects, which include poverty and inequality, are still discernible in present-day South Africa.[16]

9 Section 19 of the Union of South Africa Act.
10 Section 59 of the Union of South Africa Act.
11 Section 137 of the Union of South Africa Act.
12 Margaret Cornell, 'The Statutory Background of Apartheid: A Chronological Survey of South African Legislation' (1960) 16 The World Today 181, 182.
13 Assented to on 16 June 1913 and came into effect of 30 June 1913. See, for further reading, Harvey M. Feinberg, 'The 1913 Native Land Act in South Africa: Politics, Race, and Segregation in the early 20th Century' (1993) 26 The International Journal of African Historical Studies 65.
14 Cherryl Walker, *The Land Question in South Africa. 1913 and Beyond* (Oxford Research Encyclopedia of African History 2017) 2.
15 William P. Van Schoor, *The Origin and Development of Segregation in South Africa* (Unity Movement History Series 1951) 20–21.
16 See, for example, Ruth Hall, 'The Legacies of the Natives Land Act of 1913' (2014) 113 Scriptura 1.

The Race Problem

Race relations in South Africa have always been complicated – particularly since the settlement of Europeans in that part of the world.[17] The Europeans, particularly the nationalists, were determined to dominate the Natives and non-Whites who lived in the Union.[18] There were various reasons for this stance. For instance, Whites (Europeans or *blankes* in Afrikaans)[19] were of the view that they were the superior race that brought Christianity and European civilisation to a dark continent.[20] The White supremacists believed that Natives were on earth to serve the Whites.[21] Furthermore, they viewed Natives as an inferior race,[22] child-like,[23] and, thus, in need of guidance and control of the Europeans. This thinking is closely linked to the 'European trusteeship of the Natives' approach followed at that time.[24] It is a close associate of the notions of separation and segregation in that they are a part of the so-called old traditional standpoint,[25] namely: '[S]egregation, separation and trusteeship as

17 See, for example, Aborigines Protection Society, *The Native Question in South Africa: Outlines of a Suggested Charter for Natives under British Rule in South Africa* (Submitted to Her Majesty's Government on behalf of the Aborigines Protection Society 1900); Alice Werner, 'The Native Question in South Africa' (1905) 4 Journal of the Royal African Society 441; Jan C Smuts, 'Problems in South Africa' (1917) 16 Journal of the Royal African Society 273; Earl Buxton, 'South Africa and its Native Problem' (1921) 20 Journal of the Royal African Society 161; Patrick Duncan, 'Race Questions in South Africa' (1927) Foreign Affairs 293; Max Yergan, 'The Status of the Native in South Africa' (1939) 24 The Journal of Negro History 44; William O. Brown, 'White Dominance in South Africa: A Study in Social Control' (1940) 18 Social Forces 406; Heaton Nicholls, 'South African Native Policy' (1945) 44 African Affairs 73; Margaret Ballinger, 'South African native policies' (1950) 49 African Affairs 32; Feinberg (n 13) 65.

18 The so-called proper handling of the race problem was perceived as 'a matter of life and death to the inhabitants of South Africa'. After all, Whites were outnumbered five to one. Robert H. Brand, *The Union of South Africa* (Oxford at the Clarendon Press 1909) 98 and 100. See, for further reading, Brown (n 17) 406.

19 Elizabeth S. Landis, 'South Africa Apartheid Legislation I: Fundamental Structure' (1961) 71 The Yale Law Journal 1, 4.

20 See, for instance, Johannes J. Venter, 'H.F. Verwoerd: Foundational Aspects of his Thought' (1999) 64 Koers 415, 417.

21 See Venter (n 20) 439.

22 Brand (n 1) 97.

23 For instance, Brand ([n 1] 110–111), reflecting on the sentiments of that era, argued that a Native 'cannot be treated as an equal or as a child. But in the complexity of modern civilization it must be confessed that at present he is more of a child than a man'. Buxton ([n 17] 173) referred to Natives as 'these Child Races of the Empire' which 'are a great asset, but also a grave responsibility'. Smuts, commenting on the African race, averred that: 'This type has some wonderful characteristics. It has largely remained a child-type, with a child psychology and outlook. A child-like human cannot be a bad human, for are we not in spiritual matters bidden to be like unto little children?' Jan C. Smuts, 'Native Policy in Africa' (1930) 29 Journal of the Royal African Society 248, 249.

24 Union of South Africa, Debates of the House of Assembly (Second Session – Ninth Parliament (20th January to 12th June, 1945) (Parliamentary Printers 1945) 5428, 5631, 5671, 6886.

25 ibid 5428.

far as non-Europeans and concerned'.[26] Premised on the so-called Christian guardianship[27] ideology, the White supremacists went as far as using religious scriptures to justify their views. For instance, Afrikaners ('*Boers*' or farmers),[28] descendants of the Dutch settlers and French Huguenots refugees, deemed themselves as God's chosen race.[29] This reasoning was fundamental to their justification of their racial domination doctrine. Nationalists, who rose to power in 1948, such as Dr DF Malan viewed the notion of treating Natives as equals as a 'Black menace' that had to be fought.[30] Strengthened by the parliamentary sovereignty principle, the Parliament of the Union enacted a variety of laws[31] to ensure White dominance over all aspects of the lives of non-Whites.[32]

26 ibid.

27 Landis (n 19) 2.

28 ibid 4.

29 Christopher W.M. Gell 'Hard Choices in South Africa' (1953) 31 Foreign Affairs 287, 292–293 points out: 'Biblical fundamentalists and Calvinist predestinarians by religion, the Afrikaners explicitly reject the doctrine of "the equal and inalienable rights of all members of the human family", which forms part of the U.N. Declaration of Human Rights. They are certain, on the contrary, that a man gets what he deserves only when it is allotted to him by God. In their surroundings the Afrikaner settlers found abundant justification for their conviction that "everyone should be treated according to what God ordained for him after the pattern of inequality which He Himself created". Early and naturally, their consciousness of being chosen took on a racial aspect. Genesis IX 25 ("a servant of servants") and Joshua IX 23–27 ("hewers of wood and drawers of water") were cited as scriptural sanction for the view that "God not only willed the existence of different races with different functions, but gave to each people a specified epoch and a place in which to live". All available evidence supported the view that South Africa had been selected for the Afrikaner people to rule'.

30 Gell (n 29) 292.

31 These laws, which formed legislative foundation for segregation (*segregasie* in Afrikaans) and the apartheid system, include the following: Immorality Act 5 of 1927 (prohibited illicit carnal intercourse between Europeans and Natives), Prohibition of Mixed Marriages Act 55 of 1949 (proscribed marriages between Whites and other races), Immorality Amendment Act 21 of 1950 (prohibited adultery, attempted adultery, or related immoral acts (extra-marital sex) between White and Black people), Population Registration Act 30 of 1950 (created a national race register and the Race Classification Board), Group Areas Act 41 of 1950 (created different residential areas for different races), Native Building Workers Act 27 of 1951 (made it a criminal offence for Bantu to perform skilled work in urban areas except in sections designed for Black occupation), Bantu Authorities Act 68 of 1951 (made provision for the homelands), Native Labour (Settlement of Disputes) Act 48 of 1953 (prohibited strike action by Blacks), Bantu Education Act 47 of 1953 (made provision for racially segregated education facilities), Native (Prohibition of Interdicts) Act 64 of 1956 (denied Blacks an opportunity to appeal to the courts against forced removals), and Extension of University Education Act 45 of 1959 (stopped Black students from attending White universities). See, for an analysis of a selection of statutes which supported apartheid by defining the fundamental relations between Whites and non-Whites, Landis (n 19) 1.

32 See, for example, Tameshnie Deane, 'Understanding the Need for Anti-Discrimination Legislation in South Africa' (2005) 11 Fundamina 2, 4–11; Landis (n 19) 1 and Cornell (n 12) 181.

Social Security

Preliminary Observations

The earnest Union of South Africa's social security construction efforts are traceable back to the late 1920s.[33] These endeavours, which were energised by among others the great depression and the seminal work of the Commission on Old Age Pensions and National Insurance and the Carnegie Commission of Inquiry Reports on the Poor White Problem in South Africa (hereinafter the Carnegie Commission), led to a well-advanced social security system for a middle-income country of that time.[34] The Commission on Old Age Pensions and National Insurance was required to:

> examine and report upon: (a) The payment of pensions by the State to necessitous aged and permanently incapacitated persons who are unable to maintain themselves and for whom no provision at present exists. (b) A system of National Insurance as a means of making provision for the risk of sickness, accident, premature death, invalidity, old age, employment and maternity.[35]

The findings of the Commission were contained in three reports, namely: First Report of the Commission on Old Age Pensions and National Insurance, Second Report on Old Age Pensions and National Insurance, and Third Report on Old Age Pensions and National Insurance.[36] The Carnegie Commission, which was non-governmental and financed by the Carnegie Corporation of

33 The key turning point when the term 'social security' was officially used in the Union of South Africa was with the establishment of the Social Security Committee in 1943. The Social Security Committee was established to investigate and report on the subject of social security in the Union of South Africa. Union of South Africa, *Report of the Social Security Committee and Report No. 2 of the Social and Economic Planning Council* (Union of South Africa 1944) 5. The Committee defined 'social security' as 'the provision of benefits in cash and in kind at levels to be determined from time to time with due regard to the current economic capacity of the country and its population groups – (a) to individuals not gainfully occupied because they are too young, too disabled, too old, temporarily disabled, permanently disabled or for other causes not due to their own volition; (b) to individuals gainfully occupied but unable to maintain themselves and their dependants at levels to be determined; (c) in certain circumstances to needy mothers, with young children, as it is undesirable that they be fully occupied; (d) in respect of injury or disease sustained in employment; and (e) to assist in meeting the costs of births and funerals'. ibid 5.

34 See, for example, Servaas Van der Berg 'South African Social Security Under Apartheid and Beyond' (1997) 14 Development Southern Africa 481.

35 Union of South Africa, *First Report of the Commission on Old Age Pensions and National Insurance* (Cape Times 1927) 7.

36 Union of South Africa (n 35); Union of South Africa, *Second Report on Old Age Pensions and National Insurance* (The Government Printer 1928); and Union of South Africa, *Third Report on Old Age Pensions and National Insurance* (The Government Printer 1929).

New York, produced a five-volume report published in 1932. The report focused on the economic, psychological, educational, health, and sociological aspects of the poor White problem.[37] Both commissions, indeed, set the foundation for the present-day social security system of South Africa, which covers both social assistance and social insurance. Their findings, particularly those pertaining to the poor Whites problem,[38] encouraged the Afrikaner nationalists to strive towards the freeing of the poor Whites,[39] who relied on kin and/or the church,[40] from the throngs of poverty.[41] The main concern was that many White families faced the risk of crumpling under the increasing pressure of providing support and care to their elderly members.[42] Thus, the government of the day began to invest in the expansion of social welfare services from public funds.[43]

Social Assistance

Prior to and shortly after the formation of the Union, the state's involvement in social assistance was largely limited to poor relief.[44] Churches and the philanthropic organisations took care of, *inter alia*, the aged, sick, orphaned, blind, and deaf.[45] As pointed out by Patterson:

37 'The "Poor-White" Problem in South Africa' (1933) 2 The British Medical Journal 296.

38 In 1933, the total population of the poor Whites in the Union of South Africa was estimated at 300,000 out of a total European population of 2,000,000. 'The "Poor-White" Problem in South Africa' (n 37) 296, 297.

39 The notion of 'poor White' has been explained as follows: 'As the term "poor White" implies, the European inhabitants of the country traditionally have a higher standard of living than the non-European. The majority of poor Whites are still imbued with the conviction that they are superior to the Bantus, and this feeling has played an important part in preventing intermarriage between the races. There was an insufficient supply of European labour at the time when modern economic development began in South Africa. Consequently, the economic system has been organized on a basis of cheap Native labour, and this has hindered the poor White from being absorbed in the new industrial system. The unrestricted competition on the labour market between unskilled bantu and the poor White, and the low wages the European then receives, create conditions of poverty which have a demoralizing effect on the Europeans'. 'The "Poor-White" Problem in South Africa' (n 37) 296–297.

40 Jeremy Seekings, '"Not a Single White Person Should be Allowed to go Under": Swartgevaar and the Origins of South Africa's Welfare State, 1924–1929' (2007) 48 The Journal of African History 375, 379–380.

41 Jeremy Seekings, 'The Carnegie Commission and the Backlash Against Welfare State Building in South Africa, 1931–1937' (2008) 34 Journal of South African Studies 515, 516; Seekings (n 40) 378.

42 Andreas Sagner, 'The 1944 Pension Laws Amendment Bill: Old-age Security Policy in South Africa in Historical Perspective, ca. 1920–1960' (1998) 7 Southern African Journal of Gerontology 10, 11; Andreas Sagner, 'Ageing and Social Policy in South Africa: Historical Perspectives with Particular Reference to the Eastern Cape' (2000) 26 Journal of Southern African Studies 523, 526.

43 Seekings (n 41) 516; Sagner, 'Ageing and Social Policy in South Africa' (n 42) 526.

44 Sagner, 'Ageing and Social Policy in South Africa' (n 42) 525.

45 See, for example, Sagner, 'Ageing and Social Policy in South Africa' (n 42) 525.

> Before 1928 social assistance was available in the Union only in the form of poor relief, some medical treatment, and support for mothers and children under the Children's Protection Act; the costs were borne by the Provinces, private welfare organisations and the churches.[46]

The findings of the Commission on Old Age Pensions and National Insurance and the Carnegie Commission, particularly around the issue of the growing numbers of poor Whites, played an important role in the introduction of the social pensions in South Africa.[47] In its first report, the Commission on Old Age Pensions and National Insurance recommended 'the inauguration of a system of Invalidity and Old Age Pensions to provide for the wants of those who are incapacitated and infirm and whose means are insufficient for their maintenance'.[48] From the recommendation, it is clear that the proposed scheme was to be needs-based. The Commission on Old Age Pensions and National Insurance recommended further that:

> pending the further enquiries into the institution of a contributory scheme . . . , that for those who have already attained the pensionable age, or who will attain it before such a Contributory Scheme is instituted, and whose means are inadequate for their maintenance, a system of non-contributory pensions should be introduced without delay.[49]

From the reading of the aforementioned recommendation, it appears that the proposed non-contributory scheme was to be a temporary arrangement pending the introduction of a more ambitious scheme, most probably, of a contributory nature.[50] The general view was that the Union of South Africa should follow a 'staged' approach in its quest to provide social security to its population.[51] This stance was because the national income per head was low to shoulder a contributory scheme.[52] In addition, the prevalent view was that introducing a contributory old age pension scheme would create difficulties with the existing state and private pension funds. Another point raised was that the cost of establishing a contributory old age pension scheme would

46 Sheila Patterson, *Colour and Culture in South Africa* (Routledge and Kegan Paul Limited 1952) 114.

47 Nicoli Nattrass and Jeremy Seekings, 'Citizenship and Welfare in South Africa: Deracialisation and Inequality in a Labour-Surplus Economy' (1997) 31 Canadian Journal of African Studies 452, 458; Seekings (n 40) 377.

48 Union of South Africa (n 35) 7.

49 Union of South Africa (n 35) 15.

50 Rand Daily Mail, 'Scheme for Old Age Pensions – Commission's Report' (14 May 1927) 10.

51 John L. Gray, 'The Application of Social Security Principles to the Union of South Africa' (1943) XL South African Journal of Science 342, 344.

52 ibid.

be excessive.[53] Estimates were that government would have to deal with an increase in expenditure of roughly £4 million per annum within a year should it introduce a compulsory contributory scheme.[54] A further argument made in favour of a non-contributory scheme was that the Union could ill-afford waiting for individuals to acquire the right to pensions by means of contributions.[55] Thus, a non-contributory scheme would provide immediate respite to the eligible poor Whites.[56]

The legislative framework for the establishment of a non-contributory old age pension scheme was set out in the Old Age Pensions Act 22 of 1928. The old age pensions' scheme covered Whites and Coloured persons. The exclusion of Natives was justified on the basis that their addition to the scheme would be costly as their number far exceeded those of the Whites.[57] In addition, Parliament was not prepared to finance benefits for Natives through general government revenue.[58] One of the arguments put forth was that Natives could rely on their community and kinship-based coping mechanisms.[59] This assumption was not entirely correct. The truth of the matter is that:

> In administrative circles the assumption held sway that dependent Africans should be cared for in their rural places of origin. But although traditional sources of social security were still effective in most rural areas, progressive underdevelopment of the reserve economies, landlessness, increasing social stratification and growing dependence on wage labour made an ever-increasing part of the rural African population susceptible to fluctuations in the economy and in need of more formal social-security programmes. In the early 1940s the issue of old-age pensions – and besides that, of old-age homes – had become prominent in many reserves.[60]

53 JR 'Social Security in South Africa' (1944) 21 Bulletin of International News 512.
54 John D. Rheinallt-Jones, 'Social Welfare' in E. Hellman (ed), *Handbook on Race Relations on South Africa* (Cape Town 1949) 21.
55 Seekings (n 40) 388.
56 ibid.
57 ibid 390. See also Sagner, 'Ageing and Social Policy in South Africa' (n 42) 532.
58 Van der Berg (n 34) 486.
59 See, for example, Seekings (n 40) 390; Van der Berg (n 34) 486–487. It is interesting to note that these sentiments were also expressed elsewhere about developing African countries in general. See eg Victor Gerdes 'Social Security in Developing African Nations' (1965) 32 The Journal of Risk and Insurance 455, 460 remarking: 'A contributory program cannot be undertaken at this time. . . . The effect of the lack of pension programs is somewhat offset because the elderly often remain under the umbrella of tribal protection an dare thereby assured of some care although the level may be far below what might be desired'.
60 Sagner, 'The 1944 Pension Laws Amendment Bill' (n 42) 11.

In the end, the exclusion of the Natives from the scheme was motivated by segregation policies of that time.[61] From a political perspective, there was nothing to gain from including the disenfranchised Natives in the scheme.[62] At a practical level, the difficulties in ascertaining the age of the Natives and distinguishing between the rural and urban Natives came handy in the government's quest to bolster its decision to exclude that group.[63] Unlike the Natives, Coloureds had some political currency in the form of votes. As a result, they were included in the scope of coverage of the old age pensions scheme to build a support-base amongst the Coloured voters and to turn them against the Natives.[64] The exclusion of Indians was part of an endeavour 'to disfranchise them, prohibit them from competing with White traders, restrict their land ownership and even, ultimately, return them to India'.[65]

The old age pensions scheme provided benefits subject to compliance with a set age of eligibility, ie 65 years. This age, which was lowered to 60 for women at some stage,[66] is the pensionable age of that era. This presupposed that beneficiaries received the benefit on the premise that they were too old to participate in the labour market and, ultimately, unable to provide for themselves. As Sagner puts it, 'the Old Age Pension Act centred on the "deserving" poor, who, due to age and family circumstances could not be expected to earn a minimal living, the pension legislation did not undermine the policy emphasis on the value of work in gaining social security'.[67] The pension scheme was regarded as 'a method of income-maintenances which saved the deserving elderly poor from the stigmatisation of poor relief without adding too greatly to state expenditure'.[68] In addition, the scheme followed the residence and domicile requirement.[69] Furthermore, the benefits provided under the scheme were means-tested. This requirement ensured that only the needy benefited from the scheme. This form of targeting was preferred above a universal approach because a universal scheme was deemed too costly, and a means-test was in accord with the public opinion of the time.[70] The general administration of the Old Age Pensions Act fell under the jurisdiction of the Commissioner of Pensions.[71]

61 See Seekings (n 40) 391; Sagner, 'Ageing and Social Policy in South Africa' (n 42) 530.
62 Stephen Devereux, 'Social Pensions in Southern Africa in the Twentieth Century' (2007) 33 Journal of Southern African Studies 539, 542.
63 Sagner, 'Ageing and Social Policy in South Africa' (n 42) 529.
64 Seekings (n 40) 390.
65 ibid.
66 Act 34 of 1937.
67 Sagner, 'Ageing and Social Policy in South Africa' (n 42) 529.
68 ibid 526.
69 Section 1(a)-(e) of the Old Age Pensions Act 22 of 1928.
70 Seekings (n 40) 386.
71 Section 2(1) of the Old Age Pensions Act 22 of 1928. The Commissioner of Pensions was a public servant appointed by the governor-general and reported to the Minister of Finance or other minister administering the act.

The scope of coverage of the old age pensions' scheme was broadened, to cover the Indians and Natives, following the amendment of the Old Age Pensions Act of 1928 by Act 48 of 1944. The extension of coverage resulted from increased pressure in the 1930s from, amongst others, White liberals, African organisations, and parliamentary commissions.[72] The government justified its decision to extend coverage by using Christian and human values.[73] It essentially argued that it was their Christian and human duty as a society to care for Africans.[74] This argument was perceived to be in accordance with the principle of trusteeship.[75] Furthermore, the government deemed the move as a 'moral obligation between the state and the African population'.[76] In some quarters, poverty and the lack of social security were seen as the catalyst for communism, which was regarded as a danger against South Africa. It was asserted that:

> there was only one way in which the Government could safeguard the country and avoid Communism. It must provide proper social security for the population, it must not allow the poor to sink into despair, because despair is a fruitful breeding ground for Communism.[77]

Those against the extension of the pension scheme to Natives were of a view that the inclusion of Natives would result in an untenable tax burden on the European taxpayers.[78] Some argued that this move would render Natives 'less amenable drawers of water and hewers of wood'.[79]

A Social Security Commission, established in 1943 to review the social welfare programmes of the Union, recommended the broadening of the old age pensions scheme's scope of coverage as well as the provision of social assistance to the vulnerable groups of persons such as the blind and persons with disabilities. The welfare needs of the blind persons were catered for through payment of a tax-financed pension. This was legislated for in the Blind Person's Act 11 of 1936. Provision for the blind was prioritised ahead of other forms

72 Sagner, 'The 1944 Pension Laws Amendment Bill' (n 42) 11.

73 Sagner, 'Ageing and Social Policy in South Africa' (n 42) 537. 'Human values' were raised as a ground of justification for social security for all in the Re-United Nationalist Party's socio-economic policy as follows: 'If the whole nation is to be held responsible for a decent living for everyone of its members and if human values are always to rank higher than financial interests, no want shall he allowed owing to causes over which the individual or the community has any control, and in that case every individual must be protected as far as possible against physical retrogression and disease. The Re-United Nationalist Party is therefore of opinion that social welfare and national health must be of fundamental importance to the nation and the state'. Union of South Africa (n 24) 80.

74 Sagner, 'Ageing and Social Policy in South Africa' (n 42) 537.

75 ibid.

76 ibid.

77 Union of South Africa (n 24) 1422.

78 ibid 490.

79 ibid 490–491.

of disability because '[b]lindness evokes special sympathy'.[80] The blind persons' pension was initially disbursed for the promotion of the welfare of White and Coloured blind persons.[81] The Commissioner of Pensions administered this tax-financed scheme. Its benefits were payable subject to the means-test. The age of eligibility remained one of the qualifying conditions for the old age pension. Just like the needy elderly, the blind persons covered under the scheme could not eke a living in the labour market. The disability grants were provided to Whites, Coloureds, Indians, and Natives[82] who, owing to physical or mental disabilities, were unable to provide for themselves.[83] The administration of the scheme as regards persons other than Natives resorted to the Minister of Social Welfare and Demobilization. The administration of the scheme as regards the Natives fell under the jurisdiction of the Minister of Native Affairs. Public funds financed the disability grant. The 'relevant circumstances' of the applicant were taken into account when determining the value of the disability grant.[84] The value of the grant varied in accordance with the race of the recipient. Whites received the most favourable amount while the Natives the lowest amount.[85] Reasons provided for this stance were that Natives paid lower taxes[86] and had lower living costs or standards.[87] It is interesting to note that Southern Rhodesia was averse to emulating the Union's approach in its social security proposals. This was largely due to the following reasons:

> 1. Standards of living vary more directly with income than with race. 2. Discrimination will lead to resentment on the part of those discriminated against, amongst whom are many who contribute appreciably to revenue. 3. Discrimination will lead to 'a dangerous complacency among the least efficient and energetic Europeans, who will feel that their higher benefits represent the higher estimation in which they are held by the community regardless of their services'.[88]

Irrespective of the grounds of justification advanced in response to the differentiation between the various racial groups in the Union, this was in congruence with the racial segregation policies of the time. As discriminatory as this

80 Union of South Africa Report of the Social Security Committee and Report No. 2 of the Social and Economic Planning Council (Union of South Africa 1944) 57.
81 This was in accordance with the Blind Persons Act 11 of 1936.
82 Section 1 of the Disability Grants Act 36 of 1946.
83 Preamble of the Disability Grants Act 36 of 1946.
84 Section 9(1) of the Disability Grants Act 36 of 1946.
85 ibid.
86 Sagner, 'Ageing and Social Policy in South Africa' (n 42) 531.
87 Devereux (n 62) 543.
88 Edward Batson 'Some Points of Comparison Between the Social Security Proposals for the Union and for Southern Rhodesia' (1945) The South African Journal of Economics 43, 44.

may be, there is some solace in some aspects of the 1944 old age pension law amendments. As averred by Sagner: '[A]lthough the 1944 pension law contained discriminatory clauses to the disadvantage of older Africans, it marked a milestone in the development of public old-age security policy, in South Africa as well as in Africa at large'.[89] Gray, on the other hand, argued that:

> The extension of old age pensions to all sections of the population presents no difficulties. Objectionable in principle, racial differentiation in rates of pension is in practice easy to administer. It is also possible to reduce the discrepancy between different racial pension-rates to a proportion lower than that which holds between, average earned standards of living, thus serving the cause of distributive justice. No rate at present can be adequate wholly to remove want and anxiety from the lives of any section of the aged population. The cost of attempting it would be colossal and the effort misdirected. In a poor country the claims of the productive and potentially productive age-groups must come first. Moreover, we must be careful not to start with too high a rate, since the cost will steadily rise, owing both to the increasing age-composition of the population and to later claims for higher benefits.[90]

As regards children, the government did make provision for the care and maintenance of destitute children. This is traceable back to the Children's Protection Amendment Act 26 of 1921. Section 11(1) of the aforementioned Act made provision of the payment of a grant (ie Maintenance Grant to Children) to assist certain parents and guardians for the support of a destitute child through general government revenue. These were discretionary funds and were subject to a recommendation by a magistrate or judge to the relevant minister.[91] The Children's Act 31 of 1937, which repealed the Children's Protection Act 25 of 1913, made provision for financial support from public funds for the care of needy children.[92] The Children's Act 33 of 1960 repealed Act 31 of 1937. It provided for the payment of children's grant. The purpose of the grant was to maintain children in need of care.[93] It was non-contributory and funded from the general government revenues. In addition, it was subject to conditions such as school attendance.[94] The notable thing about the grant is that it was paid to Europeans and Coloureds. This was in line with the discriminatory policies of that era.

In conclusion, it can be summarised that law regulated the old age, blind, and disability benefits. These benefits were a legal entitlement availed to eligible

89 Sagner, 'The 1944 Pension Laws Amendment Bill' (n 42) 10.

90 Gray (n 51) 345.

91 Children's Protection Amendment Act 26 of 1921.

92 Section 84(1) of the Children's Act 31 of 1937.

93 Regulation 58(1)(b) of the Regulations made under the Children's Act, 1960 of 15 April 1977.

94 Regulation 62(1)(c) of the Regulations made under the Children's Act, 1960 of 15 April 1977.

persons and not a charity. The targeting mechanism used (ie means-test) indicated the fact that the scheme followed a needs-based approach. In addition, the non-contributory nature of the scheme brought it under the category of the social assistance instead of social insurance. Lastly, these social assistance benefits were a means to safeguard the covered individuals against the loss of earning ability because of the covered contingency, eg old age or blindness.

Social Insurance

UNEMPLOYMENT

The first national compulsory unemployment insurance scheme in South Africa came into existence in 1937.[95] The primary objectives of this contributory scheme were to provide benefits to workers, in certain industries, who are capable of and available for work but are unemployed.[96] The Unemployment Benefit Act 25 of 1937 was passed due to the negative impact of the depression and the lack of resources.[97] For example, in 1930, 400,000 Whites out of a total population of 2 million Whites were alleged to live in poverty.[98] The Unemployment Benefit Act made provision for the establishment of separate funds for individual industries.[99] The scope of coverage of the unemployment benefit scheme was limited.[100] The act excluded persons whose contract of

95 The unemployment insurance scheme came into existence pursuant to the Unemployment Benefit Act 25 of 1937, assented to on 24 of April 1937. The Unemployment Benefit Act was repealed by Section 57 of the Unemployment Insurance Act 53 of 1946. This act was enacted to provide for the establishment of an Unemployment Insurance Fund (UIF) and the payment of benefits to certain unemployed persons; repeal the Unemployment Benefit Act, 1937; provide for the transfer of the officials of unemployment benefit funds established under the said act to the service of the Union Government, and for matters incidental thereto (Preamble of the Unemployment Benefit Act 25 of 1937). Similarly to its predecessor, the Unemployment Insurance Act of 1943 excluded certain categories and groups of persons from its scope of coverage. It should be recalled that the Union of South Africa signed and ratified the Unemployment Convention 2 of 1919 on 20 February 1924. This convention is still in force.

96 Preamble of the Unemployment Benefit Act 25 of 1937.

97 *The Complete Wiehahn Report* (Lex Patria Publishers 1982) 312.

98 Suzanne Klausen, 'The Uncertain Future of White Supremacy and the Politics of Fertility in South Africa – 1920–1939', paper presented at the Wits Institute for Social and Economic Research, University of the Witwatersrand, 2 November 2002.

99 *The Complete Wiehahn Report* (n 97) 312.

100 Among those who were excluded from the ambit of the scheme were the following persons: labourers, persons employed by an employer at irregular intervals for less than one day in any one calendar week, persons employed during the same calendar week by more than one employer unless such employers are engaged in the same scheduled industry, persons employed by the Government of the Union (including the Railway Administration) or a provincial administration. Section 2(a)-(i) of the Unemployment Benefit Act 25 of 1937. The exclusion of the aforementioned categories of persons was largely due to the fact that they did not fall within the categories of persons regarded as contributors in accordance with Section 2 of the Unemployment Benefit Act.

service or labour fell under the regulatory purview of the Native Labour Regulation Act 15 of 1911 and persons employed in agriculture.[101] The overall effect of this limitation was that large numbers of Native workers fell outside the scope of coverage of the Unemployment Benefit Act. This is not surprising because the state was only concerned about the eradication of poverty among Whites. Widespread poverty among the White population was, for a variety of reasons, viewed as a big problem – hence the phenomenon was widely referred to as the 'Poor White' problem.

The recommendations of the Commission on Old Age Pensions and National Insurance influenced the nature and scope of coverage of the scheme. Those recommendations were that the Union of South Africa should consider introducing a compulsory unemployment insurance scheme instead of a scheme where participation is on a voluntary basis.[102] The reason for this recommendation was mainly that a system of voluntary insurance against unemployment was unlikely to succeed in South Africa. It argued further that:

> Of late years there has been a tendency towards the introduction of some form of compulsion into funds which originally started on a voluntary basis. This points to the fact being realised that voluntary schemes cannot be relied on to meet the needs of the workers and that any schemes which may be started in the future with the object of providing insurance against unemployment for the general body of workers must be on a compulsory basis.[103]

In addition, the Commission recommended that: '[A]n insurance scheme cannot, under the present circumstances, be applied in the rural and tribal areas of the Union'. It observed that it was satisfied that it could assume that there is practically no unemployment for Natives.[104] It argued further that:

> In rural areas the unskilled work is almost entirely in the hands of the native races the evidence of the last few years would seem to show that there is no likelihood of unemployment being rife in these areas, as anyone who finds himself unemployed in a rural area betakes himself either to an industrial centre or to the mines, where he is at all times able to secure employment.[105]

101 Section 2(a)-(i) of the Unemployment Benefit Act 25 of 1937.
102 Union of South Africa (n 35) 36.
103 ibid 23.
104 ibid 24–25.
105 ibid 25.

As regards the financing of the scheme, the Commission argued that both employers and employees should contribute. It averred that:

> Unemployment insurance has been defined as a device for meeting a portion of the loss in wages during normal periods of unemployment. The payment of an insurance benefits to an unemployed person is not poor relief, but is the payment of part wages to him whilst he is waiting for another situation. It is generally accepted that in any insurance scheme the persons who are to reap the benefits should be called upon to make a substantial contribution towards the cost of it. . . . Employers are usually required to contribute a part of the funds in any scheme of compulsory insurance, and this is justified on the grounds that if industry requires a reserve of labour it has some responsibility for maintaining the worker whilst he is unemployed. The sponsors of the original scheme considered that if employers were required to share the cost of unemployment insurance they would be compelled, in their own interests, to endeavour to solve the problem of unemployment by organizing the labour and stabilising production.[106]

Another important point to note as regards the creation of an unemployment insurance scheme in the Union of South Africa is that, the Commission on Old Age Pensions and National Insurance 'obtained from the International Labour Office a statement in which it summarised the provisions of the laws of the various countries which have passed legislation dealing with insurance against the risk of unemployment'.[107] In addition, the Commission on Old Age Pensions and National Insurance consulted the International Labour Conference proposals concerning 'the question of preventing, or providing against, unemployment'.[108] This makes sense as the Union of South Africa ratified the International Labour Organization (ILO) Unemployment Convention 2 of 1919 on 20 February 1924. In addition, the Unemployment Recommendation 1 of 1919[109] recommended that:

> each Member of the International Labour Organisation establish an effective system of unemployment insurance, either through Government system or through a system of Government subventions to associations whose rules provide for the payment of benefits to their unemployed members.[110]

106 ibid 35.

107 Union of South Africa, *Third Report* (n 36) 9.

108 ibid.

109 Adopted in Washington at the 1st International Labour Conference Session of 28 November 1919 and withdrawn by decision of the International Labour Conference at its 90th Session in 2002.

110 Article III of the Unemployment Recommendation 1 of 1919.

Thus, the establishment of an unemployment insurance scheme endeavoured to comply with South Africa's obligations in terms of the Unemployment Convention.

The Unemployment Insurance Act 53 of 1946 repealed the Unemployment Benefit Act. It was felt by some that the foundation of social security subsequent to a war desired by the public is the 'benefit of employment' and not 'unemployment benefit'. Thus, the Unemployment Insurance Act, which created an Unemployment Insurance Fund,[111] sought to prevent unemployment and to connect employers with unemployed persons who wished to work. Its scope of coverage was limited.[112] The act, for example, excluded Natives employed in gold or coal mines who were fed and accommodated by their employers. In addition, it excluded certain employment sectors that mainly engaged the Natives. These included domestic work in private households and certain agricultural sectors. The government opposed the inclusion of domestic and farmworkers in the scheme because it believed that it would be difficult to collect contributions from such workers.[113] The unemployment insurance scheme initially made provision for ordinary unemployment benefits. It made provision for illness benefits in 1952.[114] This was pursuant to some criticism that the scheme did not provide benefits to contributors who were unemployed due to an illness.[115] The illness allowances essentially served as a form of protection against the loss of earnings because of illness. Maternity benefits were introduced in 1954 to alleviate the hardship endured by women due to a prohibition of employment during certain periods before and after giving birth.[116] This development had its detractors. For instance, the *Rand Daily Mail* reported that:

> Mr. M.J. Van Den Berg (N.P., Krugersdorp) said that the Unemployment Benefit Fund should be used strictly for the purpose for which it had been created – to provide for unemployment. It was not correct in principle that it should be used to pay benefits to expectant mothers. A separate fund should be created for this. This form of benefit was a continuous drain on the fund; even if there was no unemployment at all, there will still be expectant mother applying for benefits.[117]

111 The Unemployment Insurance Fund was managed by the Unemployment Insurance Board consisting of representatives of employees, employers, and government.

112 See Section 2(a) – (p) of the Unemployment Insurance Act 53 of 1946.

113 Rand Daily Mail, 'Disappointment for Many in UIF Report' (25 November 1960) 2.

114 *The Complete Wiehahn Report* (n 97) 313.

115 ibid.

116 ibid.

117 Rand Daily Mail, 'Trollip May Alter Workless Bill' (17 April 1962) 2.

The dependants' benefits came into effect in 1957. This was an allowance which was made available to the dependants of a deceased contributor. The reason for the introduction of this allowance as part of the unemployment scheme was that 'the greatest unemployment is prevalent in a home where the breadwinner has suddenly died. Then there is the greatest unemployment and the greatest difficulty in surviving the initial shock, when the breadwinner dies'.[118]

WORK INJURIES

Unlike unemployment insurance, compensation schemes aimed at providing some protection to workers injured on duty existed even prior to the establishment of the Union of South Africa. The Native Labour Regulation Act 15 of 1911 was the first law in the Union that dealt with worker's compensation. It made provision for compensation for permanent, total, or partial incapacity and death.[119] The employer paid the compensation to the director appointed in terms of this act on behalf of the Native labourer.[120] The director would then pay any amount received to the Native labourer concerned or his widow and children in the case of death.[121] The scope of the Native Labour Regulation was limited. It is for this reason that Parliament enacted the Workmen's Compensation Act 25 of 1914. This legislation endeavoured to consolidate all the relevant laws that existed prior to the existence of the Union.[122] The liability to pay compensation to the workmen or their dependants fell squarely on the shoulders of the employers.[123] It made no provision for medical aid. This changed when Act 59 of 1934 substituted the Workmen's Compensation Act. The 1934 legislation obliged employers to insure themselves with an approved insurance company. Benefits payable under this act included reasonable medical expenses incurred by a worker who suffered an injury during the course and scope of his employment. The Workmen's Compensation Act 30 of 1941, in turn, replaced the 1934 law. It substituted the system of insurance provided by private companies with a mutual insurance fund. The mutual insurance fund operated under the auspices of the state.

118 Union of South Africa, Debates of the House of Assembly (Hansards) (Fifth Session – Eleventh Parliament (18th January to 22nd June, 1957) (Cape Times 1957) 1072.

119 ibid.

120 ibid.

121 Section 22(4) of the Native Labour Regulation Act 15 of 1911.

122 Namely, Workmen's Compensation Act 40 of 1905 (Cape of Good Hope), Employer's Liability Act 12 of 1896 (Natal) and Workmen's Compensation Act 36 of 1907 (Transvaal).

123 Section 1 of the Workmen's Compensation Act 25 of 1914.

The Workmen's Compensation Commissioner administered the compensation scheme.[124] The 1941 legislation did away with the common law claim in delict against the employer by employees who suffered a work accident, contracted work-related diseases during the course and scope of employment, or passed away due to a work injury or occupational disease.[125] Instead, employers contributed to the fund from which employees and their dependants could claim benefits. Only employers contributed to the fund. The benefits were payable in the case of temporary partial or total disablement,[126] permanent disablement,[127] and death.[128] This approach favoured the workers and their dependants in that claims could be resolved without protracted and expensive court cases. Secondly, it ensured that workers and dependants still receive benefits in cases where the employer might have become insolvent or left the country.

The 1941 Act did not cover workers engaged in the agricultural, mining, and domestic sectors. As neutral as this exclusion may seem, the truth of the matter is that it mainly affected Natives. The majority of persons employed in these sectors were Natives. Some members of Parliament argued strongly against the exclusion. Their argument essentially hinged on the reality that there were dangers inherent in the work done by workers in the excluded sectors.[129] Thus, the workers' compensation had to be applied equally to cover the affected workers. Those opposed to the inclusion of the workers engaged in the agricultural and domestic sectors argued that it would be 'absolutely impracticable and inoperative' to introduce compulsory insurance' to such sectors.[130] For instance, it was argued that the seasonal nature of agricultural work and the associated challenge of guaranteeing a profit and that there are no losses make it difficult to extend cover to such workers.[131] The legislative amendments introduced by Act 27 of 1945 removed the exclusion. Nevertheless, the schedule of benefits varied according to race. That meant, as typical of that era, benefits payable to Natives were the lowest of all the races. At the same time, Europeans received the most favourable benefits in comparison to those provided to other races.

124 Section 12 of the Workmen's Compensation Act 30 of 1941.

125 Section 37 of the Workmen's Compensation 30 of 1941 provided that: 'Compensation shall be paid to any workman entitled thereto either (a) by the employer individually liable; or (b) by the commissioner from the accident fund'.

126 Section 38 of Workmen's Compensation Act 30 of 1941.

127 Section 42 of Workmen's Compensation Act 30 of 1941

128 Section 40 of Workmen's Compensation Act 30 of 1941.

129 Union of South Africa (n 24) 5388–5389.

130 ibid 5389–5390.

131 ibid.

Union of South Africa in Global Arenas

International Labour Organisation, League of Nations, and United Nations

The Union of South Africa participated in World War I (1914–1918). Thus, General Louis Botha (Minister of Native Affairs and Prime Minister of the Union of South Africa) and Lieutenant-General Jan Christian Smuts (Minister of Defence of the Union of South Africa) represented it at the peace conference of Versailles in France.[132] The Union of South Africa, through Lieutenant-General Jan Christian Smuts, played a pivotal role in the drafting of the Covenant of the League of Nations. Accordingly, the Union of South Africa was a founding member of the League of Nations and the ILO.[133] Smuts drafted the initial opening lines of the preamble of the Charter of the United Nations of 1945.[134] The United Nations succeeded the League of Nations after World War II (1939–1945). The United Nations retained the ILO as a specialised agency of the United Nations. Members of Commission on Old Age Pensions and National Insurance travelled to the International Labour Conference to learn about the social insurance system. The following exposition of the influence of the ILO on the development of social security, particularly social insurance, on the African continent is equally true for South Africa:

> the influence of international organisations, especially the International Labour Organisation, with its broad experience, capable consultation, storehouse of knowledge, prestige and resources has shaped the ultimate course of social security in Africa as an instrument for human social betterment and alleviation of human miseries.[135]

The Race Question and the United Nations

The Indian population in the Union of South Africa[136] was ill-treated in the same way as the Natives. In as much as a revered political leader of Smuts' calibre advocated for human rights, it is clear that the sentiment in the Union

132 Treaty of Peace with Germany (Treaty of Versailles). Treaty and protocol signed at Versailles on 28 June 1919 and protocol signed by Germany at Paris on 10 January 1920.

133 The International Labour Organisation was established by Part XIII of the Treaty of Versailles.

134 Peter Marshall, 'Smuts and the Preamble to the UN Charter' (2001) 358 The Round Table 55.

135 Gerdes (n 59) 459.

136 The Indian population comprised of the descendants of Indians who migrated to the Union of South Africa between 1860 and 1911. See Marian Neal, 'The United Nations and the Union of South Africa' (1953) 7 Journal of International Affairs 151, 152.

of South Africa was that of non-alignment with the 'principle of respect for human rights without distinction on the ground of race'.[137] This was contrary to the provisions of the Charter of the United Nations dealing with human rights and basic freedoms.[138] India's early attempts to get the United Nations to deal decisively with the Indian question in the Union of South Africa were futile. The Union of South Africa considered any steps taken by the United Nations to be illegal and unjustifiably interfering in domestic affairs.[139]

Ratification of Pertinent International Labour Organisation Instruments

The Union of South Africa signed and ratified a number of International Labour Organisation instruments.[140] The ratification of the ILO instruments may explain to some degree the early introduction of social security schemes such as the unemployment insurance in the Union of South Africa.

The Influence of Developments in Other Jurisdictions

The Union of South Africa actively took note of social security developments in other countries as it endeavoured to develop its social security system. This included study tours by members of social security commissions and committees to countries such as Germany.[141] Furthermore, from time to time social security developments in South Africa were compared to those in Britain.[142] It is argued by some commentators that the introduction of a means-test in the South African old age pensions' scheme was influenced by the British experience.[143] To conclude, South Africa had close ties and linkages with other countries.[144] This was particularly the case due to World War II which is credited

137 Neal (n 136) 154.

138 ibid 152.

139 ibid 153.

140 Unemployment Convention 2 of 1919, Night Work (Women) Convention 4 of 1919, Equality of Treatment (Accident Compensation) Convention 19 of 1925, Minimum Wage-Fixing Machinery Convention 26 of 1928, Marking of Weight (Packages Transported by Vessels) Convention 27 of 1929, Night Work (Women) Convention (Revised) 41 of 1934, Workmen's Compensation (Occupational Diseases) Convention (Revised) 42 of 1934, Underground Work (Women) Convention 45 of 1935, Convention concerning Statistics of Wages and Hours of Work 63 of 1938 (Excluding Parts II and IV) and Night Work (Women) Convention (Revised) 89 of 1948.

141 See, for example, Union of South Africa (n 35), Union of South Africa, *Second Report* (n 36) and Union of South Africa, *Third Report* (n 36).

142 See, for example, Ellison Kahn, 'The Report of the Social Security Committee: Some Reflections' (1944) South African Journal of Economics 64; Gray (n 51) 342; Seekings (n 40) 387–388.

143 Nattrass and Seekings (n 47) 460; Van der Berg (n 34) 482–483.

144 See Devereux (n 62) 541: 'Given close historical and cultural linkages between the White South African regime and Western Europe South Africa's adoption of social welfare principles and programmes in the early twentieth century is perhaps better explained by diffusion theory ("social

for bringing the Union in 'greater contact with Britain and the United States where state interventions and social planning were well established'.[145]

Republic of South Africa (1961 to 1994)

General Overview

The Republic of South Africa and the Apartheid System

South Africa terminated constitutional relations with the British when it became the Republic of South Africa in 1961. The Constitution of the Republic of South Africa, 1961 substituted the Union of South Africa Act.[146] The state president elected by parliament replaced the queen and the appointed governor-general. This constitution became the basic law of the Republic of South Africa until it was repealed in 1983. English and Afrikaans were the official languages. This marginalised native languages and their speakers one more time. Indeed, the discrimination and unfair treatment experienced by the Natives during the Union of South Africa era continued unabated. Apartheid, which negatively affected every facet of life of mainly Africans,[147] crystallised as an official state policy in 1948. The apartheid system was an attractive policy for its supporters for the simple reason that it empowered the White minority[148] to retain absolute control of the affairs of the Republic.[149] The arguments advanced previously to justify discriminatory practices and White domination

institutions are culturally diffused from some societies to others") than by the convergence hypothesis (an empirical observation that countries at similar levels of industrialisation tend to introduce similar social programmes). The Boer Republics, for instance, were directly influenced by Bismarck's introduction of formal social security programmes to Germany in the 1880's, not least because many Dutch citizens were employed as civil servants by the Zuid-Afrikaansche Republic, while the civil services of the Cape and Natal were dominated by people of British decent, and their social policies influenced by the harsher attitudes embodied by the British Poor Law and *laissez-faire* liberalism' (italics in the original).

145 David Duncan, 'The Origin of the "Welfare State" in Pre-Apartheid South Africa' (unpublished seminar paper 1993).

146 Act 32 of 1961.

147 See, for example, United Nations Educational, Scientific and Cultural Organisation (UNESCO), *Apartheid* (United Educational, Scientific and Cultural Organisation 1967); United Nations, *Segregation in South Africa: Questions and Answers on the Policy of Apartheid* (United Nations 1969).

148 The total number of Whites was lesser than one-fifth of the total population. United Nations (n 147) 1.

149 United Nations (n 147) 1. As Deane (n 32) 3–4 puts it: 'The founders of the Herenigde National Party invented apartheid as a means to cement their power over the economic and social system. Initially, the aim of apartheid was to maintain a White domination while extending racial separation. This was in response to Africans' increasing participation in the country's economic life and their assertion of political rights. The principles of segregationists thinking evolved in response to economic, social and political pressures of the time'.

were used to defend the apartheid policy. These include flawed arguments such as Blacks were on earth to serve the Whites and that, 'it was the duty of Whites to protect and defend Western civilisation'.[150]

The Bantustans

The apartheid government adopted the Bantustans or African reserves policy as one of the mechanisms to physically separate races and individual African tribes.[151] Thus, the Bantustans such as Transkei, Bophuthatswana, Venda, and Ciskei, were an integral part of the apartheid segregated homeland policies. Laws such as the Group Areas Act 41 of 1950 enforced these policies.[152] The apartheid government's justification for the Bantustans policy was that it is about separate development[153] and creation of areas where tribal life can thrive.[154] Therefore, this was ideal for 'orderly coexistence whereby each racial group may freely exercise its rights'.[155] This argument landed itself more towards the 'separate but equal' notion. In reality, this was not the case. For instance, the scheme 'meant that Africans will lose all of equal rights in 87 per cent of the country in return for self-government of 13 per cent'.[156] Another point to note is that the Bantustans lacked the requisite resources to support their populace adequately.[157]

Social Security

Social Assistance

The social assistance framework during the apartheid era comprised of four key social pensions, namely: Old age pension, blind persons pension, disability grant, and the children's grant. The aforementioned benefits, which were established during the Union of South Africa period, were financed through the general tax revenue[158] and were administered by the state. The means-test continued to play a pivotal role in the determination of needs.[159]

150 United Nations (n 147) 1.
151 ibid 4–5.
152 Landis (n 19) 20–29.
153 ibid 2.
154 ibid 18.
155 United Nations (n 147) 6.
156 ibid 7.
157 ibid.
158 See, for example, Section 8 of the Old Age Pensions Act 38 of 1962 on the determination of the amount of the pension.
159 See Section 8 of the Old Age Pensions Act 38 of 1962 on the determination of the amount of the pension.

Thus, the pensions were needs-based. The laws outlining the legislative framework for the three social pensions were either amended or repealed.[160] Even so, their scope of coverage included the Indians and Bantu.[161] However, in conformity with segregation policies of the time, the benefits provided to the Indians and Bantu were lower than that provided to the White and Coloured persons.[162]

It was during the dying days of apartheid that the legislature enacted the Social Assistance Act 59 of 1992. This Act repealed all the other apartheid social assistance laws[163] and consolidated the various social assistance benefits, inclusive of the children's grant.[164] The benefits continued to be funded through taxes and remained to be needs-based with the means-test used as the key targeting mechanism. The uniformity of social pensions in South Africa, which included the harmonisation of the grant amount for different racial groups, was realised in 1993.[165] The introduction of the Social Assistance Act is regarded as the first attempt at significantly reforming a discriminatory social assistance system in South Africa.

Social Insurance

The two prominent social insurance schemes during the apartheid era were the workmen's compensation scheme and the unemployment insurance scheme.

WORKMEN'S COMPENSATION SCHEME

The workmen's compensation scheme focused on the payment of compensation to workers who were disabled or contracted an industrial disease in the course of their employment.[166] It also provided compensation for death

160 The Old Age Pensions Act 38 of 1962 repealed the Old Age Pensions Act 22 of 1928. It consolidated the laws relating to old age pensions. The Blind Persons Act 39 of 1962 repealed the Blind Persons Act 11 of 1936 and consolidated the laws relating to the payment of pensions to blind persons and of grants-in-aid for the promotion of the welfare of such persons and matters incidental thereto. The Disability Grants Act 41 of 1962 repealed the Disability Grants Act 36 of 1946. It consolidated the laws relating to disability grants.

161 See Section 2(1) of the Old Age Pensions Act 38 of 1962 and Section 3 of the Blind Persons Act 39 of 1962.

162 Francie Lund, 'State Social Benefits in South Africa' (1993) 46 International Social Security Review 5, 9.

163 Schedule – Repealed Acts of the Social Assistance Act 59 of 1992.

164 Section 2 of the Social Assistance Act 59 of 1992.

165 Jean D. Triegaardt, 'Social policy domains: Social welfare and social security in South Africa' (2002) 45 International Social Work 325; 333; Francie Lund, *Changing Social Policy: The Child Support Grant in South Africa* (Human Sciences Research Council Press 2008) 15.

166 Preamble of the Workmen's Compensation Act 30 of 1941.

resulting from such accidents and diseases.[167] The Workmen's Compensation Commissioner administered the scheme.[168] The common law claim generally available to the employee was discarded. This is a claim in delict against the employer by employees who suffer a work accident, contract occupational diseases during the course and scope of employment, or pass away due to a work injury or occupational disease.[169] Instead, employers contributed to the compensation fund from which employees and their dependants could claim benefits. Only employers contributed to the fund. The benefits were payable in the case of temporary partial or total disablement,[170] permanent disablement,[171] and death.[172] This approach favoured the workers and their dependants in that claims could be resolved without protracted and expensive court cases. Secondly, it ensured that workers or dependants still receive benefits in cases where the employer might have become insolvent or left the country.

UNEMPLOYMENT INSURANCE

The Unemployment Insurance Act 30 of 1966 regulated the unemployment insurance scheme. It repealed the Unemployment Insurance Act 53 of 1946.[173] This piece of legislation consolidated the laws relating to the Unemployment Insurance Fund, the payment of benefits to certain persons, and the payment of certain amounts to dependants of certain deceased persons, and the combatting of unemployment. The act specifically excluded from its ambit, among others, the following workers: farmworkers, domestic workers, casual workers, seasonal workers, pieceworkers, contract workers, civil servants, and South African Transport Service workers.[174] The scheme was administered by the Unemployment Insurance Fund that comprised of, among others, the contributions of employers and contributors, any amounts of money paid as penalties and any interest from investments of the fund.[175] The fund is used for, *inter alia*, the payment of benefits over a predefined time period.[176] Payments payable under the

167 ibid.

168 Section 12 of the of the Workmen's Compensation Act 30 of 1941.

169 Section 37 of the Workmen's Compensation 30 of 1941 provided that: 'Compensation shall be paid to any workman entitled thereto either (a) by the employer individually liable; or (b) by the commissioner from the accident fund'.

170 Section 38 of Workmen's Compensation Act 30 of 1941.

171 Section 42 of Workmen's Compensation Act 30 of 1941

172 Section 40 of Workmen's Compensation Act 30 of 1941.

173 Section 65 of the Unemployment Insurance Act 30 of 1966.

174 Section 2 of the Unemployment Insurance Act 30 of 1966.

175 ibid.

176 Section 7(a) of the Unemployment Insurance Act 30 of 1966.

unemployment insurance scheme as follows: unemployment benefits,[177] illness allowances,[178] maternity benefits,[179] and benefits for the dependants of deceased contributors.

Legacies of the Apartheid Social Policies

The main legacies of the apartheid social policies were that the Native reserves established through the various laws served as a reservoir of manpower. The migrant labour scheme was central to the system. The living arrangements of many African families suffered tremendously due to the system.[180] In addition, welfare regimes were racially exclusive with the Whites being the best looked after section of the population of South Africa. The prevalent assumption was that traditional social forms of social security would substitute state-provided social security.[181] Furthermore, the system secured the property rights of the minority White. Aligned to this was the dispossession and marginalisation of indigenous populations. Moreover, it laid a foundation for the South African social security system as we know it today.

Global Arenas: International Labour Organisation and United Nations Organisation

The United Nations and its agencies put a great deal of pressure on the Republic of South Africa to force it to abandon its apartheid policies. The government of South Africa, which consistently maintained that the United Nations efforts amounted to interference in its internal affairs,[182] withdrew from the ILO on 14 March 1964. As regards the ratification of the ILO instruments, only the Final Articles Revision Convention 116 of 1961 was ratified during the apartheid era.[183] South Africa ratified the instrument on 9 August 1963.

177 Section 37 of the Unemployment Insurance Act 30 of 1966.

178 Section 38 of the Unemployment Insurance Act 30 of 1966.

179 Section 39 of the Unemployment Insurance Act 30 of 1966.

180 See, for example, Ria Smit, 'The impact of the labour migration on African families in South Africa: Yesterday and today' (2001) 32 Journal of Comparative Family Studies 533; Ronald P. Mazibuko, *The Effects of Migrant Labour on the family System* (University of South Africa 2000); Anne Case and Angus Deaton, 'Large cash transfers to the elderly in South Africa' (1998) 108 The Economic Journal 1330, 1341.

181 Nicoli Nattrass and Jeremy Seekings, 'Citizenship and welfare in South Africa: Deracialisation and inequality in a labour-surplus economy' (1997) 31 Canadian Journal of African Studies 452, 460.

182 Neal (n 136) 154.

183 This Convention concerned the partial revision of the conventions adopted by the General Conference of the International Labour Organisation at its first thirty-two sessions for the purpose of standardising the provisions regarding the preparation of reports by the Governing Body of the International Labour Office on the working of conventions. It entered into force on 5 February 1962.

Post-Apartheid Republic of South Africa (1994 to date)

Post-Apartheid Constitution: General Overview

The need for a new constitution for a democratic South Africa was identified and agreed on during the Convention for the Democratic South Africa (hereinafter the CODESA).[184] Twenty-six parties participated in the Multi-Party Negotiating Process, which drafted the interim Constitution[185] and adopted the thirty-four Constitutional Principles which were to guide the Constitutional Assembly when drafting the final Constitution. These principles covered key issues such as constitutional supremacy, equality, fundamental rights, and diversity of language and culture. The interim Constitution made provision for values such as 'equality between men and women and people of all races'.[186] In addition, it recognised eleven languages as official languages.[187] It added nine African languages to the two that were recognised by the apartheid Constitutions of 1961 and 1983, namely English and Afrikaans. Furthermore, it declared the constitution to be the supreme law of the country.[188] This was a significant departure from the apartheid approach of parliamentary sovereignty.[189] Another

184 This is highlighted in the Convention for the Democratic South Africa Declaration of Intent of 20 December 1991 as follows: 'We, the duly authorised representatives of political parties, political organizations, administrations and the South African Government, coming together at this first meeting of the Convention for a Democratic South Africa, mindful of the awesome responsibility that rests on us at this moment in the history of our country, declare our solemn intent . . . to set in motion the process of drawing up and establishing a constitution that will ensure, *inter alia*: (a) that South Africa will be a united, democratic, non-racial and non-sexist state in which sovereign authority is exercised over the whole of its territory; (b) that the Constitution will be the supreme law and that it will be guarded over by an independent, non-racial and impartial judiciary; (c) that there will be a multi-party democracy with the right to form and join political parties and with regular elections on the basis of universal adult suffrage on a common voters roll; in general the basic electoral system shall be that of proportional representation; (d) that there shall be a separation of powers between the legislature, executive and judiciary with appropriate checks and balances; (e) that the diversity of languages, cultures and religions of the people of South Africa shall be acknowledged; (f) that all shall enjoy universally accepted human rights, freedoms and civil liberties including freedom of religion, speech and assembly protected by an entrenched and justiciable Bill of Rights and a legal system that guarantees equality of all before the law'.

185 Constitution of the Republic of South Africa Act 200 of 1993 (hereinafter the interim Constitution). The interim Constitution was assented to on 25 January 1994 and came into effect of 27 April 1994.

186 Preamble of the interim Constitution.

187 These languages are as follows: Afrikaans, English, isiNdebele, Sesotho sa Leboa, Sesotho, siSwati, Xitsonga, Setswana, Tshivenda, isiXhosa, and isiZulu.

188 Section 4 of the interim Constitution.

189 See, for further reading, about the notion of constitutional supremacy, Jutta Limbach, 'The concept of the supremacy of the constitution' (2001) 64 Modern Law Review 1. By adopting constitutional supremacy, South Africa broke away from the parliamentary sovereignty system. In accordance with the parliamentary sovereignty doctrine, the South African parliament was at

key departure from the previous constitutions is that the interim Constitution had a chapter on the Bill of Rights.[190] All the rights entrenched in the Bill of Rights were justiciable and not absolute.[191] In many ways, the interim Constitution was the first crucial legal step towards correcting the wrongs of the past, which were legislated in the erstwhile constitutions and apartheid laws.[192]

The Constitution of the Republic of South Africa, 1996 (hereinafter the final Constitution) was drafted by the National Assembly in line with the provisions of Chapter 5 of the interim Constitution which dealt with the adoption of the new constitution.[193] It was adopted by the Constitutional Assembly on 8 May 1996. The final Constitution, unlike the Union of South Africa and the Apartheid Constitutions, had to be credible and acceptable to all South Africans. To achieve this goal the following measures were adopted:

> the process of drafting the Constitution involved many South Africans in the largest public participation programme ever carried out in South Africa. After nearly two years of intensive consultations, political parties represented in the Constitutional Assembly negotiated the formulations

liberty to enact any law(s) it deemed fit. See, for further reading, about the concept of parliamentary sovereignty, Denis V Cowen, 'Legislature and judiciary: Reflections on the constitutional issues in South Africa (Part I)' (1952) 15 Modern Law Review 282; Denis V. Cowen, 'Legislature and judiciary: Reflections on the constitutional issues in South Africa (Part II)' (1953) 16 Modern Law Review 273; Hamish R. Gray, 'The sovereignty of parliament today' (1953) 10 University of Toronto Law Journal 54.

190 Chapter 3 (Sections 7–35) of the interim Constitution of 1993.

191 Section 33 of the interim Constitution of 1993.

192 Accordingly, it professed in the postscript aptly titled 'National Unity and Reconciliation' that: 'This Constitution provides a historic bridge between the past of a deeply divided society characterised by strife, conflict, untold suffering and injustice, and a future founded on the recognition of human rights, democracy and peaceful co-existence and development opportunities for all South Africans, irrespective of colour, race, class, belief or sex. The pursuit of national unity, the well-being of all South African citizens and peace require reconciliation between the people of South Africa and the reconstruction of society. The adoption of this Constitution lays the secure foundation for the people of South Africa to transcend the divisions and strife of the past, which generated gross violations of human rights, the transgression of humanitarian principles in violent conflicts and a legacy of hatred, fear, guilt and revenge. These can now be addressed on the basis that there is a need for understanding but not for vengeance, a need for reparation but not for retaliation, a need for ubuntu but not for victimisation. In order to advance such reconciliation and reconstruction, amnesty shall be granted in respect of acts, omissions and offences associated with political objectives and committed in the course of the conflicts of the past. To this end, Parliament under this Constitution shall adopt a law determining a firm cut-off date, which shall be a date after 8 October 1990 and before 6 December 1993, and providing for the mechanisms, criteria and procedures, including tribunals, if any, through which such amnesty shall be dealt with at any time after the law has been passed. With this Constitution and these commitments, we, the people of South Africa, open a new chapter in the history of our country. Nkosi sikelel' iAfrika. God seen Suid-Afrika Morena boloka sechaba sa heso. May God bless our country Mudzimu fhatutshedza Afrika. Hosi katekisa Afrika'.

193 See Sections 68–74 of the interim Constitution of 1993.

> contained in this text, which are an integration of ideas from ordinary citizens, civil society and political parties represented in and outside of the Constitutional Assembly.

The final Constitution, in the spirit of the interim Constitution, is clear about its aim to fix the injustices of the past. It states in its preamble the following:

> We, the people of South Africa, Recognise the injustices of our past; Honour those who suffered for justice and freedom in our land; Respect those who have worked to build and develop our country; and Believe that South Africa belongs to all who live in it, united in our diversity. We, therefore, through our freely elected representatives, adopt this Constitution as the supreme law of the Republic so as to – Heal the divisions of the past and establish a society based on democratic values, social justice and fundamental human rights; Lay the foundations for a democratic and open society in which government is based on the will of the people and every citizen is equally protected by law; Improve the quality of life of all citizens and free the potential of each person; and Build a united and democratic South Africa able to take its rightful place as a sovereign state in the family of nations. May God protect our people.

As evident from the preamble, it is because of the unpleasant past practices that the drafters deemed it fit to include such a preamble. In *S v Makwanyane*[194] the Constitutional Court remarked that

> the Constitution . . . provides a historic bridge between the past of a deeply divided society characterised by strife, conflict, untold suffering and injustice, and a future founded on the recognition of human rights, democracy and peaceful co-existence and development opportunities for all South Africans, irrespective of colour, race, class, belief or sex.

Constitutional Values

South Africa is founded on, among others, the following constitutional values: human dignity, non-racialism and non-sexism, and supremacy of the constitution and the rule of law.[195] The courts are enjoined by the constitution to promote the values that underlie an open and democratic society

194 1995 (3) SA 391 (CC).
195 Section 1 of the Constitution of the Republic of South Africa of 1996.

based on human dignity, equality, and freedom.[196] These values underpin social protection provisioning endeavours in South Africa. The point is that they formulate the conceptual foundation from which endeavours to provide, transform and develop social protection in South Africa should be based. Furthermore, they give meaning to the socio-economic rights enshrined in the Bill of Rights.

The effect of the supremacy of the constitution is that law or conduct inconsistent with the constitution is invalid[197] and the obligations imposed by it must be complied with.[198] As put differently by the Constitutional Court in *Du Plessis and Others v De Klerk and Another*, 'the Constitution is elevated to supremacy overall law, and then all organs of state are enjoined to honour and enforce that supremacy'.[199] In addition to the aforementioned values,[200] there are other equally significant values such as those that originate from culture. One such value, which was also mentioned in the postscript of the interim Constitution, is ubuntu. Ubuntu is an important constitutional value which 'broadly means that an individual's humanity is expressed through his relationship with others and theirs in turn through a recognition of his humanity'.[201]

Social Rights

Social rights are entrenched in Chapter 2 of the constitution. This chapter is the Bill of Rights. The following rights are guaranteed: The right to have access to housing;[202] the right to have access to health care services;[203] the right to have access to sufficient food and water;[204] the right to have access to

196 Section 39(1)(a) of the constitution.

197 The effect of the supremacy of the constitution was explained in Section 4(1) of the Constitution of the Republic of South Africa 200 of 1993 (the interim Constitution) as follows: 'This Constitution shall be the supreme law of the Republic and any law or act inconsistent with its provisions shall, unless otherwise provided expressly or by necessary implication in this Constitution, be of no force and effect to the extent of the inconsistency'.

198 Section 2 of the constitution.

199 1996 (3) SA 850 at paragraph 128.

200 See, for further reading about the South African constitutional values, Arthur Chaskalson, 'Human dignity as a fundamental value of our constitutional order' (2000) 16 South African Journal on Human Rights 193 and Hiroshi Nishihara 'The significance of constitutional values' (2001) 4 Potchefstroom Electronic Law Journal 1.

201 George Barrie, 'Ubuntu Ungamuntu Ngabanye Abantu: The Recognition of Minority Rights in the South African Constitution' (2000) 2 TSAR 271. See, for the meaning of the concept of ubuntu and social values it represents, Yvonne Mokgoro, 'Ubuntu and the Law in South Africa', Paper presented at the first Colloquium Constitution and Law held in Potchefstroom, South Africa, 31 October 1997.

202 Section 26 of the constitution.

203 Section 27(1)(a) of the constitution.

204 Section 27(1)(b) of the constitution.

social security;[205] every child's right to basic nutrition, shelter, basic health care services;[206] and the right to education.[207] The subject entitled to protection is outlined in the constitution. The Bill of Rights uses the phrases '[e]veryone has a right (of access) to . . .'[208] and 'every child has a right to . . .'[209] The rights contained in the constitution are not absolute. They can be limited in terms of the general limitation contained in Section 36 of the constitution. Furthermore, social rights such as the right of access to housing and social security are subject to the availability of resources.

Furthermore, other fundamental rights buttress social rights. These rights include the right to equality,[210] the right to human dignity,[211] the right to life,[212] the right to privacy,[213] the right of access to housing,[214] the right of access to health care,[215] the right of access to food and water,[216] and the right to education.[217] These rights are interconnected and, as a result, reinforce one another.[218] For example, the Constitutional Court pointed out in *S v Makwanyane*[219] that:

> The right to life, thus understood, incorporates the right to dignity. Therefore, the rights to human dignity and life are intertwined. The right to life is more than existence, it is a right to be treated as a human being with

205 Section 27(1)(c) of the constitution.
206 Section 28(1)(c) of the constitution.
207 Section 29 of the constitution.
208 See, for example, Sections 26(1) and 27(1) of the constitution.
209 See, for example, Section 28(1) of the constitution.
210 Section 9 of the constitution. It provides that: '(1) Everyone is equal before the law and has the right to equal protection and benefit of the law. (2) Equality includes the full and equal enjoyment of all rights and freedoms. To promote the achievement of equality, legislative and other measures designed to protect or advance persons, or categories of persons, disadvantaged by unfair discrimination may be taken. (3) The state may not unfairly discriminate directly or indirectly against anyone on one or more grounds, including race, gender, sex, pregnancy, marital status, ethnic or social origin, colour, sexual orientation, age, disability, religion, conscience, belief, culture, language and birth. (4) No person may unfairly discriminate directly or indirectly against anyone on one or more grounds in terms of subsection (3). National legislation must be enacted to prevent or prohibit unfair discrimination. (5) Discrimination on one or more of the grounds listed in subsection (3) is unfair unless it is established that the discrimination is fair'.
211 Section 10 of the constitution. See Chaskalson (n 200) 193.
212 Section 11 of the constitution. See *S v Makwanyane* 1995 3 SA 391 (CC).
213 Section 14 of the constitution.
214 Section 26 of the constitution.
215 Section 27(1)(a) of the constitution.
216 Section 27(1)(b) of the constitution.
217 Section 29 of the constitution.
218 *Khosa and Others v Minister of Social Development and Others; Mahlaule and Another v Minister of Social Development* 2004 (6) SA 505 (CC) para 41; *Government of the Republic of South Africa and Others v Grootboom and Others* 2001 (1) SA 46 para 23.
219 1995 (3) SA 391 para 326.

dignity: without dignity, human life is substantially diminished. Without life, there cannot be dignity.

Role of Courts

Rights entrenched in the Bill of Rights, inclusive of the socio-economic rights, are fully enforceable.[220] As remarked by the Constitutional Court: '[T]hey cannot be said to exist on paper only'.[221] The following persons may approach a court: (a) anyone acting in their own interest; (b) anyone acting on behalf of another person who cannot act in their own name; (c) anyone acting as a member of, or in the interest of, a group or a class of persons; (d) anyone acting in the public interest; and (e) an association acting in the interest of its members.[222] A judge may grant appropriate relief, including a declaration of rights.[223] One of the practical effects of the justiciability of socio-economic rights is that (an) affected person(s) or parties with an interest may approach a competent court alleging that a right in the Bill of Rights has been infringed or threatened.[224] This means that the socio-economic rights are subject to 'the "hard protection" offered by the binding decisions which courts can take'.[225]

Social Security

Social Assistance

The Social Assistance Act 13 of 2004, which repealed the Social Assistance Act 59 of 1992, regulates social assistance in South Africa. The act makes provision for the payment of social grants, namely: child support grant, care dependency

220 Section 38 of the constitution.

221 *Government of the Republic of South Africa v Grootboom* 2001 (1) SA 46 (CC) para 20.

222 ibid. Also see the *Certification of the Constitution of the Republic of South Africa* 1996 (4) SA 744 (CC); 1996 (10) BCLR 1253 (CC) – a Constitutional Court case where it was found that socio-economic rights are indeed justiciable. The justiciability of socio-economic rights is of great significance in South Africa. See also Sandra Liebenberg, 'South Africa's evolving jurisprudence on socio-economic rights: An effective tool in challenging poverty?' (2002) 6 Law, Democracy & Development 160: 'The inclusion of socio-economic rights as *justiciable* rights indicates that the Constitution envisages an important role for the judiciary in their enforcement. The jurisprudence will define the nature of the state's obligations in relation to socio-economic rights, the conditions under which these rights can be claimed, and the nature of the relief that those who turn to the courts can expect. The evolving jurisprudence is not only significant for future litigation aimed at enforcing socio-economic rights, but also in guiding the adoption and implementation of policies and legislation by government to facilitate access to them. It is also important to the monitoring and advocacy initiatives by civil society, the South African Human Rights Commission (SAHRC) and the Commission for Gender Equality' (italics in the original).

223 Section 38 of the constitution.

224 ibid.

225 Christof Heyns and Danie Brand, 'Introduction to Socio-economic Rights in the South African Constitution' (1998) 2 Law, Democracy & Development 155.

grant, foster child grant, disability grant, older persons grant, and war veteran's grant and grant-in-aid.[226] Thus, the social grant system follows a categorical approach. That is to say that they are paid to certain categories of persons. These are the indigent persons who are, apart from being poor, too young, or too old, or too disabled to eke a living in the labour market. The social grants are non-contributory and means-tested. There have been talks about making the older persons grant universal. The main reason for such a step is that the number of the elderly in South Africa is low enough to use such a targeting approach. Furthermore, money appropriated by Parliament finance the social grants scheme.[227] The South African Social Security Agency, established by the South African Social Security Agency Act, administers the social grants scheme.

The post-apartheid social assistance scheme retained the disability and elderly persons grants. In addition, it featured the child support grant, which substituted the Maintenance Grants to Children in 1998.[228] The child support grant was introduced with the intention of reaching the poorest children in deep rural areas.[229] The state maintenance grants system was regarded as 'complex and unreliable'.[230] Furthermore, it was based on 'the model of the nuclear family, [which] had become inappropriate'.[231] It is important to note that the scheme did away with the apartheid inequities. A person's race is no longer a determining factor when it comes to the rate of social assistance benefits. This is in line with constitutional values and rights such as equality and human dignity. Most importantly, the current social assistance scheme gives effect to the right of access to social security.[232] The social assistance programme is the largest poverty alleviation programme in South Africa.

Selected Basic Needs: General Principles and Values

There are basic needs, which are covered by tax-financed programmes, that are entrenched as fundamental rights in the constitution. The state must through the implementation of reasonable measures strive towards the realisation of these basic needs. They concern access to housing,[233] health care,[234] and water.[235] In addition, the constitution provides every child with

226 Section 4 of the Social Assistance Act 13 of 2004.
227 ibid.
228 See, for further reading, Lund (n 165).
229 Triegaardt (n 165) 332.
230 Department of Welfare, *White Paper for Social Welfare* (Department of Welfare 1997).
231 Lund (n 165) 80.
232 Preamble of the Social Assistance Act 13 of 2004.
233 Section 26 of the constitution.
234 Section 27(1)(a) of the constitution.
235 Section 27(1)(b) of the constitution.

the right to shelter, basic health care services, and social services.[236] These entitlements, which are enforceable, have been adjudicated by the South African courts on several occasions. The seminal decision of the *Government of the Republic of South Africa v Grootboom and others*[237] dealt with the right of access to housing and shelter of persons who lived under intolerable conditions while waiting for their turn to be allocated low-cost housing.[238] The Constitutional Court found that there was a link between the severe shortages of housing experienced and apartheid.[239] In so doing, the court emphasised the importance of understanding rights contained in the Bill of Rights in their social and historical context.[240] The Constitutional Court re-affirmed the inter-relationship between the rights entrenched in the constitution,[241] particularly the socio-economic rights and the right to dignity.[242] It argued that:

> All rights in our Bill of Rights are inter-related and mutually supporting. There can be no doubt than human dignity, freedom and equality, the foundational values of our society, are denied those who have no food, clothing or shelter.[243]

In acknowledging the state's obligation to provide access to adequate housing, the court highlighted the important fact that such a duty is dependent upon the context, which may vary from one setting to another. Therefore, what is expected of the state in a rural area may differ from what is expected in urban environments.[244] The court found that 'human beings are required to be treated as human beings'[245] and the state is obligated by the constitution 'to devise and implement within its available resources a comprehensive and coordinated programme progressively to realise the right of access to adequate housing'.[246]

236 Section 28(1)(c) of the constitution.
237 2001 (SA) 46.
238 See, for further reading, Daniel Schneider, 'The Constitutional Right to Housing in South Africa: The Government of the Republic of South Africa v Irene Grootboom' (2004) 45 International Journal of Civil Society Law 45.
239 *Government of the Republic of South Africa v Grootboom and others* 2001 (SA) 46 (CC) para 6.
240 ibid para 22.
241 ibid para 24. Also see *City of Cape Town v Persons who are presently unlawfully occupying erf 1800, Capricorn: Vrygrond Development and others* 2003 (8) BCLR 878 (C).
242 See Anne Hughes, *Human Dignity and Fundamental Rights in South Africa and Ireland* (Pretoria University Law Press 2014); Sandra Liebenberg 'The Value of Human Dignity in Interpreting Socio-Economic Rights' (2005) 21 South African Journal on Human Rights 1.
243 *Government of the Republic of South Africa v Grootboom and others* 2001 (SA) 46 (CC) para 23.
244 ibid para 37.
245 ibid para 83.
246 ibid para 99.

The decision of *Soobramoney v Minister of Health (Kwazulu-Natal)*[247] concerned an indigent unemployed man who was in the final stages of chronic renal failure. He was denied access to treatment at a public hospital due to the shortage of resources, which entailed the prioritisation of patients suffering from renal failure that could be treated and remedied. The Constitutional Court found that it should 'be slow to interfere with rational decisions taken in good faith by the political organs and medical authorities whose responsibility it is to deal with such matters'.[248] The court found that suffering from chronic renal failure is not an emergency that calls for immediate medical attention.[249] It argued further that the right to life[250] could not be constitutionally extended to 'encompass the right indefinitely to evade death'.[251]

Minister of Health and Others v Treatment Action Campaign and Others (No. 2)[252] dealt with the provision of antiretroviral drugs to an expectant mother to prevent the transmission of HIV from mother-to-child. The Constitutional Court held that '[w]here a breach of any right has taken place, including a socio-economic right, a court is under a duty to ensure that effective relief is granted'.[253] The court found further that the government's policy failed to meet constitutional standards. The reason behind this point of view was that the policy excluded 'those who could reasonably be included where such treatment is medically indicated to combat mother-to-child transmission of HIV'.[254] However, it pointed out that such a view does not imply the wholesale provision of treatment although such a situation would be desirable. It directed that every effort must be made to ensure full coverage as soon as reasonably possible even if this will entail increases in the budget.[255]

The case of *Mazibuko and Others v City of Johannesburg and Others*[256] concerned the right of access to water. The applicants challenged the City of Johannesburg's Free Basic Water policy. The policy entitled all households in Johannesburg to free 6 kilolitres of water on a monthly basis.[257] In addition, it provided for the installation of pre-paid water meters in the areas where the applicants lived.[258] The applicants argued that the manner in which the policy was implemented was unlawful, unreasonable, unfair, and in violation of their constitutional right to sufficient water. They argued that an amount

247 1998 (1) SA 765 (CC).
248 ibid para 29.
249 ibid para 21.
250 Section 11 of the constitution.
251 *Soobramoney v Minister of Health (Kwazulu-Natal)* 1998 (1) SA 765 (CC) para 57.
252 2002 (5) SA 721 (CC).
253 ibid para 106.
254 ibid para 125.
255 ibid.
256 2010 (4) SA 1 (CC).
257 ibid para 6.
258 ibid.

of 50 litres per day is essential for 'dignified human life'.[259] The view held by the applicants was that the court should 'adopt a quantified standard determining the content of the right not merely its minimum content'.[260] The Constitutional Court found that there were many answers as to what constitutes 'sufficient water'. Therefore, it was of the view that '[c]ourts are ill-placed to make these assessments for both institutional and democratic reasons'.[261] As regards the installation of pre-paid meters, the court ruled that the applicants failed to show that the implementation of such a system was unlawful[262] and discriminated unfairly.[263] In addition, the court acknowledged the significance of litigation on social and economic rights in a democracy by stating that:

> The purpose of litigation concerning the positive obligations imposed by social and economic rights should be to hold the democratic arms of government to account through litigation. In so doing, litigation of this sort fosters a form of participative democracy that holds government accountable and requires it to account between elections over specific aspects of government policy.[264]

The court maintained further that:

> When challenged as to its policies relating to social and economic rights, the government agency must explain why the policy is reasonable. Government must disclose what it has done to formulate the policy: its investigation and research, the alternatives considered, and the reasons why the option underlying the policy was selected. The Constitution does not require government to be held to an impossible standard of perfection. Nor does it require courts to take over the tasks that in a democracy should properly be reserved for the democratic arms of government. Simply put, through the institution of the courts, government can be called upon to account to citizens for its decisions. This understanding of social and economic rights litigation accords with the founding values of our Constitution and, in particular, the principles that government should be responsive, accountable and open. Not only must government show that the policy it has selected is reasonable, it must show that the policy is being reconsidered consistent with the obligation to 'progressively realise' social and economic rights in mind. A policy that is set in stone and never

259 ibid para 56.
260 ibid.
261 ibid para 62.
262 ibid para 158.
263 ibid para 157.
264 ibid para 160.

revisited is unlikely to be a policy that will result in the progressive realisation of rights consistently with the obligations imposed by the social and economic rights in our Constitution.[265]

Social Insurance

The current social insurance programme in South Africa caters for both occupational injuries and diseases as well as unemployment.

OCCUPATIONAL INJURY AND DISEASES

The current legislative basis of the South African employment injury and diseases scheme is contained in two statues, namely: The Compensation for Occupational Injuries and Diseases Act 130 of 1993 and Occupational Diseases in Mines and Works Act 78 of 1997. The Compensation for Occupational Injuries and Diseases Act provides for a 'no-fault' occupational injuries and diseases scheme. The Compensation Fund consists of, *inter alia*, the assessments paid by the employers;[266] penalties and fines imposed; any interest on investments of the compensation fund and the reserve fund; any amounts transferred from the reserve fund; and any other amounts to which the compensation fund may become entitled.[267] Its scope of coverage is broad.[268] The definition of 'employee' contained in Section 1(xix)(v) of the Compensation for Occupational Injuries and Diseases Act was declared by the High Court of South Africa in *Mahlangu and the South African Domestic Service and Allied Workers Union v The Minister of Labour and Others* (Case no: 79280/15) to be unconstitutional and invalid. The scheme previously excluded domestic employees employed as such in a private household. This was mainly due to the difficulty in administering the act with regard to such an employment relationship which takes place largely in private, particularly in a private household. The Compensation for Occupational Injuries and Diseases Act is administered by the Director-General of the Department of Labour.[269] The Director-General is assisted by the Compensation Commissioner as well as

265 Para 161–62.

266 Section 1 of the Compensation for Occupational Injuries and Diseases Act 130 of 1993.

267 Section 15 (2) of the Compensation for Occupational Injuries and Diseases Act 130 of 1993.

268 The Compensation for Occupational Injuries and Diseases Act defines an employer as: 'any person, including the State, who employs an employee, and includes (a) any person controlling the business of an employer; (b) if the services of an employee are lent or let or temporarily made available to some other person by his employer, such employer for such period as the employee works for that other person; (c) a labour broker who against payment provides a person to a client for the rendering of a service or the performance of work, and for which service or work such person is paid by the labour broker'. Section 1(i)-(v) of the Compensation for Occupational Injuries and Diseases Act 130 of 1993.

269 Section 2(1) of the Compensation for Occupational Injuries and Diseases Act 130 of 1993.

other officers and employees appointed by the Minister of Labour.[270] An employee covered by Compensation for Occupational Injuries and Diseases Act is entitled to claim compensation for occupational injuries or occupational diseases. The following benefits can be claimed in accordance with the Compensation for Occupational Injuries and Diseases Act: Temporary disablement benefits,[271] permanent disablement,[272] dependants' benefits,[273] and medical aid.[274] Alongside the Compensation Fund, the Compensation for Occupational Injuries and Diseases Act does make provision for the existence of two mutual associations, namely, the Rand Mutual Assurance Company Limited and the Federated Employers' Mutual Limited.[275] The Rand Mutual Assurance Company Limited operates in the mining industry and the Federated Employers' Mutual Limited functions in the construction industry.

UNEMPLOYMENT INSURANCE

The post-apartheid unemployment insurance framework is set out in two pieces of legislation, namely: The Unemployment Insurance Act 63 of 2001 and Unemployment Insurance Contributions Act 4 of 2002. Its purpose is to 'establish an unemployment insurance fund to which employers and employees contribute and from which employees who become unemployed or their beneficiaries, as the case may be, are entitled to benefits and in so doing alleviate the harmful economic and social effects of unemployment'.[276] The purpose of the Unemployment Insurance Contributions Act is to provide for 'the payment of contributions for the benefit of the Unemployment Insurance Fund; and procedures for the collection of such contributions'.[277] The unemployment insurance laws apply to all employers and employees with the exception of the groups and categories of persons mentioned in the next paragraph.[278] The unemployment insurance laws define an employee as 'any natural person who receives remuneration or to whom remuneration accrues in respect of services rendered or to be rendered by that person, but

270 ibid.
271 Section 47 of the Compensation for Occupational Injuries and Diseases Act 130 of 1993.
272 Section 49 of the Compensation for Occupational Injuries and Diseases Act 130 of 1993.
273 Section 54 of the Compensation for Occupational Injuries and Diseases Act 130 of 1993.
274 Chapter VIII of the Compensation for Occupational Injuries and Diseases Act 130 of 1993.
275 Section 30 of the Compensation for Occupational Injuries and Diseases Act 130 of 1993.
276 Section 2 of the Unemployment Insurance Act 63 of 2001.
277 Section 2 and preamble of the Unemployment Insurance Contributions Act 4 of 2002.
278 Section 3(1) of the Unemployment Insurance Act 63 of 2001 and Section 4(1)(a) of the Unemployment Insurance Contributions Act 4 of 2002.

excludes any independent contractor'.[279] The Unemployment Insurance Act binds the state.[280]

The following groups of persons are excluded from the unemployment insurance scheme: Employees employed for less than 24 hours per month with a particular employer as well as their employers;[281] and members of parliament, cabinet ministers, deputy ministers, members of provincial executive councils, members of provincial legislatures, and municipal councillors.[282] Domestic workers are also included in the scope of coverage of the unemployment insurance scheme. The administrative and institutional framework of the South African unemployment insurance system are largely set out in the Unemployment Insurance Act and Unemployment Insurance Contributions Act. The Unemployment Insurance Act makes provision for, among others, the establishment and functions of the Unemployment Insurance Board, the establishment of the Unemployment Insurance Fund, and the designation of the Unemployment Insurance Commissioner as well as the appointment of claims officers.

Seven different types of benefits can be found in the South African unemployment insurance system, namely: the unemployment benefits, the illness benefits, the maternity benefits, the adoption benefits, the dependants' benefits, the parental benefits, and the commissioning parental benefits.[283] The unemployment benefits, the illness benefits, the maternity benefits, the adoption benefits, and the dependants' benefits provided for in the repealed Unemployment Insurance Act of 1966 were carried forward in the current legislation. The parental benefits and the commissioning parental benefits were inserted by Section 8 of the Labour Laws Amendment Act 10 of 2018 after the introduction of parental leave[284] and commissioning parental leave[285] in South Africa.[286] The unemployment insurance is largely financed by three participants, namely: The insured (employee), the employer, and the state. It must be born in mind that there are additional sources of revenue, such as donations and bequests. An employer and his or her employee each contribute 1 percent of the employee's salary which is remitted to the Unemployment Insurance Fund or South African Revenue Service.

279 Section 1 of the Unemployment Insurance Act 63 of 2001 and Section 1 of the Unemployment Insurance Contributions Act 4 of 2002.

280 Section 72 of the Unemployment Insurance Act 63 of 2001.

281 Section 3(1)(a) of the Unemployment Insurance Act 63 of 2001 and Section 4(1)(a) of the Unemployment Insurance Contributions Act 4 of 2002.

282 Section 3(2) of the Unemployment Insurance Act 63 of 2001 and Section 4(1)(c) – (f) of the Unemployment Insurance Contributions Act 4 of 2002.

283 Section 12 of the Unemployment Insurance Act 63 of 2001.

284 Section 25A of the Basic Conditions of Employment Act 75 of 1997.

285 Section 25C of the Basic Conditions of Employment Act 75 of 1997.

286 See *MIA v State Information Technology Agency (Pty) Ltd* (2015) 36 ILJ 1905 (LC).

OLD AGE AND HEALTH CARE

From a contributory point of view, old age and health care are provided for mainly through private (occupational) schemes. South Africa is yet to introduce a national contributory retirement scheme despite having touted this scheme from the inception of the tax-financed old age pension scheme. The lack of such contributory national schemes is attributable to the difficulties attendant to efforts to construct a proper social security system during the apartheid period. Kahn has outlined the situation at that time succinctly as follows:

> In the nature of things, a realistic scheme for social security in South Africa must be difficult to fashion due to the different races, our undeveloped system of social insurance, the absence of adequate labour statistics, our divided system of government and many other complicity factors, all operation only slightly if at all in other lands.[287]

As regards health care, it is pleasing to note that plans are at an advanced stage towards the introduction of a contributory National Health Insurance scheme. The National Health Insurance Bill was published from public comments on 21 June 2018. The rationale behind the introduction of such a scheme is to achieve the progressive realisation of the rights of access to social security in South Africa.[288]

South Africa in the Global Arena

The United Nations readmitted South Africa on Thursday 23 June 1994. This was subsequent to the holding of the first multiparty and multiracial national election, which signalled the demise of apartheid in that country. To mark its return to the international community of nations South Africa signed and ratified a number of social security and labour law (related) international (United Nations and ILO) instruments, which include the following: Forced Labour Convention 29 of 1930 (5 May 1997), Freedom of Association and Protection of the Right to Organise Convention 87 of 1948 (19 February 1996), Right to Organise and Collective Bargaining Convention 98 of 1949 (19 February 1996), Equal Remuneration Convention 100 of 1951 (5 March 1997), Abolition of Forced Labour Convention 105 of 1957 (5 March 1997), Discrimination (Employment and Occupation) Convention 111 of 1958 (5 March 1997), Minimum Age Convention 138 of 1973 (30 March 2000), and Worst Forms of Child Labour Convention 182 of 1999 (7 June 2000). In addition, new labour laws and social security laws were enacted/amended

287 Kahn (n 142) 64.
288 Preamble of the National Health Insurance Bill of 2018.

to give effect to the provisions of the Constitution of the Republic of South Africa, 1996 and the country's international obligations.

Conclusion

South Africa has, by emerging economy standards, a well-developed social security scheme. This system, which is set in law, makes provision for both social assistance and social insurance. It evolved from an era characterised by 'separation' and 'segregation' based on racial domination. Despite that, many approaches developed during that era influence(d) the current social security framework. For example, the old age benefits are still payable subject to a means-test in South Africa. It is interesting to note that the envisaged contributory old age scheme, touted at the introduction of the old age pensions scheme, never saw the light of day. In the social insurance sphere, the various benefits provided for under the Union and apartheid unemployment insurance schemes, as odd as the inclusion of some of those benefits (eg maternity and adoption benefits) in such a scheme may be, have been retained in the post-apartheid unemployment insurance programme. All said and done, the South African social security system has evolved over a long period, through interesting changes and phases, from an unjust to a value- and human rights-based scheme. Ellison Kahn once characterised the efforts to develop social security in South Africa as 'a brave attempt to do what is almost impossible – to devise Social Security for the common man in a poor and racially divided country'.[289] It took decades to ensure that a 'common man' is not excluded from the South African social security system because of unfair grounds such as racism. In today's terms, such an unfair system will not thrive in South Africa. The constitution, through its values, rights, and enforcement mechanisms, jealously guards against that.

289 Kahn (n 142) 66.

Chapter 6

Southern Welfare

From Social Insurance to Social Security

Ulrike Davy

Introduction: Framing the Making of Comparisons

The making of comparisons has a long-standing tradition in a multitude of disciplines in Europe and other Western countries, including law. The tradition started at the end of the nineteenth century and has produced abundant comparative studies dealing with all sorts of subjects. The long history notwithstanding, the making of comparisons was contested from early on. Critical anthropologists warned Western scientists against jumping to conclusions too quickly, in particular, against detecting a grand scheme or general laws significant for mankind as a whole, when and where the data, objects, or people compared were not fully understood in their specific contexts.[1] Indeed, making comparisons across countries or across world regions is tricky. The act of comparing involves at least two entities which are being compared (*comparata*) and an angle or a perspective that informs and determines the outcome of the comparison (*tertium*), such as length, weight, beauty, knowledge, or amounts of income. In addition to that, the act of comparing presupposes that it is possible, or that it makes sense, to compare *comparatum* A to *comparatum* B (assumption of comparability or commensurability). Comparability (commensurability) may be assumed when the *comparata* share at least some characteristics deemed relevant while differing in other respects. A and B can only be compared, and ranked according to their weight, if both A and B can, one way or the other, be put on a weight-machine with the effect that the weight-machine assigns weight to A as well as to B. Against that theoretical background, the making of comparisons across countries or across world regions fails if the entities supposed to be compared – in our case, ideas (concepts, values, beliefs) relating to social policy – lack relevant commonalities. Moreover, the making of comparisons will produce unbiased and meaningful results only if the commonalities regarding the ideas are not simply read into the findings by an investigator

1 Seminal Franz Boas, 'The Limitations of the Comparative Method of Anthropology' (1896) 4 Science (New Series) 901; from the perspective of law Günter Frankenberg, 'Critical Comparisons: Re-thinking Comparative Law' (1985) 26 Harvard International Law Journal 411.

DOI: 10.4324/9781003242826-6

who proceeds according to preconceived expectations. Poignantly, investigators with a Western eye and equipped with Western notions of, let's say, social security or social protection, might misinterpret their findings and overlook local peculiarities.[2] What needs to be done is putting all assumptions regarding comparability on the table while being aware that these assumptions are nothing but abstract starting points. Findings must primarily draw on country-specific sources and the meanings they convey in their contexts.

When preparing our country studies, we wanted the authors to be able to report on some basic commonalities regarding the ideational foundations of social policy, otherwise the making of comparisons would have failed. But we also wanted the authors of the country studies to have plenty of room for presenting differences, idiosyncrasies, counter-ideas, or the outright rejection of ideas as inappropriate in their context. That is why we concentrated on instruments of social policy that have, from the late nineteenth century onward, been discussed in political circles around the globe at the national level as well as in international organisations, namely state-regulated contribution-based social insurance on the one hand, and state-provided means-tested benefits supposed to cover basic human needs, such as food, clothing, housing, water, and health care, on the other hand.[3] According to our concept, the essential characteristics of social insurance are state involvement; a link between benefits and certain contingencies; some social element, such as contributions by the insured, but not necessarily in cash, and not by the insured only; lack of risk-based calculation. The essential elements of means-tested benefits are state provision (ie tax-financed benefits); some sort of targeting of the poor; and benefits in cash or in kind. With the focus on these flagship instruments of social policy, the country studies aim to give an account on when relevant policies in Brazil, China,

2 See Jean D'Aspremont, 'Comparativism and Colonizing Thinking in International Law' (2019) 57 Canadian Yearbook of International Law 89, 102, warning against unilaterally defining, silencing, or speaking on behalf of an 'other'. On contingencies and power-relations implicated in practices of comparing see also Ulrike Davy and Antje Flüchter, 'Concepts of Equality: Why, Who, What for?' in Ulrike Davy and Antje Flüchter (eds), *Imaging Unequals, Imagining Equals. Concepts of Equality in History and Law* (Bielefeld University Press 2022) 11.

3 For early discussions in Brazil see Lena Lavinas, 'The Anatomy of the Social Question and the Evolution of the Brazilian Social Security System, 1919–2020' in Lutz Leisering (ed), *One Hundred Years of Social Protection. The Changing Social Question in Brazil, India, China, and South Africa* (Palgrave Macmillan 2021); see also A. Tixier, 'Sickness Insurance at the International Labour Conference' (1927) 16 International Labour Review 773; Moises Poblete-Troncoso, 'Labour Legislation in Latin America: I' (1928) 17 International Labour Review 51; Moises Poblete-Troncoso, 'Labour Legislation in Latin America: II' (1928) 17 International Labour Review 204. For China see Albert H.Y. Chen, Chapter 3 in this volume; see also Ta Chen, 'The Labour Movement in China' (1927) 15 International Labour Review 339. For India see Ernest C. Low, 'India and the Washington Conference' (1922) 5 International Labour Review 3; Henry W. Wolff, 'The Co-operative Movement and Labour in India' (1922) 5 International Labour Review 229; Rajani Kanta Das, 'Labour Legislation in India' (1930) 22 International Labour Review 599; P.P. Pillai, *India and the International Labour Organisation* (Patna University 1931); Sarbani Sen, Chapter 4 in this volume.

India, and South Africa first emerged and then were developed further. The main questions to be answered were: When and how were instruments sharing these characteristics introduced? What were the political ideas that prompted the states to move toward the introduction of those instruments? What were the concepts underlying those instruments? Were the states paying attention to models elsewhere? When and how were those instruments developed further? Were there changes in the design of those instruments? If so, what ideas triggered the change? The questions already indicate what our *comparata* and our *tertia* are. The *comparata* are made of the social policy instruments the states have resorted to, the ideas that were advanced in relevant political discourses, the design of the instruments, and the concepts underpinning the (concrete) design of the instruments. Important *tertia* comprise, for instance, the weight assigned to the contingencies in the context of considering the introduction of social insurance (has there been some form of prioritisation), the weight given to the ideas pondered in politics (have some ideas been more important than others), the weight accorded to social policy in relation to other policies, or the extent to which states assumed responsibility for the individual well-being of the people residing in their territories.

This chapter encompasses five main sections. The first section deals with the policies negotiated under the umbrella of the International Labour Organisation (ILO), the main facilitator and mediator with respect to ideas relating to social and labour policies, becoming operative in the aftermath of World War I. The focus of the first section is, however, not on the question of how ideas spread around the globe, also reaching Brazil, China, India, and South Africa. The focus is on how Brazil, China, India, and South Africa have influenced what has been debated at the level of the ILO in the 1920s and the 1930s and, through that, have influenced some of the ideas that became, eventually, part of the official ILO policies. However, we also want to look behind the surface of official ILO policies that materialise in the texts of resolutions, recommendations, or draft conventions. We want to give an account on the positions of the delegates coming from the four countries, and to make their voices heard, also with a view to policies pursued at the national level: Are national policies reflected in the debates on international policy (law) making? The question of how internationally conceived elements of social policy find their way to the national level will be dealt with in the other sections of the chapter where the making of comparisons is central. The second section turns to the emergence of social policies in Brazil, China, India, and South Africa: When and how did Brazil, India, China, and South Africa consider and implement instruments that can be identified as social insurance or tax-financed means-tested benefits targeting the poor? What were the arguments brought forward to legitimise such a move, and what were the aims and the aspirations? The third section traces the trajectories of social policy chosen and followed (or abandoned) by policy makers at the national level: What became of the social policy instruments once they had been introduced? Did new ideas prompt policy changes?

The fourth section concentrates on the role of constitutional courts: What can be said about the role of constitutions and constitutional courts? How did constitutional courts influence the ideational foundations of social policies? Each section of the chapter puts these questions – addressed to the national levels of the four countries – in context, for one, with respect to policies at the level of the international level (ILO), for another with respect to policies in the global North, in particular to policies in Europe (Germany or the United Kingdom serve as the model welfare states) and, at certain points, the United States. The final section summarises the findings of the various comparisons: What characterises the social policies pursued by Brazil, China, India, and South Africa? Can we detect a distinct narrative (condensing emergence and trajectories of social policies) that differs from the narrative rehearsed in Europe or at the level of the ILO?

ILO Social Policy: Colonial Powers Encounter Brazil, China, and India, 1920–1944

Foundations

Since the late 1890s, non-governmental organisations specialising in labour questions had campaigned for the introduction of international labour standards. In 1919, when the Allied and Associated Powers met in Paris to negotiate a peace that would end World War I,[4] they finally succeeded. Against the fear that European states might soon face a series of left-wing revolutions (similar to the one taking place in Russia), the Allied and Associated Powers were willing to give in to one of most important workers' demands, namely the establishment of a permanent international organisation tasked to deal with international labour.[5] Each of the peace treaties brokered in Paris – the peace treaty with Germany signed in Versailles serving as a template – contained a part on 'Labour'.[6] The part was primarily concerned with organisational matters, such as formally establishing the ILO as a permanent organisation, listing the principal organs (the General Conference of Representatives, later termed

4 Among the Allied and Associated Powers were the United States of America, the British Empire, France, Italy, Japan (the Principal Allied and Associated Powers), and Belgium, Bolivia, Brazil, China, Cuba, Ecuador, Greece, Guatemala, Haiti, The Hedjaz, Honduras, Liberia, Nicaragua, Panama, Peru, Poland, Portugal, Roumania, The Serb-Croat-Slovene State, Siam, Czecho-Slovakia, and Uruguay.

5 James T. Shotwell, 'The International Labor Organization as an Alternative to Violent Revolution' (1933) 166 Annals of the American Academy of Political and Social Science 18; Edward J. Phelan, 'The Commission on the International Labour Legislation' in James T. Shotwell (ed), *The Origins of the International Labor Organization, vol 1 History* (Columbia University Press 1934) 127.

6 Treaty of Peace between the Allied and Associated Powers and Germany, signed at Versailles, June 28, 1919, British Treaty Series No. 4, Articles 387–427.

International Labour Conference, consisting of delegates sent by governments, employers, and workers; the Governing Body; and the International Labour Office), outlining procedures, and defining membership in the organisation.[7] Regarding substantive matters, the Versailles Treaty indicated that – differences in climate, habits, and customs notwithstanding – the standards negotiated and agreed upon at the International Labour Conference were meant to being applied by all industrial communities (Article 427). Universal labour and social policy standards were clearly envisioned as a political aim, even though the treaty explicitly conceded that 'immediate attainment' of uniformity was unrealistic. Universality was to be attained (only) gradually. The idea of the universality of standards was additionally thwarted by a treaty clause concerned with the overseas (dependent) territories of the European colonial powers. Pressed by the French labour movement, the treatymakers agreed to a clause obliging the members of the ILO to apply the ILO conventions, once ratified, also to their overseas territories (termed 'colonies, protectorates and possessions which are not fully self-governing') (Article 421). Yet, the obligation to apply the standards to overseas territories was partly withdrawn by a proviso saying that members were free to refrain from applying the standards when, according to their judgement, the standards were inapplicable due to 'local conditions' or in need of 'modifications' that would adapt the standards to 'local conditions' (Article 421).[8] In practice, the principle of universality soon became a focal point in the debates taking place at International Labour Conferences, most of them held in Geneva. Delegates from the South were the main actors confronting and challenging the European colonial powers, and delegates from China and India were at the forefront.

Membership

Brazil, China, India, and South Africa were among the founding members of the ILO listed in the Annex following the final article of part I of the Versailles Treaty. Yet India was, in 1919, neither a self-governing Dominion (like Australia, Canada, New Zealand, or South Africa listed under the heading 'British Empire') nor any other internationally recognised self-governing entity. However, against the background of India's contribution to the war effort, Indian political movements demanding self-government had gained considerable strength, and the demands had gained legitimacy.[9]

7 Regarding the composition of the International Labour Conference, the Versailles Treaty stated in Article 389(1): 'It shall be composed of four Representatives of each of the Members, of whom two shall be Government Delegates and the two others shall be Delegates representing respectively the employers and the workpeople of each of the Members'.

8 On the background of the Versailles treaty clause concerned with the overseas territories of the European colonial powers see Phelan (n 5) 171.

9 Arthur Berriedale Keith, *A Constitutional History of India 1600–1935* (Methuen & Co Ltd 1936) 240.

Negotiations with the British government on constitutional issues started long before the Paris peace talks opened. The negotiations ended in an act of the British parliament adopted in December 1919.[10] The British government were prepared to enhance the representation of Indians in the Government of India, to introduce some kind of legislative bodies at the central and provincial level, and to enhance the power of the local (provincial) governments as first tentative political steps. At that point in time, the British government were not prepared to grant full self-government in one big leap. Self-government was to be attained progressively.[11] Still, at the 1919 Paris peace talks, the British government made sure that India, even though its status was different, was being treated on an equal footing with the fully self-governing Dominions which were – also for the first time in history – separately represented within the British Empire delegation.[12] Indian officials attended the talks, signed the peace treaties, and became a 'member' of the League of Nations and the ILO. A new constitutional arrangement was found in 1935, when India was turned into a federation and the British Crown retained limited powers mostly relating to external affairs, but – to some extent – also to executive matters.[13] Only in 1947 did India attain the status of a fully self-governing dominion and an independent state.[14] China's statehood was not contested at the end of World War I, the internal struggles and the incursions into its territories through a system of concessions and leases (foreign settlements) notwithstanding.[15] China participated in the Paris peace talks, as one of the smaller nations. However, China did eventually not sign the Versailles treaty, protesting the decision taken by the principal Allies to hand some of the German concessions in China (linked to Shantung) over to

10 Government of India Act 1919 (9 & 10 Geo 5 c 101).

11 The official formula spoke of 'gradual development of self-governing institutions with a view to the progressive realization of responsible government in India as an integral part of the British Empire'. Keith (n 9) 243. The relationship created by the various acts of government in India in the second half of the nineteenth century had a dual structure. India was, on the one hand governed by a secretary of state (advised by the Council of India) located in London and, on the other hand, by a governor-general (advised by the Council of the Governor-General of India) located in India (first Calcutta, then Delhi). Prior to the establishment of legislative assemblies, the governor-general was vested with administrative and legislative powers.

12 Robert Borden, *Canada in the Commonwealth. From Conflict to Cooperation* (Clarendon Press 1929) 92.

13 Government of India Act 1935 (26 Geo 5 c 2).

14 Indian Independence Act 1947 (10 & 11 Geo 6 c 30) creating two new dominions, India and Pakistan; L. Oppenheim and H. Lauterpacht, *International Law. A Treatise, vol 1. Peace*, 7th edn (Longmans, Green and Co 1948) 190.

15 On the historical background see Edmund S.K. Fung, 'The Chinese Nationalists and the Unequal Treaties 1924–1931' (1987) 21 Modern Asian Studies 793; Alison Adcock Kaufman, 'In Pursuit of Equality and Respect: China's Diplomacy and the League of Nations' (2014) 40 Modern China 605, 609.

Japan instead of restoring China's rights over the peninsula.[16] But China did sign the peace treaty with Austria at Saint-Germain-en-Laye and – through this – became an original member of the League of Nations and the ILO, like Brazil, India, or South Africa.[17]

The decision to set up the International Labour Office in Geneva and to hold (almost) all international labour conferences in Geneva clearly favoured the European states. Travelling was short, costs low. Non-European members had to shoulder considerably higher costs and to endure long and tiresome journeys.[18] Still, India's delegations were, in the 1920s and 1930s, always complete ones. The workers' delegates were generally Indian natives nominated by unions. The employers' delegates were until the late 1920s British natives with business interests in India, afterwards Indian natives nominated by employers' associations. The two government delegates were high-ranking officials (high commissioners for India; members of the Council of India), usually one British, one Indian, and very often based in London. Sir Louis James Kershaw, for instance, served as a delegate for the government of India for many years, and so did Atul Chandra Chatterjee. Kershaw was Secretary of the India Office in London, then Assistant Under Secretary of State. Chatterjee was Chief Secretary in the United Provinces Government, then Secretary to the Government of India, then member of the Council of the Governor-General, then High Commissioner for India in London, then member of the Council of India in London. China sent delegations to the International Labour Conference, starting with the first session in 1919, but the first complete delegation – comprising government, employers', and workers' delegates – was sent in 1929.[19] Prior to that, China had sent only government delegates and, in the early 1920s, barely communicated with the International Labour Office or the European colonial powers. Distrust reigned. Things changed when the Guomindang government (Chiang Kai-shek) was established in Nanjing in 1928. Brazil also participated in the conferences from early on, but sending complete delegations seemed not a high priority.[20] Brazil commenced sending complete delegations from 1930 onwards. In 1926, Brazil (and Spain) decided to leave the

16 S.K. Hornbeck, 'Shantung at the Peace Conference' in Harold Temperley (ed), *A History of the Peace Conference of Paris* (Oxford University Press 1924) 368; Robert T. Pollard, *China's Foreign Relations 1917–1931* (The Macmillan Company 1933) 67. For the Chinese position see N.N., 'Questions for Readjustment Submitted by China to the Peace Conference' (1920) 5 Chinese Social and Political Science Review 116.

17 Treaty of Peace between the Allied and Associated Powers and Austria, signed at Saint-Germain-en-Laye, September 10, 1919, British Treaty Series No. 11; Pollard (n 16) 84.

18 Under Article 399 of the Versailles Treaty, travelling costs of the delegates were not to be paid out of the general funds of the League of Nations.

19 League of Nations, International Labour Conference, 12th Session 1929, vol I, XXXVII.

20 On the reluctance of Latin American states to actively participate in the work of the League of Nations see Don Augustin Edwards, 'Latin America and the League of Nations' (1929) 8 Journal of the Royal Institute of International Affairs 134.

League of Nations.[21] The decision became effective in 1928, after the two years notice period had expired. Yet, Brazil was willing to further cooperate under the framework of the ILO and, after legal uncertainties had been resolved by way of interpretation, Brazil continued to attend the International Labour Conferences and to fulfil its duties under the ILO framework.[22] South Africa – at the relevant time the Union of South Africa[23] – shared the status of the other British dominions that were fully self-governing and had gained international standing in the aftermath of World War I: Dominions were states of their own and had a position in international law of their own, even if they were still part of the British Empire, and that made their exact status difficult to define.[24]

Politics and Ideas

From the perspective of willingness to ratify the draft conventions brokered by the International Labour Conferences in the 1920s and 1930s, India took the lead (fifteen ratifications), followed by China (thirteen ratifications), Brazil (twelve ratifications), and South Africa (seven ratifications). The conventions that were eventually ratified by the four countries signal preferences with regard to social policies, also from the perspective of ideas. The four countries barely ratified an ILO-brokered convention concerned with matters pertaining to social insurance, such as workmen's compensation in case of accidents or occupational diseases, sickness insurance, old age insurance, invalidity insurance, or unemployment insurance, although the ILO had been quite active in the field in the 1920s and 1930s. The four countries were focused on labour standards, yet not on all labour standards the ILO had on offer.[25] Clearly, the four countries were interested in restrictions regarding

21 League of Nations, International Labour Conference, 10th Session 1927, vol II, Report of the Director presented to the Conference, 3. Brazil and Spain felt that, when Germany was admitted to the League of Nations and given a permanent Council seat, they should be treated the same. For details Edwards (n 20) 143.

22 Statement of the Secretary-General, 14 June 1929, International Labour Conference 1929 (n 19) 291.

23 South Africa Act 1909 (9 Edw 7 c 9). The act united several 'British Colonies' under one government in a legislative union under the Crown of Great Britain and Ireland, namely the Cape of Good Hope, Natal, the Transvaal, and the Orange River Colony. See Letlhokwa George Mpedi, Chapter 5 in this volume.

24 L. Oppenheim and Ronald F. Roxburgh, *International Law. A Treatise, vol 1. Peace*, 3rd edn (Longmans, Green and Co 1920) 170. The other self-governing dominions listed among the original members of the League of Nations were Australia, Canada, and New Zealand.

25 India's focus, for instance, was on hours of work in industrial undertakings; unemployment; employment of women during the night; night work of young persons in industry; minimum age for admission of children to employment in industry (with reservations) and sea; compulsory medical examination of children and young persons employed at sea; right of association of agricultural workers; weekly rest in industry; workmen's compensation for occupational diseases; equality of treatment (workmen's compensation); inspection of emigrants of bord of ship; weight of packages

night work for women and young persons and in employment of young persons at sea, hence in core labour standards, with a focus on work deemed very stressful and workers deemed vulnerable. The countries abstained from ratifying conventions dealing with maternity protection, hours of work (in particular, in commerce, offices, and coal mines), night work more generally, or the minimum age of admission to employment in industry or agriculture. From the perspective of policies and ideas actively pursued, four topics were prominent: Brazil, China, India, and South Africa joined forces in their dislike for European colonialism. The countries differed strongly in their positions when questions of equality were raised and debated. The need for development, in particular economic development, was emphasised by all of them. And all but South Africa championed regionalism under the ILO framework. The following provides a brief sketch on these four topics.

Anti-Colonialism

Anti-colonial sentiment surfaced when the delegates to the International Labour Conference gathered for the first time in Washington in November 1919. A (preparatory) *ad hoc* commission had proposed that the Governing Body of the ILO be asked to appoint an international commission tasked with considering the measures to be adopted to regulate the migration of workers out of their own states and to protect the interests of wage earners residing in a state other than their own.[26] The proposal triggered fierce criticism of the Versailles Treaty provisions concerned with the composition of the Governing Body. Under these provisions (Article 393), the Governing Body was to comprise 24 persons, twelve representing governments, six representing employers, and six representing workers. Of the twelve persons representing governments, eight were to be nominated by the members considered to be 'of the chief industrial importance', and four were to be nominated by the government delegates to the conference (excluding the delegates of the eight members considered to be of chief industrial importance). The first to voice his criticism was an employers' delegate from South Africa (William Gemmill) who said he wanted to 'draw the attention of the conference to the amazing fact that the government body contains, out of 24 representatives, 20 from the European Continent'.[27] Gemmill doubted that the interests of the countries of immigration (the countries of the 'new world', as he liked to call them) would duly be

transported by vessels; seamen's articles of agreement; underground work in mines (women). China's and Brazil's preferences were similar. South Africa's narrow focus was on employment of women during the night; unemployment; equality of treatment (workmen's compensation); creation of minimum wage fixing machinery; weight of packages transported by vessels; underground word in mines (women); statistics of wages and hours of work (with reservation).

26 League of Nations, International Labour Conference, First Annual Meeting 1919, 237.

27 International Labour Conference 1919 (n 26) 137.

represented in that international commission. While the conference was able to find a compromise on the composition of the migration commission,[28] the composition of the Governing Body remained an issue for sessions to come. Under the lead of South Africa and other countries (including Brazil, China, and India), the first International Labour Conference adopted a formal protest against the composition of the Governing Body; the conference also moved to amend Article 393 of the Treaty of Versailles with a view to enlarge the number of seats assigned to the Governing Body in order to accommodate the wishes of the non-European states.[29] In addition, India complained that it had not been given a seat among the eight countries of chief industrial importance.[30] India was, because of its intervention, eventually admitted in 1922 to the group of eight members of the Governing Body considered to be of chief industrial importance.[31] The 1922 conference adopted an amendment to Article 393, which became effective in 1934.[32]

India and China continued to express discontent with colonial politics. India's discontent was primarily voiced by workers' delegates. The speeches by Narayan Malhar Joshi, Lala Lajpat Rai, Chaman Lall, and Benegal Shiva Rao in the 1920s clearly stick out. Protests focused on the politics of the British government as well as on the politics of the Government of India (which was dominated by British officials). China targeted European countries more broadly. China's criticism aimed at the countries which operated 'foreign settlements' or held 'concessions' on China's soil, and at what China perceived as Western imperialism.[33] China's anti-colonial stance gained momentum in the late 1920s and could still be heard throughout the 1930s. Governments' as well as workers' delegates from China dominated the speeches. The strategies of the workers' delegates from India and the strategies of the delegates from China were similar. Both groups pursued a politics of scandalising the situation on the ground, thus blaming and shaming the European countries as the

28 The conference agreed that the representation of European states on the commission ought to be limited to one-half of the total membership of the commission. International Labour Conference 1919 (n 26) 151, 153.

29 International Labour Conference 1919 (n 26) 197, 275; International Labour Office, Official Bulletin, vol I (1919–1920) 458.

30 Official Bulletin 1919–1920 (n 29) 456.

31 International Labour Office, Official Bulletin, vol VI (1922) 590.

32 Official Bulletin 1922 (n 31) 603; International Labour Office, Official Bulletin, vol XIX (1934) 62.

33 Generally Edmund S.K. Fung, 'The Sino-British Rapprochement, 1927–1931' (1983) 17 Modern Asian Studies 79; Edmund S.K. Fung, 'Anti-Imperialism and the Left Guomindang' (1985) 11 Modern China 39; William C. Johnstone, 'International Relations: The Status of Foreign Concessions and Settlements in the Treaty Ports of China' (1937) 31 The American Political Science Review 942. In the 1930s, special rights and privileges were held by Great Britain, the United States, Japan, France, Italy, Norway, Sweden, Denmark, the Netherlands, Spain, Portugal, Peru, Mexico, and Switzerland. Prior to 1919, special rights and privileges had, additionally, been held by Germany and Austria-Hungary.

ones responsible for what happened in their territories. The Indian workers' delegates were more outspoken and tended to stress the backwardness of India's industries and the miserable living conditions of the Indian people. The main message of the Indian workers' delegates was: The British have failed in what they called their civilising mission. At the 1925 International Labour Conference, for instance, Benegal Shiva Rao said:

> India to-day is a land of slaves; it consists of workers and peasants who are living on the starvation line. . . . You find in the cotton mills women working ten hours a day and getting Rs. 19 a month. . . . You find men, women and children working on the tea plantations, the men getting Rs. 8 a month, the women Rs. 6 and the children Rs. 4. . . . The jute workers in Calcutta are getting Rs. 5 a week as wages, while similar work done in Dundee in similar mills . . . is paid at the rate of £3 a week. The result is that the owners close down their mills in Dundee . . . and start fresh mills in Calcutta, because there they can get cheap labour and cheap raw material. . . . This is glorious India, the great eastern empire, which is the substratum of the system which is known as the British Empire.[34]

The Indian workers' delegates had no trust in the British Empire's colonial politics. Again, in the words of Benegal Shiva Rao:

> We in India are familiar with the theory of trusteeship. . . . We have endured the trusteeship of a foreign Power for more than a century and a half . . . we have seen how the trustee has grown steadily richer and more prosperous at the expense of the ward.[35]

The delegates from China concentrated on the working conditions in the foreign settlements they deemed inhumane. The delegates mainly complained about not being able to implement the standards adopted by the International Labour Conferences. The main message was: Only if and when China's full sovereignty is restored (and the Europeans are driven out of the country) will China be able to live up to its ILO membership duties. Early demands were raised by Chu Chao-Hsin, a government delegate, at the 1927 International Conference, rather politely:

> [Some] industries have been established in China by foreign capitalists, who take advantage of the plentiful supply of raw materials and cheap labour. Chinese labour regulations do not apply to them, because they

34 League of Nations, International Labour Conference, 7th Session 1925, vol I, 173.
35 International Labour Conference 1929 (n 19) 46.

> are located in the international settlements and foreign concessions where extra-territoriality is being abusively enjoyed.[36]

At the 1934 International Labour Conference, An Fu-Ting, a Chinese workers' delegate, was more straightforward:

> The foreign settlements and concessions . . . are merely profitable trade territories for foreign employers, where they work temporarily for a certain period of years and return to their homeland with bank-notes soaked with the sweat and blood of the Chinese workers. To them there is no such thing as social justice, and thus they do not care a bit for the welfare of the workers.[37]

In 1929 and in 1933, China failed in prompting the International Labour Conference to adopt a resolution supporting China's wish to extend its labour laws to the foreign settlements. Eventually though, in 1937, China got the votes needed for the adoption of a resolution requesting the Governing Body to consider steps which might ensure the application of a uniform system of protection for the workers in all undertakings situated on Chinese territory.[38] The system of foreign settlements and concessions was finally abandoned in the 1940s.[39]

Clearly, India and China used the ILO labour conferences as public venues for advancing their demands regarding self-government (India) and the restoration of full sovereignty over the territory (China).

Equality

Equality issues were, at least partly, related to anti-colonial politics. Demands regarding the representation in international forums drew on the idea of equality among states. That is true for the arguments related to the distribution of seats in the Governing Body. The non-European countries felt that, given the initial distribution of seats, their interests were valued less than the interests of the European states. China's claim that full sovereignty over its territories be restored was based on the argument that foreign settlements

36 League of Nations, International Labour Conference, 10th Session 1927, vol I, 144. Time and again, China's delegates stressed the idea of equality: 'China considers it is necessary to have the Chinese labour laws enforced throughout China, irrespective of whether the factories are directed by foreigners or by Chinese. It considers that the same labour laws should apply throughout the country'. Statement of Thomas Tchou, 21 June 1929, International Labour Conference 1929 (n 19) 621.

37 League of Nations, International Labour Conference, 18th Session 1934, vol I, 214.

38 League of Nations, International Labour Conference, 23rd Session 1937, vol I, 488. For the text of the resolution see International Labour Office, Official Bulletin, vol XXII (1937) 146.

39 Dong Wang, 'The Discourse of Unequal Treaties in Modern China' (2003) 76 Pacific Affairs 399.

and concessions had their basis in what China called 'unequal treaties'. And India wanted to gain a status equal to the status of the British dominions that had been granted full self-government or equal to the status of fully independent states. But equality issues were also raised with respect to equality among human beings. India and China were again the main protagonists. In that context, the protagonists mainly came from the group of workers' delegates. The linchpin of the debates was the 'universality' of labour standards. Under the constitutional framework, universality of standards was certainly a political aim the ILO was striving for (Article 427). Yet, the clause on special countries (Article 405) left room for setting different standards for countries such as China, India, or Japan. And the clause on dependent territories (Article 421) left room for the European powers to not apply the ILO standards to their colonial territories. In fact, ILO standards were either not extended to the colonial territories or modified with the effect that the standards were lower. Likewise, the (British dominated) Government of India made sure that international labour standards remained lower for India, for instance with a view to child labour, even when the government was prepared to ratify an ILO convention, though with reservations. At the national level, the standards applicable to 'native' workers (in India or the colonies) differed greatly from the standards applicable to European workers. In the 1920s and 1930s, the universality of international standards was an aspiration, no reality on the ground. Unequal standards were the rule. These inequalities, sanctioned by law, and their underlying assumptions regarding the (in)equality of human beings, became the target of the workers' delegates from India and China, even in the early years of the ILO.

When arguing against inequalities in labour conditions, the workers' delegates from India and China used two main arguments. One argument was fundamental. The argument directly addressed the European attitude of supremacy and made the claim that non-Europeans (non-European workers) were deserving of the respect that Europeans were (rightfully) used to expect from lawmakers or employers. Put simply, the argument said, both non-Europeans and Europeans were human beings, and that common nature warranted the same kind of respect. To give but a few examples of how the argument was played out in context: When the delegates to the 1929 International Labour Conference were poised to accept that forced labour would continue in colonial territories (whereas in Europe, forced labour had been abolished), the workers' adviser from India, Shiva Rao, intervened: 'I should like to remind this Conference that its two basic principles are justice and humanity for all workers. I ask you to consider whether there is any justice or any humanity in forced labour'.[40] Rao's argument had little effect. The conference (dominated by European powers) decided that forced labour

40 International Labour Conference 1929 (n 19) 46.

was still to be tolerated in colonial territories for a transition period.[41] Or, when the delegates to the International Labour Conference debated whether the minimum age of admission to employment (the threshold that defined child labour) should be 10 years in India instead of the (European) standard of 14 years, the workers' delegate from India, Ramaswamy Moodaliar, first attacked the Government of India: 'It is sad to realise that even to this day no serious attempt is being made by the state to impart to the Indian child the benefits of compulsory education'.[42] That, so Moodaliar continued, was the reason why illiteracy was rampant and children were idle at an early age. Then Moodaliar addressed the conference:

> I do not think it necessary to remind this gathering that the question of the welfare of the child is a universal one, transcending race, class and creed. The child's psychology is just the same whether in the East or in the West . . . in the name of the children of the world . . . we should all unite to provide the necessary facilities for their natural development.[43]

Again, the intervention failed. At the request of the Government of India, the age limit was set at 10 years for India.[44] Finally, at the 1934 International Labour Conference, the workers' delegate from China, An Fu-Ting, attacked what he called the contract system:

> In Asia there is a system of labour recruitment known as the contract system. . . . [Under] this system the workers are employed in certain industries or mines, through a contractor, at low rates of wages. There is no direct relation between the employers and the workers, who are treated by the employers not as human beings, but as economic commodities. . . . The contract system is inhuman from a humanitarian point of view, unjust from the social point of view, and detrimental from the economic point of view. . . . Therefore, in the name of humanity, in the name of social justice and in the name of economic peace, I demand that the Conference should pay close attention to this problem, which is a dark spot in our civilisation.[45]

41 Draft Convention concerning forced or compulsory labour (C029), Article 1 reading: 'With a view to this complete suppression, recourse to forced or compulsory labour may be had, during the transitional period, for public purposes only and as an exceptional measure, subject to the conditions and guarantees hereinafter provided'.

42 League of Nations, International Labour Conference, 15th Session 1931, vol I, 436.

43 International Labour Conference 1931 (n 42) 438.

44 Draft Convention concerning the age for admission of children to non-industrial employment (C033), Article 9.

45 International Labour Conference 1934 (n 37) 213.

In each of these instances, the speaker described a practice (forced labour, child labour, contract system) that did not occur in any European country, demanding – in the name of a (shared) humanity – that these practices be eradicated everywhere. In practical terms, the Asian workers' delegates launched a series of resolutions pressing for an enquiry into the conditions of 'native labour' in Africa and 'Asiatic labour' in the Asian countries in the 1920s.[46] Eventually, the International Labour Conferences adopted the texts of four important conventions that (at least partly) accommodated the demands of the workers' delegates.[47]

The other argument was not about claiming 'equal worth' based on (assumed) commonalities. The argument was about 'equal treatment'. The argument was most skilfully advanced by Chinese and Indian seamen serving as workers' delegates to the International Labour Conference. Chinese and Indian seamen were usually employed on ships flying a European flag. There was no genuine shipping industry in China or India. The argument tabled by the Chinese and Indian seamen focused on differences made by the (European) employers, differences that were brought to light through numerous comparisons. The contention was that these differences were not legitimate. From the perspective of the Chinese or Indian seamen, the only legitimate option was equal treatment. The debate on equal treatment gained momentum in June 1929 when Ma Cheu-Chun, a union leader, complained about the 'inequality of treatment between Chinese and foreign seamen, and the general contempt for Chinese seamen shown by the foreign companies'.[48] Seamen, so Ma held, were particularly sensitive about differences in treatment as they were 'the most touched by Western ideas'.[49] An important bone of contention were the wages paid to various groups of seamen. At the October 1929 conference, Wu Chau Chit spoke on behalf of 160,000

46 The series commenced in 1925 with a resolution concerning an enquiry into conditions of labour in Asiatic countries, submitted by Narayan Malhar Joshi, and in 1926 with a resolution concerning an enquiry into conditions of native labour, submitted by Lala Lajpat Rai, International Labour Conference 1925 (n 34) 837; League of Nations, International Labour Conference, 8th Session 1926, vol I, 431.

47 Draft Convention concerning forced or compulsory labour (C029) adopted in 1930; Draft Convention concerning the regulation of certain special systems of recruiting workers (C050) adopted in 1936; Draft Convention concerning the regulation of written contracts of employment of indigenous workers (C064) adopted in 1939; Draft Convention concerning penal sanctions for breaches of contracts of employment by indigenous workers (C065) adopted in 1939. Whereas the United Kingdom quickly ratified the conventions, other European colonial powers were reluctant. The United Kingdom, for instance, ratified the Forced Labour Convention in 1931, the Netherlands followed suit in 1933, France in 1937, Belgium in 1944, Portugal in 1956. The Penal Sanctions Convention, to take another example, was ratified by the United Kingdom in 1944, yet not ratified by Belgium, France, the Netherlands, and Portugal.

48 International Labour Conference 1929 (n 19) 206.

49 ibid.

Chinese seamen employed by foreign shipowners, pointing out with respect to Chinese or Indian sailors on the one hand and non-Asiatic seamen on the other performing the same kind of work:

> Non-Asiatic sailors receive about £9 or £10 monthly, or even more, but Asiatic seamen receive only £2 to £3. In the case of firemen the situation is just the same. Similarly, the Asiatic and non-Asiatic stewards are unequally paid. We can find no reason for such unequal treatment.

Clearly, the argument relates to the argument asserting 'equal worth'. Someone who complains about being treated with contempt complains about not being treated with the kind of respect human beings owe each other. Still, the thrust of the argument is not (simply) about being treated respectfully or being treated as a human being. The argument aims at equal pay for equal work.

Arguments demanding equal treatment were met with fierce resistance, especially in the 1920s and 1930s. Delegates from South Africa often took the lead when it came to dampen the momentum advancing the idea of equality. In the early years, South African delegates stressed how alien and different Asians were compared to Europeans, implying that Asians and Europeans were of differing kinds and no equals.[50] Later, the South African delegates relied on a narrative that no longer contested the existence of some basic commonalities but emphasised the backwardness of the non-European populations living under European rule.[51] Hence, the South African delegates were against any enquiry into 'native' or 'coloured' or 'Asiatic' labour (because of the consequences that might ensue), and they were opposed to considering the abolition of forced labour or penal sanctions for a breach of the labour contract. In many instances, the delegates from South Africa were joined by delegates from the Netherlands and Belgium. That is why debates on equal worth and equality of treatment

50 At the 1919 International Labour Conference, Archibald Crawford, a workers' delegate, argued against the need to introduce some kind of maternity protection for 'native' women, saying: 'There are women in South Africa belonging to the native tribes for which the performance of the function such as is under consideration to-day [ie giving birth to a child] is not a matter of hardship or difficulty at all. They belong to a different stage of civilization entirely'. International Labour Conference 1919 (n 26) 175. Consequently, South Africa abstained from ratifying the Draft Convention concerning the employment of women before and after childbirth (C003).

51 In 1926, when Lala Lajpat Rai proposed to launch an enquiry into 'native labour', Clarence Wilfred Cousins, a South African government delegate, was fiercely opposed, holding that South Africa's policies were certainly impeccable: '[Distinctions] of civilisation . . . cannot diminish . . . our common humanity, and where, as in South Africa, two orders of civilisation so widely divergent as those represented by the Dutch and English populations . . . on the one side . . . and by the virile races of the Bantu on the other, just emerging from conditions of savagery into the elementary scale of civilisation [exist] . . . in such circumstances the responsibility is as high as . . . the difficulties are great. Of one thing, however, this Conference . . . may be assured that rigid justice and, more than that, real generosity has been the keynote of South African native administration'.

remained on the agendas of the International Labour Conference well into the 1940s and 1950s. The debates then focused on non-discrimination clauses, obliging ILO members to pursue – at the national level – a policy of equal treatment regarding access to employment and labour conditions.[52]

Regionalism

The idea that ILO policies should, to some extent, allow for regional peculiarities is linked to equality thinking. From early on, non-European members of the ILO felt that the ILO regime was biased in favour of the European countries: The constitution of the ILO was part of treaties that had ended a war that originated in Europe, had taken place in Europe, and had mainly involved European powers. The League of Nations – somehow the mother-organisation of the ILO – was preoccupied with European questions, such as European border issues, European minority questions, and European refugee issues.[53] The ILO was equally dominated by European powers and 'their' problems, such as the side effects of industrialisation or unemployment or labour relations. The conferences were regularly held in Geneva, easy to reach for European delegates, difficult and costly to reach for non-European delegates. Non-Europeans felt under-represented not only in terms of seats, but also in regard of issues and matters, and that feeling grew stronger as the years went by.

The Asian states were the first to form a coalition on the issue of regionalism, stressing that their interests were being neglected by the International Labour Conference. Criticism began to be voiced in the second half of the 1920s,

52 The war and the war effort, including the efforts of people from Asia and Africa, changed the political climate considerably. Unequal treatment along 'racial lines' had lost its legitimacy, also against the background of the horrors caused and inflicted on numerous peoples by the racist Nazi regime. At the 1944 International Labour Conference taking place in Philadelphia, the delegates adopted a declaration affirming that 'all human beings, irrespective of race, creed or sex, have the right to pursue both their material well-being and their spiritual development'. Declaration concerning the aims and purposes of the International Labour Organisation, International Labour Office, Official Bulletin, vol XXVI (1944) 1. At the 1944 Philadelphia conference, when the ILO had to re-invent itself in order to find a place in a new international order mapped out and dominated by the United Nations, the consensus had strong anti-colonial overtones. Many delegates from non-European countries demanded that any future international policy be a policy that would no longer recognise discrimination based on race. And indeed, the 1944 conference adopted a Recommendation concerning minimum standards of social policy in dependent territories (R70), saying in Article 41(2): 'Discrimination directed against workers for reason of race, colour, confession or tribal association, as regards their admission to public or private employment shall be prohibited'. In 1947, the non-discrimination clause became part of a convention targeting non-metropolitan territories. Convention concerning social policy in non-metropolitan territories (C082), Article 18. In 1958, non-discrimination in labour contexts became a universal norm. Convention concerning discrimination in respect of employment and occupation (C111).

53 Edwards (n 20); Arthur Sweetser, 'The First Ten Years of the League of Nations' (1930) 13 International Conciliation 1.

when Asian states demanded that labour conditions in Asiatic countries be thoroughly investigated, with a view to making these conditions known in the ILO and to the European public.[54] Asian states also pushed for visits by high ILO officials so that officials could study local conditions on the spot, and for the establishment of a regional ILO office.[55] Yet, their most important request was that, in addition to the yearly sessions of the International Labour Conference, an 'Asiatic session' be held, with a focus on labour problems in Asia.[56] Pressure was stepped up in the 1930s and the early 1940s, when it became clear that Western powers favoured regional conferences in Latin America over regionalism in Asia. The International Labour Conference adopted a series of resolutions in the 1930s and 1940s expressing growing discontent.[57] The first Asian Regional Conference finally took place in 1947 in Delhi.[58] The main reason for the Asian states (most prominently among them China, India, and Japan) to opt for additional regional conferences was, primarily, a shared belief that their problems were either being ignored or not understood by the delegates gathering in Geneva, given the Western dominance in the conference. Early in the debate, the Asian delegates stressed the lack of knowledge on the side of their fellow delegates, also with respect to Asian culture and civilisation. In the 1930s, Asian delegates emphasised that national policies, in particular policies with a view to industrialisation, were being thwarted by the exploitation their countries have been and still were subjected to during Western modernisation. The 'lifting up' of the standards of living in their countries to an international level became more and more important.[59] And industrialisation was deemed

54 See eg International Labour Conference 1925 (n 34) 837.

55 In 1927, the director of the International Labour Office, Albert Thomas, eventually announced that a National Correspondent's Office would be set up in Delhi in 1928. International Labour Conference 1927 (n 21) 30.

56 The idea was first tabled at the 1927 session by Bunji Suzuki, a workers' delegate from Japan. International Labour Conference 1927 (n 36) 61.

57 Resolution concerning the convocation of an advisory conference of Asiatic countries, submitted by Mr. Bakhale, Indian Workers' Delegate, International Labour Conference 1931 (n 42) 746; Resolution concerning the improvement of conditions of work in Asiatic countries, submitted by Mr. Fulay, Indian Workers' Delegate and Mr. Kono, Japanese Workers' Delegate, League of Nations, International Labour Conference, 20th Session 1936, vol I, 742; Resolution concerning the calling of an Advisory Tripartite Labour Conference of Asiatic Countries and the establishment of an Asiatic Committee, submitted by Mr. Chu Hsueh-Fan, Chinese Workers' Delegate, Mr. Sen, Indian Workers' Delegate, and Mr. Koizumi, Japanese Workers' Delegate, League of Nations, International Labour Conference, 23th Session 1937, vol I, 787; Resolution concerning social security in Asiatic countries, International Labour Conference, 26th Session 1944, Record of Proceedings (International Labour Office 1944) 216, 393, 413, 538.

58 *Preparatory Asian Regional Conference of the International Labour Organisation, New Delhi, October – November 1947, Record of Proceedings* (International Labour Office 1948).

59 See eg the statement of Tadao Kikukawa, a Japanese workers' delegate at the 1934 conference, International Labour Conference 1934 (n 37) 264, pointing out that 'the world must share in the responsibility for the slow progress in Asia, for the normal development of her people has been

key in the process, even at the cost of postponing ILO policies which, because of national priorities, could not at once be carried out in their entirety in Asiatic countries.[60] D.G. Mulherkar, an employers' adviser from India, was quite outspoken:

> We have all along been pointing out that . . . laws and regulations which might have proved suitable for countries which are industrially in the saddle, might possibly have no application to the less fortunate countries which are now only beginning to industrialise themselves. The principle of regionalism . . . will correct this wrong perspective.[61]

India was, therefore, not willing to accept the draft proposals on social security tabled at the 1944 conference, which were, from the perspective of the ILO, fundamental for the re-gaining of (new) legitimacy under a future global framework under the aegis of the United Nations.[62] Against the background of the resistance by Asian delegates, the 1944 conference adopted a resolution conceding that the proposals concerning social security were 'for the most part inapplicable to Asiatic countries . . . in their present stage of industrial development'.[63] The resolution recommended the holding of an Asiatic regional conference that would deal with the question of the organisation of social security in the countries concerned.

American regionalism – the second form of organised regionalism in the interwar period – was very different from the regionalism requested by the Asian countries. For one, American regionalism became prominent only in the second half of the 1930s. Second, American regionalism focused on social security and was rather the outcome of the initiative of the Director of the International Labour Office, Harold B. Butler, and the political quest of the United States. Latin American States did not push for regionalism at International Labour Conferences. Third, American regionalism became an iconic symbol for the global rise of the concept of social security that was, prior to 1936, unknown in the working context of the ILO. To cut a long story short: American regionalism, focused on social security promoted and orchestrated by the International Labour Office and the United States, was basically a protective response to the fast-growing aggression characterising

hindered either by foreign domination or by artificial obstacles preventing the free movement of people and of goods'. The 1937 resolution (n 57) was then exclusively concerned with promoting 'far-reaching improvements in conditions of life and labour in Asiatic countries'.

60 Statement of Samuel Runganadhan, government delegate from India, International Labour Conference 1944 (n 57) 62.

61 International Labour Conference 1944 (n 57) 74.

62 The proposals were eventually adopted in the form of a recommendation. See Recommendation concerning income security (R67).

63 International Labour Conference 1944 (n 57) 538.

German and Italian politics after the rise of National Socialism and Fascism. The drive toward American regionalism had a political undertone: America as a continent was supposed to stand together and uphold the ideas of freedom and democracy, against the odds of extreme nationalism.[64] The *quid pro quo* was economic cooperation in the region and, in the logic of the Roosevelt's New Deal and Getúlio Vargas' *estado nôvo*, the promise of social security for the people, mindful of the special interests of the people of the Latin American countries, such as immigration, nutrition, housing, living conditions of indigenous populations, health, or education.[65]

Development

The ideational framework of regionalism – Asian and American – combined two sub-ideas, the idea that workers ought to be protected against loss of income when certain risks materialise (workers' insurance) and the idea that social standards and economic development ought to be pursued in tandem. The former idea upheld the traditional objective of the ILO (to promote adequate labour standards and social legislation), and the latter was novel and due to political pressures exerted by non-European countries, primarily Asian countries, whose delegates left no doubt that their continuing support following the demise of the League of Nations at the end of the war would depend on a re-focusing of ILO policies. D.G. Mulherkar asserted:

> It has always been a matter of great disappointment to Asiatic countries that, in spite of the . . . support that Asia has always accorded to the I.L.O., the Organisation has never thought it worth while to take note of Asia's legitimate rights . . . or of its special economic needs.[66]

64 For details see Daniel Maul, *The International Labour Organization. 100 Years of Global Social Policy* (Walter de Gruyter GmbH 2019) 85; Jill Jensen, 'From Geneva to the Americas: The International Labor Organization and Inter-American Social Security Standards, 1936–1948' (2011) 80 International Labor and Working Class History 215; Sandrine Kott, 'Fighting the War or Preparing for Peace? The ILO during the Second World War' (2014) 12 Journal of Modern European History 359, 370. On the political background Earl R. Beck, 'The Good Neighbour Policy, 1933–1938' (1939) 1 The Historian 110; Karl Loewenstein, *Brazil under Vargas* (The Macmillan Company 1942) 332; Uwe Lübken, '"Americans All": The United States, the Nazi Menace, and the Construction of a Pan-American Identity' (2003) 48 Amerikastudien/American Studies 389.

65 The first Labour Conference of the American States which are Members of the International Labour Organisation took place in Santiago de Chile in January 1936; the second conference took place in Havana in November 1939; the third conference took place in Lima in December 1940; the fourth conference took place in Santiago de Chile in September 1942. The fourth conference established a permanent Inter-American Conference on Social Security and a Permanent Inter-American Committee on Social Security. For an overview see Wilbur J. Cohen, 'The First Inter-American Conference on Social Security' (1942) 4 Social Security Bulletin 4.

66 International Labour Conference 1944 (n 57) 74.

Aftab Ali, a workers' advisor from India, seconded:

> Frankly, our relationship with the I.L.O. is becoming really difficult, if not impossible. I must therefore request this Conference and our newly appointed Governing Body to act, and act quickly, if the I.L.O. is to justify its existence as an international organisation for securing social justice.[67]

The arguments and the critique put forward by the Asian delegates bore fruit, though in steps and at a rhetorical level. The 1944 International Labour Conference adopted a recommendation addressing explicitly the relation between social policies in dependent territories, economic development, and the responsibilities of the European colonial powers.[68] Colonial powers were asked to direct all policies primarily to the well-being and development of the peoples of dependent territories (Article 1), and to secure financial and technical assistance in the economic development of these territories, in particular by making adequate funds available for development purposes (Article 2). The recommendation also enumerated the fields believed to need improvement, such as public health, housing, nutrition, education, the welfare of children, the status of women, conditions of labour, or social security. In 1947, these principles became part of the Convention concerning social policy in non-metropolitan territories (C082). In 1962, the principles became part of yet another Convention, this time a universal convention, as many of the dependent territories had become newly independent states.[69] All these international norms mirror demands and expectations, but do, of course, not change the realities on the ground.

What the Asian delegates had to struggle for – international cooperation regarding economic development so that they could overcome an appalling poverty of the masses – was freely given to the Latin American states. When the end of the war drew nearer (and in the face of the final war efforts), an Inter-American Conference on Problems of War and Peace was convened in Mexico end of February 1945 at the initiative of the Pan American Union.[70] The delegates to the Conference adopted two important resolutions regarding regional cooperation, a Declaration on Reciprocal Assistance and American Solidarity (also called the Act of Chapultepec) and, prompted by the United States of

67 International Labour Conference 1944 (n 57) 173–174.

68 Recommendation concerning minimum standards of social policy in dependent territories (R70).

69 Convention concerning basic aims and standards of social policy (C117).

70 For details on the background of the conference see Manuel S. Canyes, 'The Inter-American System and the Conference of Chapultepec' (1945) 39 American Journal of International Law 504; David Efrón, 'Latin American Labor Comes of Age' (1945) 240 The Annals of the American Academy of Political and Social Science 116; Robin Humphreys, 'The Pan American System and the United Nations' (1946) 22 International Affairs 75.

America, an Economic Charter of the Americas.[71] The Declaration intended to deepen Inter-American cooperation and solidarity beyond actual wartime. The Economic Charter envisaged an Inter-American economic programme aimed at rising levels of living standards and, based on economic liberty, encouraging full production and employment. One of the pillars of the programme included 'the sound economic development of the Americas through the development of natural resources; increased industrialization; improvement of transportation; modernization of agriculture; . . . and the improvement of labour standards and working conditions'.[72]

Fighting poverty and raising the standard of living for all people was a number one priority for Asian and Latin American states alike. Economic development, in particular industrialisation, was deemed indispensable for achieving that goal.

The Emergence of Social Policies: Poor Relief and Social Insurance

European Welfare

According to welfare state theory, a 'welfare state' emerges once states resume responsibility for the (individual) welfare of the people staying in their territories and intervene in their living conditions to alleviate hardship or plight (as opposed to accepting living conditions as the will of God, as destiny, as an act of nature, or as a concern left to the care of private charities).[73] Against that background, the British and the German welfare state – my European probing grounds – emerged in layers, one premodern (poor relief, *Armenwesen*, social assistance), the other modern (workers' insurance, *Arbeiterversicherung*, social insurance). From the perspective of underlying ideas, the two branches of social legislation were not connected; they emerged and evolved quite separately.

In Britain and Germany, poor relief (*Armenwesen*) emerged in the fifteenth and sixteenth centuries, and in both countries state intervention came in gradually. Taking care of the poor had, for long, been in the hands of churches (primarily at parish level). Churches collected alms and ran hospitals for the poor.

71 For the text of the Declaration (Act of Chapultepec) and the Economic Charter of the Americas see *Inter-American Conference on Problems of War and Peace. Mexico City February 21 – March 8, 1945. Report Submitted to the Governing Board of the Pan American Union by the Director General* (Pan American Union 1945) 30, 82. For the United States draft of the Economic Charter see U.S. Proposals at Mexico City Parley for a Hemisphere Charter, New York Times, 27 February 1945, 15; (1945) 12 Department of State Bulletin 347.

72 Economic Charter (n 71) 84 (Declaration of Objectives).

73 Harry K. Girvetz, 'Welfare State' in David L. Sills (ed), *International Encyclopedia of the Social Sciences*, vol 16 (The Macmillan Company & The Free Press 1968) 512.

The first British statute to intervene in the traditional state of affairs was the Statute of Labourers of 1349, prohibiting the giving of alms to 'valiant beggars', and tacitly allowing almsgiving to others.[74] In 1388, a statute issued by Richard II addressed 'impotent beggars', allowing them to stay where they were at the time of the proclamation of the statute or move on to their place of birth (and nowhere else), but stopped short of saying something about relief to be given in either place.[75] In 1535, Henry VIII ordered that certain secular officials (such as mayors, bailiffs, constables) ought to receive 'valiant vagabonds' and to provide relief, yet ought to do so by handing out voluntary charitable alms.[76] After the breaking-away from the Catholic Church (which caused distress from the perspective of poor relief because monasteries and churches were suppressed, and many poor were left to their own devices), the Crown pursued a two-pronged approach, punishment of the 'vagabonds' on the one hand, and relief for the 'poor' on the other.[77] Local church officials (parsons, vicars) were asked to draw up lists containing the names of the 'impotent poor', and secular officials (mayors) were asked to help collectors collect charitable alms at the end of church services. Under Elizabeth I, the approach of linking punishment and relief was refined: Bishops and justices were ordered in 1562 to remind church goers of their duties to extend their charities towards the relief of the poor.[78] In 1572, Elizabeth I took resort to extreme punishments targeting the 'rogues, vagabonds, and sturdy beggars' and – with a view to poor relief – ordered justices to levy and collect a tax to be able to provide for the poor.[79] In 1575, Elisabeth I introduced 'correction houses'. Finally in 1601, the existing poor law was consolidated: 'Overseers of poor' were introduced and given the power to collect taxes; the law outlined the purposes the money was supposed to be used for; and the law empowered justices to commit to 'correction houses' poor persons who would not 'employ themselves to work'. Hence, after early attempts of giving just a legal framework for legitimate begging while relying on private charities, in 1601, every important aspect of poor relief was in the hand of the secular powers. There is only one important subsequent development to be mentioned here: In 1834, after an explosion of outdoor relief expenses caused by what was deemed a widespread maladministration, the Poor Law Amendment Act gave strict priority to indoor relief (or workhouse-relief) for the

74 23 Edw 3, quoted in George Nicholls, *A History of the English Poor Law, in Connexion with the Legislation and other Circumstances Affecting the Condition of the People*, vol 1 (John Murray 1854) 36.

75 Nicholls (n 74) 59.

76 Nicholls (n 74) 121.

77 The title of a statute by Edward VI, proclaimed in 1547, is telling. The title read 'for the punishment of vagabonds, and for the relief of the poor and impotent persons'. 1 Edw 6 c 3, quoted in Nicholls (n 74) 131.

78 5 Eliz 1 c 3, quoted in Nicholls (n 74) 156.

79 14 Eliz 1 c 5, quoted in Nicholls (n 74) 162.

able-bodied, a measure that led to a quick drop of numbers of relief recipients, to be followed by a surge in numbers again around 1900.[80]

The development in the German territories was quite parallel, yet state involvement grew stronger and stronger at the local level, in particular the cities (*Reichsstädte*).[81] In the sixteenth century, the magistrates took over from the churches; almsgiving was slowly replaced by tax-paying. The (Roman) Emperor accepted and sanctioned the development in a series of *Reichspolizeiordnungen* (imperial police orders), acknowledging the principle: '*daß eyn jede statt und Cummun ire armen selbst erneren und underhalten [mußl]*' (that each city and parish must provide a living for their poor).[82] When, in the eighteenth century, the *Landesherren* (heads of Länder) had eventually gained an (almost) supreme power, the Länder accroached responsibility for relieving the poor. In Prussia, for example, the *Allgemeine Landrecht* (General Laws Applicable in the Prussian States) put it simply in 1794, saying: 'It is incumbent on the state to provide food and care for those citizens who cannot provide for themselves, and who do not receive aid from other private persons who are obliged by law to do so' (translation by the author).

Regarding social insurance, Germany was a forerunner, not only in relation to Great Britain, but worldwide. In the second half of the nineteenth century, two processes proved important for prompting a change in German politics, one political, the other intellectual. First, the labour movement, gaining strength despite oppression, voiced a growing discontent with the constitutional arrangements; the works and pamphlets of, for instance, Ferdinand Lasalle, Karl Marx, Friedrich Engels, August Bebel, or Karl Liebknecht were widely read. The German Empire, which had been proclaimed in 1871 in Versailles after a war was won against France, seemed to slide into a phase of inner destabilisation. The 'social question' – how to deal with the labour movement – was at the centre of politics.[83] Second, the writings and suggestions generated by the members of the *Verein für Socialpolitik* (society for the promotion of social

80 *Poor Law Commissioners' Report of 1834. Copy of the Report Made in 1834 by the Commissioners for Inquiring into the Administration and Practical Operation of the Poor Laws* (Cmd 2728, 1905); George Nicholls, *A History of the English Poor Law, in Connexion with the Legislation and other Circumstances Affecting the Condition of the People*, vol 2 (John Murray 1854) 286, 343.

81 For details see Ingomar Bog, 'Über Arme und Armenfürsorge in Oberdeutschland und in der Eidgenossenschaft im 15. und 16. Jahrhundert' (1974/75) 34/35 Jahrbuch für fränkische Landesforschung 983; Thomas Fischer, *Städtische Armut und Armenfürsorge im 15. und 16. Jahrhundert* (Verlag Otto Schwartz & Co 1979); Karl Otto Scherner, 'Das Recht der Armen und Bettler im Ancien régime' (1979) 96 Savigny-Zeitschrift, Germ Abt 55.

82 Reichspolizeiordnung 1530 under the header '*von bettlern und müssig gengern*' (concerning beggars and idlers), printed in Matthias Weber, *Die Reichspolizeiordnungen von 1530, 1548 und 1577. Historische Einführung und Edition* (Vittorio Klostermann 2002) 161.

83 At the turn of the nineteenth century, political problems used to be framed as questions that need to be answered in order to avoid crisis. See Holly Case, *The Age of Questions* (Princeton University Press 2018); more specifically Holly Case, 'The "Social Question," 1820–1920' (2016) 13 Modern Intellectual History 747.

policy) became so prominent that politicians started listening to the intellectuals, most of whom were economists, such as Gustav von Schmoller, Adolph Wagner, and Lujo Brentano.[84] Eventually, the German Emperor agreed that a compromise be found and some of the expectations of the labour movement be met. The compromise reached in the early 1880s in the German parliament (representing primarily the bourgeoisie) drew on economic concepts relating to private insurance, ie self-help, on the one hand and state intervention, ie state responsibility, on the other: German lawmakers introduced a mandatory regime of insurance targeting certain categories of workers only. The regime was meant to step in if and when workers lost their ability to secure income through work in case of certain (specified) contingencies (sickness, industrial accidents, invalidity, old age).[85] Yet, as contributions to such an insurance regime were deemed beyond what workers could afford, employers and, to some extent, the state (*das Reich*) were obliged by law to participate in the shouldering of the financial burden.[86] Burden-sharing became the task of many (and many potent) contributors, not just of the (eventual) beneficiaries. The British called the German regime – with good reasons – 'state-aided assurance'.[87] In 1927, the regime was brought to the full by introducing an insurance scheme providing an income in case of unemployment, entitling beneficiaries to receive (for a defined period of time) a contribution-based benefit and, after expiry of that period, a tax-financed benefit that was less onerous for the beneficiaries than poor relief (emergency benefit).[88]

84 Franz-Xaver Kaufmann, *Sozialpolitisches Denken* (Suhrkamp 2003) 49. Adolph Wagner gave a programmatic lecture in 1871. Adolph Wagner, *Rede über die sociale Frage gehalten auf der freien kirchlichen Versammlung evanglischer Männer in der K. Garnisonkirche zu Berlin am 12. October 1871* (Verlag von Wiegandt & Grieben 1871).

85 The regime of a workers' insurance was introduced in the early 1880s when parliament adopted three acts that formed an interrelated package. See Gesetz, betreffend die Krankenversicherung der Arbeiter (Act concerning the sickness insurance for workers), RGBl 1881, 73; Unfallversicherungsgesetz (Act on workers' compensation in case of industrial accidents), RGBl 1884, 69; Gesetz, betreffend die Invaliditäts- und Altersversicherung (Act on invalidity and old age insurance), RGBl 1889, 97. All associations propagating social-democratic, socialist, or communist ideas had been prohibited in 1878. Gesetz gegen die gemeingefährlichen Bestrebungen der Sozialdemokratie (Act combating social-democratic endeavours that endanger public safety), RGBl 1878, 351. The act was still in force when the parliament adopted the package that introduced what came to be known as workers' insurance. Social Democrats had, therefore, little influence in shaping the package.

86 The idea that the burden of insurance should be 'nationalised' met considerable political opposition. See Adolph Wagner, 'Der Staat und das Versicherungswesen. Principielle Erörterungen über die Frage der gemeinwirthschaftlichen oder privatwirthschaftlichen Organisation dieses wirthschaftlichen Gebiets im Allgemeinen' (1881) 37 Zeitschrift für die gesamte Staatswissenschaft 102.

87 William M. Casson, *Old-Age Pensions Act, 1908* (Charles Knight & Co. 1908) ix.

88 Gesetz über Arbeitsvermittlung und Arbeitslosenversicherung (Act on placement agencies and unemployment insurance), RGBl I 1927, 187. The tax-financed benefit depended on need (*Bedürftigkeit*), but need was not as narrowly defined as in the context of poor law, and the beneficiaries still had a right to receive that benefit if statutory requirements were met.

Great Britain moved to endorse 'social insurance' at the beginning of the twentieth century. When Great Britain did so, government and parliament responded to a question of their own, a question coined the question of 'pauperism'.[89] 'Pauperism' was short for the phenomenon that a growing portion of the population had to rely on poor relief, which was still mainly provided as workhouse relief. Pauperism was perceived to be a problem because the numbers of recipients were soaring, giving rise to a whole 'class of paupers' with little hope of ever being able to make their own living, although many of them were – admittedly – hardly responsible for their dire straits.[90] Pauperism among the aged was a case in point. Pauperism among the aged was deemed considerable. Estimates assumed that (even under the stressful conditions imposed by poor law) about 27 percent of the population aged 65 or more had to rely on poor relief.[91] Other cases in point were the unemployed and people who had fallen ill and needed medical care but could not afford it. The liberal government of the day assumed that about '30 per cent. of the pauperism [was] attributable to sickness'.[92] In the opinion of the government, unemployment and sickness were 'circumstances over which [the people concerned] have no control'.[93] That is why the British government eventually decided to intervene. In 1908, Great Britain introduced an old age pension regime, giving a right to a pension to all people over the age of 70 who fulfilled the statutory requirements (residence; income not exceeding a certain threshold).[94] The pensions were tax-financed, and recipients were no longer expected to work, no matter how they could fare in the labour market when pressed. In 1911, the British parliament adopted the National Insurance Act, introducing a 'system of national insurance which would invoke the aid of the state and the aid of the employer to enable the workman' to make provision for himself for sickness and, in certain industries, against unemployment, as David Lloyd George put

89 Helen Bosanquet, *The Poor Law Report of 1909. A Summary Explaining the Defects of the Present System and the Principal Recommendations of the Commission, so far as Relates to England and Wales* (Macmillan and Co. Ltd. 1911 reprint).

90 ibid 17, holding: 'Nearly one-third of the whole number relieved in the year 1906–7 were practically permanent paupers. . . . This class is made up chiefly of the aged, the chronic sick, and orphan and deserted children'.

91 Casson (n 87) xvii; for details regarding numbers George R. Boyer, '"Work for their Prime, the Workhouse for their Age": Old Age Pauperism an Victorian England' (2016) 40 Social Science History 3. See also Royal Commission on the Aged Poor, *Report of the Royal Commission of the Aged Poor*, vol 1 (Cmd 7684, 1895).

92 David Lloyd George, Chancellor of the Exchequer, before the House of Commons, HC Deb 4 May 1911, vol 25, col 609.

93 ibid, col 612.

94 Old Age Pensions Act 1908 (8 Edw 7 c 40). On the background Helen Leland Witmer, 'The Influence of Old Age Pensions on Public Poor Relief in England and Wales' (1930) 4 Social Service Review 587.

it when presenting the bill to the House of Commons.[95] The act was clearly modelled along the lines of the German prototype, and even overtook Germany by including a regime covering unemployment.

International Welfare

In the 1920s and 1930s, state-provided welfare propagated by the ILO drew almost exclusively on the idea of social insurance targeting workers. A German institution (*Arbeiterversicherung*, workers' insurance) thought to be vanguard had quickly become an international model. Tax-financed benefits were not in the mind of international lawmakers.

Starting in the second half of the 1920s, the International Labour Conference adopted treaty texts concerned with sickness insurance, old age insurance, invalidity insurance, and survivors' insurance.[96] A bit belated, the International Labour Conference adopted a draft convention ensuring benefits or allowances in case of unemployment in 1934.[97] The texts dealing with insurance obliged (once ratified) the member states to set up or continue compulsory insurance schemes. The texts also defined the beneficiaries. When outlining the schemes, the texts replicated the core of the German concept: A right to cash benefits or medical treatment if certain contingencies materialised (sickness, invalidity, old age, death); burden-sharing between workers and employers with respect to contributions; administration of the schemes by self-governing institutions (separation of insurance funds from other public funds); participation of workers' representatives in the administration. With respect to industrial accidents and industrial diseases, the conventions left room for discretion to be filled by the ratifying member states: Workmen's compensation was to be shouldered by the employers, designated insurers, or insurance institutions, as member states to the convention thought fit.[98] And regarding unemployment, member states to the convention could opt between an insurance model (like the primary benefit under the German model) or an allowance model that was conceptualised as neither contribution-based insurance nor poor relief (like the emergency benefit under the German model).

95 HC Deb 4 May 1911, vol 25, col 613. National Insurance Act 1911 (1 & 2 Geo 5 c 55).

96 Draft Convention concerning sickness insurance for workers (industry) (C024); Draft Convention concerning sickness insurance (agriculture) (C025); Draft Convention concerning old-age insurance (industry) (C035); Draft Convention concerning old-age insurance (agriculture) (C036); Draft Convention concerning compulsory invalidity insurance (industry) (C037); Draft Convention concerning compulsory invalidity insurance (agriculture) (C038); Draft Convention concerning compulsory widows' and orphans' insurance (industry) (C039); Draft Convention concerning compulsory widows' and orphans' insurance (agriculture) (C040).

97 Draft Convention ensuring benefit or allowances to the involuntarily unemployed (C044).

98 Draft Convention concerning workmen's compensation for accidents (C017); Draft Convention concerning workmen's compensation for occupational diseases (C018).

Southern Welfare

In Brazil, China, India, and South Africa – my probing grounds for Southern welfare – social policies (including the idea of state-led welfare) took root in the 1920s, though at a varying pace and in differing shapes and intensities. That does not come as a surprise, given the circumstances the countries found themselves in: China was torn by internal unrest, fighting between warlords, and political instabilities (no functioning central authority). India was under British colonial rule, with barely a saying regarding politics or economics, though constitutional arrangements changed in the mid-1930s, and native Indians gained more power. South Africa pursued a policy of state-organised racial discrimination in all possible areas (politics, economy, land, education, labour) but was not yet internationally ostracised. And Brazil was in a phase of early post-colonial industrialisation, in the 1930s a well-esteemed member of American regionalism, the turn toward nationalism under Vargas notwithstanding.

To give a summary of what is important for my context: In China, the emergence of state-led welfare was connected to the thinking of Sun Yat-sen and the establishment of a nationalist government after his death in Nanjing in 1928. The third of Sun Yat-sen's three (political) principles promised a right of the people to livelihood or decent conditions of life.[99] Accordingly, the first congress of the Guomindang (1924) asserted that it was the duty of the state to improve the conditions of workers and peasants, to provide assistance in old age, sickness, and invalidity.[100] A Factory Law was introduced in 1923.[101] That law was (also) an important lever in China's international struggle against the unequal treaties.[102] Eventually, the Sun Yat-sen principles, including the third, became part of the 1946 Constitution of the Republic of China. Article 155 of the constitution obliged the state to enforce a social insurance and to provide assistance and relief to the aged, the weak, and the disabled who were unable to earn an income, and to victims of disasters.[103] Policy makers of the time envisaged a code that was supposed to include, along with a part on rules on labour conditions, a part on social assistance and a part on social insurance.[104] In India, the (British dominated) Government of India launched a series of labour laws. The Government of India also adopted a law providing for the compensation in case of industrial accidents (1923). The payment of maternity benefits was introduced at province level (Bombay 1929; Central Provinces

99 Albert H.Y. Chen, Chapter 3 in this volume; C.S. Chan, 'Social Legislation in China under the Nationalist Government' (1929) 19 International Labour Review 60.

100 Chan (n 99) 61.

101 P. Henry, 'Some Aspects of the Labour Problem in China' (1927) 15 International Labour Review 24; Chen, 'The Labour Movement in China' (n 3).

102 On the so-called unequal treaties see p. 174, 179 in this chapter.

103 Albert H.Y. Chen, Chapter 3 in this volume.

104 Chan (n 99) 68.

1930).[105] Yet, government involvement remained thin. Central and provincial lawmakers provided a framework under which employers were obliged to make payments in case of accidents or maternity. Neither the (central) state nor the provinces were involved in the administration of the schemes. Other branches of welfare (eg, medical aid, child welfare, unemployment relief) were left to private initiatives, such as charities, employers, or workers' organisations. State-led aid was confined to famine relief. The Government of India thought it could not afford to do more.[106] Brazil responded to a public discourse in the early 1920s on what had been termed the 'social question', similarly to politics in Germany in the second half of the nineteenth century.[107] For Brazil, the year 1923 marked the beginning of a step-by-step introduction of social insurance schemes, eventually covering old age, invalidity, sickness, and death of breadwinner, following the German model and the model propagated by the ILO, first for defined categories of workers, starting with railway workers and dock workers who were well organised and able to amass political power, later for whole branches of industry, eventually encompassing all organised urban workers. Poor relief was not introduced in Brazil. South Africa's social policy also started in the late 1920s but was narrowly focused. The policy concentrated on what had been termed the 'poor White problem', in other words, lawmakers concentrated their attention almost exclusively on 'White persons' and 'Coloured persons'. The first act to address the problem of (racially charged) poverty in old age was the 1928 Old Age Pensions Act, granting an 'entitlement' to 'every White person' and 'every Coloured person' to receive an old age pension if certain statutory requirements were met (age, residence, income below threshold),[108] akin to the British 1908 Old Age Pension Act.[109] In the 1930s, South Africa introduced the first 'grant', targeting 'White' and 'Coloured' blind persons whose income did not exceed a certain threshold (1936 Blind Persons Act). South Africa also introduced an unemployment insurance (1937 Unemployment Benefit Act), providing for flat-rate benefits, financed by contributions of employers and employees, targeting 'labourers' and persons whose income remained below a defined threshold. Again, 'Natives' were denied access to the benefit.

105 Sarbani Sen, Chapter 4 in this volume; Das (n 3) 616; Rajani Kanta Das, 'Woman Labour in India: II' (1931) 24 International Labour Review 536, 560.

106 Ravi Ahuja, 'A Beveridge Plan for India? Social Insurance and the Making of the "Formal Sector" (2019) 64 International Review of Social History 207, 214; Ravi Ahuja, 'Minoritarian Labour Welfare in India: The Case of the Employees' State Insurance Act of 1948' in Lutz Leisering (ed), *One Hundred Years of Social Protection. The Changing Social Question in Brazil, India, China, and South Africa* (Palgrave Macmillan 2021) 157, 164.

107 James M. Malloy, *The Politics of Social Security in Brazil* (University of Pittsburgh Press 1979) 19; Lavinas (n 3) 305; Octávio Luiz Motta Ferraz, Chapter 2 in this volume.

108 Letlhokwa George Mpedi, Chapter 5 in this volume.

109 See p. 194 in this chapter.

Ideational Foundations

State Responsibility

All the countries under investigation assume, beginning in the 1920s and 1930s, that the state is (at least to some extent) responsible for the individual welfare of the people living in the territory. Sometimes, that assumption is expressed in political statements preceding legislation, sometimes through legislative action (the adoption of laws granting benefits), sometimes even by way of promises or guarantees embedded in the constitution (we can call these processes legalisation and constitutionalisation of state responsibility). The 1934 Constitution of Brazil, for instance, was one of the first non-European constitutions that deliberately incorporated ideas of social policy making: The constitution demanded that all law dealing with the economy or labour ought to pay attention to 'the social protection of the worker' (Article 121).[110] The 1946 Constitution of Brazil promised 'social justice' and 'work that enables a dignified existence' (Article 145), including assistance to the unemployed and 'previdência social' against the consequences of old age, invalidity, illness, or death, based on contributions from the Union, the employers and the employees (Article 157). Clearly, state responsibility reached differing levels of intensity. In Europe, Germany assumed more responsibility than Great Britain, where poor relief was, until 1908, the main regime people could rely on when in need. Insurance regimes were confined to sickness and unemployment. Germany created – in addition to *Armenrecht* (poor law) – a comprehensive second pillar aimed to prevent people from having to turn to poor relief (workers' insurance; later, social insurance). Brazil and China were prepared to give more guarantees than South Africa, where even poor relief was exclusionary in racial terms and limited to elderly people and blind people (things changed, when South Africa introduced the unemployment benefit in 1937). India (under British rule) relied primarily on welfare regimes based on private initiative (family, charities, workers associations, employers). State involvement was confined to enacting frameworks for employers' liabilities. In Europe as well as in the global South, the assumption of state responsibility was often triggered by 'questions' (or, more generally, problems) that demanded solutions (Germany, Brazil: the growing strength of the labour movement; Great Britain: pauperism; South Africa: poverty among the Whites; India: the existing conditions of labour in industrial undertakings and plantations; China: the labour conditions in the foreign settlements). That connection to country-specific problems explains why the emergence of social policies was time and again linked to other ideational goals, such as national unity, political stability, independence and home rule, or the ending of unequal treaties.

110 Octávio Luiz Motta Ferraz, Chapter 2 in this volume.

When acting on their responsibility for individual welfare, states used to choose between two modes of financing, contributions on the one hand, tax revenues on the other. Contribution-based regimes regularly relied on the idea of insurance, in the European context originally inspired by the expanding private insurance regimes of the nineteenth century, in the Southern context by the models promoted by the ILO (which were a replica of the German prototype). The ILO was indeed instrumental for spreading the idea that state responsibility should primarily take the form of social insurance. The ILO influenced policies in Brazil, China, India, and (to some extent) South Africa accordingly. Tax-financed regimes evolved around the idea of poor relief or its off-springs (in Europe, national assistance; welfare (*Fürsorge*); social assistance; in the global South, grants, social assistance). Tax-financed pension regimes (Great Britain, South Africa) take a middle ground, combining elements of 'poor relief' (way of financing) and elements of 'insurance' (granted as of right).

Insurance: Risks, Contributions, Burden-Sharing

Like private assurance, social insurance is focused on the idea of risk and the idea of pooling money given by the people who are at risk (contributions), with the intention that that money would be redistributed to the ones whose resources are lost when the risk materialises. Early examples of private assurance regimes are regimes covering the risk of foundering of ships or the risk of loss of housing or businesses through fire. In a nutshell, the idea is: Everyone who is – like specified others – at risk, shoulders a burden (payment of contributions) and takes an advantage once the risk materialises: The amount that is redistributed in case of risk occurrence might be many times higher than the total amount of contributions paid. That economical background explains, why 'social insurance' had (and still has) such a strong focus on 'risks' or 'contingencies'. Social insurance reacts to defined risks, namely the risk of loss of income in case of events that were (by political consensus, in parliament) accepted to be risks that ought to be covered by a regime of mandatory contributions, ie so-called social risks (*soziale Risiken*).[111] Social risks have always been limited in number. Among the risks usually accepted as 'social' were the risk of loss of income in case of sickness, invalidity, old age, death of breadwinner, and unemployment. Adolph Wagner, one of the masterminds behind the German regime of social insurance, believed that – unlike in the case of premiums paid to private assurance companies – the insured would not be able to cover the costs arising from social risks by way of contributions. Social insurance regimes were meant to target workers whose risks were considerable,

111 Karl Pribram, 'Social Insurance in Europe and Social Security in the United States' (1937) 36 International Labour Review 742.

but whose incomes were meagre.[112] That is why most regimes of social insurance opted for burden-sharing when it came to the making of contributions, obliging employees, employers, and – at times – public bodies to take a share in contributing to the regime that was deemed fair or necessary.

Poor Relief: Need, Labour, Correction, Minimum

Poor relief (later, national assistance, social assistance) has a long-standing tradition in Europe; it goes back for centuries. In the global South, state-led premodern relief was mainly confined to catastrophes (famines; floods). In Europe, poor relief responded to destitution (lack of income and assets). Also, poor relief was often linked to the idea of need: Lawmakers directed relief towards people who could be seen as being in need of the help of others, and, since the aspect of need had normative implications, as 'deserving' of help or worthy of help. British poor law emphasised the aspect of need and deservingness particularly strongly: Even very early statutes prohibited almsgiving to 'valiant beggars', ie beggars who could engage in work instead of loitering and begging.[113] Early statutes ordered 'vagabonds' and 'feitors' to be put in jail. Later, statutes grew more outspoken in condemning 'idle' persons, in particular the statutes under Elizabeth I. A 1572 Elizabethan statute, for instance, complained that 'all parts of . . . England and Wales be presently with rogues, vagabonds, and sturdy beggars exceedingly pestered, . . . to the great annoyance of the common weal'.[114] Under Elizabeth I, the punishments became exceedingly drastic (whipping; burning through the ear; death in case of repeated offenses). German poor law never went that far. German poor law rather preferred the withholding of the relief and the (local) expulsion of beggars who were not old, weak, or disabled. Also, the normative undertones varied. British poor law emerged as the flip side of statutes sanctioning forced labour. British monarchs pursued a policy of making sure that all able-bodied people worked, eventually for the greater good of the commonwealth, against the background of a (perceived) labour-shortage after slavery and villeinage had begun to die out in the fourteenth century, and many people began to leave their former places.[115] 'Correction houses' were meant to make people work under the rule of wardens, thus, to make people become accustomed to work. The workhouses established after 1834 were intended to drive people to work under

112 Wagner (n 86) 150, 155.

113 See p. 191 in this chapter.

114 Nicholls (n 74) 161.

115 Nicholls (n 74) 31, 45. A 1349 statute ordered that all able-bodies persons (who did not earn a living) 'shall be bound to serve him which him shall require'. ibid 37. An Elizabethan statute of 1562 ordained that 'every unmarried person, and every married person under thirty, not having 40 shillings per annum . . . shall be compelled to serve as a yearly servant in the trade to which he was brought up; and none are permitted to quit such service'. ibid 158.

the conditions offered by the labour market, even under conditions deemed unpalatable, due to the deliberately harsh conditions prevailing in the workhouses. British workhouses made social control visible and tangible.[116] German poor law rather drew on an ethics of work, yet not in a strict manner. In Catholic territories, the idea of deservingness or worthiness was practically absent. According to the principle of *caritas*, it was the act of giving that mattered (in relation to God), not a particular state of the receiving person, deserving or non-deserving.[117] The idea of need (lack of ability to make a living) and an ethics of work grew stronger when the German cities became the main providers of poor relief, and the local citizenry got a saying in determining who should be given relief.[118] The idea that state intervention should aim at the moral betterment of the poor gained ground, and the *Arbeitshaus* (workhouse) was the preferred venue for doing so.[119] Of all the countries of the global South under investigation, only pre-apartheid and apartheid South Africa had a similar regime in place.[120] The South African regime of grants targeting blind persons of 1936 and later the grant regimes for disabled persons and children seem to reflect the idea of need rooted in an ethics of work, even in a strict form. South African lawmakers took pains to define the classes of people they wanted to be deemed in need, ie unable to work. People who did not fall in one of the defined classes were not worthy of relief. And throughout history, in Europe and in South Africa, relief for the poor (later, national assistance, social assistance) aimed to provide a bare minimum (food, housing, clothing, basic medical care).

The British and the South African non-contributory old age pensions (introduced in 1908 and 1928 respectively) are an interesting case. These pensions followed the idea of need. The elderly could – by law and without further inquiries – easily and plausibly be classified as deserving from the perspective of an ethics of work. Elderly could no longer be expected to work. There seemed to be a consensus on that. The pensions also followed the idea of a minimum level of provision: The pensions were granted if the income of the elderly did not exceed a threshold, and the amount of the benefit aimed to secure a minimum of subsistence. The fact that beneficiaries were 'entitled' by law and discretion in decision-making was, at least in Great Britain, reduced (in comparison to poor relief) cannot undo that the main characteristics of poor relief persisted. Against the background of the political intention to exempt a certain

116 On the notion of social control see early Edward Alsworth Ross, 'Social Control' (1896) 1 American Journal of Sociology 513. In 1909, however, experts declared the workhouse concept to have failed. Bosanquet (n 89) 95, 100.

117 Fischer (n 81) 43, 45, 149.

118 Bog (n 81) 996; Fischer (n 81) 245.

119 Rudolf Endres, 'Das Armenproblem im Zeitalter des Absolutismus' (1974/75) 34/35 Jahrbuch für fränkische Landesforschung 1003, 1011; Fischer (n 81) 245.

120 See Letlhokwa George Mpedi, Chapter 5 in this volume.

category of people – the elderly – from the harsh regime of the British poor law, the pensions remained a variant of poor relief. The pension affirmed the notion of worthiness underlying traditional poor law. The elderly were simply declared deserving by law, and then no longer stigmatised as 'paupers'.[121] In South Africa, the grants similarly affirmed the strong notion of self-reliance prevalent among the ruling minority of 'White persons'. In Great Britain, the introduction of an old age insurance was indeed debated around 1900, but eventually discarded. In South Africa, introducing an old age insurance was seemingly not among political options.

Development

Economic development was an important and explicit goal in policy making in Brazil, China, and India. The goal became prominent in the 1930s. Still, the relation between economic development and other national policy goals differed. For Brazil, economic development was part and parcel of the cooperation evolving in the context of American regionalism. Economic development came in easily. Social policies were rather spurred, certainly not hampered, by policies promoting economic development. For nationalist China, economic development was part and parcel of a national policy that was about implementing the programme envisaged by Sun Yat-sen (economic democracy), at a moment when about 80 percent of the population depended on agriculture and poverty was widespread. At International Labour Conferences, Chinese government delegates often referred to what they called the 'reconstruction of China', 'national reconstruction', and 'new industries' in China.[122] China's grand goal was the improving of the standards of living. However, apart from large-scale public work programmes, social policies remained policies in the making, given the circumstances (internal unrest, most existing industries in the hand of foreigners, war with Japan).[123] India's take emphasised the importance of economic development even stronger. At the international level, India deplored the legacy of colonial politics: 'The condition of life and work is miserable'.[124] The nationalist response prioritised creating a new state and economic development.[125] Social policy had barely a place on the political agenda of the newly independent India and for decades to come.

121 Derek Fraser, *The Evolution of the British Welfare State. A History of Social Policy since the Industrial Revolution* (Macmillan 1984) 153.

122 League of Nations, International Labour Conference, 16th Session 1932, vol I, 87 ('reconstruction of China'); League of Nations, International Labour Conference, 19th Session 1935, vol I, 282 ('new industries'); International Labour Conference 1937 (n 57) 131 ('vast plan of national reconstruction').

123 R.H. Tawney, *Land and Labour in China* (George Allen & Unwin Ltd. 1932) 121.

124 Statement of R.R. Bhole, International Labour Conference 1944 (n 57) 202.

125 Sarbani Sen, Chapter 4 in this volume.

Exclusion

Emerging welfare states, in Europe as well as in the global South, were all but universal. According to the relevant domestic logics, lawmakers confined social insurance to certain classes of (blue collar) workers; other workers were excluded (non-manual workers earning more; rural workers; workers in small manufacturing units; workers in the informal sector; the self-employed). At best, excluded categories of workers or self-employed were integrated into the regime as time went by. Poor relief, if existing, targeted categories of the poor perceived to be in need and worthy, and excluded many others, such as the able-bodied; people thought to be unwilling to work; people called 'natives'; disabled people, who were not blind; and children.

The Trajectories of Social Policies: Social Security

Once social policies were instituted at the national and the international level, initial policies slowly evolved into trajectories. Some trajectories continued along the original lines, some took turns, some broke off, followed by a new beginning. Some developments also affected the ideational foundations underlying social policies. I concentrate on what I think has been the most important turn, in policies and ideational foundations: Franklin D. Roosevelt's New Deal introduced a concept and a term – social security – that affected post-World War II social policies in Europe, policies at the international level, and policies in countries of the global South, even the social policies of the Peoples' Republic of China (PRC), the shortcomings of the programme providing social security at the United States level notwithstanding.[126] The concept of social security spread because it was open to new ideas.

Starting Point: New Deal

Around 1900, experts and practitioners in the United States followed the emergence of social insurance regimes in Europe closely, particularly the emergence of the German variant.[127] In the 1910s, a debate on whether the United

126 For a critical evaluation of the New Deal and its outcomes in the United States as well as further sources on the subject see Walter I. Trattner, *From Poor Law to Welfare State. A History of Social Welfare in America*, 6th edn (The Free Press 1999) 273; Robert Leighninger and Leslie Leighninger, 'Social Policy of the New Deal' in James Midgley and Michelle Livermore (eds), *The Handbook of Social Policy*, 2nd edn (Sage 2009) 133; Andrew Morris, 'The Great Depression and World War II' in Daniel Béland, Kimberly J. Morgan and Christopher Howard (eds), *Oxford Handbook of US Social Policy* (Oxford University Press 2014) 59, 68. For a contemporary, conservative critique see Herbert Hoover, *American Ideals versus the New Deal* (The Scribner Press 1936); I.M. Rubinow, *The Quest for Security* (Henry Holt and Company 1934).

127 John Graham Brooks, *Compulsory Insurance in Germany including an Appendix Relating to Compulsory Insurance in Other Countries in Europe. Fourth Special Report of the Commissioner of Labor*, 2nd edn

States should join these developments started but led nowhere.[128] The Great Depression and Franklin D. Roosevelt's gift to attract a broader audience to his political ideas eventually convinced lawmakers to make a move in the 1930s. Public debates on the usefulness of social insurance regimes resumed, when the government moved to launch a comprehensive public works programme in 1933 (eg, Federal Emergency Relief Act; Civil Works Administration). In June 1934, Roosevelt addressed the Senate, promising to place 'the security of the men, women, and children of the Nation' first and to further 'the security of the citizen and his family through social insurance'.[129] The Economic Security Committee – installed by the president late in June 1934 – produced a report and a bill (short-titled the Economic Security Bill), both were submitted to the House of Representatives in January 1935.[130] At the beginning of April 1935, the short title of the bill was changed to Social Security Bill.[131] The bill passed quickly through the House and the Senate and was signed into law by the president in August 1935.[132] The 1935 Social Security Act combined several elements of social legislation, some traditional, some innovative. First, the act introduced a social insurance regime. The insurance regime provided for contribution-based benefits in old age ('old age benefit') and in case of unemployment ('unemployment compensation'). Second, the act introduced an offspring of poor law, coined 'assistance' or 'aid' by the act (eg, Sections 1 and 401) and 'public assistance' by scholars.[133] The assistance regime targeted, for immediate and tax-financed relief, the elderly ('old age assistance'), children ('aid to dependent children'), and blind persons ('aid to the blind'). Third and novel, the act introduced 'services', ie benefits in kind, such as maternal and child health services; services for 'crippled children' (medical, surgical, or corrective services; care; hospitalisation); child-welfare services for the protection and care of homeless or neglected children; and public health services more generally. As the act moved clearly beyond what was known as social insurance, United States lawmakers had to come up with a new term to denote the area of social legislation covered by the act. Their final choice was 'social security',

(Government Printing Office 1895); Lee K. Frankel and Miles M. Dawson, *Workmen's Insurance in Europe* (Charities Publication Committee 1910); I.M. Rubinow, *Social Insurance with Special Reference to American Conditions* (Henry Holt and Company 1913).

128 Henry Rogers Seager, *Social Insurance. A Program of Social Reform* (The Macmillan Company 1910); Alpheus H. Snow, 'Social Insurance' (1910) 59 University of Pennsylvania Law Review 283; William F. Willoughby, 'The Problem of Social Insurance: An Analysis' (1913) 3 American Labor Legislation Review 153.

129 78 Cong Rec 10,770–10,771.

130 *Report to the President of the Committee on Economic Security* (United States Government Printing Office 1935); HR 4120, 74th Cong, 1st Sess (1935).

131 HR 7260, 74th Cong, 1st Sess (1935); HR Rep No 615, 74th Cong, 1st Sess (1935).

132 Social Security Act, 49 Stat 620 (1935).

133 Maurice Stack, 'The Meaning of Social Security' (1941) 23 Journal of Comparative Legislation and International Law 113, 114.

after experimenting with the term 'economic security'. Practitioners in the field of relief liked to use the term 'public aid' as an umbrella term for a sample of 'constructive' and 'preventive' measures on offer, ranging from vocational training and education to public work programmes, to cash benefits, and to health services.[134]

European Welfare

In Europe, Germany was not inclined to follow the American path. The invention of the term 'social security' (which would translate into *soziale Sicherheit*) had basically no impact on the traditional concepts of social insurance on the one hand and social assistance (*Sozialhilfe*; formerly poor law, *Armenwesen*) on the other, at least at the national level. The term 'social security' was (and is) used mainly in international agreements entered into by Germany with a view to coordinate the various regimes of social insurance for migrant workers, primarily at the level of the Council of Europe or bilateral level (with the home countries of the major groups of migrant workers residing in Germany, such as Spain, Greece, Portugal, or Turkey, ie countries that were – at the relevant time – not participating in the European Communities).[135]

In Great Britain, 'social security' became one of the most important legal categories structuring social policy and the ensuing social legislation, long before the United Kingdom joined the European Communities. When outlining what was to become the British welfare state, William Henry Beveridge put 'social security' at the very centre of the policy to come, although the term did not make it into the title of his report to the British parliament.[136] Without mentioning the social policies under the New Deal even once, the report's terminology was – nonetheless – similar to the terminology typical for social policies developed under the New Deal. According to Beveridge's concept, social insurance was an element of social security, but social security reached beyond insurance. At its core, social security was conceptualised as based on

134 Committee on Long-Range Work and Relief Policies, *Security, Work, and Relief Policies*, HR Doc No 128 Part 3, 78th Cong, 1st Sess (1941) 8–9.

135 For the agreements and conventions brokered by the Council of Europe see the early European Interim Agreements of Social Security, ETS No 12 and 12A, and later the European Convention on Social Security, ETS No 78. For the bilateral conventions see BGBl II 1961 S 599 (Spain); BGBl II 1963 S 679 (Greece); BGBl II 1965 S 1170 (Turkey); BGBl II 1968 S 474 (Portugal). At the level of the European Union (EU), 'social security' is a familiar term, and for decades so. Like in international treaty law, the term refers to norms concerned with social insurance and family allowances that EU law seeks to coordinate so that rights accrued at the domestic level are not lost simply because migrants move to another EU member state. On the development of EU social policy and pertinent EU terminology see Ulrike Davy, 'Sozialpolitik der Union' in Matthias Niedobitek (ed), *Europarecht Grundlagen und Politiken der Union*, 2nd edn (de Gruyter 2020) 1447, 1449.

136 William Beveridge, *Social Insurance and Allied Services. Report* (Cmd 6404, 1942).

three instruments, namely, social insurance for basic needs, means-tested and tax-financed national assistance for special cases, and voluntary insurance for add-ons to the basic provision secured by the state.[137] Beveridge left no doubt that 'social security' could only be achieved if certain additional instruments were in place, such as children's allowances, comprehensive health services, and a state-driven employment policy preventing mass unemployment. Hence, all in all, Beveridge suggested five pillars of state-led social policy (social insurance, national assistance, children's allowances, health services, employment policy), complemented by a framework for voluntary (private) insurance. Within just a few years, the British parliament enacted a series of bills to implement Beveridge's plan. In 1945, family allowances were introduced, followed in 1946 by the introduction of a national insurance scheme, providing benefits in case of unemployment, sickness, maternity, retirement, or death, and the establishment of a national health service.[138] A national assistance scheme was enacted in 1948 that eventually replaced the still existing poor law.[139] Occupational and private pension schemes were, for the first time, officially connected to state-organised social insurance in 1959.[140] British lawmakers obviously took some effort to avoid any resemblance to the German terminology by preferring the use of the adjective 'national' over the adjective 'social' in their choice of wording. It took a while until 'social security' became a term used in an act of parliament. In 1966, the British parliament moved to appoint a 'Minister of Social Security' and to transfer to that position the functions of the Minister of Pensions and National Insurance as well as the administering of the benefits provided under the 1948 National Assistance Act.[141] The 1966 Act was indeed the first act to make provisions with a view to national insurance on the one hand and to national assistance on the other. It was in line with Beveridge's terminology, in that case, for lawmakers to opt for the term 'social security' as an umbrella term. In 1970, non-contributory and not means-tested benefits were introduced for certain categories of persons in need, continuing the trajectory introduced by the 1908 Old Age Pensions Act.[142] In 1992, the Social Security Contributions and Benefits Act finally fulfilled Beveridge's vision of

137 Beveridge (n 136) 120.

138 Family Allowances Act 1945; National Insurance Act 1946; National Health Service Act 1946.

139 National Assistance Act 1948.

140 National Insurance Act 1959, s 7 (allowing insured persons to opt out of the state pension scheme). For details on the link between state pensions and occupational and private pensions Leslie Hannah, *Inventing Retirement. The Development of Occupational Pensions in Britain* (Cambridge University Press 1986) 46; Ulrike Davy, 'Systeme der nicht-staatlichen Alterssicherung in Großbritannien' in Monika Schlachter, Ulrich Becker and Gerhard Igl (eds), *Funktion und rechtliche Ausgestaltung zusätzlicher Alterssicherung* (Nomos 2005) 35.

141 Ministry of Social Security Act 1966.

142 National Insurance (Old persons' and widows' pensions and attendance allowance) 1970, targeting classes of the elderly and severely disabled people. For the trajectory introduced by the 1908 Old Age Pensions Act see p. 194 in this chapter.

social security: The provisions on contributory, non-contributory (not means-tested), and means-tested benefits became part of one single act (though they grouped in different parts of that act). The term 'national insurance' and the term 'national assistance' came out of use and lost their significance in the course of a few decades following World War II.

International Welfare

At the international level, the term 'social security' spread quickly in the 1940s, globally and regionally. The term appeared for the first time in 1941 in the Atlantic Charter, then 1948 in the Universal Declaration of Human Rights, 1966 in the International Covenant on Economic, Social and Cultural Rights, 1961 in the European Social Charter, and 1988 in the Additional Protocol to the American Convention on Human Right in the Area of Economic, Social and Cultural Rights ('Protocol of San Salvador'). None of these political or legal documents elaborated on the meaning of the term. However, prior to human rights law-making under the aegis of the United Nations, the notion of social security was debated by the Inter-American Conference on Social Security in the early 1940s and by the International Labour Conference taking place in Philadelphia in 1944.

As American regionalism gained strength under the United States initiative of a 'good neighbour policy', the ILO initiated and supported a series of conferences bringing together the American States which were then members of the ILO.[143] The first two conferences were tagged 'labour' conferences. The first labour conference took place in Santiago (Chile) in 1936, the second in 1939 in Havana (Cuba).[144] At the third conference taking place in 1940 in Lima (Peru), the delegates decided that a permanent organisation should be established. The next meeting in 1942 in Santiago was organised as the First Inter-American Conference on Social Security.[145] Other conferences followed

143 On American regionalism see p. 187 in this chapter.

144 Warren Irvin, 'Labor Conference of American States, Santiago, Chile 1936' (1936) 42 Monthly Labor Review 690; N.N., 'The Labour Conference of the American States which are Members of the International Labour Organisation, Santiago de Chile, 2–14 January 1936: I' (1936) 33 International Labour Review 479; N.N., 'The Labour Conference of the American States which are Members of the International Labour Organisation, Santiago de Chile, 2–14 January 1936: II' (1936) 33 International Labour Review 646; *Report on the Action Taken to Give Effect to the Resolutions Adopted by the Santiago Conference* (International Labour Office 1939).

145 Cohen (n 65); Wilfried C. Jenks, 'The First Inter-American Conference on Social Security' (1943) 37 American Journal of International Law 120; Hugo A. Garciamarín Hernández, *The Foundation of the Inter-American Conference on Social Security* (Inter-American Conference on Social Security 2020). In Spanish, the conference was termed 'Conferencia Interamericana de Seguridad Social', in Portuguese, the conference was termed 'Conferência Interamericana Segurança Social', and in French, the conference was termed 'Conférence interaméricaine de sécurité sociale'. English, Spanish, Portuguese, and French were the four languages that were, at the time of the founding of the conference, officially spoken in the American countries.

suit (1947 Rio de Janeiro; 1951 Buenos Aires); and since 1952, the headquarter of the conference is located in Mexico City. The 1942 Conference adopted several resolutions, among them the Declaration of Santiago, outlining the meaning of social security.[146] The resolutions adopted in Santiago in 1936 had mentioned 'social security' in passing, briefly holding that 'compulsory social insurance . . . is at once the most rational and most effective means of affording to the workers the social security to which they are entitled'.[147] The 1942 Declaration of Santiago was more specific. Against the background of the horrors of a global war, the declaration promised 'social and economic security', emphasising that a 'new inspiration' would have to be based on the 'moral objective of a just social order':

> Each country must create, conserve and build up the intellectual, moral and physical vigour of its active generation, prepare the way for its future generations, and support the generation that has been discharged from productive life. This is social security: a genuine and rational economy of human resources and values.[148]

Social insurance was recognised as 'an expression of social security'. Yet, the programme outlined by the declaration was not limited to envisioning security provided for by the state in case of defined employment-related contingencies or risks. The declaration aimed at security with respect to employment, health, food, housing, and clothing:

> A policy of social security for the Americas should comprise measures for promoting employment and maintaining it at a high level, for increasing the national income and sharing it more equitably, and for improving health, nutrition, clothing, housing and general and vocational education for workers and their families.

The far-reaching vision of the 1942 Declaration of what 'social security' ought to entail inspired, just two years later, the debates at the International Labour Conference taking place in Philadelphia in May 1944. The labour conference was special, because – at that point in time – there was no doubt that the order established under the League of Nations would soon be history. A new global regime was about to emerge, and that regime would be fleshed out by the victorious United Nations. Whether or not there would be a place

146 Inter-American Conference on Social Security, *The Inter American Committee on Social Security* (International Labour Office 1950) 62.

147 Labour Conference of the American States which are Members of the International Labour Organisation, *Record of Proceedings* (International Labour Office 1936) 270 (Resolution concerning the fundamental principles of social insurance, preamble).

148 Inter-American Conference on Social Security (n 146) 62–63.

for the ILO under the new regime had not yet been decided upon. With good reasons, the Philadelphia conference has been called 'a turning point' in the ILO's history, the outcome of the conference even 'a second founding' of the ILO.[149] The ILO had to re-invent itself and to find a new purpose. The ILO indeed did so, drawing heavily on the idea of social security. The newly defined ILO goals, proclaimed in the Declaration concerning the aims and purposes of the ILO,[150] included, *inter alia*, the extension of social security measures to provide a basic income of all in need of such protection and comprehensive medical care; provision for child welfare and maternity protection; and the provision of adequate nutrition, housing, and facilities for recreation and culture. Finally, the concept of social security also made its way into the wording of the rights listed in the 1948 Universal Declaration of Human Rights and in the 1966 International Covenant on Economic, Social and Cultural Rights (ICESCR), not least because of the insistence of the Latin American countries.[151]

Southern Welfare

Brazil and India were the first of the four Southern countries under investigation that made 'social security' a term used in the text of their constitutions, even though the text of the Brazilian constitutions used varying terms in Portuguese. The language of the 1946 Brazilian Constitution, for instance, differed considerably from the language of the 1988 Constitution, to mention the most important texts. But the meanings were by and large the same over time. The People's Republic of China constitutions of 1954, 1975, 1978, and 1982 did not specifically mention 'social security', unlike the 1946 Constitution of the Republic of China (Articles 152 through 157). Only in 2004 did the term 'social security' (*shehui baozhang*) become part of constitutional law of the PRC. Still, the concept that has – in various contexts after World War II – been epitomised in the term 'social security' was present in the PRC even before 2004, at least at an ideational level. Following the political turn from apartheid to non-racialism, South Africa was the last of the countries under investigation to embed 'social security' into its 1996 Constitution. In each of the four countries, 'social security' has a broad meaning, encompassing a whole

149 Maul (n 64) 135. See also Kott (n 64); Sandrine Kott, 'Organizing World Peace. The ILO from the Second World War to the Cold War' in Stefan-Ludwig Hoffmann and others (eds), *Seeking Peace in the Wake of War Europe, 1943–1947* (Amsterdam University Press B.V. 2015).

150 Declaration (n 52).

151 Universal Declaration of Human Rights, 8 December 1948, UN Doc A/RES 217 (III); International Covenant on Economic, Social and Cultural Rights, 16 December 1966, 993 UNTS 3. On Latin American contributions to human rights law-making see Ulrike Davy, 'How Human Rights Shape Social Citizenship: On Citizenship and the Understanding of Economic and Social Rights' (2014) 13 Washington University Global Studies Law Review 201, 218.

range of measures, including regimes of work-related social insurance, but also non-contributory measures responding to all sorts of economic insecurities.

Brazil

In Brazil, the constitutions of 1934 and 1937 used the word 'proteção social' (social protection) as an umbrella term for labour and social policy issues explicitly referred to in various articles, such as working hours, a minimum age of admission to employment, a weekly rest, annual vacations with pay, but also medical assistance, social insurance, or maternity protection (1934 Constitution, Article 121; 1937 Constitution, Articles 136, 137). The 1946 Constitution introduced the term 'seguro e previdência social' as a particular field of prospective legislation, distinct from the legislation in the field of labour ('trabalho'). The 1946 Constitution was seemingly inspired by the terminology evolving at the level of the Inter-American Conferences on Social Security (Article 5 XV b; Article 157; later, 1967 Constitution, Article 8 XVIII c).[152] According to the list given by the 1946 Constitution, 'seguro e previdência social' was concerned with medical assistance (for the workers), maternity protection, social insurance, assistance to the unemployed, or security of employment. Also, the family was guaranteed special protection of the state, including assistance to mothers, infants, and adolescents, and assistance with regard the education of children (1946 Constitution, Articles 163, 168, 172; 1967 Constitution, Articles 158, 167, 168). And indeed, in the 1960s, Brazilian social legislation provided means of support in case of certain contingencies, assistance in the event of childbirth and assistance for families, medical services, food services (low-cost restaurants, retail food stores, nutritional supplements), and housing assistance.[153] Around 1960, the number of insured persons had reached 4 million; however, about 48 million workers and their families, mostly living in the rural areas, were not (yet) covered.[154]

Finally, the 1988 Constitution of Brazil changed the terminology for a third time. For one, the constitution expressly granted social rights ('direitos sociais'), comprising rights regarding education ('educação'), health ('saúde'), work ('trabalho'), rest ('lazer'), security ('segurança'), social insurance ('previdência social'), protection of mothers and infants ('proteção à maternidade e à infância), and assistance to the unemployed ('assistência aos desamparados'). For another, the 1988 Constitution dedicated a whole title to the social order

152 See also the language used in the Portuguese part by the Inter-American Committee on Social Security, *Inter-American Handbook of Social Insurance Institutions* (International Labour Office 1945) 45.

153 Moacyr Vellosos Cardoso De Oliveira, 'Social Security in Brazil' (1961) 84 International Labour Review 376. For the second half of the 1940s see Arthur J. Altmeyer, 'The Progress of Social Security in the Americas in 1944' (1945) 51 International Labour Review 699, 703.

154 De Oliveira (n 153) 386–387.

('ordem social'), structured according to a new terminology: One chapter dealt with 'seguridade social' (social security), a term that had no forerunners in prior constitutions, but had – in Spanish – a long tradition at the regional (American) level ('seguridad social'). A second chapter dealt with education, culture, and sports; a third with science and technology; a fourth with social communication; a fifth with the environment; a sixth with family, children, adolescents, and the elderly; and a seventh with the Indians. Of all chapters, the chapter on 'seguridade social' is of particular interest in our context. The chapter comprised, apart from a sub-chapter on general provisions, three sub-chapters, one on 'saúde' (health), one on 'previdência social' (social insurance), and one on 'assistência social' (social assistance). The wording of the 1988 Constitution of Brazil suggests that, after some searching for an adequate terminology, 'seguridade social' (social security) rests on three pillars: First, the provision of health care; second, social insurance providing contribution-based cash benefits in the case of illness, disability, or death (including those caused by work accidents), maternity, old age, or unemployment; and third, non-contributory benefits rendering protection and assistance to families, parents, children, the elderly, including assistance with respect to food and housing, and the promotion of the integration into the labour market. When taken together, these three pillars comprise 'social security' as outlined by the 1942 Declaration of Santiago.[155]

India

The terminology of the Indian Constitution is less complex. The Directive Principles of State Policy in Part IV of the constitution include core elements of social policy, such as securing the right of all citizens to an adequate means of livelihood (Article 39[a]), the right to work, to education, and to public assistance in cases of unemployment, old age, sickness and disablement, and in other cases of undeserved want (Article 41), and to maternity relief (Article 42). A reference to 'social security' is conspicuously missing in Part IV. The term 'social security' appears only once in the constitution, namely in a list contained in Schedule 7 that briefly enumerates the matters that may be dealt with by the (central) parliament as well as by the legislatures of the states (concurrent legislative powers). In the process of constitution-making, the reference to 'social security' came in last minute, namely in October 1948, when the Drafting Committee accepted suggestions put forward by the Ministry of Labour in order to bring the draft in line with a 'modern tendency' that preferred the use of a 'comprehensive term', covering 'unemployment insurance, social insurance, provident fund, invalidity pensions, old age pensions,

155 On the 1942 Declaration of Santiago see p. 208 in this chapter.

employers' liability and workmen's compensation'.[156] Prior to that, the February 1948 draft constitution had – like the 1935 Government of India Act before – referred to 'welfare of labour; conditions of labour; provident funds; employers' liability and workmen's compensation; health insurance, including invalidity pensions; old age pensions' (item 26) and – insofar moving beyond the 1935 Act – to 'unemployment and social insurance' (item 27).[157]

The change in the wording of the concurrent list between 1935 and February 1948, when the first draft constitution was released (insertion of 'social insurance'), reflects the changing role of the state in welfare provision around 1940. Prior to 1940, expert reports had regularly asserted that, in India, a regime of social insurance would not exist and could not be introduced, given the circumstances prevalent in the country.[158] But perceptions were moving. In its infancy, around 1900 and up to the 1920s, social legislation in India strongly relied on making employers responsible, for instance, for paying compensation in the case of work-related accidents, for protecting the health of workers employed in factories, or – at the provincial level – for granting maternity benefits to women.[159] Welfare provision was mainly in the hands of employers, municipalities, the emerging trade unions, and private charities. That kind of welfare provision was voluntary and had no basis in law, apart from statutory law dealing with private insurance or provident funds. Some employers indeed engaged voluntarily in providing welfare, for one in the case of certain contingencies that made wage-earning impossible, such as paying gratuities or allowances in the case of sickness, or old age, for another in the field called 'welfare of labour' more generally, such as providing medical services for the employed, providing crèches for the very young children of employed women, providing for the education for the older children, housing for the workers, or access to food.[160] By and large, however, experts and organised workers found living and working conditions in India to be deploring, in almost every respect. Starting

156 Shiva B. Rao, *The Framing of India's Constitution. Select Documents*, vol 4 (The Indian Institute of Public Administration 1968) 319.

157 Shiva B. Rao, *The Framing of India's Constitution. Select Documents*, vol 3 (The Indian Institute of Public Administration 1967) 670.

158 *Report of the Bombay Strike Enquiry Committee, 1928–29*, vol 1 (Government Central Press 1929) 158; Royal Commission on Labour in India, *Report of the Royal Commission on Labour in India* (Calcutta Government of India) 267; International Labour Office, *Industrial Labour in India* (International Labour Office 1938) 205.

159 See Sarbani Sen, Chapter 4 in this volume; Das (n 3) 612, 616; Rajani Kanta Das, 'Woman Labour in India: I' (1931) 24 International Labour Review 376, 401; Royal Commission on Labour in India (n 158) 263.

160 On allowances or gratuities Das (n 105) 559; Royal Commission on Labour in India (n 158) 268, 269; on welfare work Das (n 105) 562 (crèches), 563 (medical aid); International Labour Office (n 158) 310 (general welfare activities); Rajani Kanta Das, 'Child Labour in India: II' (1934) 29 International Labour Review 43, 66 (housing); International Labour Office (n 158) 296 (housing), 313 (grain stores, workmen's stores).

in the 1930s, demands for a stronger involvement of the state and, hence, an expansion of social legislation grew stronger, most notably demands for the introduction of certain branches of social insurance, such as unemployment insurance and sickness insurance.[161]

Against that political background, the suggestion during constitution-making of the Ministry of Labour to use the 'modern' and 'comprehensive' term 'social security' makes good sense. In my reading, the final versions of the relevant items of the concurrent list addressed two different concepts of welfare provision: One item dealt with the (then prevailing) concept that it was primarily the responsibility of the employer to provide for individual welfare. Like the corresponding item listed in the 7th Schedule of the 1935 Government of India Act, item 24 of the 7th Schedule of the 1949 Constitution of India enumerated matters that were in the focus of (voluntary or mandatory) employers' activities or labour laws, namely 'welfare of labour including conditions of work, provident funds, employers' liability, workmen's compensation, invalidity and old age pensions, and maternity benefits'. In contrast, item 23 of the 7th Schedule enumerated matters that presume that it is for the state to provide for individual welfare and to finance and administer benefits, namely 'social security and social insurance; employment and unemployment'. The term 'social security' mentioned in item 23 opened a room for manoeuvring for the state to expand social legislation into fields that were – hitherto – left to private initiatives and did not fit the narrow and technical notion of social insurance. The Indian lawmakers acted accordingly, but tentatively and persistently with limited range of coverage: Even before the adoption of the constitution, lawmakers introduced a sickness insurance regime for workers in factories (1948 Employees' State Insurance Act). In the 1950s, lawmakers adopted an act providing a framework for market-based provident funds and pension funds run under the control of the central government (Employees' Provident Funds Act). In the 1960s, lawmakers made the payment by the employer of (non-contributory) maternity benefits obligatory (1961 Maternity Benefit Act). In the 1970s, lawmakers obliged employers to pay a gratuity (ie a lump sum) upon retirement, thus

161 With a view to unemployment see cautiously the report of the Bombay Strike Enquiry Committee (n 158) 98, 159, and the report of Royal Commission on Labour in India (n 158) 35. Both reports emphasised the idea of an employers' responsibility for making workers redundant and, thus, for financing unemployment allowances. State involvement should be confined to providing public work, a system that had been devised to deal with famine in rural areas. For more forceful demands see *Report of the Textile Labour Inquiry Committee, vol 2, Final Report* (Government Central Press 1940) 208, 401, 416. For the introduction of a sickness scheme see Royal Commission on Labour in India (n 158) 268; Report of the Textile Labour Inquiry Committee, 292, 321. For a unionist's perspective see Shiva B. Rao, 'Labor in India' (1944) 233 Annals of the American Academy of Political and Social Science 127; for a government perspective see Atul C. Chatterjee, 'Federalism and Labour Legislation in India' (1944) 49 International Labour Review 415, 432.

introducing a non-contributory retirement benefit (1972 Payment of Gratuity Act). Except for the 1948 Employees' State Insurance Act, all these acts were based on the legislative powers attributed to the central parliament by item 24 of the 7th Schedule of the constitution. The 1990s then saw the emergence of central government sponsored social assistance programmes and a renewal of the food subsidies programmes, though not in the form of a statutory enactment. In the 2000s, lawmakers introduced a legal basis for a public work regime for rural areas, granting a right to work and remuneration (2005 National Rural Employment Guarantee Act). Lawmakers also provided a legal basis for existing (and possibly, future) assistance and micro-insurance schemes under one roof (2008 Unorganised Workers' Social Security Act), and a legal basis for the provision of food grains and meals as well as for a right to receive a food security allowance (2013 National Food Security Act). Clearly, these more recent acts are concerned with 'social security' in a very broad sense, whatever their shortcomings are, when scrutinised from a political angle.[162] The governments formed under Narendra Modi after the electoral victory of the Bharatiya Janata Party in 2014 couched the aims of social policies in a new rhetoric, putting emphasis on 'empowerment' instead of 'entitlement', which had been the trademark of the Congress-led coalition from 2004 through 2014.[163] But action did not follow rhetoric. Entitlements have not been rolled back. Interestingly, in 2020, the Modi government initiated the enactment of a Social Security Code, introducing a narrower and India-specific concept of social security that encompasses regimes of social insurance (for workers in the formal and informal sector) and labour welfare regimes drawing on employers' responsibilities (maternity benefits, gratuities, provident funds, compensation for work injuries).

China

The 1946 Constitution of the Republic of China dedicated Part IV of Chapter XIII (Fundamental National Policies) to 'social security' (*shehui anquan*). The concept of social security underlying Part IV of Chapter XIII included the implementation of employment policies (most notably the provision of opportunity of employment), the improvement of the livelihood of labourers and farmers, the protection of women and children engaged in labour, the promotion of the welfare of women and children more generally (as foundation

162 Sony Pellissery and Armando Barrientos, 'Expansion of Social Assistance: Does Politics Matter?' (2013) 48 Economic & Political Weekly 47, 48; Tina Dutta and Parthapratim Pal, 'Politics Overpowering Welfare: Unorganised Workers' Social Security Act 2008' (2012) 47 Economic & Political Weekly 26; Ashima Majumdar and Suandarjya Borbora, 'Social Security System and the Informal Sector in India: A Review' (2013) 48 Economic & Political Weekly 69.

163 Sarbani Sen, Chapter 4 in this volume.

of national existence and development), and the improvement of national health. Constitution-makers envisioned three main instruments for the state to promote social security (*shehui anquan*): For one, the state was supposed to enforce a 'social insurance system' (*shehui baoxian*) (Article 155 sentence 1). For another, the state was supposed to extend appropriate assistance (*fuzhu*) and relief (*jiuji*) to the aged, the infirm, and the disabled among the people who were unable to earn a living, and to victims of unusual calamities (Article 155 sentence 2). Finally, the state was supposed to establish sanitation and infant health protection enterprises, and a system of socialised medical service (Article 157). Hence, 'social security' (*shehui anquan*) comprised employment policies, social insurance, social assistance, disaster relief, medical services, and regimes of special protection for mothers and infants.

The first constitution of the People's Republic of China, adopted in 1954, avoided any reference to 'social security'. In Chapter 3 on the fundamental rights and duties of citizens, the 1954 PRC Constitution proclaimed a corresponding right, namely a right of the 'working people' to 'material assistance in old age, and in case of illness or disability' (Article 93 sentence 1: *wuzhi bangzhu*). The 1954 PRC Constitution envisaged three instruments to ensure this right: social insurance (*shehui baoxian*), social assistance and relief (*shehui jiuji*), and public health services (Article 93 sentence 2). When compared to the description given by the 1946 Constitution of the Republic of China, the notion of 'material assistance' seems to be narrower than the notion of 'social security' under the 1946 Constitution, at least at first glance. Yet, from the perspective of the protection circumscribed in other provisions of Chapter 3, the difference between the 1954 PRC Constitution and the 1946 Constitution of the Republic of China is not as big as it seems: The 1954 PRC Constitution also expected the state to engage in employment policies: Article 91 envisaged a state which, by planned development of the national economy, gradually provided more employment, improved the working conditions, and increased wages, amenities, and benefits. The 1954 PRC Constitution also guaranteed that the state would protect the institution of marriage, the family, and the mother and child (Article 96). The only element that was missing of what the 1946 Constitution of the Republic of China had termed 'social security' (*shehui anquan*) was the explicit promise of relief in the case of calamities.

That the 1954 PRC Constitution avoided the use of the term 'social security', is – so it seems to me – due to the fact that the constitution was closely modelled along the lines of the 1936 USSR Constitution, the so-called Stalin constitution. The 1936 USSR Constitution did not use the term 'social security' either. In Article 120, the 1936 USSR Constitution promised 'материальное обеспечение' ('material'noe obespechenie'), and the meaning of 'obespechenie' is difficult to translate. In English, several terms are used, as such assistance, security, relief, maintenance, welfare, or protection.[164] Hence, 'material assistance' (*wuzhi bangzhu*) is one convenient way to translate 'obespechenie' into the Chinese language. And it is clear from the texts of both constitutions that 'wuzhi bangzhu' and 'obespechenie' were targeting 'workers' (not citizens or residents). It is also clear that the measures were supposed to address certain human conditions (old age; sickness; inability to work). And it is clear that 'social insurance' (*сотсиальное стракхование; sotsial'noe strakhovanie*; *shehui baoxian*) was not the only remedy constitution-makers had in mind. The 1954 PRC Constitution mentioned, additionally, medical services and social assistance. The 1936 USSR Constitution mentioned health related instruments only (medical help, health resorts). In Stalin's Russia, social assistance (*сотсиальное обеспечениеь, sotsial'noe obespechenie*) had some tradition. Social assistance was introduced in October 1918, but social assistance was barely given as a right, let alone a constitutional right.[165] The 1954 PRC Constitution was less reluctant to guarantee a right to social assistance. Social insurance, social assistance, and medical services were essential dimensions of 'social security', according to the contemporary meaning of the term. 'Social security' was present, though hidden in the term 'material assistance' (*wuzhi bangzhu*). The PRC Constitution of the reform era, adopted in 1982, did not change very much. The right to material assistance was now to be found in Article 45(1), as one of the rights listed in Chapter 2 on the fundamental rights and duties of citizens. The right holders were no longer workers only, but the citizens of the PRC. The content of the right, however, remained unchanged. Two paragraphs were added, obliging the state and society to ensure the livelihood of military personnel and their families, and to arrange work, livelihood, and education for people with disabilities (blind, deaf-mutes, and other handicapped persons).

Eventually, the term 'social security' (*shehui baozhang*) indeed entered into the text of the 1982 PRC Constitution, by an amendment adopted in 2004. The last paragraph of Article 14 of the constitution – an article located in Chapter 1 (general principles) that deals with economic development and the raising of

164 A. Abramson, 'Social Insurance in Soviet Russia' (1929) 37 Journal of Political Economy 377, 381 (relief); Gaston V. Rimlinger, 'The Trade Union in Soviet Social Insurance: Historical Development and Present Functions' (1961) 14 Industrial and Labor Relations Review 397, 399 (social security); Bernice Madison, 'Social Welfare: Soviet Model' (1964) 38 Social Service Review 191, 194 (social assistance); Bernice Q. Madison, *Social Welfare in the Soviet Union* (Stanford University Press 1968) 79 (welfare); Sally E. Ewing, *Social Insurance in Russia and the Soviet Union, 1912–1933: A Study of Legal Form and Administrative Practice* (Princeton University (Dissertation) 1984) 175 (social security); Dorena Caroli, 'Bolshevism, Stalinism, and Social Welfare (1917–1936)' (2003) 48 International Review of Social History 27, 33 (protection); Maria Cristina Galmarini-Kabala, *The Right to Be Helped. Deviance, Entitlement, and the Soviet Moral Order* (Northern Illinois University Press 2016) 31 (social assistance).

165 On the tensions between the concept of social insurance and the concept of social assistance see Galmarini-Kabala (n 164) 36.

labour productivity – now reads: 'The state builds and improves a social security system that corresponds with the level of economic development'.[166] That is a declaration of political intent (not an individual right), and the declaration is conditioned: The realisation of social security depends on economic progress. The amendment to Article 14 of the constitution was adopted, when the People's Republic of China moved, in the early 2000s, to ratify the ICESCR. The ICESCR was, like the 1966 International Covenant on Civil and Political Rights, conceptualised as one of the twin-parts of an international bill of human rights. In 2001, the People's Republic of China decided to adhere to the social rights-part of the bill, but not to the civil and political rights-part.[167] When confronting the obligation to participate in the control mechanism established under the ICESCR, China seemingly intended to attune its constitution to the international human rights language. At the hearings before the committee established under the ICESCR, China continually stresses its willingness to abide by its international human rights obligations, also by embedding its human rights obligations at the domestic level.[168]

South Africa

The constitution-makers of South Africa decided in 1996 to include a 'right to social security' in the 'Bill of Rights', contained in Chapter 2 of the constitution. Among the socio-economic rights enshrined in Chapter 2 are rights that relate to health care, food, water, and social security (Section 27). Section 27(1)

166 For details on the terminology in the Chinese language see Albert H.Y. Chen, Chapter 3 in this volume.

167 Multilateral Treaties Deposited with the Secretary-General, <https://treaties.un.org/Pages/ViewDetails.aspx?src=TREATY&mtdsg_no=IV-3&chapter=4&clang=_en> accessed 28 February 2022.

168 The People's Republic of China submitted its first report under ICESCR on 27 June 2003 (UN Doc E/1990/5/Add 59), the second report on 30 June 2010 (UN Doc E/C.12/CHN/2), the third report on 19 December 2019 (UN Doc E/C.12/CHN/3). In their dealings with the Committee established under the ICESCR, the representatives of the PRC regularly face questions regarding the incorporation of the ICESCR into domestic law and its applicability in court. See the lists of issues handed over by the Committee, UN Doc E/C.12/Q/CHN/1 (2004), E/C.12/WG/CHN/Q/2 (2013); E/C.12/CHN/Q/3 (2021). After some criticism was voiced by the Committee in its concluding observations to the first state party report, the PRC emphasised in its second report under the ICESCR that on 14 March 2004 the constitution had been amended so as to incorporate human rights into the PRC Constitution, commenting that, when doing so, 'the construction of a human rights legal system in China had entered a new stage of historical development'. UN Doc E/C.12/CHN/2 (2010) 6; see also the summary record of the Committee meeting on 8 May 2014, UN Doc E/C.12/2014/SR.17, 2. On the Chinese understanding of 'social security' from a political and domestic perspective see Shih-Jiunn Shi, 'Social Security: The Career of a Contested Social Idea in China During the Reform Era, 1978–2020' in Lutz Leisering (ed), *One Hundred Years of Social Protection. The Changing Social Question in Brazil, India, China, and South Africa* (Palgrave Macmillan 2021) 91.

guarantees to 'everyone' the right to have access to health care services, sufficient food and water, and 'social security, including, if they are unable to support themselves and their dependants, appropriate social assistance'.

The Bill of Rights leaves no doubt that the rights listed in the bill – including the socio-economic rights – involve as a flip-side responsibilities on the side of the state. Section 7(2) of the constitution states: 'The state must respect, protect, promote and fulfil the rights in the Bill of Rights'. Still, when it comes to the rights enumerated in Section 27, the state is given some leeway regarding the promotion and the fulfilment of the rights. According to Section 27(2), the state must take 'reasonable legislative and other measures, within its available resources' – and not more – to 'achieve the progressive realisation of each of these rights'. The Constitutional Court of South Africa asserted early that constitutionally embedded socio-economic rights were justiciable, like other embedded rights.[169] However, even the Constitutional Court pays its respect to that leeway granted to the state by the constitution, at least to some extent. The court admits that the obligations imposed on the state by Articles 26 or 27 of the constitution – and the corresponding individual rights – are dependent on available resources and hence limited.[170] Also, the court assumes that, under the constitution, the state was empowered to choose among a wide range of possible measures; and if the state would be able to show that the measure chosen was reasonable, the constitutional requirements would be deemed met.[171] Nonetheless, if it comes to determining the (substantive) content of the rights, international law – and human rights law in particular – provides important guidance for the court's interpretation. Paying attention to international law conforms with Section 39(1)(b) of the constitution and established case-law.[172]

Against that backdrop, elaborating the meaning of 'social security' under Section 27 of the Constitution of South Africa must (also) be guided by the meaning given to the term by Article 9 ICESCR and by the Committee established under the ICESCR in its General Comment No. 19 on the right to social security.[173] Broadly speaking, 'social security' under the ICESCR and, as a consequence, under the Constitution of South Africa encompasses access to benefits that secure protection primarily (but not exclusively) from '(a) lack of work-related income caused by sickness, disability, maternity, employment injury, unemployment, old age, or death of a family member; (b) unaffordable

169 *Government of the Republic of South Africa v Grootboom and others* 2001 (1) SA 46 (CC) para 20.

170 *Soobramoney v Minister of Health Kwazulu-Natal* 1998 (1) SA 765 (CC) para 11.

171 *Grootboom* (n 169) para 41; see also *Minister of Health and Others v Treatment Action Campaign and Others* 2002 (5) SA 721 (CC) para 37–38.

172 Regarding the interpretation of the term 'social security' see *Mahlangu and Another v Minister of Labour and Others* 2021 (2) SA 54 (CC) paras 41, 58.

173 General Comment No. 19 on the right to social security (art 9) was adopted on 23 November 2007, UN Doc E/2008/22, 126.

access to health care; (c) insufficient family support, particularly for children and adult dependents'.[174] That notion of social security, summarised in General Comment No. 19, reflects closely the notion given to the term by the ILO at the end of World War II, when the ILO reacted to developments that had taken place at the (American) regional level and the global level (demise of the League of Nations).[175] The notion combines instruments of risk-based social insurance – the traditional focus of the ILO – with other instruments of providing income security (tax-financed benefits), and access to health care. The notion is, however, not as comprehensive as the one developed under American regionalism.

Ideational Foundations

Social Security

From the perspective of terminology and concepts, the main development following the end of World War II was the invention of the term 'social security' and the evolving meaning of the term. The term was, rather by coincidence, invented in 1935 in the United States and, according to Arthur Altmeyer, no-one dared to define the term at that point in time because it was basically unknown.[176] Seemingly, the (German-inspired) idea of social insurance was easier to sell to a critical public in the United States when couched in the notion of social security. 'Social insurance' was believed to involve strong government responsibilities and strong government interventions in private affairs, which was deemed at odds with the American tradition.[177] In stark contrast to the 'risk'-oriented language used in German politics at the end of the nineteenth century, the meaning of 'social security' took its starting point from the diagnosis that many people (workers and self-employed farmers alike) had to face 'economic insecurity' caused by a variety of factors such as market forces (unemployment; drop of market prices), consequences of low income (sickness bills amounting to one-half of the family income; large number of family members, entailing high costs for even a simple living), or dependency

174 ibid para 2.

175 See p. 208 in this chapter.

176 Arthur J. Altmeyer, *The Formative Years of Social Security* (The University of Wisconsin Press 1966) 4. Abraham Epstein, *Insecurity. A Challenge to America* (Harrison Smith & Haas Robert 1933) used the term 'social security' occasionally in his book, but primarily to advocate the introduction of 'social insurance' also in the United States 'as a feasible method of social security', so he stated openly in the foreword.

177 For criticism raised against social insurance see C.A. Kulp, 'The Relation of Government to Social Insurance' (1935) 178 Annals of the American Academy of Political and Social Science 53; Frances Perkins, 'Social Security Here and Abroad' (1935) 13 Foreign Affairs 373, 374; Jesse Frederick Steiner, 'Social Security and American Traditions' (1936) 14 Social Forces 461. See also the arguments raised against the New Deal by Hoover (n 126).

in young or old age – all circumstances that went beyond what was commonly called a 'social risk' meant to be covered by social insurance.[178] The remedy envisioned was an 'assured income', mainly through employment and, in certain cases, through cash benefits, some contribution-based, some tax-financed. That already went beyond 'social insurance', as traditionally understood by the ILO or in Germany. The potential of the term 'social security' unfolded even further when the Latin-American countries pressed to add additional meaning to the term.[179] The Inter-American Conferences on Social Security added access to health care, nutrition, clothing, housing, and education to the agenda of a policy providing 'social security'. Lack of access to health care, food insecurity, deplorable housing conditions, or the lack of education can certainly be constructed as causes for 'insecurity', yet barely as 'risks' to be covered by a regime of 'insurance', social or private.[180]

Attempts at conceptualising social security broadly have been met by attempts aimed to keep the concept narrow, even in the 1940s. A programmatic ILO paper on the concept of social security published 1942 suggested to confine 'social security' to a regime comprising two elements, traditional social insurance on the one hand, and social assistance on the other, the latter conceptualised as a system of tax-financed cash benefits, means-tested or – under certain circumstances – not means-tested (a re-conceptualised poor law).[181] Social insurance was construed as based on 'compulsory mutual aid', social assistance as 'representing the unilateral obligation of the community towards its dependent groups'.[182] In short, social security was meant to provide income security, no more. The 1944 International Labour Conference accepted a meaning that was a bit broader, against the backdrop of social policy initiatives taking place in certain English-speaking countries, such as Great Britain (Beveridge report), Australia, or New Zealand, and the aspirations of the Latin American countries and Asian countries, such as India and China.[183] The conference compromised, nonetheless. The notion of social security underlying the 1944 Philadelphia Declaration on the (future) aims and purposes of the ILO comprised income security (social insurance plus social assistance) as well as access to medical

178 *Report to the President* (n 130) 1–3.

179 See p. 207 in this chapter.

180 The ILO opened to the idea of broadening its mandate in 1941, after having relocated its offices from war-torn Europe to Montreal. See International Labour Office, *The I.L.O. and Reconstruction* (International Labour Office 1941) 88: 'To-day the programme [responding to the social objective] is far wider. . . . It covers not the comparatively narrow domain of conditions of work but the infinitely more extensive area of conditions of life'. See also Oswald Stein, 'Building Social Security' (1941) 44 International Labour Review 247.

181 International Labour Office, *Approaches to Social Security. An International Survey* (International Labour Office 1942).

182 ibid 2. In a similar vein Stack (n 133) 113.

183 International Labour Conference, 26th Session, Director's Report, Report VII (International Labour Office 1944) 50.

care, not more, but also not less.[184] The idea that the provision of adequate food, housing, child welfare, maternity protection, or child protection was also part of the ILO agenda was, however, not discarded. These dimensions of social policy were indeed listed in the catalogue of goals to be achieved by programmes launched by the ILO, but as separate goals, not as goals that come under the heading of 'social security'.

Human rights law reflects a similar systematic arrangement. One article of the ICESCR grants a right to 'social security, including social insurance' (Article 9); other articles deal with protection of mothers and child welfare (Article 10), with the right to an adequate standard of living, including food, clothing, housing (Article 11), with the right to health (Article 12), and with the right to education (Article 13). The close similarity to the systematic arrangements underlying the 1944 ILO Declaration of Philadelphia may explain why the committee established under the ICESCR chose to follow the ILO model when elaborating on the meaning of 'social security' (Article 9) in its General Comment No 19.[185]

The semantic variations indicate that – in the aftermath of World War II – two notions of social security crystallised, one notion covering income security (social insurance and social assistance) and medical care (narrow notion), one notion covering a broad range of social policies, such as income security, medical care, employment policies, public work programmes, placement strategies, family allowances, food subsidies, and affordable housing policies (broad notion). The semantics prevailing in Brazil, China, India, and South Africa match the varying notions according to political preferences at the national level. China and South Africa prefer the narrow notion, Brazil and India the broader one. In any case, the term 'social security' indicates a huge expansion of state responsibilities, compared to the beginning of social policy in Europe.

Development and Equality

At the international level, countries of the global South – including Brazil, China, and India – fought tirelessly for the universalisation of the idea of equality, also in the context of social policies.[186] Likewise, China and India insisted that the implementation of social policies required a certain level of economic development, and that economic development required assistance.[187] On both

184 The particular goal listed in Part III para f of the 1944 Philadelphia Declaration read: 'extension of social security measures to provide a basic income to all in need of such protection and comprehensive medical care'. Two recommendations adopted by the International Labour Conference at the same time elaborated on the meaning of 'basic income' and 'medical care'. See Recommendation concerning income security (R67); Recommendation concerning medical care (R69).

185 See p. 209 in this chapter.

186 See p. 177, 180 in this chapter.

187 See p. 188 in this chapter.

accounts, the countries eventually succeeded. In the aftermath of World War II, the International Labour Conference adhered to the idea that equality demanded universal standards or, put differently, that differing labour standards according to 'race' or 'nationality' went against the very core of the idea of equality and the ILO mandate. Moreover, the International Labour Conference accepted that economic development was necessary for the implementation of social policies. The Convention C117 left no doubt, stating in the preamble that 'economic development must serve as a basis for social progress', a term that included social policies.

Still, at the domestic level, concepts of equality (as an important aim of social policies) and economic development proved difficult to balance, especially in China and India. At the first session of the Plenary Conference of the Tripartite Labour Organisation in India, taking place in Delhi in September 1943, B.R. Ambedkar addressed the tension openly:

> It will not be enough to make the industrial development of India our goal. We have to agree that any such industrial development shall be maintained at a socially desirable level. . . . We shall have to agree not merely to recognise the basic right of all Indians to share in that wealth as a means of a decent and dignified existence but to devise ways and means to ensure them against insecurity.[188]

After independence, Indian politics nevertheless favoured economic development over equality and universal social policies, and it did so for decades.[189]

The 1949 Constitution of India embedded 'directive principles of state policy', asserting that 'it shall be the duty of the state to apply these principles in making laws' (Article 37). But policy makers were given a free rein in deciding which principles would be implemented and, if so, when. Article 37 also declared that the Directive Principles were not enforceable by any court. Hence, policy makers needed not to worry about courts meddling with politics. Likewise, Article 41 of the constitution obliged the state to secure socio-economic rights, such as the right to work, to education, and to public assistance, but added a drawback clause: The state had to act under Article 41 only 'within the limits of its economic capacity and development'. That

188 N.N., 'Conference Report: First Session of the Plenary Conference of the Tripartite Labour Organisation in India' (1944) 49 International Labour Review 494, 496. On the tensions between economic development (growth) and equality against the background of the turn to reform and opening in China see Elizabeth J. Perry and Christine Wong, 'Introduction: The Political Economy of Reform in Post-Mao China: Causes, Content, and Consequences' in Elizabeth J. Perry and Christine Wong (eds), *The Political Economy of Reform in Post-Mao China* (Harvard University Press 1985) 1, 21; Cecilia L.W. Chan and Nelson W.S. Chow, *More Welfare after Economic Reform? Welfare Development in the People's Republic of China* (University of Hong Kong 1992) 48.

189 See Sarbani Sen, Chapter 4 in this volume.

constitutional framework provided the basis for favouring industrial workers in the so-called organised sector when introducing sickness insurance or a framework for pension funds, such as workers employed in plantations, the mining industry, heavy industries, banks, insurance businesses, railways, or factories producing consumer goods. Agricultural workers and workers employed in the so-called unorganised sector (home-based workers engaged in household manufacturing, wage workers or self-employed workers engaged in small-scale production, the sale of goods, or the provision of services) were excluded.

Politics began to change in 2004, when a Congress Party-led United Progressive Alliance government came to power.[190] In 2005, parliament introduced a right to paid employment in rural areas, for a limited number of days, thus securing income, at least for a certain period and to some extent. In 2008, parliament obliged the central government to formulate welfare schemes for unorganised workers covering disability, health, maternity, and old age. And in 2013, parliament made provision for food security, targeting eligible households in urban and rural areas, not workers. Yet, apart from that, people not qualifying as workers depended on government programmes without a basis in statutory law. Social security and equality do not rank high in Indian politics, despite the far-reaching ambitions announced in the 1940s.[191]

The constitutional framework of the People's Republic of China preceding the reform era was more explicit. The PRC constitutions prior to the reform era (1954, 1975, 1978) officially proclaimed that the industrialisation of the country had priority over all other policy goals: The 1954 PRC Constitution announced – with regard to the so-called transition period (ie the period preceding the socialist society) – as the first task to be achieved the bringing about of 'the socialist industrialisation of the country', and thereafter, step by step, of the socialist transformation of agriculture, handicrafts, and capitalist industry and commerce (preamble). The PRC constitutions of 1975 and 1978 asserted, when elaborating on the development of the socialist economy, that the state would take 'agriculture as the foundation and industry as the leading factor' (Article 10 of the 1975 Constitution; Article 11[2] of the 1978 Constitution). The 1982 PRC Constitution finally proclaimed and still proclaims that the 'state sector of the economy is the socialist sector . . . and . . . the leading force in the national economy' (Article 7; similarly, Article 5 of the 1954 Constitution). Accordingly, social policies as envisioned by the constitutions continuously favoured industrial workers over peasants. Workers enjoyed more rights and more reliable social security. The right to 'material assistance in old age,

190 On the political background of the policy change see Yamini Aiyar and Michael Walton, *Rights, Accountability and Citizenship: Examining India's Emerging Welfare State* (Centre for Policy Research 2014); see also Sarbani Sen, Chapter 4 in this volume.

191 On social assistance programmes at the level of the Indian states see Louise Tillin, 'Does India have Subnational Welfare Regimes? The Role of State Governments in Shaping Social Policy' (2022) 10 Territory, Politics, Governance 86.

and in case of illness or disability' was accorded to 'working people', ie people who labour (Article 93 PRC Constitution of 1954). Social insurance, social assistance, and public health services were, therefore, confined to working people. Yet, even if peasants could potentially qualify as people who labour according to the letter of the law, in practice, treatment was not equal. Peasants were accorded some social security through land reform and the peoples' communes, and through the 'Five Guarantees' (*wubao*), but the systems were inferior to the security given workers.[192] For decades, industrialisation was furthered and pushed on at the expense of the livelihood of peasants.[193] In addition to that, the right to equality before the law granted under the 1954 PRC Constitution was not open to people called traitors, counter-revolutionaries, or feudal landlords (preamble; Article 86). Article 100 of the 1954 PRC Constitution demanded that, to be able to rely on the rights embedded in the constitution, citizens had to abide by the constitution and other laws, and observe labour discipline. The right to equality in the PRC was not a universal concept; it was a particular concept.[194] The constitutions of 1975 and 1978 (debated at the height of Mao's era) drew the consequence of such a limited concept of equality; the constitutions abstained from even mentioning a right to equality before the law.

The era of reform and opening in the PRC (de-collectivisation of agrarian production; marketisation and privatisation of enterprises; abandonment of socialist social insurance) brought a change in politics toward acceptance of a universalisation of social security. The politics of universalisation began in the 1990s and was stepped up in the 2000s: The domains of social insurance were expanded, eventually covering old age, sickness, work injury, maternity, and – a novelty – unemployment. Social insurance became based on contributions by employers, employees, and the state. Social insurance schemes were, step by step, extended to cover all employees, including migrant workers and informal workers, at first in urban areas, then in rural areas. Sickness insurance was even extended to cover all urban residents and rural populations. The Minimum Livelihood Guarantee (a form of social assistance) was extended from urban areas to rural areas. In short, and without going into details: The gradual universalisation of the regimes resulted

192 Albert H.Y. Chen, Chapter 3 in this volume.

193 Social policies in the Soviet Union were similarly preferential towards workers. See Galmarini-Kabala (n 164) 36, 45.

194 On universal and particular concepts of equality see Ulrike Davy, 'Minority Protection under the League of Nations: Universal and Particular Equality' in Ulrike Davy and Antje Flüchter (eds), *Imagining Unequals, Imagining Equals Concepts of Equality in History and Law* (Bielefeld University Press 2022) 131. The ideological commitment of the PRC to the ending of exploitation, fraternity, and equality is often overrated. See eg Chan and Chow (n 188) 21, 41, 68.

in a new balance of development and equality. Yawning equality gaps have been closed.[195]

The tension between economic development and equality was less pronounced in Brazil and South Africa. For one, Brazil's economy could take advantage of American regionalism, even after World War II. Politics was not faced with a dire trade-off, like the dilemma faced by politics in China or India. And Brazilian social policy moved to expand the social security regimes gradually. Such expansionist policies were pursued by right-wing as well as by left-wing governments.[196] In the 1960s, basically all urban workers in the formal sector were integrated into one unified system (with few exceptions, such as civil servants).[197] In the 1970s, regimes for agricultural workers were introduced, followed by the creation of regimes for (small-scale) self-employed entrepreneurs in the 1980s.[198] Since the late 1990s and early 2000s, governments introduced various forms of non-contributory (means-tested) benefits, addressing the elderly and families, most famously *bolsa família*, a conditional cash benefit targeting poor families.[199] In short, social security measures are no longer preserved to certain strata of society (formal workers, civil servants, the military), even if the move toward universalisation may remain precarious and piecemeal or lacks redistributive effects.[200] For another, South Africa adhered to a narrow concept of equality based on hierarchies according to racialised thinking (apartheid) until the early 1990s. As far as industrialisation relied on mining, agriculture, the building industry, or heavy industry, South Africa could take advantage of its racialised labour policies that kept wages down

195 On the inequalities accepted or constructed by the welfare regimes in China and India – past and present – see Nara Dillon, 'Parallel Trajectories: The Development of the Welfare State in China and India' in Prasenjit Duara and Elizabeth J. Perry (eds), *Beyond Regimes. China and India Compared* (Harvard University Asia Center 2018) 173.

196 Octávio Luiz Motta Ferraz, Chapter 2 in this volume.

197 Cardoso de Oliveira (n 153) 383.

198 Carlos Alberto G. Chiarelli, 'Social Security for Rural Workers in Brazil' (1976) 113 International Labour Review 159; James M. Malloy, 'Authoritarianism and the Extension of Social Security Protection to the Rural Sector in Brazil' (1977) 14 Luso-Brazilian Review 195; Rogério Nagamine Costanzi, Edvaldo Duarte Barbosa and Julimar da Silva Bichara, 'Extending Social Security Coverage to Self-Employed Workers in Brazil' (2013) 152 International Labour Review 549.

199 Wendy Hunter, 'Making Citizens: Brazilian Social Policy from Getúlio to Lula' (2014) 6 Journal of Politics in Latin America 15; Jonathan Tepperman, 'Brazil's Antipoverty Breakthrough: The Surprising Success of Bolsa Família' (2016) 95 Foreign Affairs 34; Fabián A. Borges, *Human Capital versus Basic Income. Ideology and Models for Anti-Poverty Programs in Latin America* (University of Michigan Press 2022) 46.

200 For critical voices see eg Octávio Luiz Motta Ferraz, Chapter 2 in this volume; Lena Lavinas, *The Takeover of Social Policy by Financialization. The Brazilian Paradox* (Palgrave Macmillan 2017); Lena Lavinas, 'The Collateralization of Social Policy under Financialized Capitalism' (2018) 49 Development and Change 502.

in an exploitative manner in important sectors.[201] In the 1960s and 1970s, South Africa's industry was by far the most advanced industry of the whole contingent.

Social Insurance for Work

For several decades, the People's Republic of China provided social security according to a concept that could be called a socialist form of social insurance. The concept was obviously inspired by the USSR approach to social insurance. Under Marxist-Leninist thinking, social insurance was deemed a *quid pro quo* for work that contributed to the furtherance of the state and the economy.[202] The state owed the provision of social insurance to all who were engaged in productive work and thus earned the benefits granted under the system. Providing social insurance benefits was not an act of grace or the outcome of a power struggle between labour and industry, but – like wages – the complement of or an equivalent to a contribution in kind (work) to the common good made by the workers. From a Marxist-Leninist perspective, there was no room for the idea that workers could be asked to make (further) contributions in money to the functioning of the social insurance regime. The functioning of the regime was the sole responsibility of the state and the state enterprises. Prior to the era of reform and opening, the PRC adhered to such a Marxist-Leninist model of a social insurance: The Labour Insurance Regulations, promulgated in 1951, established a system of insurance that operated under the sole responsibility of the employers (state-owned enterprises); similar regimes were established for government officials and cadres.[203] The concept of a socialist social insurance was abandoned when the PRC overhauled its entire social insurance regime in the 1990s and introduced a tripartite contribution system that required employees to also make contributions to the financing of the regime. With hindsight, the socialist form of social insurance was short-lived, in China and the USSR.

Poverty: Absence of Stigma, Dignity

In the context of European welfare, attaching stigma to needs-based, non-work-related, and tax-financed benefits was part of the concept of poor relief that dominated the delivery of those benefits well into the twentieth

201 O.F. Raum, 'Der Afrikaner in der südafrikanischen Industrie' (1970) 20 Sociologus 97; Fred Curtis, 'Contradiction and Uneven Development in South Africa: The Constrained Allocation of African Labour-Power' (1984) 22 Journal of Modern African Studies 381.

202 Galmarini-Kabala (n 164) 36.

203 Albert H.Y. Chen, Chapter 3 in this volume.

century.[204] The provision of poor relief was orchestrated in a manner that was supposed to make recipients feel debased and humiliated. Humiliating the recipients of relief was a particularly strong feature of the British poor law. For centuries, British poor law relied on corporal punishment to reproach people who preferred taking alms to being engaged in work they declined to do. Beggars believed to be able-bodied were whipped in public, branded, put in the correction house and subjected to forced labour, or even put to death. When given, relief was provided under circumstances that only people in real need would accept (workhouse). Humiliation thus had a function. Humiliation was meant to discourage (unwanted) idleness. Humiliation was also present in nineteenth century German poor law, though official reactions to begging and alms taking were less drastic. Cities regularly took resort to expelling beggars who were not licensed and, hence, suspected of trickery and treasury. However, both traditions have something in common: In Great Britain and in Germany, dependency on poor relief was met with suspicion. Recipients were made to understand that granting relief was underpinned by a suspicion, namely the suspicion that the recipients had failed to live up to the expectations of society and the state and were, hence, worthy of contempt. In Great Britain, idleness was deemed a threat to the commonwealth and a burden to the community.[205] In Germany, the emphasis was on the failure to comply with bourgeois virtues (in particular, in protestant territories), such as industriousness, punctuality, reliability, and eagerness regarding work.[206] In Great Britain as well as in Germany, poor relief aimed to make recipients better humans, ie to enhance their will to accept the idea of self-reliance or their will to adhere to civic morals.

Southern social assistance regimes differ. For one, social assistance regimes are a recent phenomenon in Brazil, China, India, and South Africa. Prior to and even after 1945, the countries' social policies concentrated on work-related social insurance, in accordance with ILO strategies. Social assistance regimes became a significant element of social policy only in the 1990s. Brazil started experimenting with conditional cash transfers (which later became *bolsa família*)

204 See p. 190 in this chapter.

205 For the sixteenth century see Nicholls (n 74) 115, 162, for the eighteenth century, Nicholls (n 80) 37.

206 Endres (n 119) 1011. On the difficulties to conceive of the poor or of paupers as comrades or equals in early nineteenth century pre-industrial Germany, when nationalism was about to take roots, see Helmut Walser Smith, '"A Deep, Horizontal Comradeship?". Early Nineteenth Century German Nationalism and the Problem of Poverty' in Ulrike Davy and Antje Flüchter (eds), *Imagining Unequals, Imagining Equals Concepts of Equality in History and Law* (Bielefeld University Press 2022) 103.

and a non-contributory pension scheme.[207] China introduced the Minimum Livelihood Guarantee, first in big cities, later in rural areas too.[208] India established a National Social Assistance Programme at a national level, though as a government programme.[209] And South Africa overhauled the grant system inherited from the time of apartheid.[210] Apart from disaster or famine relief, there was no centuries-long tradition of poor relief in these countries. For another, and more importantly, the discursive link between social assistance and an ethic that generates suspicion if people were not able to sustain themselves was either weak or absent. In the case of India and South Africa, the absence of such a link seems obvious: In both countries, the problem to be solved was (and is) 'poverty', and 'poverty' was constructed in a manner that had nothing to do with a reproachable idleness on the side of the poor or an unwillingness to work. In 1902, Romesh Chunder Dutt set the tone in India for the decades to come:

> The poverty of the Indian population at the present day is unparalleled in any civilised country; the famines which have desolated India within the last quarter of the nineteenth century are unexampled in their extent and intensity in the history of ancient or modern times. By a moderate calculation, the famines [in recent years] . . . have carried off fifteen millions of people. The population of a faired-sized European country has been swept away from India within twenty-five years.[211]

For these catastrophes, the British rulers were to blame, not the Indian people. Dutt was unmistakeably clear about the root causes of widespread and horrendous poverty:

> [In] many ways, the sources of national wealth in India have been narrowed under British rule. . . . [The] East Indian Company and the British Parliament . . . discouraged Indian manufacturers . . . in order to encourage the rising manufacturers in England. Their fixed policy . . . was to make India subservient to the industries of Great Britain, and to make the Indian people grow raw produce only.[212]

207 Octávio Luiz Motta Ferraz, Chapter 2 in this volume. See also Lavinas (n 3) 328, 332; Lena Lavinas, Denise Gentil and Barbara Cobo, *The Controversial Brazilian Welfare Regime. UNRISD Working Paper 2017–10* (United Nations Research Institute for Social Development 2017) 6; Borges (n 199) 46.

208 Albert H.Y. Chen, Chapter 3 in this volume.

209 Sarbani Sen, Chapter 4 in this volume.

210 Letlhokwa George Mpedi, Chapter 5 in this volume.

211 Romesh Dutt, *The Economic History of India Under Early British Rule*, vol 1 (Kegan Paul, Trench, Trübner 1902) viii.

212 ibid ix.

In September 1943, with independence and the end of World War II in sight, the delegates of a tripartite labour conference taking place in Delhi translated their vision of social security 'into terms which the common man could understand', namely,

> peace, a house, adequate clothing, education, good health, and above all the right to walk with dignity on the world's great boulevards.[213]

From the point of view of the ideational foundations of politics, linking poverty in such a manner with dignity was fundamentally non-European. Indeed, if the problem of poverty was being conceived of from the perspective of dignity (its neglect in the first place as well as its restoration), the idea that recipients of relief could be unworthy is absent from the ideational framework.[214] The focus is on restoring dignity through a change in living conditions.

After the fall of the apartheid regime, South Africa faced its own kind of legacy, namely, the legacy of racism. That legacy made recent politics concentrate on equality and equity. A pivotal policy paper of 1994 laid out the task in just a few words:

> South Africa has inherited a fragmented and inequitable welfare system which requires restructuring. . . . Co-ordination of programmed alleviating the needs of people living in poverty and marginalised circumstances will be essential to maximise individual potential and minimise the extent of dependency on the State.[215]

The task awaiting the new and democratic regime in South Africa was considered huge. Another policy paper of 1997 gave numbers of people affected:

> About a third (35.2%) of all South African households, amounting to 18 million people, are living in poverty. African households, households in rural areas, especially those headed by women in rural areas, are the most affected. Over half (54%) of all South Africa's children live in poverty.[216]

213 N.N. (n 188) 496.

214 For a cultural perspective see Sarbani Sen, Chapter 4 in this volume; Leemamol Mathew and Sony Pellissery, 'Film and Literature as Social Commentary in India' in Elaine Chase and Grace Bantebya-Kyomuhendo (eds), *Poverty and Shame: Global Experiences* (Oxford University Press 2014) 48; Sony Pellissery and Leemamol Mathew, 'Persistence of Shaming in a Hierarchical Society' in Elaine Chase and Grace Bantebya-Kyomuhendo (eds), *Poverty and Shame: Global Experiences* (Oxford University Press 2014) 231.

215 Government of National Unity, *White Paper on Reconstruction and Development*, Government Gazette, 23 November 1994, No 16085, 27.

216 Department of Welfare, *White Paper for Social Welfare* (Department of Welfare 1997) para 1.

Again, poverty or being poor was not met with suspicion or contempt by those responsible for making policies. Being poor was simply the reality of a considerable part of the South African population. Blaming the poor for being poor was not merely far-fetched, it would have seemed irrational and is unheard of.[217]

The case of China and Brazil is not as clear-cut as the Indian and the South African case. Both China and Brazil constitutionalised – at some point in history or currently – individual duties vis-à-vis the community and the state. The constitutional framework of the People's Republic of China embeds a strong notion of work as a value and has done so from the early days of the PRC. The 1936 USSR Constitution served again as a model. Article 12 of the 1936 USSR Constitution epitomised the sanctity of labour under socialism, detesting the leisure certain classes of capitalists were able to afford themselves through income generated by the work of others: 'Work in the USSR is the obligation and matter of honour of each citizen capable of working, according to the principle "He who does not work shall not eat"'. Several PRC constitutions rehearsed that strong version of the value of work. Article 8 of the 1949 Common Programme of the Chinese People's Political Consultative Conference stated: 'It is the duty of every national . . . to observe labour discipline'. Article 16 of the 1954 PRC Constitution then declared: 'Work is a matter of honour for every citizen of the People's Republic of China who is capable of working'. Article 6 of the 1982 PRC Constitution asserts, after having stated that 'the system of exploitation of man by man' had been abolished by the system of socialist public ownership: 'The principle of "from each according to his ability, to each according to his work" is applied in this system'. Finally, Article 42(3) of the constitution of 1982 proclaims: 'Work is the glorious duty of every able-bodied citizen'.

Still, the Chinese concept of poverty is all but similar to the European concept of poverty where the focus was, for centuries, on the willingness of individuals to engage in paid labour. Morally laden notions such as the 'idle poor' did not exist in traditional China. Starvation, ailments, or the lack of clothes was attributed to fate rather than to individual responsibilities. Unlike in Europe, poverty was not construed as a 'social problem', manifest in an identifiable category of people called the 'poor'.[218] The notion of poverty (and the notion of 'social problems') gained relevance in political circles only at the beginning of the

217 On the framing of poverty in post-apartheid South Africa see Jeremy Seekings, '(Re)formulating the Social Question in Post-apartheid South Africa: Zola Skweyiya, Dignity, Development and the Welfare State' in Lutz Leisering (ed), *One Hundred Years of Social Protection. The Changing Social Question in Brazil, India, China, and South Africa* (Palgrave Macmillan 2021) 263, pointing out that the notion of self-reliance is also dominant in some circles of the governments led by the African National Congress.

218 Janet Y. Chen, *Guilty of Indigence. The Urban Poor in China, 1900–1953* (Princeton University Press 2012) 5.

twentieth century when China's 'weakness' (vis-à-vis Western powers; vis-à-vis Japan) became the number one political question among elites. Inspired by Western sociology, a prevalent answer to this vexing question linked 'weakness' to 'poverty', holding that widespread poverty constituted one of the greatest perils that threatened the very existence of China.[219] Linking 'weakness' in such a manner to 'poverty' already implied the remedy against China's weakness: If China wanted to overcome its weakness, widespread poverty needed to be overcome; and in order to overcome poverty, every one (who could) needed to contribute to the national effort of creating wealth. From that perspective, the value of labour was supposed to strengthen a collective effort, namely the effort aimed to avoid national extinction. In other words, in the Chinese context, the appraisal of the value of work was just loosely connected to individual virtues (unlike in the context of an ethic of work). The thrust of the appraisal was on national survival, hence a collective good.[220] To be sure, the Chinese approach to poverty constructed two categories of the 'poor': For one, the 'poor' who could not be blamed for living in a state of poverty; and the 'poor' who, because they were unwilling to join in the national effort, were branded as parasites, vermin, or paupers, who could legitimately be punished or sent to workhouses for re-education (work relief).[221] The important point is: Ideological contempt did not address the poor, but a particular section of the people, who might or might not be poor. That distinction then reoccurred in Maoist thinking, in particular in the belief that the poor (as a class living in a state of exploitation) had an important role to play in overthrowing feudalism, capitalism, and imperialism, and were, therefore, highly respected. Maoist scorn targeted the ones who did not live up to nationalist expectations.

The constitutions of Brazil also incorporated individual duties regarding work, yet in a less assertive manner than the PRC constitutions. Article 136 of the 1937 Constitution read: 'Labour is a social duty'. Article 136, however, added immediately a counter-duty to be fulfilled by the state: 'Intellectual, technical and manual labour has the right to protection and special care of the State'. The duties were obviously connected. The individual duty corresponded with a state duty (protection). The 1946 Constitution linked the individual right to work to a corresponding individual duty to work: 'Everyone is assured work that enables a dignified existence. Work is a social obligation' (Article 145, sole paragraph). Under the short-lived democratic Constitution of 1946,

219 ibid 16, 49.

220 See also Aiqun Hu, 'The Early Rise of Social Security in China: Ideas and Reforms, 1911–1949' in Lutz Leisering (ed), *One Hundred Years of Social Protection. The Changing Social Question in Brazil, India, China, and South Africa* (Palgrave Macmillan 2021) 55, 58 stressing that Republican China emphasised collectivistic notions rather than individualist notions of social problems and social policy; similarly, Shih-Jiunn Shi, 'Reviving the Dragon: Social Ideas and Social Policy Development in Modern China' (2017) 53 Issues and Studies 1.

221 Chen (n 218) 9, 17, 47, 53.

the obligation to work was construed as the flip-side of a right addressed to the state that implicated a duty on the side of the state (to provide work), similarly to the concept underlying the 1936 Constitution. The 1967 Constitution then turned away from speaking of 'duty' or 'obligation'. Under the rule of the military, work was no longer the object of an individual duty, but a constitutional value: In Article 157, the 1967 Constitution enumerated several principles that were supposed to characterise the economic and social order, among them the 'appreciation of labour as a condition of human dignity' (the other principles were: Freedom of initiative, the social function of property, harmony and solidarity among the factors of production, and economic development). Likewise, the (current) liberal Constitution of 1988 lists the 'social values of labour and of the free enterprise' among the founding principles of the Federative Republic of Brazil, which also include sovereignty, citizenship, the dignity of the human person, and political pluralism. Article 170 of the 1988 Constitution speaks of the 'appreciation of human work' as one of the foundations of the economic order. In short, work is clearly valued by the Brazilian constitutions, but not linked to strong expectations regarding work which might, if not fulfilled, legitimate grave repercussions based on moral contempt.

Poverty: Categorisation of Beneficiaries

Social assistance regimes in the global South – exemplified in the regimes of Brazil, China, India, and South Africa – differ from European regimes of poor law (and their offspring such as welfare relief, national assistance, and social assistance) in yet another dimension. Social assistance regimes in the global South tend to rely on a mechanism – the categorisation of beneficiaries – that attenuates debates about failures attributable to the poor even if societies underwrite an ideology that specifically values work.

Social assistance regimes in Brazil, China, India, and South Africa are not open to all people who are in need and present in their territories. The lawmakers of all countries under investigation decided to explicitly enumerate the categories of persons who have access to social assistance, provided their income does not exceed certain defined thresholds. Brazil targets poor senior citizens (aged 65 or older), people with disabilities in poor families, and children living in poor households. The Indian national social assistance programme targets the elderly (aged 60 or older), widows, people with disabilities, and families, and eligibility requires that beneficiaries live below the poverty line. The means-tested South African regime of social grants addresses the need of children, people with disabilities, the elderly, and war veterans. China is about to enumerate nine categories of people entitled to social assistance, such as families covered by the Minimum Livelihood Guarantee; the destitute; low-come families; poor families (according to income and expenditures on essential items); victims of natural disasters; vagrants and beggars without means of livelihood; families or persons facing temporary difficulties; persons of unknown identity or unable to make payments who need emergency assistance; and other families or persons with special difficulties as determined by the provincial authorities. Even though the laws of the countries vary as they define people who ought to have access to social assistance, the laws have something in common: The laws concentrate on the elderly, on people with disabilities, and on children in families, who qualify – according to an applicable yardstick – as being in need of help. Obviously, these categories constitute the core consensus among states. Enumerating categories of beneficiaries in such a manner, so it seems, serves a purpose: The various lists seek out people who can barely be blamed for not being engaged in work, at least from the perspective of and the consensus among lawmakers. One could also say: These categories are placed beyond dispute. In any case, contempt or scorn is not a feature of providing help.[222]

Constitutional Courts and Social Policy

Courts and Ideational Foundations

Courts called upon to elaborate authoritatively on the meaning of social rights or social values that ought to be respected or implemented greatly contribute to the shaping and re-shaping of the ideational foundations underpinning social policies at the national level. That is particularly true for constitutional courts. In most of the countries under investigation – in Germany, Brazil, China, India, and South Africa – social rights or social principles form part of the (written) constitutional law and, apart from China, individuals or juristic persons may turn to a court empowered to review state actions (or inaction) from the angle of constitutional rights or values. When interpreting those constitutional norms, the courts necessarily concretise the meaning of the text of the constitutions. Concretisation of textual meaning again involves taking part in the shaping of the content of the constitutional norms. As courts concretise the meaning of constitutional norms, they may affirm the existing meaning, they may augment the meaning, they may narrow the meaning down, or they may clarify what has (so far) been contentious. Whatever courts do when they interpret and apply constitutional norms to the peculiarities of a case, their doing has a dimension of law-making.[223] That is why constitutional courts

222 Whether means-testing *per se* or behavioural conditionalities infringe upon the dignity of the beneficiaries is a different and highly contested question. Against the backdrop of *bolsa família* (conceptualised as conditional cash transfer targeting poor families) see eg Wendy Hunter and Natasha Borges Sugiyama, 'Transforming Subjects into Citizens: Insights from Brazil's Bolsa Família' (2014) 12 Perspectives on Politics 829; Cristian Pérez-Muñoz, 'What is Wrong with Conditional Cash Transfer Programs?' (2017) 48 Journal of Social Philosophy 440.

223 From the point of view of legal theory Hans Kelsen, *General Theory of Law and State* (Harvard University Press 1945) 133, 134; from the point of view of judicial activism P.N. Bhagwati, 'Judicial Activism and Public Interest Litigation' (1985) 23 Columbia Journal of Transnational Law 561.

influence the content of social rights and of social values (principles, directives) when they adjudicate.

It is impossible for me to even attempt to give an overview on how the constitutional courts of Germany, Brazil, India, and South Africa have influenced the social policies on the ground and how the constitutional case law compares across countries. There is, meanwhile, an abundance of literature that does so, and this literature includes the case-law of the Constitutional Court of Brazil (*Supremo Tribunal Federal*), the Federal Constitutional Court of Germany (*Bundesverfassungsgericht*), the Supreme Court of India, and the Constitutional Court of South Africa.[224] What I present here is modest: I shall concentrate on themes that I have already touched upon from the perspective of the ideational foundations of social policies, though so far with a focus on statutory law. Now, the focus is on constitutional case law, and I'll specifically focus on case law that reflects tensions between politics and the judiciary. Such tensions seem to arise and get strong in three contexts: Where policy makers and lawmakers try to exclude social policy making from the realm of judicial review; where fundamental questions of dignity are at stake; and where questions of equality are touched upon. I shall give examples for each of these contexts.

Rights and Review

In Germany, it was not self-understood throughout history that the recipients of poor relief or welfare relief (*Armenpflege*, *Fürsorge*) could bring their case before the courts if relief had been denied, maybe arbitrarily denied. There was a court system in place for matters of social insurance, but none for poor relief: From the turn to the nineteenth century onward, statutory law obliged certain administrative authorities at the local level to take care of the poor.[225] But taking care of the poor was believed to be in the discretion of the administrative authority; when relief was granted, it was not granted as of a right held by the person in need.[226] According to the prevalent concept of poor relief, the

224 See eg the contributions in Fons Coomans (ed), *Justiciability of Economic and Social Rights. Experiences from Domestic Systems* (Intersentia 2006); Varun Gauri and Daniel M. Brinks (eds), *Courting Social Justice. Judicial Enforcement of Social and Economic Rights in the Developing World* (Cambridge University Press 2008); Malcolm Langford (ed), *Social Rights Jurisprudence. Emerging Trends in International and Comparative Law* (Cambridge University Press 2008); Daphne Barak-Erez and Aeyal M. Gross (eds), *Exploring Social Rights. Between Theory and Practice* (Hart Publishing 2011); Katharine G. Young, *Constituting Economic and Social Rights* (Oxford University Press 2012); Jeff King, *Judging Social Rights* (Cambridge University Press 2012); Katie Boyle, *Economic and Social Rights Law. Incorporation, Justiciability and Principles of Adjudication* (Routledge 2020).

225 See p. 192 in this chapter.

226 Prussian statutory law (Gesetz über die Verpflichtung zur Armenpflege, 31 December 1842, preußische Gesetzessammlung 1842, 8) unmistakably stated in Section 33: 'Einen Anspruch auf Verpflegung kann der Arme gegen einen Armenverband niemals im Rechtsweg, sondern nur bei der Verwaltungsbehörde geltend machen' (a poor person is not empowered to take the

authority's obligation was just that: An obligation on the side of the authority, with no corresponding individual right as the flip-side of the duty which could be legally enforced. The authority's duty was meant to exist vis-à-vis the state. Consequently, people in need of help were not empowered to take the administrative authority to court and raise a claim. The only kind of litigation provided for by statutory law in matters of poor relief involved the various administrative authorities. The authority which had in fact provided help in a particular case was entitled to take another authority to court, claiming that it had been the duty of this other authority to provide help in the case concerned. Hence, courts were meant to become involved only when and where administrative authorities quarrelled about the width of their respective duties and the ensuing financial burdens. Courts were not meant to decide on the legitimacy of the claim of an individual that help ought to be provided in his or her case. These principles remained in place even after the major reform of 1924, when poor relief (*Armenpflege*) became welfare relief (*Fürsorge*).[227] After the reform of 1924, relevant statutory law no longer explicitly ruled out that recipients bring in a petition and take the administrative authority to court. Still, traditional thinking continued to dominate practice. Lawmakers saw no reason to intervene and overturn the practice, not in the 1930s, not in the 1940s. In 1954, the Federal Administrative Court (*Bundesverwaltungsgericht*) stepped in, holding: 'In the matter of poor relief individual rights do exist'.[228] The court's main argument was that, under the German constitution of 1949 (*Grundgesetz*), it was no longer possible to assume that people in need were simply the object of a duty of a state organ, a duty that existed vis-à-vis the state and was not linked to the people concerned. The fundamental rights granted under the constitution and the rule of law demanded, so the court argued, that the recipients of relief be construed as legal subjects (also when in receipt of relief) and, therefore, as the holders of rights that would be violated if welfare authorities neglected their duties under welfare law. That judgement of the *Bundesverwaltungsgericht* opened the door to (individual) litigation in the matter of welfare relief.[229]

In the 1940s, the constitution-makers in India compromised on the legal status of socio-economic rights, ie constitutional norms involving a (positive)

administrative authority to court; a claim may be raised only before the administrative authority). See also G.A. Grotefend, *Lehrbuch des Preußischen Verwaltungsrechts, vol 2 Das innere Verwaltungsrecht in Preußen* (Verlag von Carl Habel 1892) 68; Fritz Stier-Somlo, *Deutsche Sozialgesetzgebung. Geschichtliche Grundlagen und Krankenversicherungsrecht* (Verlag von Gustav Fischer 1906) 56; much later Otto Mayer, *Deutsches Verwaltungsrecht*, vol 2 (Duncker & Humblot 1924) 386, asserting that the then existing statutory law on welfare relief would still put public poor relief on a par with alms giving.

227 Verordnung über die Fürsorgepflicht (Regulation on the obligation to provide welfare), 13 February 1924, BGBl I S 100.

228 Bundesverwaltungsgericht, judgement of 24 June 1954, V C 78.54.

229 In 1961, the right to social assistance became eventually part of statutory law. See Bundessozialhilfegesetz (law on social assistance), 30 June 1961, BGBl I S 815.

duty on the side of the state to make arrangements relating to employment (employment policies), social security, social assistance, family protection, health, or education.[230] There was no consensus among constitution-makers to enumerate social rights explicitly in the list of the Fundamental Rights contained in Part III of the constitution, most of which were civil or political in character, such as the right to equality before the law; freedom of expression; freedom to form associations; freedom of religion; and right to property. Also, there was no consensus to not mention social rights at all. In the end, constitution-makers agreed to include in the constitution a Part IV dealing with 'directive principles of state policy' where reference was made to issues of (individual) welfare, yet not from the angle of individual rights, but from the angle of government policy and government duties. Most of the articles enshrined in Part IV of the constitution address the state. Under Article 38, for instance, the state 'shall strive to promote the welfare of the people'. Or, to give another example, under Article 39 the state shall 'direct its policy securing', *inter alia*, 'that the citizens, man and women equally, have the right to an adequate means of livelihood'. Hence, the state was meant to be the actor under Part IV; individuals and rights were addressed in an indirect manner only, namely, as the object of a state duty. Of all articles, Article 37 of the constitution embeds the very heart of the political compromise: On the one hand, the article states that the Directive Principles are 'fundamental in the governance of the country' and that it would be 'the duty of the State to apply these principles in making laws'. On the other hand, Article 37 emphasises that the provisions of Part IV 'shall not be enforceable by any court'. In short, the compromise reached late in 1949 seemed to say: The state was bound to act according to the principles laid down in Part IV, but it was up to the (central and state) governments to decide when and how to act. Courts ought not to have a say in this.

The view that courts were excluded from taking part in social policy making was, in the 1950s and the following decades, by and large accepted by the Supreme Court of India and many other Indian courts.[231] In an indirect manner however, the Supreme Court was present in social policy making, and quite strongly so. When adjudicating on the (abstract) relationship between the Fundamental Rights (Part III) and the Directive Principles (Part IV), the court stressed in the 1950s that Fundamental Rights were 'sacrosanct and not

230 On the constitutional history see Granville Austin, *The Indian Constitution: Cornerstone of a Nation* (Clarendon Press 1966) 52, 75; K.C. Markandan, *Directive Principles in the Indian Constitution* (Allied Publishers Private Limited 1966); Bertus de Villiers, 'Directive Principles of State Policy and Fundamental Rights' (1992) 8 South African Journal on Human Rights 29; Sarbani Sen, Chapter 4 in this volume. Succinctly Gautam Bhatia, 'Directive Principles of State Policy' in Sujit Choudhry, Madhav Khosla and Pratap Bhanu Mehta (eds), *Oxford Handbook of the Indian Constitution* (Oxford University Press 2016) 644.

231 Bhatia (n 230) 645.

liable to be abridged . . . , except to the extent provided in . . . Part III'.[232] If the state wanted to implement Directive Principles, the state had to make sure that those acts conformed with the rights under Part III. Directive Principles were deemed to 'run as subsidiary to the Chapter of Fundamental Rights', not as something more powerful.[233] The Fundamental Rights had to be respected under all circumstances. That position of the court made social reform – guided by the Directive Principles – fragile. Courts could intervene and stop the implementation of policy programmes, holding the programmes would be inconsistent with Fundamental Rights. When the government and the law-makers moved to amend the constitution in the 1970s with a view to making Directive Principles prevail over Fundamental Rights (the government wanted to move on with land reform plans), the Supreme Court of India insisted: The power of the parliament to amend the constitution would not 'enable Parliament to abrogate or take away Fundamental Rights or to completely change the fundamental features of the Constitution so as to destroy its identity'.[234] The amendment was partially declared unconstitutional.[235]

In the 1980s, the Supreme Court of India moved away from the position held in the 1950s. The departure from the early consensus had several dimensions. At a principled level, the Supreme Court of India recalibrated its take on the relationship between the Fundamental Rights (Part III) and the Directive Principles (Part IV). The Supreme Court now emphasised that Fundamental Rights and Directive Principles were of equal importance and that the court, therefore, should adopt 'the principle of harmonious construction', implicating that both Fundamental Rights and Directive Principles had to be weighed against each other.[236] Courts should attempt, so the Supreme Court ruled now,

232 *State of Madras v Srimathi Champakam Dorairajan*, 1951 SCR 525, 531.

233 ibid.

234 *Kesavananda Bharati Sripadagalvaru v State of Kerala* (1973) 4 SCC 225, para 506. The political and legal conflict began in 1971, when the Indian parliament adopted the Constitution (25th Amendment) Act, headed 'Saving of laws giving effect to certain directive principles'. The intention of the parliament was to bar the courts from questioning the constitutionality of laws from the perspective of Article 14 of the constitution (equality) or the perspective of Article 19 of the constitution (rights regarding certain freedoms, *inter alia*, the right to practise any profession, or to carry on any occupation, trade or business), if those laws, according to a declaration, specifically aimed to give effect to certain Directive Principles, in particular the principle that ownership and control of material resources be distributed so as to best serve the common good, and the principle that there be no concentration of wealth and means of production to the common detriment. Also, courts were explicitly barred from questioning whether such laws would indeed give effect to the Directive Principles involved in the declaration attached to the law.

235 The Supreme Court of India took issue with the part of the 25th Amendment which barred the courts from questioning the law on the ground that it would (in fact) not give effect to the directive principle involved. On what was called 'radical constitutional amendments' in the early 1970s see also Granville Austin, *Working a Democratic Constitution. The Indian Experience* (Oxford University Press 1999) 236; Sarbani Sen, Chapter 4 in this volume.

236 *Minerva Mills Ltd v Union of India*, 1981 SCR (1) 206, 326.

to give effect to both as much as possible. That change in principled positions had consequences. First, courts in India accepted that the values encapsulated in the Directive Principles constituted 'public interest' that could legitimise the restriction of Fundamental Rights.[237] Second, courts assumed that statutory provisions ought to be interpreted in such a manner as to conform with Directive Principles.[238]

The Supreme Court of India went even further. In the 1980s, the Supreme Court of India commenced to read into some Fundamental Rights (Part III) certain aspects of social policy that had, by the constitution-makers, been written into Part IV of the constitution, thus making the content of Directive Principles part of the content of Fundamental Rights. In that respect, the change in the reading of Article 21 of the constitution stands out. Article 21 of the constitution states: 'No person shall be deprived of his life or personal liberty except according to the procedure established by law'. In 1985, the Supreme Court of India faced petitions lodged by a number of men and women who were threatened to be expelled from pavements in Mumbai (than Bombay) where they were dwelling, contending that they have, under the constitution, a right to live, and that the right to live could not be exercised without the means of livelihood.[239] Given their circumstances, so the petitioners contended further, they would have no other option but to flock to big cities, which provided the means of bare subsistence, and they would only choose a pavement or a slum which was nearest to their place of work. The court took side with the petitioners, holding:

> The sweep of the right to life conferred by Article 21 is wide and far reaching. It does not mean merely that life cannot be extinguished or taken away as, for example, by the imposition and execution of the death sentence, except according to procedure established by law. That is but one aspect of the right to life. An equally important facet of that right is the right to livelihood because, no person can live without the means of living, that is, the means of livelihood. If the right to livelihood is not treated as a part of the constitutional right to life, the easiest way of depriving a person

237 Bhatia (n 230) 649 citing cases dealing with restrictions placed on employers by labour law in the interest of employees. See also *Chameli Singh v State of Uttra Pradesh*, AIR 1996 SC 1051 concerned with a restriction of property rights.

238 See, as an early example, Allahabad High Court in *Eveready Flashlight Co v Labour Court*, AIR 1962 All 497 para 16, holding – when interpreting a provision of an Indian Trade Unions Act concerned with 'unfair practice' – that 'any practice which violates the principles of Article 43 of the Constitution and other articles declaring decent wages and living conditions for workmen and which if allowed to become normal would tend to lead to industrial strife should be condemned as unfair labour practice'. See also Supreme Court of India, *S Subramaniam Balaji v Goverment of Tamil Nadu* (2013) 9 SCC 659, interpreting the words 'public purpose' in Article 282 of the constitution.

239 *Olga Tellis v Bombay Municipal Corporation*, 1985 SCR Supl (2) 51.

> of his right to life would be to deprive him of his means of livelihood to the point of abrogation. Such deprivation would . . . make life impossible to live.[240]

The reasoning of the Supreme Court in *Olga Tellis v Bombay Municipal Corporation* tightly linked a Fundamental Right (right to life guaranteed under Article 21) and a Directive Principle (principle that the state ought to secure the right to an adequate means of livelihood under Article 39[a]). That linking blurred the demarcation line between the rights embedded in Part III and the principles laid down in Part IV, at least in the context of the right to life. If the right to livelihood was a dimension of the right to life, the right to livelihood had to be seen as being incorporated in a 'Fundamental Right' and, as such, enforceable before a court of law.[241] And indeed, the Supreme Court of India continued to go against the demarcation line that had – historically – been drawn by the constitution-makers: In *Olga Tellis v Bombay Municipal Corporation*, the Supreme Court of India confronted a situation where people had been dwelling on pavements and the state wanted to intervene (expulsion). The court's judgement required the municipal authorities to refrain from expelling people without much ado. The court demanded that the authorities proceeded according to certain rules, in particular procedural rules, making sure that the people would be heard, and their interests would be taken into account by the authorities in the course of decision making. In *Chameli Singh v State of Uttar Pradesh*, the Supreme Court faced an appeal lodged by landowners who complained about having been given notification under the Land Acquisition Act, an administrative act informing them of the intention of the state to take possession of their lands in order to build houses for the Dalits.[242] The Supreme Court first held rather sweepingly: 'Right to live guaranteed by any Civilised society implies the right to food, water, decent environment, education, medical care and shelter. These are basic human rights known to any civilised society'.[243] Then the Supreme Court turned to India and its constitution:

> Right to shelter when used as an essential requisite to the right to live, should be deemed to have been guaranteed as a fundamental right. As is

240 ibid 79.

241 See also Jayna Kothari, 'Social Rights Litigation in India: Developments in the Last Decade' in Daphne Barak-Erez and Aeyal M. Gross (eds), *Exploring Social Rights Between Theory and Practice* (Hart Publishing 2011) 171, 174; Arun Thiruvengadam, 'Revisiting The Role of the Judiciary in Plural Societies (1987). A Quarter-Century Retrospective on Public Interest Litigation in India and the Global South' in Sunil Khilnani, Vikram Raghavan and Arun K. Thiruvengadam (eds), *Comparative Constitutionalism in South Asia* (Oxford University Press 2012) 341, 349; Young (n 224) 200.

242 AIR 1996 SC 1051.

243 ibid para 8.

> enjoined in the Directive Principles, the State should be deemed to be under an obligation to secure it for its citizens, of course subject to its economic budgeting.[244]

The Supreme Court of India obviously envisioned Article 21 of the constitution when making that statement, possibly also Article 19(1)(e), conceptualising these articles of Part III of the constitution as the source of an (enforceable) individual right as well as of a corresponding state duty. In the end, the landowners lost their case; their appeals were dismissed.

In its orders guiding the authorities on how to deliver what they owed to the poor, the Supreme Court of India got involved even in the details of delivery. For instance, in *People's Union for Civil Liberties v Union of India*, the court issued an order dated 23 January 2012, asserting: 'The State owes to the homeless people to ensure at least minimum shelter as part of the State obligation under Article 21'.[245] Following that statement, the Supreme Court directed certain states of India to 'ensure that at least temporary night shelters are provided to protect and preserve the lives of the people in consonance with . . . Article 21 of the Constitution'. In another renowned order released on 28 November 2001 in the context of a food campaign – *People's Union for Civil Liberties v Union of India* – the Supreme Court of India issued a long list of directions, aimed at enhancing food security for India's poor, such as the directive to complete the identification of families below the poverty line, to issue cards, and to commence the distribution of a certain amount of grains per family and month by 1 January 2002 the latest; or the directive to ensure that application forms were freely available and an effective mechanism was in place to ensure redressal of grievances; or the directive to provide a mid-day meal for every child in every government and government assisted primary school, with a minimum content of 300 calories and 8 to 12 grams of proteins, each day of school for a minimum of 200 days.[246]

The judgements and orders delivered by the German *Bundesverwaltungsgericht* and the Indian Supreme Court of India indicate the extent to which courts are willing to contribute to the shaping of the ideational foundations. Seemingly, courts tend to intervene where courts feel that politics fails to correct a situation perceived as wrong by the justices. In the cases mentioned before, the wrong involved the denying of enforceable individual rights in matters of social policy, which is a wrong that implicitly also negates the watch-dog function of the judiciary. Obviously, discontent with politics may reach various degrees

244 ibid.

245 Order of 23 January 2012 in Writ Petition (Civil) No 196 of 2001. When confronting a food crisis similarly judgement of 11 May 2016 in Writ Petition (Civil) No 857 of 2015.

246 Order of 28 November 2001 in Writ Petition (Civil) No 196 of 2001. On the background of the case see Lauren Birchfield and Jessica Corsi, 'Between Starvation and Globalization: Realizing the Right to Food in India' (2009) 31 Michigan Journal of International Law 691.

of intensity. Judicial discontent was considerably stronger in India than in Germany, prompting Indian courts to resume a very active role in promoting social justice, a move that was also met with criticism.[247]

Dignity

The notion of dignity inspired adjudication in matters of social policy, again predominantly in cases relating to welfare relief, in Germany, in India, and in South Africa. At the international level, questions relating to 'equal worth' and humane conditions of work were among the constant concerns of the non-European members of the ILO, especially the delegates coming from China and India.[248] After independence (India), the establishment of a People's Republic (China), the end of the military regime (Brazil), and the demise of apartheid (South Africa), 'dignity' became a cornerstone of the respective constitutions. In Brazil's 1988 Constitution, dignity is listed among the foundational values of the Federal Republic (Article 1) and among the goals of the economic order (Article 170). The PRC 1982 Constitution declares the personal dignity of citizens of the People's Republic of China to be inviolable (Article 38). India's 1949 Constitution promises, *inter alia*, to secure 'fraternity' with a view to 'assuring the dignity of the individual and the unity of the Nation' (preamble). South Africa's 1996 Constitution mentions 'human dignity' among the foundational values (Section 1[a] and Section 7). Additionally, the South African Constitution grants every person 'the right to respect for and protection of his or her dignity' (Section 10), a right listed among the non-derogable rights. The 1949 Constitution of Germany (*Grundgesetz*) states in Article 1: 'Human dignity is inviolable. To respect and protect it shall be the duty of all state authority'. The political context of the clauses and the legal nature of the clauses vary considerably. The Constitution of India is mindful of the struggles preceding independence, South Africa's constitution responds to the legacy of apartheid,

247 For favourable opinions see Bhagwati (n 223); Jagat Narain, 'Judicial Law Making and the Place of Directive Principles in Indian Constitution' (1985) 27 Journal of the Indian Law Institute 198; de Villiers (n 230); Bertus de Villiers, 'The Socio-Economic Consequences of Directive Principles of State Policy; Limitations on Fundamental Rights' (1992) 8 South African Journal on Human Rights 188; Bhatia (n 230). For rather critical voices see Madhav Khosla, 'Making Social Rights Conditional: Lessons from India' (2010) 8 International Journal of Constitutional Law 739; Farrah Ahmed and Tabunabh Khaitan, 'Constitutional Avoidance in Social Rights Adjudication' (2015) 35 Oxford Journal of Legal Studies 607; Gaurav Mukherjee, 'The Supreme Court of India and the Inter-Institutional Dynamics of Legislated Social Rights' (2020) 53 VRÜ/World Comparative Law 411; Sourya Bandyopadhyay, '"A Noble Tree that Bore Bitter Fruits?": The Supreme Court of India, Judicial Activism and Judicialization of Politics' (2020) 11 Indian Journal of Law and Justice 120. For an account on the historical background of judicial activism in India see Nick Robinson, 'Expanding Judiciaries: India and the Rise of the Good Governance Court' (2009) 8 Washington University Global Studies Law Review 1.

248 See p. 177, 180 in this chapter.

and Germany's constitution responds to the crimes committed under National Socialism. Whatever the background, 'dignity' ranks high across the countries, either as a foundational value or as a right. The case law of the constitutional courts involved reflects the position accorded to dignity by the constitutional framework.

When constitutional courts adjudicate on questions relating to individual welfare, dignity serves (at least) three important purposes.

First, where constitution-makers were reluctant to explicitly embed individual socio-economic rights (India, Germany), the dignity clause occasionally serves as a vehicle for making certain aspects of social security enforceable through a court of law, eventually the constitutional court. The Supreme Court of India, for instance, used the notion of dignity to bridge the gap (wilfully created by the constitution-makers) between the Fundamental Rights enumerated in Part III of the constitution and the Directive Principles laid down in Part IV of the constitution.[249] The Supreme Court now consistently holds that Fundamental Rights and Directive Principles are equally important. When the court established that position, the idea of dignity was essential: In *Minerva Mills Ltd v Union of India* the Supreme Court stressed that Fundamental Rights were 'not an end in themselves but . . . the means to an end'. And, so the court continued, the end was 'specified in Part IV'.[250] For the court, both Fundamental Rights and Directive Principles were 'intended to carry out the objectives set out in the preamble of the Constitution and establish an egalitarian social order', thereby 'ensuring dignity of the individual not only to a few privileged persons but to the entire people . . . including the have-nots and the handicapped, the lowliest and the lost'.[251] Dignity appears to be the most far-reaching of all ends. According to the court, dignity extended to the whole population: In *Minerva Mills Ltd v Union of India* the Supreme Court of India clearly envisioned 'dignity of the individual' to become a 'living reality' for all, and that required the 'socio-economic structure envisaged in the Directive Principles' to become real, because 'only then [the Fundamental Rights] can become meaningful and significant for the millions of our poor and deprived people'.[252] Through linking rights and principles in the concept of dignity, the Supreme Court of India made socio-economic rights a legitimate issue in courts of law.[253] In Germany,

249 On the gap and the ensuing tensions see p. 222, 236 in this chapter.

250 *Minerva Mills Ltd v Union of India*, 1981 SCR (1) 206, 255.

251 ibid 320.

252 ibid 325.

253 On the Supreme Court's approach to human dignity and the relation between the Fundamental Rights enshrined in Part III of the constitution and the Directive Principles embedded in Part IV see Pritam Baruah, 'Logic and Coherence in *Naz Foundation*: The Arguments of Non-Discrimination, Privacy, and Dignity' (2009) 2 National University of Judicial Sciences 505, 520.

constitution-makers were similarly unwilling to include socio-economic rights in the list of fundamental rights embedded in Part I of the constitution. And, quite similarly to the Supreme Court of India, the German Federal Constitutional Court (*Bundesverfassungsgericht*) relied on the dignity clause contained in Article 1(1) of the constitution to engage in questions relating to social assistance (formerly welfare relief), contending that the dignity clause incorporated – in conjunction with Article 20(1) of the constitution – a right to a subsistence minimum that conforms with human dignity.[254] The *Bundesverfassungsgericht* too connected a fundamental right (Article 1, respect of human dignity) with a non-forceable principle (Article 20[1], welfare state principle), enabling people to get access to constitutional review in matters of social assistance, and enabling the *Bundesverfassungsgericht* to intervene in politics, at times to the disliking of policy makers.[255]

Secondly, the notion of dignity inspires the interpretation of fundamental rights and statutory law. When the Supreme Court of India held that the right to life (Article 21 of the constitution) was not confined to a narrow meaning, but included 'the right to live with human dignity and all that goes along with it',[256] the door was opened to all aspects of basic human needs, to adequate nutrition, clothing, shelter, health, education, or commingling with fellow human beings.[257] These aspects mirror almost exactly the dimensions of human dignity as guaranteed under Article 1(1) of the German constitution, which the *Bundesverfassungsgericht* summarily calls the socio-cultural subsistence minimum (*sozio-kulturelles Existenzminimum*), encompassing food, clothing, household items, housing, heating, health, building and keeping relations with other human beings, education, and the like.[258] The South African Constitutional Court joins in the interpretation when elaborating on the content of the right to

254 Bundesverfassungsgericht, judgement of the First Senate, 9 February 2010, 1 BvL 1/09. For an English translation see <www.bundesverfassungsgericht.de/SharedDocs/Entscheidungen/EN/2010/02/ls20100209_1bvl000109en.html> accessed 28 February 2022.

255 See eg Bundesverfassungsgericht, judgement of the First Senate, 5 November 2019, 1 BvL 7/16, declaring the withdrawal of benefits securing the existence minimum to be partly unconstitutional. For an English translation see <www.bundesverfassungsgericht.de/SharedDocs/Entscheidungen/EN/2019/11/ls20191105_1bvl000716en.html> accessed 28 February 2022.

256 *Francis Coralie Mullin v The Administrator, Union Territory of Delhi*, 1981 SCR (2) 516.

257 See also *Bandhua Mukti Morcha v Union on India*, 1984 SCR (2) 67, where the Supreme Court of India – confronting the still common practice of bonded labour in some Indian states, mainly involving labourers belonging to lower castes and tribes – held that Article 21 of the constitution included 'protection of the health and strength of workers . . . and of the tender age of children against abuse, opportunities and facilities for children to develop in healthy manner and in conditions of freedom and dignity, educational facilities, just and humane conditions of work and maternity relief'.

258 Bundesverfassungsgericht, judgement of the First Senate, 9 February 2010, 1 BvL 1/09, paras 90, 135 (English translation).

access to social security. In *Louis Khosa and others v Minister of Social Development and others*, the court stressed:

> The importance of the right . . . cannot be gainsaid. It is a right that goes to one of the core values of our Constitution – human dignity. The state has an obligation to ensure that its citizens have access to basic needs such as food, clean water and shelter.[259]

As a constitutional value or as a right, either way, human dignity relates to basic human needs, and that meaning influences the content of other rights. The courts agree on that.

Thirdly, human dignity serves a source for moral judgements delivered by the courts as they give reasons for their (legal) judgements or their orders. Sometimes, justices show signs of anger or outrage as they confront details of the cases pending before the court. In *Maharashtra Ekta Hawkers Union v Municipal Corporation, Greater Mumbai*, the Supreme Court of India said in introducing the case, apparently with discontent:

> Unfortunately, the street vendors/hawkers have received raw treatment from the State apparatus before and even after the independence. They are a harassed lot and are constantly victimized by the officials of the local authorities, the police, etc., who regularly target them for extra income and treat them with extreme contempt. The goods and belongings of the street vendors/hawkers are thrown to the ground and destroyed . . . if they are not able to meet the demands of the officials. Perhaps these minions in the administration have not understood [the] meaning of the term dignity enshrined in the preamble of the Constitution.[260]

The Constitutional Court of South Africa emphasises the humiliation that poverty might imply for people in need. In *Louis Khosa and others v Minister of Social Development and others*, the Constitutional Court of South Africa was asked to rule on the constitutionality of a statute that excluded non-nationals (yet permanent residents) from the grant system open to nationals. The Constitutional Court contended – with compassion – when describing the effects of the law:

> The exclusion of permanent residents in need . . . forces them into relationships of dependency upon families, friends and the community in which they live. . . . These families or dependants, who may be in need

259 *Louis Khosa and others v Minister of Social Development and others* 2004 (6) SA 505 (CC) para 114.

260 *Maharashtra Ekta Hawkers Union v Municipal Corporation, Greater Mumbai*, order of 9 September 2013 in Civil Appeals Nos 4156–4157 of 2002, para 4.

> of social assistance themselves, are asked to shoulder burdens not asked of other citizens. . . . Apart from the undue burden that this places on those who take on this responsibility, it is likely to have a serious impact on the dignity of the permanent residents concerned who are cast in the role of supplicants.[261]

Yet, humiliation, disrespect, or shame are not the only aspects courts have in mind when talking emotionally about human dignity. The Supreme Court of India as well as the Constitutional Court of South Africa insist on paying their respect as they go along in their reasoning. In *Maharashtra Ekta Hawkers Union v Municipal Corporation, Greater Mumbai*, the Supreme Court of India also stresses the worth of street vendors, from the perspective of the common good:

> The importance of street vendors and hawkers can be measured from the fact that millions of urban poor across the country procure their basic necessities mainly from street vendors/hawkers because the goods, viz., cloths, hosiery items, plastic wares, household items, food items, etc., sold on pavements or through push carts, etc., are cheap. The lower income groups also spend a large proportion of their income in purchasing goods from street vendors/hawkers.[262]

A similar combination of reprimand for disrespect and, at the same time, a show of respect can be found in *Sylvia Bongi Mahlangu and others v Minister of Labour and others* where the Constitutional Court of South Africa was called upon to decide on the constitutionality of a statute that (expressly) excluded domestic workers from the definition of 'employee', with the effect that domestic workers – mainly women – were not entitled to receive benefits in the case of an occupational injury or death.[263] On the one hand, the Constitutional Court deplored:

> The exclusion of domestic workers from the protection under [the act] has resulted in a situation where domestic workers have for decades into our democracy, had to bear work-related injuries or death without compensation. They are a category of workers that have been lamentably left out and been rendered invisible. Their lived experiences have gone unrecognised.[264]

261 *Louis Khosa and others v Minister of Social Development and others* 2004 (6) SA 505 (CC) para 76.

262 *Maharashtra Ekta Hawkers Union v Municipal Corporation, Greater Mumbai*, order of 9 September 2013 in Civil Appeals Nos 4156–4157 of 2002, para 3.

263 *Sylvia Bongi Mahlangu and others v Minister of Labour and others* 2021 (2) SA 54 (CC).

264 ibid para 103.

On the other hand, the Constitutional Court of South Africa spoke highly of domestic workers, attributing value to their work and to them as persons:

> One can only imagine the pain of these women who work graciously, hard and with pride only for their work and by consequence them, to go unrecognised. This amounts to domestic workers themselves not being treated with dignity.[265]

The reference to graciousness, hard work, and pride resonates in the first sentence of the judgement, stating: 'Domestic workers are the unsung heroines in this country and globally'.[266] Obviously, the court wanted to pay respect and indeed paid respect, visibly and for all to read.

Emotional statements like the ones just quoted certainly express discontent with politics. But they express more. The statements underline that a grave wrong had been occurring for a long time and was now being righted by the court, possibly against the will of policy makers. Reference to human dignity and emotions thus add legitimacy to what the courts are doing when they intervene and demand state action.[267] Also, the statements enact the recognition that had, so far, been denied to the people concerned.

Equality

Equality is the last concept I want to touch upon. Courts take resort to human dignity to ensure that individuals are provided (by the state) with a modicum that covers basic human needs. Courts take resort to equality to ensure universality of provision. To put it shortly: In the context of social policy, raising a claim under the right to equality, often means saying: I, too, want to be among the beneficiaries. Again, the ruling of the Constitutional Court of South Africa in *Sylvia Bongi Mahlangu and others v Minister of Labour and others* is a good case in point, and so is *Louis Khosa and others v Minister of Social Development and others*. Yet, this time, I approach these cases from a different perspective.

The cases have in common that lawmakers had acted and, by statute, introduced specific regimes of social security. In the former case, the lawmakers had introduced a regime providing benefits in the case of occupational injury or death. In the latter case, lawmakers had introduced a social assistance regime, providing social grants to South African citizens. Both statutes excluded – by way of definition – certain categories of people. The law on occupational injuries

265 ibid para 108.

266 ibid para 1.

267 See Sandra Liebenberg, 'The Value of Human Dignity in Interpreting Socio-Economic Rights' (2005) 21 South African Journal on Human Rights 1, 15 stressing that a relational concept of human dignity can help the courts to identify the urgency of the needs of the poor and to get a better understanding of the seriousness of the impact of poverty.

explicitly excluded domestic workers from the definition of 'employees'. The law on social assistance excluded all non-nationals, including non-nationals who were permanent residents, though not explicitly, but implicitly by preserving the grants to South African citizens. In both cases, the Constitutional Court of South Africa accepted that the exclusion could be challenged from the perspective of equality, in *Sylvia Bongi Mahlangu and others v Minister of Labour and others* in addition to the challenge from the perspective of human dignity. In each case, the court declared the exclusion to be unconstitutional. Consequently, the court extended the circle of beneficiaries under the relevant statutes, in one case by simply striking the provision relating to domestic workers out of the law, in the other case by reading the words 'or permanent residents' into the law. In both cases, the court's ruling contributed to the universalisation of the benefits involved, but the benefits did not become universal. In one case, domestic workers became entitled to the benefits provided for under the 1993 Compensation for Occupational Injuries and Diseases Act. Still, other employees remained excluded, in particular certain classes of state employees who were adequately protected by other statutory regimes. In the other case, permanent residents got access to social grants in addition to South African citizens, but other residents remained excluded, in particular, all kinds of temporary residents.

Conclusion: Southern Welfare

If one accepts that developments in Brazil, China, India, and South Africa give insights into the characteristics of Southern welfare, I would like to point to five peculiarities. The peculiarities relate Southern welfare to Northern welfare, but also demarcate stark differences.

First, in the four countries, the emergence of the welfare state seems intrinsically linked to Northern welfare concepts, in particular, European concepts, German as well as British. In the early twentieth century, local elites studied the Bismarckian variant of the welfare state closely. Core elements of Northern welfare were transplanted to the local context. Early republican China sticks out as an example. These processes of transplantation or intellectual diffusion were greatly supported by the politics of the ILO in the 1920s and 1930s. Brazil stands out as an example for such a politics of dissemination, triggered and guided by the ILO in the early twentieth century. However, Brazil is certainly not the only example. The ILO opened regional offices in all the countries involved in our study and sent its officials to disseminate on the spot the ideas favoured by the organisation. Again, these ideas drew heavily on the Bismarckian model of social insurance.[268] In short, Southern welfare emerged against the

268 Sandrine Kott, 'Constructing a European Social Model: The Fight for Social Insurance in the Interwar Period' in Jasmien van Daele and others (eds), *ILO Histories: Essays on the International Labour Organization and Its Impact on the World During the Twentieth Century* (Peter Lang 2010) 173.

backdrop of Northern welfare and involved a process of constant testing and weighing of Northern ideas against the local concepts and the local interests.

Second and equally important, Southern welfare was and is shaped by colonial politics and, as a (local) reaction to colonial politics, by anti-colonial struggle: In India and South Africa, it was the colonising powers who made the first move toward introducing nascent regimes of individual welfare in the 1920s and early 1930s, partial and racist as these regimes may have been. For China, the enactment of the first domestic labour laws and their implementation provided an opportunity and a stage in the battle against the European powers running the foreign settlements in Chinese ports. And Brazil was – for a Western observer – a country that had just begun to emerge from nineteenth century semi-feudalism grounded in agriculture and slave work and was, under Vargas, about to embark on a course of rapid industrialisation, willing to gain the support of urban workers by covering work-related risks through social insurance.[269] At the international level, Brazil, China, and India joined forces in their struggle against European dominance in ILO institutions, a dominance that mirrored colonial power relations and made sure that the interests of the colonial powers persevered in the negotiations on labour standards and social policy in the interwar period. Finally, China and India joined forces to end the (long-standing) ILO practice of double labour standards, one standard for European workers and workers in Europe, another for so-called native workers in colonial territories.

Third, and turning to the content of Southern welfare: The early welfare regimes in Brazil, China (until the 1930s), India, and (to some extent) South Africa clearly bear the imprint of the ILO politics of the inter-war period: The first steps involved the adoption of factory laws, of laws concerned with workmen's compensation, or of sickness insurance. India and South Africa, however, adhered more to the idea of employers' responsibility than, for example, Brazil. And the People's Republic of China eventually introduced its own concept of socialist social insurance (sole responsibility of the employer for bearing the costs). Financial difficulties may explain why the regimes first concentrated on certain categories of workers, even though political aspirations went further. The concept of poor relief played no role in ILO politics, and that was in line with the 1919 ILO mandate, with its strong focus on the conditions of industrial life and labour. Consequently, regimes of poor relief were not specifically promoted and sponsored by ILO officials.[270] Regimes of poor relief also had little local tradition in the countries, apart from disaster relief. The colonising powers showed no interest

269 Loewenstein (n 64) 332.

270 ILO politics stayed focused on work-related social policies after World War II. See Daniel Maul, '"Help Them Move the ILO Way": The International Labor Organization and the Modernization Discourse in the Era of Decolonization and the Cold War' (2009) 33 Diplomatic History 387; Daniel Roger Maul, 'The "Morse Years": The ILO 1948–1970' in Jasmien van Daele, Marcel van der Linden and Magaly Rodriguez Garcia (eds), *ILO Histories Essays on the International Labour*

either. Hence, regimes of poor relief were absent on the ground. In the four countries, the welfare state started as a state that introduced (nascent) regimes of social insurance. Poverty was a blind spot in policy making, if not as a problem, then as a problem that needed to be prioritised. It was exactly that blind spot that attracted the attention of Latin American and Asian countries in the 1930s and 1940s. In the late 1930s, Latin American countries picked up on the United States-grown term 'social security', even before the term was used by Beveridge, and added new meaning to the term. Asian countries soon followed suit. Attaching new meaning to the term 'social security' was, so it seems to me, the most important and lasting contribution of non-European countries to welfare state thinking and practice. For Latin American and Asian countries, the term 'social security' captured much better than any other term the goals the countries wanted to achieve in their social policies, given the realities on the ground, for instance, regarding housing, nutrition, education, health, employment, living costs, and standard of living. The political aspiration was 'social security', not only a narrowly defined 'social insurance' for some or even all categories of workers. After World War II, the ILO adjusted to the new thinking, in the 1940s a bit reluctantly (introducing the concept of income security and the concept of medical care), in the 2000s more determined (introducing the concept of national floors of social protection). Surprisingly, the contribution of the non-European countries to one of the basic welfare state concepts – epitomised in the term 'social security' – has so far been ignored in ILO historiography.

Fourth and relating to the goal of ensuring social security: For decades, Southern welfare was conceptualised as the outcome of social policies that must go hand-in-hand with economic development, or even stronger: Southern actors firmly believed that social policy comes second, and economic development comes first. That is certainly true for Brazilian, Indian, and Chinese politics. The new and strong emphasis on development clearly had an impact at the international level: Promoting social progress and development became an important ILO mandate, starting in the 1950s.[271] ILO policies vis-à-vis dependent territories in the aftermath of World War II and, later, the ILO policies vis-à-vis newly independent (post-colonial) states were an outcome of this policy revision. 'Technical assistance' became the main instrument for linking policies of promoting ILO standards with policies of assisting development. Yet, at the domestic level (where development policies were implemented)

Organization and its Impact on the World During the Twentieth Century (Peter Lang 2010) 365. ILO politics changed in the 1970s. See Maul (n 64) 171.

271 Maul (n 64) 159; Kott (n 64) 371; Kott (n 149) 310. On the relationship between colonialism, decolonisation, and development policies see Frederick Cooper, 'Writing the History of Development' (2010) 8 Journal of Modern European History 5.

the emphasis on economic development had its price: The idea that economic development trumps all other political goals, in other words, that the goals to be achieved formed a hierarchy, led to a (sometimes drastic) neglect of values enshrined in social policy, such as equality or even dignity. Often and for lengthy periods of time, economic development was pursued at the cost of the exclusion of certain categories of people from social policy measures, such as peasants; workers in small enterprises; domestic workers; the unemployed; the poor. Sometimes the insistence on pushing ahead with economic development even paved the way to relying on forms of labour that had been outlawed at the international level (eg, by the ILO) at the insistence of the non-European members.[272] Only recently, policy makers (including courts) in Brazil, China, India, and South Africa pay greater attention to equality and the universalisation of social benefits.

Fifth, the concept of poverty and, consequently of the poor, that underlies Southern welfare regimes is very different from the concept that is typical for the British or the German relief regime. In Europe, poverty or being poor carries a stigma to this day. Social assistance is given to people in need. But the suspicion that people in need are in need because of their own doings continues to inform policies. Social assistance is given in a manner that signals that idleness and leisure are no options for the recipients. Recipients face an impending value judgement and a dire choice: They are expected to take up jobs irrespective of their qualifications or, if they decline, to accept contempt and loss of the benefit as a response to their failure. Southern social assistance regimes have no such implied value judgements. That is partly due to their colonial histories or ideologies that blocked the idea that the poor were to blame for their poverty. It is partly due to the mechanism of enumerating categories of beneficiaries because the mechanism makes it difficult to blame the beneficiaries (children, elderly, disabled people). And it is partly due to a concept of dignity that is highly sensitive to the disrespect, the neglect, and the shame that flourishes in (traditional) unequal power relations and in ignorance vis-à-vis the pain of others. The judgement of the Constitutional Court of South Africa in *Louis Khosa and others v Minister of Social Development and others* is a good example for a court's heightened sensitivity regarding shame and humiliation.[273] When ruling on the constitutionality of a provision that excluded foreign residents from the regime of social grants, the Constitutional Court of South Africa reflected lengthily on the repercussions the exclusion had for the relations with family, friends, or acquaintances of the excluded, for instance, when the excluded had to turn to those relations to cover

272 Maul, 'Help Them Move the ILO Way' (n 270) 401.

273 *Louis Khosa and others v Minister of Social Development and others* 2004 (6) SA 505 (CC).

their most basic needs. In those words of the court, humiliation and shame materialised and became palpable, also to the non-affected and the public. When the German Federal Constitutional Court (*Bundesverfassungsgericht*) was called upon to decide on the constitutionality of so-called sanctions – ie the partial or total withdrawal of social assistance in response to a failure on the side of the recipients – the court showed little interest in the details of deprivation the addressees of sanctions had to go through when benefits were withdrawn.[274] In a Southern context, dignity is deemed present also in simple details and, hence, might be impaired as people engage in their quotidian struggles for a livelihood.

274 Bundesverfassungsgericht, judgement of the First Senate, 5 November 2019, 1 BvL 7/16.

Index

Note: Page numbers in *italics* indicate a figure on the corresponding page.

For Product Safety Concerns and Information please contact our EU
representative GPSR@taylorandfrancis.com
Taylor & Francis Verlag GmbH, Kaufingerstraße 24, 80331 München, Germany

www.ingramcontent.com/pod-product-compliance
Ingram Content Group UK Ltd.
Pitfield, Milton Keynes, MK11 3LW, UK
UKHW022316250926
475702UK00046B/890

* 9 7 8 1 0 3 2 1 5 1 6 7 0 *